Financial Analysis

A Business Decision Guide

Third Edition

Steven M. Bragg

Copyright © 2017 by AccountingTools, Inc. All rights reserved.

Published by AccountingTools, Inc., Centennial, Colorado.

No part of this publication may be reproduced, stored in a retrieval system, or transmitted in any form or by any means, except as permitted under Section 107 or 108 of the 1976 United States Copyright Act, without the prior written permission of the Publisher. Requests to the Publisher for permission should be addressed to Steven M. Bragg, 6727 E. Fremont Place, Centennial, CO 80112.

Limit of Liability/Disclaimer of Warranty: While the publisher and author have used their best efforts in preparing this book, they make no representations or warranties with respect to the accuracy or completeness of the contents of this book and specifically disclaim any implied warranties of merchantability or fitness for a particular purpose. No warranty may be created or extended by written sales materials. The advice and strategies contained herein may not be suitable for your situation. You should consult with a professional where appropriate. Neither the publisher nor author shall be liable for any loss of profit or any other commercial damages, including but not limited to special, incidental, consequential, or other damages.

For more information about AccountingTools® products, visit our Web site at www.accountingtools.com.

ISBN-13: 978-1-938910-96-8

Printed in the United States of America

Table of Contents

Chapter 1 - Overview of Financial Analysis 1
The Purpose of Financial Analysis *1*
Key Financial Analysis Concepts *2*
Judgment in Financial Analysis *4*
Precision of Financial Analysis *5*
Death by a Thousand Cuts *5*
Monitoring Analysis *6*
Role of the Financial Analyst *7*
A Conservative Bias *8*

Chapter 2 - The Financial Statements 9
The Income Statement *9*
   Income Statement Overview 9
   The Single-Step Income Statement 12
   The Multi-Step Income Statement 13
   The Contribution Margin Income Statement 13
   The Multi-Period Income Statement 15

The Balance Sheet *16*
   Overview of the Balance Sheet 16
   The Common Size Balance Sheet 19
   The Comparative Balance Sheet 21

The Statement of Cash Flows *22*
   Overview of the Statement of Cash Flows 22
   The Direct Method 23
   The Indirect Method 24

The Statement of Retained Earnings *25*
   Overview of the Statement of Retained Earnings 25

Financial Statement Disclosures *27*

Chapter 3 - Accounting Issues Impacting the Financials 37
The Basis of Accounting *37*
   Accrual Basis of Accounting 37
   Cash Basis of Accounting 38
   Modified Cash Basis of Accounting 39

Effect of the Fiscal Year *39*
Recordation of Revenue at Gross or Net *40*
Bill and Hold Revenue *41*

Negative Cash *42*

Inventory Costing Methods *42*

Depreciation Methods *43*

Current Value Accounting *45*

Illusory Profits *46*

Financial Statement Reporting Issues *47*
    Headline Earnings 47
    Pro Forma Earnings 47
    Window Dressing 48

Auditor Certification *49*

Chapter 4 - Interpretation of Financial Statements 51

Interpretation of Financial Statements *51*

Horizontal Analysis *53*

Vertical Analysis *54*

Cash Coverage Ratio *56*

Current Ratio *57*

Quick Ratio *57*

Liquidity Index *58*

Accounts Payable Turnover Ratio *59*

Accounts Receivable Turnover Ratio *60*

Inventory Turnover Ratio *61*

Fixed Asset Turnover Ratio *62*

Sales to Working Capital Ratio *63*

Debt to Equity Ratio *64*

Fixed Charge Coverage *65*

Breakeven Point *65*

Gross Profit Ratio *66*

Net Profit Ratio *67*

Return on Net Assets *68*

EBITDA *68*

NOPAT *69*

Limitations of Ratio Analysis *70*

Chapter 5 - Cost-Volume-Profit Analysis 73

Contribution Margin *73*

Breakeven Point *75*

Margin of Safety *78*

Cost-Volume-Profit Analysis *79*

Sales Mix *81*

Chapter 6 - Pricing Decisions 84

Psychological Pricing *84*

Cost Plus Pricing *86*

Dynamic Pricing *87*

Freemium Pricing *88*

High-Low Pricing *89*

Premium Pricing *90*

Time and Materials Pricing *92*

Value Based Pricing *94*

Other Pricing Strategies *95*

When to Review Pricing *97*

Price Elasticity of Demand *98*

Cross Price Elasticity of Demand *99*

Non-Price Determinants of Demand *100*

Chapter 7 - Cost Object Analysis 102

Factors in Cost Object Analysis *102*

The Assignability of Costs *103*

The Customer Cost Object *104*
    Customer Acquisition Costs 106
    Customer Lifetime Value 107

The Employee Cost Object *108*

The Product Cost Object *109*

The Product Line Cost Object *111*

The Sales Channel Cost Object *113*

Cost Object Termination Issues *114*

Which Cost Objects to Track *114*

Chapter 8 - Constraint Analysis 116

    Overview of Constraint Analysis *117*
    The Cost of the Bottleneck *119*
    Local Optimization *120*
    Constraint Analysis Financial Terminology *121*
    Constraint Analysis from a Financial Perspective *122*
    The Constraint Analysis Model *122*
    The Decision to Sell at a Lower Price *125*
    The Decision to Outsource Production *126*
    The Capital Investment Decision *127*
    The Decision to Cancel a Product *128*

Chapter 9 - Credit Decisions **131**
    The Credit Rating *131*
    Internal Credit Rating Systems *132*
    Third Party Credit Ratings *135*
    Evaluating Credit Scores *136*
    Use of Credit Ratings *137*
    Credit Rating Errors *137*
    Indicators of Future Payment Delinquency *138*
    Ongoing Credit Monitoring Actions *139*
    Requests for Credit Increases *142*
    The Riskiest Customers *143*
    The Demanding Customer *144*
    Effects of Industry Credit Practices *145*

Chapter 10 - Financing Choices **147**
    Overview of Debt Funding *147*
    The Line of Credit *148*
    The Borrowing Base *149*
    Early Payment Discounting *150*
    Invoice Discounting *152*
    Factoring *153*
    Inventory Financing *153*
    Purchase Order Financing *154*

Leases *154*
The Long-Term Loan *155*
Bonds *156*
Agency Financing *157*
Deleveraging *158*
Overview of Equity Funding *158*
Restricted Stock *159*
Unrestricted Stock *160*
Warrants *160*
Angel Investors and Venture Capital *161*
Crowdfunding *162*
Private Investment in Public Equity *163*
Debt for Equity Swaps *163*

Chapter 11 - Financial Leverage 165
The Financial Leverage Concept *165*
Issues Impacting Leverage *168*
Leverage Risk *169*
Impact of Compensation on Leverage *170*

Chapter 12 - Capital Structure Analysis 172
Optimal Capital Structure *172*
Capital Structure Analysis *173*
Line of Credit Issues *174*
Tax Shield Effects *175*
Future Financing Flexibility *175*
Loan Covenant Issues *175*
Maturity Structure of Debt *176*
Creditor Position Considerations *177*
Debt Paydown *177*
Cost of Capital Reduction *178*
Planning for a Bond Rating *178*
Capital Structure Measurements *180*
    Interest Coverage Ratio *180*
    Debt Service Coverage Ratio *181*

 Recapitalization 182
 Timing of Changes to the Capital Structure 182

Chapter 13 - Dividend Analysis 183
 The Investor Viewpoint 183
 The Company Viewpoint 184
 The Stock Buyback Option 186
 The Stock Dividend 187

Chapter 14 - Foreign Exchange Risk Analysis 189
 Foreign Exchange Risk Overview 189
 Foreign Exchange Risk Management 191
  Take No Action 191
  Avoid Risk 192
  Shift Risk 192
  Time Compression 193
  Payment Leading and Lagging 193
  Build Reserves 194
  Maintain Local Reserves 194
  Hedging 194
 Types of Foreign Exchange Hedges 196
  Loan Denominated in a Foreign Currency 196
  The Forward Contract 196
  The Futures Contract 198
  The Currency Option 198
  The Cylinder Option 200
  Swaps 201
 Netting 201

Chapter 15 - Interest Rate Risk Analysis 203
 Interest Risk Overview 203
 Interest Rate Risk Management 203
  Take No Action 204
  Avoid Risk 204
  Asset and Liability Matching 204
  Hedging 204
 Types of Interest Rate Hedges 205
  The Forward Rate Agreement 205
  The Futures Contract 207
  The Interest Rate Swap 209
  Interest Rate Options 211
  Interest Rate Swaptions 214

Chapter 16 - Financial Forecasting 216

The Differences between a Budget and a Forecast 216

The Run Rate Concept 217

Sensitivity Analysis 218

Revenue Forecasting 219

The System of Budgets 224

The Number of Budget Scenarios 228

The Rolling Forecast 229

The Cash Forecast 233
    The Short-Term Cash Forecast 234
    The Medium-Term Cash Forecast 238
    The Long-Term Cash Forecast 239
    The Use of Averages 239
    The Use of Clearing Dates in a Forecast 240

Chapter 17 - Managing the Rate of Growth 242

The Funding of Growth 242

Contribution Margins and Sustainable Growth 244

Organic Growth 245

Step Costs and Sales Growth 245

Other Constraints on Growth 247

Negative Effects of Excessive Growth 248

The Ideal Rate of Growth 249

Chapter 18 - The Cost of Capital 251

Cost of Capital Derivation 251
    Cost of Debt 251
    Cost of Preferred Stock 252
    Cost of Common Stock 252
    Weighted Average Cost of Capital 253

Variations in the Cost of Capital 253

Adjustments to the Cost of Capital 256

Cost of Capital as a Threshold Value 257

Chapter 19 - Discounted Cash Flow Techniques 259

Time Value of Money 259

Present and Future Value Tables 261

Net Present Value 263

Internal Rate of Return 265
Incremental Internal Rate of Return 265
Terminal Value 266
Inclusions in Cash Flow Analysis 267

Chapter 20 - Capital Budgeting 269
Overview of Capital Budgeting 269
The Capital Request Form 271
The Payback Method 272
Real Options 274
Capital Budget Proposal Analysis 275
Complex Systems Analysis 277
Research and Development Funding Analysis 278
The Outsourcing Decision 279
The Post Installation Review 280

Chapter 21 - The Lease or Buy Decision 283
The Lease Arrangement 283
The Lease or Buy Decision 283
Leasing Concerns 284
Leasing Advantages 286

Chapter 22 - Acquisition Valuation 288
Liquidation Value 288
Real Estate Value 289
Relief-from-Royalty Method 289
Book Value 290
Enterprise Value 292
Multiples Analysis 292
Discounted Cash Flows 296
    Post Five-Year Cash Flows 296
    Negotiation of DCF Contents 297
Replication Value 299
Comparison Analysis 301
    The Comparison of Sales Multiples 301
    The Comparison of Cash Flows 302

    The Comparison of Contract Revenues 302
    52-Week High...303
    Influencer Price Point..303
    The Initial Public Offering Valuation 304
    The Strategic Purchase 304
    Intellectual Property Valuation...305
    Extraneous Valuation Factors 305
    The Control Premium..306
    The Earnout 306
    Synergy Analysis 308
    The Valuation Floor and Ceiling 310

Chapter 23 - The Enhancement of Shareholder Value 313
    Return on Equity 313
    Economic Value Added..316
    Cash Flow Analysis...318
    Opportunity Cost of Capital..319
    Key Success Factors..319
    Stock Price Enhancement..320
    Long-Term and Short-Term Value Considerations...321
    The Industry Setting..322

Glossary...323

Index..329

Preface

A company is constantly confronted with situations that require a detailed review of available options and a decision to proceed in a certain direction. These decisions can be supported by different types of analysis tools. In *Financial Analysis: A Business Decision Guide*, we explore many of the decision tools available to management, and how they can be employed to improve operations and financial results. The topics covered include the general areas of financial statement analysis, operational analysis, financing analysis, forecasting, and investment analysis. As examples of the topics covered, *Financial Analysis* provides answers to the following questions:

- How do inventory costing methods impact the reported results of a business?
- Which ratios should I use to interpret the information in financial statements?
- Which pricing methods would work best in my company?
- Which costs should I include when examining the profitability of customers?
- How can bottlenecks impact profitability?
- How can I employ financial leverage to enhance the return on equity?
- How can I design the optimal capital structure for my business?
- How can I reduce the risk of holding foreign exchange?
- Which issues should I consider when arriving at a reasonable rate of growth?
- When should I use discounted cash flow methods?
- Which methods should I use.to value a potential acquisition?

Financial Analysis: A Business Decision Guide is intended for managers, analysts, accountants, consultants, and students, who can benefit from its broad range of analysis topics. The book also provides references to the author's popular Accounting Best Practices podcast, which provides additional coverage of many analysis topics. As such, it may earn a place on your book shelf as a reference tool for years to come.

Centennial, Colorado
October 2017

About the Author

Steven Bragg, CPA, has been the chief financial officer or controller of four companies, as well as a consulting manager at Ernst & Young. He received a master's degree in finance from Bentley College, an MBA from Babson College, and a Bachelor's degree in Economics from the University of Maine. He has been a two-time president of the Colorado Mountain Club, and is an avid alpine skier, mountain biker, and certified master diver. Mr. Bragg resides in Centennial, Colorado. He has written the following books and courses:

7 Habits of Effective CEOs	Cost Accounting (college textbook)
7 Habits of Effective CFOs	Cost Accounting Fundamentals
7 Habits of Effective Controllers	Cost Management Guidebook
Accountant Ethics [for multiple states]	Credit & Collection Guidebook
Accountants' Guidebook	Crowdfunding
Accounting Changes and Error Corrections	Developing and Managing Teams
Accounting Controls Guidebook	Effective Collections
Accounting for Casinos and Gaming	Employee Onboarding
Accounting for Derivatives and Hedges	Enterprise Risk Management
Accounting for Earnings per Share	Fair Value Accounting
Accounting for Inventory	Financial Analysis
Accounting for Investments	Financial Forecasting and Modeling
Accounting for Intangible Assets	Fixed Asset Accounting
Accounting for Leases	Foreign Currency Accounting
Accounting for Managers	Fraud Examination
Accounting for Stock-Based Compensation	Fraud Schemes
Accounting Procedures Guidebook	GAAP Guidebook
Agricultural Accounting	Governmental Accounting
Behavioral Ethics	Health Care Accounting
Bookkeeping Guidebook	Hospitality Accounting
Budgeting	How to Audit Cash
Business Combinations and Consolidations	How to Audit Fixed Assets
Business Insurance Fundamentals	How to Audit Inventory
Business Ratios	How to Audit Receivables
Business Valuation	How to Run a Meeting
Capital Budgeting	Human Resources Guidebook
CFO Guidebook	IFRS Guidebook
Change Management	Interpretation of Financial Statements
Closing the Books	Inventory Management
Coaching and Mentoring	Investor Relations Guidebook
Conflict Management	Lean Accounting Guidebook
Constraint Management	Mergers & Acquisitions
Construction Accounting	Negotiation
Corporate Cash Management	New Controller Guidebook
Corporate Finance	Nonprofit Accounting

(continued)

Partnership Accounting	Recruiting and Hiring
Payables Management	Revenue Recognition
Payroll Management	Sales and Use Tax Accounting
Project Accounting	The MBA Guidebook
Project Management	The Soft Close
Public Company Accounting	The Statement of Cash Flows
Purchasing Guidebook	The Year-End Close
Real Estate Accounting	Treasurer's Guidebook
Records Management	Working Capital Management

On-Line Resources by Steven Bragg

Steven maintains the accountingtools.com web site, which contains continuing professional education courses, the Accounting Best Practices podcast, and thousands of articles on accounting subjects.

Financial Analysis is also available as a continuing professional education (CPE) course. You can purchase the course (and many other courses) and take an on-line exam at:

www.accountingtools.com/cpe

Chapter 1
Overview of Financial Analysis

Introduction

Almost any decision made by the manager of a corporation has a financial impact. Financial analysis is intended to unearth what this financial impact may be, and to make managers aware of the potential outcomes and consequences of their decisions. In this chapter, we delve into the purpose of financial analysis, the level of precision that can be applied to analysis, the considerable role of judgment in analyzing decisions, and certain types of analysis that are of particular concern in a modern business environment.

The Purpose of Financial Analysis

Financial analysis includes several activities that involve the examination of financial and operational information, with the intent of deriving conclusions and presenting actionable recommendations to management. This is an exceedingly broad definition of the purpose of financial analysis. More specifically, managers need someone to aggregate information for them that clarifies the issues surrounding a decision. Consider the following examples:

- *Acquisition pricing.* The board of directors is considering making an offer to acquire a competitor, and asks the financial analyst to review the fundamentals of the target company to arrive at a range of possible prices that could be offered. This may be based on comparable prices paid recently in the industry, various multiples, or an independent valuation of the target's assets.
- *Capital budgeting.* A company has $10,000,000 to invest in new capital projects, and management has been presented with $35,000,000 of proposed investments. The analyst can sort through the proposals and recommend which to accept and which to reject.
- *Capital structure.* A company is considering issuing bonds for the first time, and wants to understand the most appropriate capital structure to employ in order to earn a certain debt rating. The analyst can investigate the capital structures of similar companies with the targeted debt rating, as well as discuss the issue with consulting firms, and use this information to recommend a particular mix of debt and equity.
- *Dividend policy.* The board of directors is under pressure from investors to issue a dividend. The analyst can research similar companies to see what types of dividend policies they have, as well as the impact of a dividend payout on the company's alternative uses for cash. The result may be a rec-

ommendation for a particular amount and frequency of dividend, or an alternative, such as buying back shares.
- *Foreign exchange risk.* Management is contemplating a deal that will require the company to hold a large amount of foreign exchange for several months, and asks the analyst for options to reduce the risk of loss from adverse changes in the rate of foreign exchange. The analyst can present a range of possibilities, from doing nothing to a full hedging strategy, as well as the likely cost of each alternative.
- *Growth rate.* Management is devising a budget for the next fiscal year, and asks the analyst to estimate the most appropriate rate of growth to build into the budget. The analyst can provide an estimate based on the amount of debt and equity funding required, the presence of any bottlenecks in the organization, and other potential restrictions on growth.
- *Product terminations.* The company is reviewing ways to concentrate its activities on a small cluster of core products. The analyst can recommend which products to drop, based on their impact on cash flows and the bottleneck operation, and incorporating the effect on inventory balances and customer relations.

The broad range of these examples should make it clear that the financial analyst can become involved with people at all levels of an organization, ranging from the board of directors to the warehouse manager. Also, the sources of information to be investigated can range from general economic data to the financial statements of acquirees and even the cost structures of specific products. Further, the analyst must be conversant with every aspect of a business, since he or she may be asked to render an opinion on any area.

Key Financial Analysis Concepts

The following chapters will make it clear that a large number of analyses can be conducted on a business, and that the type of analysis used will have an impact on the analyst's recommendations. Some types of analysis are highly specific, as is found with hedging strategies for foreign exchange and interest rates. However, you will see a few general analysis themes reoccurring in the text. These themes are:

- *Constraint analysis.* The performance of a business can usually be enhanced to the greatest extent by paying close attention to whatever constrains the ability of the company from generating more profits. This may be a bottleneck in the production area, a weak sales function, the inability to obtain raw materials, or some other factor. In short, you can analyze many other projects in great detail, and yet the overall performance of a corporation will not be improved unless the constraint is addressed.
- *Pacing.* Some of the most important analyses involve the budgeted growth rate of a business, which management commonly assumes can be accelerated. This is usually not possible, due to the presence of a variety of financial

and operational constraints. The analyst should be well aware of the natural pace at which a business has proven that it can grow, and understand which factors need to be altered in order to change the rate of growth. Otherwise, a business will perpetually budget for greater change than it can actually accommodate.
- *Cash flow analysis.* Use cash flows as the basis for analysis, since cash flows reveal the true operational results of an asset or liability. In most analyses, when cash flow information is available, discard other analysis alternatives in favor of cash flows. Ultimately, the desired outcome of a business decision is an increase in cash flows, so incorporate these flows into the research supporting decisions.
- *Incremental analysis.* This involves the examination of alternative choices, based on the cost differences between them. This analysis is solely concerned with the costs that will change if one alternative is selected over another. Any costs that do not change if either alternative is selected are ignored for the purpose of deciding which alternative to pursue. For example, costs that have already been incurred (known as sunk costs) are ignored. Also, if any type of cost will be incurred for both alternatives, then it also can be ignored.

If there is any doubt regarding how to structure an analysis, see if the analysis can include one or more of these three concepts. Doing so will make it more likely that the resulting recommendation is one that will enhance the position of the business.

Another way of looking at financial analysis is that a business is comprised of many parts that must work together to achieve sales and profits. This means that a business is really a finely-meshed set of interrelated parts. Consequently, a change in one part of a business is likely to have ramifications elsewhere in the system, so the analyst must consider the complete impact of a business decision when making recommendations. For example:

- A retail chain switches from full-time to part-time sales associates to save money, and then sees sales decline when customers complain about reduced customer service.
- A consumer electronics company invests heavily in a design team in order to roll out new product versions more frequently, but then sees its inventory levels skyrocket when customers ignore old models in anticipation of new ones.
- A manufacturer in a cyclical industry decides to automate much of its production work, but finds that doing so requires a large cash investment, which reduces its cash buffer when customer orders inevitably decline during the next industry downturn.

Thus, the analyst must have a broad view of the entire system of operations, and understand how a change in one place can have a ripple effect throughout the organization. What may initially be perceived to be a minor change may in fact have a broad (and possibly negative) impact, once its full ramifications have impacted the organization.

Judgment in Financial Analysis

Much of this book is devoted to the description of specific financial analysis techniques, such as discounted cash flows and throughput analysis. However, a larger proportion of the book contains discussions of qualitative issues that must also be considered when investigating an issue and formulating a recommendation. These qualitative issues are just as important, if not more so, than any quantitative analysis.

When there is a large qualitative factor involved in a decision, the analyst must be able to exercise a proper amount of judgment in integrating these additional concepts into an analysis, and forwarding a comprehensive, well thought-out recommendation to management. The issue is expanded upon in the following examples:

- *Dividend policy*. The board of directors could ask the analyst to recommend an appropriate amount for a recurring dividend. The analysis may only include a review of the variability of company cash flows, with a view to recommending a safe amount that can still be paid out even during a worst-case scenario. However, the analyst could also consider alternative uses for the cash, and point out to the board that there are several possible investment alternatives for the funds that could generate higher returns for investors over the long term than an immediate dividend payout.
- *Growth rate*. The CFO could ask the analyst to derive a long-term average growth rate that could be built into the next version of the budget. This information could be derived from the company's ability to generate cash. However, the analyst could also review competitors to see if they are going to extremes to grab market share, whether the industry is growing faster than the company's internal rate of growth, and whether the rest of the industry is taking a more aggressive stance toward the use of debt to fund additional growth.
- *Product terminations*. If asked to recommend which products to terminate, an analyst could simply compare product prices to their variable costs. However, a more comprehensive analysis would also consider the impact on the company's entire product line if a few items were to be plucked out, and whether having an incomplete product line might drive customers toward those competitors who continue to have a broader range of offerings.

In short, the analyst must think like the chief executive officer, and consider in an analysis every possible input to a decision, as well as every area that a decision could impact. This viewpoint goes well beyond the simple application of a few ratios to financial information.

Precision of Financial Analysis

There are constant demands on the time of the financial analyst, to the extent that it is not possible to arrive at the perfect recommendation for every requested analysis. There simply is not enough time to explore each topic in a sufficient level of detail to give management an exact recommendation. Further, there is enough uncertainty surrounding most decisions that a precise recommendation is not even possible; some variables cannot be quantified. Instead, the analyst will likely have to make recommendations within a certain range. For example, the recommended price to offer for a target company could be between $10,000,000 and $13,000,000, while the recommended capital structure for a business might call for debt to be between 30% and 45% of equity.

It may be possible for the analyst to issue estimates that fall within narrower boundaries, but only at the expense of spending more time reviewing the underlying data. In essence, a greater investment of time in a project will probably produce an outcome within a narrower range, but still cannot yield an exact recommendation.

Despite the foregoing points regarding the use of ranges for answers, there are cases where the recommendation is a binary one – either yes or no. These situations tend to be simpler ones, where a relatively small amount of analysis reveals a definitive answer. Conversely, the most difficult analyses tend to be ones that have the most at stake, either in terms of the company's strategic direction or the amount of cash to be invested. Thus, in terms of time management, the analyst will likely be able to return rapid responses to some analysis requests, while reserving a large amount of time for more detailed reviews of more significant projects.

Death by a Thousand Cuts

A new financial analyst might think that the job is focused on the analysis of large issues, such as whether to acquire a company, or the decision to roll out a new line of products. While these decisions are indeed critical, there is another category of analysis that can, in total, have an equally important impact on an organization. This category is the day-to-day pricing and spending decision. Examples of these decisions are whether to raise the pay of an employee who has a particularly important skill set, whether to accept a low-price offer for a large order from a major customer, and the amount of credit to extend to a risky new customer. The cumulative impact of these decisions can easily overwhelm the supposedly more important and "sexy" decisions.

When reviewing these day-to-day decisions, the analyst should consider himself to be the guardian of the corporate margin. Many decisions are presented that may appear to have a minor cost effect when considered individually, but which can consume a large chunk of corporate profits if they are all approved. Consequently, the analyst must present a hard-nosed, conservative attitude to supplicants who want to spend just a bit more money, and uniformly recommend to management that these alternatives be turned down. Otherwise, management may find that its own decisions have led to bankruptcy by a thousand cuts, rather than one monumentally bad decision.

This attitude suggests that the work habits and mind set of the analyst be of a particular type. For example, the analyst should possess an ingrained attention to detail, constantly delving into the assumptions presented in a proposal to see if they are realistic, examining projected cash flows for faults, and generally mimicking Sherlock Holmes in delving into the details of each case. The analyst should also have sufficient social skills to have developed contacts throughout the organization, which can be called upon to provide their own views of the flaws in a proposed action. Further, the analyst must be willing to review a proposal based on worst-case scenarios, to understand the cash flow impact if a project takes a turn for the worse. Only by employing this conservative, probing, and detailed point of view can proper attention be paid to an analysis project.

Monitoring Analysis

A final type of analysis, and one that tends to be overlooked, is the monitoring of ongoing company operations and finances. This analysis is similar to a blood test given to a patient – it contains many measurements, of which most will fall within expected boundaries, and a few will be flagged for further investigation.

Monitoring the condition of a business is one of the key roles of a financial analyst, though it is not a particularly flashy activity. In essence, there should be a small number of measurements that are intended to spot any areas of the business that are showing unusual results or levels of activity. If odd results are found, the analyst conducts additional investigatory work, and presents his or her findings to management regarding the reason for each out-of-bounds result. When engaging in this monitoring function, consider the following items:

- *Targeted measurements*. Only track measurements that are specifically intended to spot problems. For example, the current ratio is much too general to provide any useful information. Instead, the dollar amount of inventory over 90 days old would give an excellent picture of the state of inventory obsolescence, while the amount of receivables over 90 days old would yield a similar view of receivables.
- *Measurement standardization*. Monitoring is most effective when measurements are tracked on a trend line for a long period of time, so that any spikes in the results are immediately obvious. However, this only works if each measurement used is compiled and calculated in exactly the same manner, every time. Consequently, the analyst should have a detailed procedure in place for deriving each measurement. Further, if the basis for a measurement is altered, the new approach should be applied to all of the periods presented, so that measurements are comparable across periods.
- *Measurement updates*. A company changes its operations and finances over time, so its measurements should change along with them. This means that the least useful measurements are dropped and replaced by ones that management can use to more precisely control the company. The review of

measurements should take place at least once a year, or whenever there is a significant change to the business, such as a major acquisition.

Though the monitoring function may not take up much of the time of the analyst, it is still an important activity, since it provides early warning that there is a problem that may require correction.

Role of the Financial Analyst

The financial analyst position occupies a key role in a business, for this person is responsible for quantifying the impact of many types of decisions, and recommending specific courses of action. In a sense, a persuasive analyst can be considered the real decision maker in a corporation. Given the magnitude of the position's influence, the analyst should be well trained in analysis concepts, able to construct complex financial models, and have a deep understanding of how an organization operates. Only with a deep level of knowledge and experience can an analyst best assist managers in arriving at optimal decisions. The following sample job description more fully outlines the requirements of the position.

Sample Financial Analyst Job Description

Basic Function: The financial analyst position is accountable for reviewing larger investments for return on investment, investigating a variety of internal financial and operational issues, and staying abreast of industry conditions and competitor activities.

Principal Accountabilities:

1. Clearly define problems to be investigated
2. Understand the limitations of all analytical tools being used and incorporate these limitations into any results generated
3. Investigate operational and financial results, and make recommendations for improvements
4. Conduct cost-benefit analyses
5. Review capital budgeting proposals and make acceptance recommendations to management
6. Review indicators of business activity published by the government and trade associations
7. Create forecasts of future business conditions using multiple scenarios
8. Review and recommend different types of investments based on risk and return analysis
9. Stay abreast of developments in those industries in which the company operates
10. Prepare and update a competitor analysis
11. Create financial models using electronic spreadsheets
12. Create presentations summarizing the results of analyses and present the results to senior management

Desired Qualifications: A master's degree in business administration or finance, with exceptional financial modeling skills and a working knowledge of statistics. Must have excellent communication and writing skills.

A Conservative Bias

The business press is full of stories about bold managers who have turned around moribund organizations with startling new business strategies that achieved outsized sales and profits. These situations appear in the press because they are so unusual. In many cases, the "bold" managers only enacted sweeping changes because they had no choice – their companies were failing.

In the real world, it can be wildly risky to enact massive changes in an organization. A business is constructed to offer a particular product or service to customers, and its underlying systems, employee training, and policies are specifically designed to maximize how those products and services are provided. When the analyst is presented with an alternative that may interrupt this closely interrelated system, pay particular attention to the impact on the underlying system, and make recommendations that incorporate the downside risk to the organization. Doing so makes it less likely that a change will be recommended that could bring about the failure of the organization. Thus, as you proceed through the remainder of this book, remember that a conservative bias should be incorporated into the more critical analyses that impact the entire organization.

Summary

Financial analysis is a critical advisory function that requires a notable amount of wisdom. The analyst must understand how a business operates, how its various parts fit together, and how a proposed action will impact that system. The analyst should use this knowledge to craft a review that informs decision makers of the alternatives available, potential risks, and the monetary impact of a decision. The result should be an organization that is continually being tweaked with carefully-considered updates, yielding a more competitive company that provides superior returns to its shareholders.

Chapter 2
The Financial Statements

Introduction

The starting point for many types of financial analysis is the financial statements. The financial statements are routinely issued by organizations at the end of each reporting period, and are intended to reveal their results of operations, financial position, and cash flows. In this chapter, we describe each of the financial statements, which include the income statement, balance sheet, statement of cash flows, and statement of retained earnings, as well as the different formats in which they can be presented. We also make note of the disclosures that accompany the financial statements, which are a rich source of information for the analyst.

The Income Statement

In most organizations, the income statement is considered the most important of the financial statements, and may even be the only one of the financial statements that is produced. Given its importance, we spend extra time in this section addressing the different income statement formats that may be encountered.

Income Statement Overview

The income statement is an integral part of an entity's financial statements, and contains the results of its operations during an accounting period, showing revenues and expenses, and the resulting profit or loss.

There are two ways to present the income statement. One method is to present all items of revenue and expense for the reporting period in a statement of comprehensive income. Alternatively, this information can be split into an income statement and a statement of comprehensive income. Smaller companies tend to ignore the distinction and simply aggregate the information into a document that they call the income statement.

> **Note:** Other comprehensive income contains all changes that are not permitted in the main part of the income statement. These items include unrealized gains and losses on available-for-sale securities, cash flow hedge gains and losses, foreign currency translation adjustments, and pension plan gains or losses.

There are no specific requirements for the line items to include in the income statement, but the following line items are typically used, based on general practice:

- Revenue
- Tax expense

- Post-tax profit or loss for discontinued operations and their disposal
- Profit or loss
- Other comprehensive income, subdivided into each component thereof
- Total comprehensive income

A key additional item is to present an analysis of the expenses in profit or loss, using a classification based on their nature or functional area; the goal is to maximize the relevance and reliability of the presented information. If expenses are presented by their nature, the format looks similar to the following:

Sample Presentation by Nature of Items

Revenue		$xxx
Expenses		
Direct materials	$xxx	
Direct labor	xxx	
Salaries expense	xxx	
Payroll taxes	xxx	
Employee benefits	xxx	
Depreciation expense	xxx	
Telephone expense	xxx	
Other expenses	xxx	
Total expenses		$xxx
Profit before tax		$xxx

Alternatively, if expenses are presented by their functional area, the format looks similar to the following, where most expenses are aggregated at the department level:

Sample Presentation by Function of Items

Revenue	$xxx
Cost of goods sold	xxx
Gross profit	xxx
Administrative expenses	$xxx
Distribution expenses	xxx
Research and development expenses	xxx
Sales and marketing expenses	xxx
Other expenses	xxx
Total expenses	$xxx
Profit before tax	$xxx

The Financial Statements

Of the two methods, the functional area presentation may be more relevant to users of the information, who can more easily see where resources are being consumed.

An example follows of an income statement that presents expenses by their nature, rather than by their function.

EXAMPLE

Milagro Corporation presents its results in two separate statements by their nature, resulting in the following format, beginning with the income statement:

Milagro Corporation
Income Statement
For the years ended December 31

(000s)	20x2	20x1
Revenue	$900,000	$850,000
Expenses		
Direct materials	$270,000	$255,000
Direct labor	90,000	85,000
Salaries	300,000	275,000
Payroll taxes	27,000	25,000
Depreciation expense	45,000	41,000
Telephone expense	30,000	20,000
Other expenses	23,000	22,000
Finance costs	29,000	23,000
Other income	-25,000	-20,000
Profit before tax	$111,000	$124,000
Income tax expense	38,000	43,000
Profit from continuing operations	$73,000	$81,000
Loss from discontinued operations	42,000	0
Profit	$31,000	$81,000

Milagro Corporation then continues with the following statement of comprehensive income:

Milagro Corporation
Statement of Comprehensive Income
For the years ended December 31

(000s)	20x2	20x1
Profit	$31,000	$81,000
Other comprehensive income		
Exchange differences on translating foreign operations	$5,000	$9,000
Available-for-sale financial assets	10,000	-2,000
Actuarial losses on defined benefit pension plan	-2,000	-12,000
Other comprehensive income, net of tax	$13,000	-$5,000
Total comprehensive income	$18,000	$76,000

The Single-Step Income Statement

The simplest format in which an income statement can be constructed is the single-step income statement. In this format, a single subtotal is presented for all revenue line items, and a single subtotal for all expense line items, with a net gain or loss appearing at the bottom of the report. A sample single-step income statement follows:

Sample Single-Step Income Statement

Revenues	$1,000,000
Expenses:	
Cost of goods sold	350,000
Advertising	30,000
Depreciation	20,000
Rent	40,000
Payroll taxes	28,000
Salaries and wages	400,000
Supplies	32,000
Travel and entertainment	50,000
Total expenses	950,000
Net income	$50,000

The single-step format is not heavily used, because it forces the reader to separately summarize information for subsets of information within the income statement. The following multi-step approach is more readable.

The Multi-Step Income Statement

The multi-step income statement involves the use of multiple sub-totals within the income statement, which makes it easier for readers to aggregate selected types of information within the report. The usual subtotals are for the gross margin, operating expenses, and other income, which allow readers to determine how much the company earns just from its manufacturing activities (the gross margin), what it spends on supporting operations (the operating expense total) and which components of its results do not relate to its core activities (the other income total). A sample format for a multi-step income statement follows.

Sample Multi-Step Income Statement

Revenues	$1,000,000
Cost of goods sold	350,000
Gross margin	$650,000
Operating expenses	
Advertising	30,000
Depreciation	20,000
Rent	40,000
Payroll taxes	28,000
Salaries and wages	380,000
Supplies	32,000
Travel and entertainment	50,000
Total operating expenses	$580,000
Other income	
Interest income	-5,000
Interest expense	25,000
Total other income	$20,000
Net income	$50,000

The Contribution Margin Income Statement

A contribution margin income statement is an income statement in which all variable expenses are deducted from sales to arrive at a contribution margin, from which all fixed expenses are then subtracted to arrive at the net profit or loss for the period. This income statement format is a superior form of presentation, because the contribution margin clearly shows the amount available to cover fixed costs and generate a profit (or loss).

In essence, if there are no sales, a contribution margin income statement will have a zero contribution margin, with fixed costs clustered beneath the contribution margin line item. As sales increase, the contribution margin will increase in conjunction with sales, while fixed costs remain approximately the same.

A contribution margin income statement varies from a normal income statement in the following three ways:

- Fixed production costs are aggregated lower in the income statement, after the contribution margin;
- Variable selling and administrative expenses are grouped with variable production costs, so that they are a part of the calculation of the contribution margin; and
- The gross margin is replaced in the statement by the contribution margin.

Thus, the format of a contribution margin income statement is:

Sample Contribution Margin Income Statement

+	Revenues
-	Variable production expenses (such as materials, supplies, and variable overhead)
-	Variable selling and administrative expenses
=	Contribution margin
-	Fixed production expenses (including most overhead)
-	Fixed selling and administrative expenses
=	Net profit or loss

In many cases, direct labor is categorized as a fixed expense in the contribution margin income statement format, rather than a variable expense, because this cost does not always change in direct proportion to the amount of revenue generated. Instead, management needs to keep a certain minimum staffing in the production area, which does not vary even if there are lower production volumes.

The key difference between gross margin and contribution margin is that fixed production costs are included in the cost of goods sold to calculate the gross margin, whereas they are not included in the same calculation for the contribution margin. This means that the contribution margin income statement is sorted based on the variability of the underlying cost information, rather than by the functional areas or expense categories found in a normal income statement.

In many businesses, the contribution margin will be substantially higher than the gross margin, because such a large proportion of production costs are fixed and few of its selling and administrative expenses are variable.

The Multi-Period Income Statement

A variation on the preceding income statement formats is a presentation over multiple periods, preferably over a trailing 12-month period. By doing so, readers can see trends in the information, as well as spot changes in the trends that may require investigation. The following sample shows the layout of a multi-period income statement over a four-quarter period.

Sample Multi-Period Income Statement

	Quarter 1	Quarter 2	Quarter 3	Quarter 4
Revenues	$1,000,000	$1,100,000	$1,050,000	$1,200,000
Cost of goods sold	350,000	385,000	368,000	**480,000**
Gross margin	$650,000	$715,000	$682,000	$720,000
Operating expenses				
Advertising	30,000	0	**60,000**	30,000
Depreciation	20,000	21,000	22,000	24,000
Rent	40,000	40,000	**50,000**	50,000
Payroll taxes	28,000	28,000	28,000	26,000
Salaries and wages	380,000	385,000	385,000	370,000
Supplies	32,000	30,000	31,000	33,000
Travel and entertainment	50,000	45,000	40,000	60,000
Total operating expenses	$580,000	$549,000	$616,000	$593,000
Other income				
Interest income	-5,000	-5,000	-3,000	-1,000
Interest expense	25,000	25,000	30,000	**39,000**
Total other income	$20,000	$20,000	$27,000	$38,000
Net income	$50,000	$146,000	$39,000	$89,000

The report shown in the sample reveals several issues that might not have been visible if the report had only spanned a single period. These issues are:

- *Cost of goods sold.* This cost is consistently 35% of sales until Quarter 4, when it jumps to 40%.
- *Advertising.* There was no advertising cost in Quarter 2 and double the amount of the normal $30,000 quarterly expense in Quarter 3. The cause

could be a missing supplier invoice in Quarter 2 that was received and recorded in Quarter 3.
- *Rent.* The rent increased by $10,000 in Quarter 3, which may indicate a scheduled increase in the rent agreement.
- *Interest expense.* The interest expense jumps in Quarter 3 and does so again in Quarter 4, while interest income declined over the same periods. This indicates a large increase in debt.

In short, the multi-period income statement is an excellent tool for spotting anomalies in the presented information from period to period.

The Balance Sheet

In most organizations, the balance sheet is considered the second most important of the financial statements, after the income statement. A common financial reporting package is to issue the income statement and balance sheet, along with supporting materials. This does not comprise a complete set of financial statements, but it is considered sufficient for internal reporting purposes in many organizations.

In this section, we explore several possible formats for the balance sheet, and also describe how to create it.

Overview of the Balance Sheet

A balance sheet (also known as a statement of financial position) presents information about an entity's assets, liabilities, and shareholders' equity, where the compiled result must match this formula:

$$\text{Total assets} = \text{Total liabilities} + \text{Equity}$$

The balance sheet reports the aggregate effect of transactions as of a specific date. The balance sheet is used to assess an entity's liquidity and ability to pay its debts.

There is no specific requirement for the line items to be included in the balance sheet. The following line items, at a minimum, are normally included in it:

Current Assets:

- Cash and cash equivalents
- Trade and other receivables
- Investments
- Inventories
- Assets held for sale

Non-Current Assets:

- Property, plant, and equipment
- Intangible assets

- Goodwill

Current Liabilities:

- Trade and other payables
- Accrued expenses
- Current tax liabilities
- Current portion of loans payable
- Other financial liabilities
- Liabilities held for sale

Non-Current Liabilities:

- Loans payable
- Deferred tax liabilities
- Other non-current liabilities

Equity:

- Capital stock
- Additional paid-in capital
- Retained earnings

Here is an example of a balance sheet which presents information as of the end of two fiscal years:

Milagro Corporation
Balance Sheet
As of December 31, 20X2 and 20X1

(000s)	12/31/20X2	12/31/20x1
ASSETS		
Current assets		
Cash and cash equivalents	$270,000	$215,000
Trade receivables	147,000	139,000
Inventories	139,000	128,000
Other current assets	15,000	27,000
Total current assets	$571,000	$509,000
Non-current assets		
Property, plant, and equipment	551,000	529,000
Goodwill	82,000	82,000
Other intangible assets	143,000	143,000

The Financial Statements

(000s)	12/31/20X2	12/31/20x1
Total non-current assets	$776,000	$754,000
Total assets	$1,347,000	$1,263,000
LIABILITIES AND EQUITY		
Current liabilities		
Trade and other payables	$217,000	$198,000
Short-term borrowings	133,000	202,000
Current portion of long-term borrowings	5,000	5,000
Current tax payable	26,000	23,000
Accrued expenses	9,000	13,000
Total current liabilities	$390,000	$441,000
Non-current liabilities		
Long-term debt	85,000	65,000
Deferred taxes	19,000	17,000
Total non-current liabilities	$104,000	$82,000
Total liabilities	$494,000	$523,000
Shareholders' equity		
Capital	100,000	100,000
Additional paid-in capital	15,000	15,000
Retained earnings	738,000	625,000
Total equity	$853,000	$740,000
Total liabilities and equity	$1,347,000	$1,263,000

An asset is classified on the balance sheet as current when an entity expects to sell or consume it during its normal operating cycle or within 12 months after the reporting period. If the operating cycle is longer than 12 months, then the longer period is used to judge whether an asset can be classified as current. All other assets are classified as non-current.

The following are all classified as current assets:

- *Cash.* This is cash available for current operations, as well as any short-term, highly liquid investments that are readily convertible to known amounts of cash and which are so near their maturities that they present an insignificant risk of value changes. Cash is not included here when its withdrawal is restricted, to be used for other than current operations, or segregated for the liquidation of long-term debts; such items are classified as longer-term.

- *Accounts receivable*. This includes trade accounts, notes, and acceptances that are receivable. Also, receivables are included from officers, employees, affiliates, and others if they are collectible within a year. Receivables are not included if there is no expectation of collection within 12 months; such items are classified as longer-term.
- *Marketable securities*. This includes those securities representing the investment of cash available for current operations, including trading securities.
- *Inventory*. This includes merchandise, raw materials, work-in-process, finished goods, operating supplies, and maintenance parts.
- *Prepaid expenses*. This includes prepayments for insurance, interest, rent, taxes, unused royalties, advertising services, and operating supplies.

A liability is classified as current when the entity expects to settle it during its normal operating cycle or within 12 months after the reporting period, or if it is scheduled for settlement within 12 months. All other liabilities are classified as non-current.

All of the following are classified as current liabilities:

- *Payables*. This is all accounts payable incurred in the acquisition of materials and supplies that are used to produce goods or services.
- *Prepayments*. This is amounts collected in advance of the delivery of goods or services by the entity to the customer. A long-term prepayment is not included in this category.
- *Accruals*. This is accrued expenses for items directly related to the operating cycle, such as accruals for compensation, rentals, royalties, and various taxes.
- *Short-term debts*. This is debts maturing within the next 12 months.

Current liabilities include accruals for amounts that can only be determined approximately, such as bonuses, and where the payee to whom payment will be made cannot initially be designated, such as a warranty accrual.

The Common Size Balance Sheet

A common size balance sheet presents not only the standard information contained in a balance sheet, but also a column that notes the same information as a percentage of the total assets (for asset line items) or as a percentage of total liabilities and shareholders' equity (for liability or shareholders' equity line items).

It is extremely useful to construct a common size balance sheet that itemizes the results as of the end of multiple time periods, so that trend lines can be constructed to ascertain changes over longer time periods. The common size balance sheet is also useful for comparing the proportions of assets, liabilities, and equity between different companies, particularly as part of an industry or acquisition analysis.

For example, if you were comparing the common size balance sheet of your company to that of a potential acquiree, and the acquiree had 40% of its assets invested in accounts receivable versus 20% by your company, this may indicate that aggressive collection activities might reduce the acquiree's receivables if your company were to acquire it.

There is no mandatory format for a common size balance sheet, though percentages are nearly always placed to the right of the normal numerical results. If balance sheet results are being reported as of the end of many periods, numerical results may be dispensed with entirely, in favor of just presenting the common size percentages.

EXAMPLE

Milagro Corporation creates a common size balance sheet that contains the balance sheet as of the end of its fiscal year for each of the past two years, with common size percentages to the right:

Milagro Corporation
Common Size Balance Sheet
As of 12/31/20x02 and 12/31/20x1

	($) 12/31/20x2	($) 12/31/20x1	(%) 12/31/20x2	(%) 12/31/20x1
Current assets				
Cash	$1,200	$900	7.6%	7.1%
Accounts receivable	4,800	3,600	30.4%	28.3%
Inventory	3,600	2,700	22.8%	21.3%
Total current assets	$9,600	$7,200	60.8%	56.7%
Total fixed assets	6,200	5,500	39.2%	43.3%
Total assets	$15,800	$12,700	100.0%	100.0%
Current liabilities				
Accounts payable	$2,400	$1,800	15.2%	14.2%
Accrued expenses	480	360	3.0%	2.8%
Short-term debt	800	600	5.1%	4.7%
Total current liabilities	$3,680	$2,760	23.3%	21.7%
Long-term debt	9,020	7,740	57.1%	60.9%
Total liabilities	$12,700	$10,500	80.4%	82.7%
Shareholders' equity	3,100	2,200	19.6%	17.3%
Total liabilities and equity	$15,800	$12,700	100.0%	100.0%

The Comparative Balance Sheet

A comparative balance sheet presents side-by-side information about an entity's assets, liabilities, and shareholders' equity as of multiple points in time. For example, a comparative balance sheet could present the balance sheet as of the end of each year for the past three years. Another variation is to present the balance sheet as of the end of each month for the past 12 months on a rolling basis. In both cases, the reader has a series of snapshots of a company's financial condition over a period of time, which is useful for developing trend line analyses.

The comparative balance sheet is not required under the GAAP accounting framework for a privately-held company, but the Securities and Exchange Commission (SEC) does require it in numerous circumstances for the reports issued by publicly-held companies, particularly the annual Form 10-K and the quarterly Form 10-Q. The usual SEC requirement is to report a comparative balance sheet for the past two years, with additional requirements for quarterly reporting.

The following is a sample of a comparative balance sheet that contains the balance sheet as of the end of a company's fiscal year for each of the past three years:

Sample Comparative Balance Sheet

	as of 12/31/20X3	as of 12/31/20X2	as of 12/31/20X1
Current assets			
Cash	$1,200,000	$900,000	$750,000
Accounts receivable	4,800,000	3,600,000	3,000,000
Inventory	3,600,000	2,700,000	2,300,000
Total current assets	$9,600,000	$7,200,000	$6,050,000
Total fixed assets	6,200,000	5,500,000	5,000,000
Total assets	$15,800,000	$12,700,000	$11,050,000
Current liabilities			
Accounts payable	$2,400,000	$1,800,000	$1,500,000
Accrued expenses	480,000	360,000	300,000
Short-term debt	800,000	600,000	400,000
Total current liabilities	$3,680,000	$2,760,000	$2,200,000
Long-term debt	9,020,000	7,740,000	7,350,000
Total liabilities	$12,700,000	$10,500,000	$9,550,000
Shareholders' equity	3,100,000	2,200,000	1,500,000
Total liabilities and equity	$15,800,000	$12,700,000	$11,050,000

The sample comparative balance sheet reveals that the company has increased the size of its current assets over the past few years, but has also recently invested in a large amount of additional fixed assets that have likely been the cause of a significant boost in its long-term debt.

The Statement of Cash Flows

The statement of cash flows is the least used of the primary financial statements, and may not be issued at all for internal financial reporting purposes. Nonetheless, the cash flows on the statement of cash flows can provide valuable information, especially when combined with the other elements of the financial statements. This section addresses the two formats used for the statement of cash flows.

Overview of the Statement of Cash Flows

The statement of cash flows contains information about the flows of cash into and out of a company; in particular, it shows the extent of those company activities that generate and use cash. The primary activities are:

- *Operating activities.* These are an entity's primary revenue-producing activities. Examples of operating activities are cash receipts from the sale of goods, as well as from royalties and commissions, amounts received or paid to settle lawsuits, fines, payments to employees and suppliers, cash payments to lenders for interest, contributions to charity, and the settlement of asset retirement obligations.
- *Investing activities.* These involve the acquisition and disposal of long-term assets. Examples of investing activities are cash receipts from the sale of property, the sale of the debt or equity instruments of other entities, the repayment of loans made to other entities, and proceeds from insurance settlements related to damaged fixed assets. Examples of cash payments that are investment activities include the acquisition of fixed assets, as well as the purchase of the debt or equity of other entities.
- *Financing activities.* These are the activities resulting in alterations to the amount of contributed equity and the entity's borrowings. Examples of financing activities include cash receipts from the sale of the entity's own equity instruments or from issuing debt, proceeds from derivative instruments, and cash payments to buy back shares, pay dividends, and pay off outstanding debt.

The statement of cash flows also incorporates the concept of cash and cash equivalents. A cash equivalent is a short-term, very liquid investment that is easily convertible into a known amount of cash, and which is so near its maturity that it presents an insignificant risk of a change in value because of changes in interest rates.

The direct method or the indirect method can be used to present the statement of cash flows. These methods are described next.

The Direct Method

The direct method of presenting the statement of cash flows presents the specific cash flows associated with items that affect cash flow. Items that typically do so include:

- Cash collected from customers
- Interest and dividends received
- Cash paid to employees
- Cash paid to suppliers
- Interest paid
- Income taxes paid

The format of the direct method appears in the following example.

EXAMPLE

Milagro Corporation constructs the following statement of cash flows using the direct method:

Milagro Corporation
Statement of Cash Flows
For the year ended 12/31/20X1

Cash flows from operating activities		
Cash receipts from customers	$45,800,000	
Cash paid to suppliers	-29,800,000	
Cash paid to employees	-11,200,000	
Cash generated from operations	4,800,000	
Interest paid	-310,000	
Income taxes paid	-1,700,000	
Net cash from operating activities		$2,790,000
Cash flows from investing activities		
Purchase of fixed assets	-580,000	
Proceeds from sale of equipment	110,000	
Net cash used in investing activities		-470,000
Cash flows from financing activities		
Proceeds from issuance of common stock	1,000,000	
Proceeds from issuance of long-term debt	500,000	
Principal payments under capital lease obligation	-10,000	
Dividends paid	-450,000	
Net cash used in financing activities		1,040,000
Net increase in cash and cash equivalents		3,360,000
Cash and cash equivalents at beginning of period		1,640,000
Cash and cash equivalents at end of period		$5,000,000

Reconciliation of net income to net cash provided by operating activities:

Net income		$2,665,000
Adjustments to reconcile net income to net cash provided by operating activities:		
Depreciation and amortization	$125,000	
Provision for losses on accounts receivable	15,000	
Gain on sale of equipment	-155,000	
Increase in interest and income taxes payable	32,000	
Increase in deferred taxes	90,000	
Increase in other liabilities	18,000	
Total adjustments		125,000
Net cash provided by operating activities		$2,790,000

The standard-setting bodies encourage the use of the direct method, but it is rarely used, for the excellent reason that the information in it is difficult to assemble; companies simply do not collect and store information in the manner required for this format. Instead, they use the indirect method, which is described next.

The Indirect Method

Under the indirect method of presenting the statement of cash flows, the presentation begins with net income or loss, with subsequent additions to or deductions from that amount for non-cash revenue and expense items, resulting in net income provided by operating activities. The format of the indirect method appears in the following example.

EXAMPLE

Milagro Corporation constructs the following statement of cash flows using the indirect method:

Milagro Corporation
Statement of Cash Flows
For the year ended 12/31/20X1

Cash flows from operating activities		
Net income		$3,000,000
Adjustments for:		
Depreciation and amortization	$125,000	
Provision for losses on accounts receivable	20,000	
Gain on sale of facility	-65,000	
		80,000
Increase in trade receivables		-250,000
Decrease in inventories		325,000
Decrease in trade payables		-50,000

		25,000
Cash generated from operations		3,105,000
Cash flows from investing activities		
Purchase of fixed assets	-500,000	
Proceeds from sale of equipment	35,000	
Net cash used in investing activities		-465,000
Cash flows from financing activities		
Proceeds from issuance of common stock	150,000	
Proceeds from issuance of long-term debt	175,000	
Dividends paid	-45,000	
Net cash used in financing activities		280,000
Net increase in cash and cash equivalents		2,920,000
Cash and cash equivalents at beginning of period		2,080,000
Cash and cash equivalents at end of period		$5,000,000

The Statement of Retained Earnings

The statement of retained earnings, also known as the statement of shareholders' equity, is essentially a reconciliation of the beginning and ending balances in a company's equity during an accounting period. It is not considered an essential part of the monthly financial statements, and so is the least likely of all the financial statements to be issued. However, it is a common part of the annual financial statements. This section discusses the format of the statement.

Overview of the Statement of Retained Earnings

The statement of retained earnings reconciles changes in the retained earnings account during an accounting period. The statement starts with the beginning balance in the retained earnings account, and then adds or subtracts such items as profits and dividend payments to arrive at the ending retained earnings balance. The general calculation structure of the statement is:

Beginning retained earnings + Net income − Dividends +/− Other changes

= Ending retained earnings

The statement of retained earnings is most commonly presented as a separate statement, but can also be added to another financial statement. The following example shows a simplified format for the statement.

The Financial Statements

EXAMPLE

The controller of Milagro Corporation assembles the following statement of retained earnings to accompany his issuance of the financial statements of the company:

Milagro Corporation
Statement of Retained Earnings
For the year ended 12/31/20X1

Retained earnings at December 31, 20X0	$150,000
Net income for the year ended December 31, 20X1	40,000
Dividends paid to shareholders	-25,000
Retained earnings at December 31, 20X1	**$165,000**

It is also possible to provide a greatly expanded version of the statement of retained earnings that discloses the various elements of retained earnings. For example, it could separately identify the par value of common stock, additional paid-in capital, retained earnings, and treasury stock, with all of these elements then rolling up into the total just noted in the last example. The following example show what the format could look like.

EXAMPLE

The controller of Milagro Corporation creates an expanded version of the statement of retained earnings in order to provide more visibility into activities involving equity. The statement follows:

Milagro Corporation
Statement of Retained Earnings
For the year ended 12/31/20X1

	Common Stock, $1 par	Additional Paid-in Capital	Retained Earnings	Total Shareholders' Equity
Retained earnings at December 31, 20X0	$10,000	$40,000	$100,000	$150,000
Net income for the year ended December 31, 20X1			40,000	40,000
Dividends paid to shareholders			-25,000	-25,000
Retained earnings at December 31, 20X1	$10,000	$40,000	$115,000	$165,000

Financial Statement Disclosures

The number of possible footnote disclosures is extremely large. The following list touches upon the more common footnotes, and is by no means even remotely comprehensive. If a company is in a specialized industry, there may be a number of additional disclosures required that are specific to that industry. A representative set of financial statement disclosures include:

- *Accounting policies.* Describes significant accounting principles followed. For example:

    Cash and Cash Equivalents

    We consider all highly liquid instruments purchased with an original maturity of three months or less to be cash equivalents. We continually monitor our positions with, and the credit quality of, the financial institutions with which we invest. As of the balance sheet dates, and periodically throughout the year, we have maintained balances in various operating accounts in excess of federally insured limits.

    Concentrations of Credit Risk

    We grant credit in the normal course of business, primarily consisting of accounts receivable and subscriptions receivable. We periodically perform credit analyses and monitor the financial condition of our major customers to reduce credit risk.

    Trade Accounts Receivable

    At the time accounts receivable originate, we consider the need for an allowance for doubtful accounts. We continually review the provision for uncollectible amounts; we adjust it to maintain the allowance at a level considered adequate to cover future losses. The allowance is our best estimate of uncollectible amounts; we determine it based on historical performance which we track on an ongoing basis. The losses we ultimately incur may differ materially in the near term from the amounts estimated in determining the allowance.

    Identifiable Intangible Assets and Goodwill

    We account for our business acquisitions using the purchase method of accounting, which allocates the total cost of an acquisition to the underlying net assets based on their respective estimated fair values. As part of this allocation process, we identify and attribute values and estimated lives to the intangible assets acquired. We amortize identifiable intangible assets with finite lives on a straight-line basis over their respective lives.

- *Bad debts.* Notes the method used to derive bad debt reserves, and the reserve amount as of the balance sheet date. For example:

The company derives an allowance for doubtful accounts based on its actual bad debt losses over the preceding year, divided by the average accounts receivable balance in the measurement period. In addition, management believes that general economic conditions are worsening, and so has increased this reserve percentage from the calculated amount of 1.9% to 2.5% of outstanding receivables. In addition, the company recognizes a 100% bad debt reserve for any receivables that are more than 120 days old. These policies resulted in an ending allowance for doubtful accounts of $329,000.

- *Business combinations.* Describes the type of combination, the reason for the acquisition, the payment price, liabilities assumed, goodwill incurred, acquisition-related costs, and many other factors. For example:

    The company acquired T-Rex Construction in July 20x4 by paying $17.25 per share for all of the common shares of T-Rex outstanding. T-Rex rents cranes and ditch-digging equipment to construction contractors on a short-term basis. The company funded this acquisition with a long-term loan for $12,000,000 and $4,500,000 from its cash reserves. The purchase was allocated to the assets acquired and liabilities assumed, based on the estimated fair value of T-Rex as of the acquisition date. As a result of the transaction, the company recorded $1,000,000 of goodwill, as well as $2,900,000 of intangible assets that are attributable to customer relationships and non-competition agreements that have useful lives of four years. The operating results of T-Rex are included in the company's consolidated financial statements as of the effective date of the acquisition.

- *Cash.* Notes any uninsured cash balances or restrictions on the use of cash. For example:

    (1) The board of directors has authorized the restriction of $500,000 as a reserve in anticipation of a groundwater pollution settlement with the Environmental Protection Agency. This left approximately $2,400,000 in restricted cash as of the balance sheet date.

    (2) The company uses cash concentration systems to maximize its investment strategy. Doing so routinely results in cash investments exceeding Federal Deposit Insurance Corporation (FDIC) insurance limits. As of the balance sheet date, $2,000,000 held as cash reserves exceeded the FDIC insurance limits.

    (3) The company maintains a $350,000 compensating balance arrangement with Bank Eastern (Eastern) under the terms of its line of credit with Eastern. The terms allow Eastern to segregate this amount in a separate account, and prohibit use of the cash unless the line of credit balance is lower than $1,000,000.

- *Contingencies and commitments.* Describes the nature of any reasonably possible losses, and any guarantees, including maximum liabilities. For example:

    (1) The company has a contingent liability related to a groundwater contamination claim at its Stillwater facility. A settlement of $15,000,000 has been established through judicial hearings, but the company's insurance provider is claiming that it has no obligation to reimburse the company for the amount of the settlement. Company counsel believes that the claim of the insurance company is not valid, and that it will be forced to pay the company for the full amount of the settlement.

    (2) The company has guaranteed a term loan held by a key supplier, under which the company is liable for both the unpaid balance of the loan and any unpaid interest, though only after the lender has made a good-faith effort to collect these amounts from the supplier. The unpaid amount of principal and interest on the loan as of the balance sheet date was $1,400,000.

- *Customers.* States whether any customers comprise a significant proportion of the company's total business, and the amount of that proportion. For example:

    The company transacts a significant amount of its business with two customers. One customer comprises 20% of net revenues for the entire business, and 40% of the revenues for the Agricultural Products segment. The second customer comprises 24% of net revenues for the entire business, and 70% of the revenues for the Government Products business.

- *Debt.* Describes loans payable, interest rates, and maturities occurring over the next five years. For example:

    (1) The company has obtained an unsecured fixed-rate loan from Bank Eastern. Under the terms of the loan, the company pays a fixed 8.0% interest rate on $3,500,000 of debt. The loan requires principal payments of $500,000 at the end of each of the first three years of the loan, with the remaining principal balance due in a balloon payment on the termination date of the loan, which is December 15, 20x4.

    (2) The company has entered into a line of credit arrangement with Bank Eastern (Eastern). Under the terms of the agreement, the company pays an interest rate equal to the Eastern prime lending rate plus one percent, which equates to a 7.25% borrowing rate as of the date of the arrangement. The company can borrow up to $3,000,000 under the line of credit, and has used $400,000 of the

facility as of the balance sheet date. There are no covenants associated with the line of credit.

- *Fixed assets.* Notes the investments in various types of fixed assets, methods of depreciation used, the amount of capitalized interest, asset retirement obligations, and impairments. A simplified summary example is:

  > We state property and equipment at cost. For all property and equipment, we calculate depreciation utilizing the straight-line method over the estimated useful lives for owned assets or to the estimated salvage value, where appropriate, or over the related lease terms for leasehold improvements. Useful lives range from 1 to 7 years. Property and equipment include the following approximate amounts:

	December 31, 20x3
Computer equipment	$580,000
Software	429,000
Furniture and fixtures	161,000
Office equipment	23,000
Leasehold improvements	78,000
Less: Accumulated depreciation	-213,000
Fixed assets, net	$1,058,000

- *Goodwill and intangibles.* Reconciles any changes in goodwill during the period, and any impairment losses. For example:

  (1) The company recorded $1,000,000 of intangible assets related to the patents that it acquired as part of the J.C. Fellows acquisition. The company is amortizing these patents over ten years, which matches the remaining term of the acquired patents.

  (2) The company has written down its goodwill asset by $900,000. The reason for the write-down is that the company has elected to exit the cellphone tower market, and the $900,000 write-down is associated with the company's purchase of the MicroTower Company, which will be closed as a result of this decision.

- *Hedging.* States the objective and strategies for using a hedging instrument, as well as the risks being hedged. For example:

  > The company designates selected futures contracts as fair value hedges of firm commitments to purchase sugar cane for ethanol production. Changes in the fair value of a derivative that is highly effective and that is classified and qualified as a fair value hedge, as well as the gain or loss on the hedged item that is attributable to the hedged risk are recorded in the results of the current period.

An ineffective hedge results from a change in the fair value of the hedge that differs from fair value changes for the hedged item. The recorded amount of ineffectiveness related to the company's designated fair value hedges was insignificant during the fiscal year.

- *Impairments.* Describes any assets that have been impaired and the amount of the impairment. For example:

    The company has written down the value of the tanning beds used in its tanning salons, on the grounds that federal regulations have significantly reduced the resale prices of these units. The company hired an independent appraiser to determine the fair market values to which the book values of the tanning beds were reduced. The impairment loss was $320,000, and was recorded within the Other Gains and Losses line item in the income statement. Following the impairment charge, the book value of the tanning beds was $800,000.

- *Inventories.* Describes any cost flow assumptions used, as well as any lower of cost or market losses. For example:

    The company uses the last in, first out (LIFO) valuation method to calculate the cost of its inventories. The company experienced a loss of $150,000 during the period that was caused by the elimination of LIFO inventory layers. The company also recorded a loss of $100,000 during the period that was caused by the write-down of the cost of inventories to market, under the lower of cost or market rule.

- *Investments.* Notes the fair value and unrealized gains and losses on investments. For example:

    (1) The company uses quoted market prices for similar instruments to derive the fair value of its investments, or it estimates the fair value based on the discounted cash flows using interest rates available for similar instruments having approximately the same remaining maturities. Based on these derivations, the company has unrealized gains of approximately $180,000 on investments having an aggregate fair value of $4,300,000.

    (2) The company liquidated $5,000,000 of securities from its held-to-maturity portfolio in order to raise cash to pay off a debt whose covenants had been breached. This liquidation resulted in the recognition of a $50,000 gain.

- *Leases.* Itemizes future minimum lease payments. For example:

    The company has entered into a variety of leases for office equipment, furniture and fixtures, all of which are recorded as operating leases. The future minimum lease payments for these leases follow:

20x1	$150,000
20x2	135,000
20x3	70,000
20x4	65,000
20x5	22,000
	$442,000

- *Liabilities.* Describes any larger accrued liabilities. For example:

    The company accrues a liability for the amount of any vacation and sick time earned but not used by its employees. The company allows employees to accumulate up to four weeks of vacation time, while the potential amount of sick time that may be accrued is not limited. The company has accrued $620,000 for this liability.

- *Pensions.* Reconciles various elements of the company pension plan during the period, and describes investment policies. For example:

    (1) The investment policy of the pension plan is to balance the maintenance of a productive capital base with superior investment results. To do so, the plan invests approximately 50% in equities and 50% in debt securities. These proportions are altered over time in reaction to market conditions related to interest rates, inflation, and other factors.

    (2) The changes in the projected benefit obligation of plan assets for the year ended December 31 were as follows:

	December 31, 20x1
Net benefit obligation – beginning of year	$472,000
Service costs incurred	5,000
Employee contributions	20,000
Interest costs on projected benefit obligations	12,000
Actuarial gain	-14,000
Gross benefits paid	-28,000
Plan amendment	1,000
Foreign currency exchange rate change	7,000
Net benefit obligation – end of year	$475,000

- *Receivables.* Notes the carrying amount of any financial instruments that are used as collateral for borrowings, and concentrations of credit risk. For example:

The company has entered into a short-term loan arrangement with Bank Eastern (Eastern). Under the terms of this arrangement, the company has pledged the full amount of its accounts receivable as collateral on a line of credit. The amount loaned by Eastern is limited to 80% of all accounts receivable less than 90 days old. As of the balance sheet date, the amount of accounts receivable subject to this arrangement was $1,400,000.

- *Related parties.* States the nature of the relationship with a related party, and the amounts due to or from the other party. For example:

    Mr. Ray Osborne is a director of the company and is also the landlord from which the company leases its headquarters building. The annual total of these lease payments is $1,200,000, which the board of directors has determined is comparable to the current market rate. The lease expires on July 31, 20x5.

- *Revenue recognition.* Notes the company's revenue recognition policies. For example:

    (1) The company sells home security monitoring services along with its electronic home security systems. Monitoring revenue is recognized ratably over the term of the monitoring agreements, which varies from 24 to 48 months. As of the balance sheet date, the company had not recognized $3,700,000 of monitoring revenues.

    (2) The company sells solar panel arrays to customers at cost, and also earns 10% of any cost savings experienced by customers for the first three years following installation. The amounts of these savings are difficult to ascertain in advance, since they are strongly impacted by weather conditions. Thus, the company only recognizes its share of cost savings after the actual savings have been calculated, which is done in the month following each calendar quarter.

    (3) The company recognizes revenue under the specific performance method, where revenue is only recognized after customers have approved specific project milestones to which billable amounts are attached in the project contract.

    (4) The company sells its products through consignment arrangements with a variety of retail stores. Under the terms of these consignment agreements, the company records revenue only after it receives notification of a sale transaction from a consignee.

- *Risks and uncertainties.* Notes the use of significant estimates in accounting transactions, as well as various business vulnerabilities. For example:

(1) Due to the large number of hurricanes that have made landfall in the Louisiana area in the past few years, it is not possible to obtain flood insurance for the company's main processing facility in Louisiana. The company has built drainage systems around the facility and also stockpiled sandbags in case of flooding. Given these risk mitigation steps, management believes that the risk of loss from a hurricane has been reduced.

(2) A key component of the company's products is tungsten, which it buys under several long-term contracts from suppliers located in central Africa. These suppliers are based in locations where civil unrest has resulted in rioting over the past few years. In the event of a complete breakdown in tungsten supplies, management believes that it can obtain adequate supplies on the spot market, but at prices approximately 40% higher than those at which it purchases tungsten under its long-term contracts.

- *Segment data.* Identifies company segments and the operational results of each one. For example:

    The company has determined that it has two reportable segments, which are direct-to-consumer and pro shops. Other unreported segments include the company's product servicing and warranty insurance businesses. The following table reveals the operations of the company's reportable segments:

	Direct to Consumers	Pro Shops	Other Segments	Total
Revenues	$3,200,000	$4,700,000	$600,000	$8,500,000
Interest revenue	200,000	100,000	0	300,000
Interest expense	50,000	300,000	150,000	500,000
Depreciation	150,000	70,000	20,000	240,000
Segment profit	175,000	200,000	-20,000	355,000
Segment assets	750,000	350,000	100,000	1,200,000

- *Stockholders' equity.* Describes any changes in equity during the period, as well as the terms of any convertible equity and dividends in arrears. For example:

    (1) As of December 31, 20x1, the capital structure of the company consisted of 5,000,000 shares of common stock authorized and 3,250,000 shares outstanding, as well as 1,000,000 shares of preferred stock authorized and 125,000 shares outstanding. Both classes of stock have par values of $0.01 per share. The preferred stockholders are entitled to a $2.50 cumulative recurring dividend by the end of each calendar year, and are entitled to the payback

of their original investments in the event of the sale of the business, and before dividends are paid to common stockholders.

(2) On October 15, 20x2, the board of directors authorized the amendment of the company's articles of incorporation to increase the number of authorized shares of preferred stock to 2,000,000 from the prior level of 1,000,000.

(3) On November 14, 20x2, the board of directors declared a cash dividend of $2.00 per share, payable on December 29, 20x2, to shareholders of record on November 29, 20x2. The distribution of this dividend does not violate any of the company's loan covenants.

(4) The board of directors deferred the payment of $1.00 per share of dividends declared on November 14, 20x2, totaling $500,000, due to a cash shortfall caused by the delayed repatriation of cash from a foreign subsidiary.

- *Subsequent events*. Discloses the nature of subsequent events and estimates their financial effect. For example:

    (1) Subsequent to the reporting period, the company issued 25,000 shares of preferred stock at an average price of $15 per share. This resulted in receipts, net of transactional fees, of $350,000. Management intends to use the funds for a possible acquisition.

    (2) From January 30 through February 12, the company repurchased 2,000,000 shares of its common stock at an average price of $9.90. The total expenditure related to this activity was $19,800,000.

    (3) The company has evaluated subsequent events through April 4, 20x1, the date when the financial statements were issued. The company is not aware of any subsequent events that would require recognition or disclosure in the financial statements.

Clearly, the sheer volume of disclosures can overshadow the financial statements themselves. When many disclosures are provided, they can be a rich source of information for the analyst, since they can reveal the detail behind the summarized information that appears in the financial statements.

Summary

This chapter has discussed each of the financial statements and revealed a number of formats in which they might be encountered. Much of the source material for the financial analysis noted in later chapters comes from the financial statements, so it makes sense to develop a deep familiarity with the layout and content of these statements, as well as the types of disclosures that are likely to accompany them.

The Financial Statements

Your level of knowledge of financial statements should be sufficient to understand when information is missing from them, or hidden by being aggregated into other line items. For example, depreciation may not have been recorded for monthly financial statements, so the reported results are skewed upward until year-end, when a massive full-year depreciation entry is recognized. Similarly, you should understand the relationships between the different line items in the financial statements, so that an unusual number in one part of the financials can be explained by information stated elsewhere. For example, a sharp decline in accounts payable could lead you to believe that a business is now being required by its suppliers to pay cash in advance, which can be supported by an examination of the amount of cash on hand (which should decline) and the amount of debt (which should increase). In short, in-depth financial analysis can only be achieved through the close examination of each of the financial statements and their accompanying disclosures.

Chapter 3
Accounting Issues Impacting the Financials

Introduction

In the last chapter, we described the types of financial statements and the various formats in which they can be reported. In this chapter, we address a number of accounting issues that can impact the information reported in those financial statements. When reviewing financials, be aware of which of the following issues may be impacting reported results, and the manner in which they can skew the financial statements.

The Basis of Accounting

Most financial statements are generated using the accrual basis of accounting, though a few may be created using alternative methods. In this section, we describe the nature of accrual basis accounting, the cash basis of accounting, and a hybrid version that includes some characteristics of both approaches. From an analysis perspective, it is important to understand which method is being used by a reporting entity, since the basis of accounting can influence the reported results and financial position of a business.

Accrual Basis of Accounting

The accrual basis of accounting is the concept of recording revenues when earned and expenses as incurred. For example, a company operating under the accrual basis of accounting will record a sale as soon as it issues an invoice to a customer. Similarly, such a company would record an expense as soon as it is incurred.

The accrual basis of accounting is advocated under both generally accepted accounting principles (GAAP) and international financial reporting standards (IFRS). Both of these accounting frameworks provide guidance regarding how to account for revenue and expense transactions in the absence of cash receipts from customers or payments to suppliers.

The accrual basis of accounting tends to provide consistent recognition of revenues and expenses over time, and so is considered by investors to be the most valid accounting system for ascertaining the results of operations, financial position, and cash flows of a business. In particular, it supports the matching principle, under which revenues and all related expenses are to be recorded within the same reporting period; by doing so, it should be possible to see the full extent of the profits and losses associated with specific business transactions within a single reporting period.

The accrual basis requires the use of estimates in certain areas. For example, a company should record an expense for estimated bad debts that have not yet been incurred. By doing so, all expenses related to a revenue transaction are recorded at the same time as the revenue, which results in an income statement that fully reflects the results of operations. Similarly, the estimated amounts of product returns, sales allowances, and obsolete inventory may be recorded.

A significant failing of the accrual basis of accounting is that it can indicate the presence of profits, even though the associated cash inflows have not yet occurred. The result can be a supposedly profitable entity that is starved for cash, and which may therefore go bankrupt despite its reported level of profitability. Consequently, pay attention to the statement of cash flows of a business, which indicates the flows of cash into and out of a business.

Cash Basis of Accounting

The cash basis of accounting is the practice of only recording revenue when cash has been received from a customer, and recording expenses only when cash has been paid out. The cash basis is commonly used by individuals and small businesses. This method has the following advantages:

- *Taxation*. The method is commonly used to record financial results for tax purposes, since a business can accelerate some payments in order to reduce its taxable profits, thereby deferring its tax liability.
- *Ease of use*. A person requires a reduced knowledge of accounting to keep records under the cash basis.

However, the cash basis of accounting also suffers from the following problems:

- *Accuracy*. The cash basis of accounting yields less accurate results than the accrual basis of accounting, since the timing of cash flows do not necessarily reflect the proper timing of changes in the financial condition of a business. For example, if a contract with a customer does not allow a business to issue an invoice until the end of a project, the company will be unable to report any revenue until the invoice has been issued and cash received.
- *Manipulation*. A business can alter its reported results by not cashing received checks or altering the payment timing for its liabilities.
- *Lending*. Lenders do not feel that the cash basis generates overly accurate financial statements, and so may refuse to lend money to a business reporting under the cash basis.
- *Audited financial statements*. Auditors will not approve financial statements that were compiled under the cash basis of accounting, so a business will need to convert to the accrual basis if it wants to have audited financial statements.
- *Management reporting*. Since the results of cash basis financial statements can be inaccurate, management reports should not be issued that are based upon it.

In short, the numerous problems with the cash basis of accounting usually cause businesses to abandon it after they move beyond their initial startup phases.

Modified Cash Basis of Accounting

The modified cash basis of accounting uses elements of both the cash basis and accrual basis of accounting. Under the cash basis, recognize a transaction when there is either incoming cash or outgoing cash; thus, the receipt of cash from a customer triggers the recordation of revenue, while the payment of a supplier triggers the recordation of an asset or expense. Under the accrual basis, record revenue when it is earned and expenses when they are incurred, irrespective of any changes in cash.

The modified cash basis establishes a position part way between the cash and accrual methods. The modified basis has the following features:

- *Records short-term items when cash levels change (the cash basis).* This means that nearly all elements of the income statement are recorded using the cash basis, and that accounts receivable and inventory are not recorded in the balance sheet.
- *Records longer-term balance sheet items with accruals (the accrual basis).* This means that fixed assets and long-term debt are recorded on the balance sheet, and depreciation and amortization in the income statement.

The modified cash basis provides financial information that is more relevant than can be found with cash basis record keeping, and generally does so at less cost than is needed to maintain a set of full-accrual accounting records. Thus, it can be considered a cost-effective approach to bookkeeping.

There are no exact specifications for what is allowed under the modified cash basis, since it has developed through common usage. There is no accounting standard that has imposed any rules on its usage.

The modified cash basis is not allowed by GAAP or IFRS, which means that a business using this basis will need to alter the recordation of those elements of its transactions that were recorded under the cash basis, so that they are now accrual basis transactions. Otherwise, an auditor will not sign off on its financial statements.

Effect of the Fiscal Year

The fiscal year is the 12-month period over which a company reports its financial results. The date range used for the fiscal year of a business can impact the information reported on its balance sheet.

Ideally, a company should use its natural business year as its fiscal year. The natural business year is the period of 12 months that terminates in a natural low point in the sales activity of the business. The natural business year is an ideal choice for being the fiscal year, since the natural low point at the end of the period should coincide with a decline in the accounts receivable, accounts payable, and inventory levels that a business states in its accounting records. These lower balances are easier to audit, and also make it easier to close the books for the year.

Two examples of natural business years are:

- Retail stores typically have their highest sales volume in December, followed by a steep decline in January. Thus, the 12 months ended January 31 is a reasonable natural business year.
- A farmer sends crops to market in the fall, after which there should be few stored crops on hand. Thus, a 12-month period ending in late fall is a reasonable natural business year.

When there is no discernible natural business year, many organizations tend to adopt the calendar year as their fiscal year.

As just noted, the assets and liabilities stated on the balance sheet tend to be at their lowest at the end of the natural business year. If a company elects to use a different range of dates for its fiscal year, the result may well be year-end balance sheet information that is much higher than what is being reported by other companies in the same industry that use a different fiscal year. Thus, when comparing the full-year results of several companies in the same industry, be aware of the effect of the fiscal year date range on the balance sheet.

Recordation of Revenue at Gross or Net

A major issue that impacts the interpretation of financial statements is whether revenues are being recorded at their gross or net amounts. Recording revenue *at gross* means that *all* of the revenue from a sale transaction is recorded on the income statement. Recording revenue *at net* means that only a commission is being recorded on a sale transaction, rather than the full amount of the sale. If there is no commission, it is still possible to report revenue at net by netting the amount billed to the customer against the amount paid to the supplier.

There are a number of accounting guidelines for whether to record a sale transaction at gross or net. It is more likely that a business reports sale transactions at gross under the following circumstances:

- The business is the primary obligor in a sale transaction. This means the business is responsible for providing the product or service.
- The business has general inventory risk. This means the company takes title to inventory before selling it to customers, and takes title to any returns from customers.
- The business gets to select suppliers. This rule implies that there is no key supplier operating in the background who is actually running the sale transaction.
- The business has credit risk, which means that the company absorbs a bad debt if the customer does not pay. Conversely, if the business only loses a commission in the event of customer non-payment, the transaction should be recorded at net.
- The business sets the price to the customer. This implies that the business has control over the entire sale transaction.

It is more likely that a business reports sale transactions at net under the following circumstances:

- The amount earned by the business is fixed. This indicates a commission structure, which is sometimes set up as a fixed payment per customer transaction. If the business earns a percentage of what the customer pays, this is also an indicator that revenue should be reported at net. In either case, the business is essentially acting as an agent for a third party.
- The supplier has credit risk, and so will bear the loss if a customer does not pay.
- The supplier is responsible for providing goods or services to the customer.

These guidelines make it fairly clear how to treat revenue in most situations. However, there are gray areas where a case could be made to record revenue either way. For example, a travel discounter negotiates with the airlines for reduced prices. The discounter then advertises the reduced rates to the public. The discounter bills the customer, and is responsible for delivering the ticket to the customer. However, once the customer receives the ticket, the airline is responsible for all subsequent service. The discounter has no inventory risk and the primary obligor is the airline, which seems to indicate that the discounter should record all sales at net. On the other hand, the discounter can set the price and bears all credit risk, which tends to point toward the recordation of revenue at gross.

Recordation at gross or net is a particular problem when comparing the results of two companies that use differing recordation methods. The business recording at gross will appear to have much more transaction volume, but a vastly lower profit percentage than the business that records at net.

Bill and Hold Revenue

A possible source of fraudulent revenue recognition is the bill and hold transaction, where the seller has not yet shipped goods to the buyer, but still records the related revenue. The Securities and Exchange Commission (SEC) allows these transactions but only under highly restricted circumstances. The SEC requires that all of the following criteria be met before a bill and hold transaction is allowed:

- The risks of ownership have passed to the buyer
- The buyer has committed in writing to buy the goods
- The buyer has requested that the seller hold the goods, and has a business reason for doing so
- There is a scheduled delivery date for the goods that is reasonable
- There are no remaining obligations that the seller must complete
- The goods cannot be used to fill orders from other customers, and so have been segregated
- The goods must have been completed

To make matters even more difficult, the SEC points out that the following additional factors be considered:

- The extent to which the seller is modifying its normal terms for this transaction
- The seller's history of employing bill and hold transactions
- The extent to which the buyer will lose if the market value of the held goods subsequently declines
- The extent to which the holding risk of the seller can be insured
- The extent to which the seller's holding of the goods really creates a contingent sale that the buyer could reject

In short, the presence of bill and hold transactions should be a cause for alarm. If it is possible to identify the amount of these transactions, the analyst would be well advised to subtract them from the sales of the company under review, to determine how the business is performing without them.

Negative Cash

It is possible for a negative cash balance to appear on the balance sheet if a business has issued checks for more funds than it has available in its bank account. When a negative cash balance is present, it is customary for the company controller to create a zero cash balance by moving the amount of the overdrawn checks into a liability account and setting up the journal entry to automatically reverse, thereby shifting the cash withdrawal back into the cash account at the beginning of the next reporting period.

When a company's balance sheet has a zero or negative cash balance, it is reasonable to assume that one of the following situations exists:

- The company has overdrawn its bank account, which brings up questions about its liquidity, and therefore its ability to continue as a going concern.
- The company is playing games with its suppliers, printing checks in order to "prove" that checks were created on time, and then holding onto the checks until there is sufficient cash to keep them from being rejected by the bank.
- The company is relying upon an overdraft arrangement with its bank to fund these additional payments, which means that it probably suffers from ongoing cash problems.

Inventory Costing Methods

There are several ways in which a business can record the cost of its inventory asset. The method chosen can alter the valuation of the inventory, which in turn impacts the cost of goods sold, and therefore the amount of reported profit. In brief, if the inventory valuation method tends to store more costs in inventory, then the cost of goods sold will be reduced and profits will increase. Conversely, if the valuation method tends to store fewer costs in inventory, then the cost of goods sold will be increased and profits will be smaller. The more commonly used inventory costing methods and their characteristics are as follows:

- *First in, first out (FIFO) method.* Under the FIFO method, a business assumes that items bought first are used or sold first, which also means that the items still in stock are the newest ones. This policy closely matches the actual movement of inventory in most companies, and so is preferable from a theoretical perspective. In periods of rising prices (which is most of the time), assuming that the earliest units bought are the first ones used also means that the least expensive units are charged to the cost of goods sold first. This means that the cost of goods sold tends to be lower, which therefore leads to a higher amount of operating earnings and more income taxes paid.
- *Last in, first out (LIFO) method.* Under the LIFO method, the assumption is that items bought last are sold first, which also means that the items still in stock are the oldest units. This policy does not follow the natural flow of inventory in most companies, which is why the method is banned under IFRS. In periods of rising prices, assuming that the last units bought are the first ones used also means that the cost of goods sold tends to be higher, which therefore leads to a lower amount of operating earnings, and fewer income taxes paid.
- *Weighted average method.* Under this method, there is only one inventory layer. This is because the cost of new inventory purchases are rolled into the cost of any existing inventory to derive a new weighted average cost, which in turn is adjusted again as more inventory is purchased. This method results in the derivation of a consistent cost of goods sold figure from period to period.
- *Specific identification method.* Under this approach, the cost of each item is separately tracked in inventory, and the specific cost of each item is charged to the cost of goods sold when that item is sold. This approach requires a massive amount of data tracking, so it is only usable for very high-cost, unique items, such as automobiles or works of art. It is not a viable method in most other situations.

From a financial analysis perspective, the main issue is whether the FIFO or LIFO method is being used, since they can alter the reported amount of profit. If the weighted average or specific identification method is used, there should not be any significant variation in the amount of inventory charged to the cost of goods sold across multiple reporting periods.

Depreciation Methods

If a company has a large investment in fixed assets, the depreciation method that it elects to use can have a significant impact on its reported level of profitability.

Consequently, be aware of the different types of depreciation and how they can affect profits.

Depreciation is the systematic reduction of the recorded cost of a fixed asset. The reason for using depreciation is to match a portion of the cost of a fixed asset to the revenue that it generates; this is mandated under the matching principle, where revenues are recorded with their associated expenses in the same reporting period in order to give a complete picture of the results of a revenue-generating transaction. The net effect of depreciation is a gradual decline in the reported carrying amount of fixed assets on the balance sheet, unless the company is committed to a long-term fixed asset replenishment program.

There are a number of methods available for depreciating fixed assets, which fall into these general categories:

- *Straight line.* The straight line method charges the same amount of depreciation to expense in every reporting period. This approach probably approximates the average usage pattern of most assets, and so is a reasonable way to match revenues to expenses. It is also the easiest depreciation method to calculate, which makes it the most commonly-used method. The use of straight-line depreciation makes the job of the financial analyst much easier, since it has a benign impact on the reported level of profitability from period to period.
- *Accelerated.* An accelerated depreciation method is designed to charge the bulk of the depreciable amount of a fixed asset to expense as soon as possible, with a rapidly-declining amount being charged to expense in later periods. This approach is useful for depressing short-term profits in order to reduce the amount of taxable income. From a financial analysis perspective, the use of accelerated depreciation can seriously skew the reported results of a business. If so, it may be better to conduct an analysis based on the statement of cash flows, rather than the income statement. The most common calculation methods for accelerated depreciation are:

Accelerated Depreciation Method	Calculation
Double declining balance	2 × Straight-line depreciation rate × Book value at the beginning of the year
150% declining balance	1.5 × Straight-line depreciation rate × Book value at the beginning of the year
Sum of the years' digits	Number of years of estimated life remaining ÷ Sum of the years' digits for the full depreciation period

- *Usage based.* A usage-based depreciation method is designed to have a variable periodic depreciation expense that is based on the amount that a fixed asset is actually used. An example of this method is the units of production method. This is the most accurate of the depreciation methods for matching actual usage to the related depreciation expense, but suffers from an inordinate amount of record keeping to track usage levels. Given this problem, it is usually restricted to the more expensive fixed assets. The impact of a usage-based methodology on financial analysis is variable; the rate will change with activity levels, which converts depreciation into more of a variable cost than a fixed cost.

The following table illustrates the differences in the amount of depreciation that would be recognized under the straight line and accelerated methods of depreciation for a $1,000 asset over a five-year period. The accelerated depreciation method used in the comparison is the sum of the years' digits method:

Depreciation Comparison for a $1,000 Asset

Year	Straight Line Depreciation	Sum of the Years' Digits Depreciation
1	$200	$333
2	200	267
3	200	200
4	200	133
5	200	67
Totals	$1,000	$1,000

In the example, note how the accelerated depreciation method distorts the reporting of expenses, so that the first two years of expense are significantly higher than the straight line method, while the last two years of expense are significantly lower.

Usage-based depreciation methods are uncommon, except in certain industries, such as forest products and airlines, where it makes sense to track usage levels at an individual asset level. In most other cases, the key concern is the use of accelerated depreciation. If used, the main issues are:

- The extent to which accelerated depreciation is being used across the various types of asset categories;
- The exact method used (since some methods are more accelerated than others); and
- How it will impact reported financial results.

Current Value Accounting

Current value accounting is the concept that assets and liabilities be measured at the current value at which they could be sold or settled as of the current date. This varies from the historically-used method of only recording assets and liabilities at the amounts at which they were originally acquired or incurred (which represents a more conservative viewpoint).

The reason for using current value is that it provides information to the readers of a company's financial statements that most closely relates to current business conditions. This is a real concern when reviewing the financial statements of older companies that may have assets and liabilities on their books from many years in the past, but is less of an issue for newer companies where this is not the case. It is a particular problem when a business has older inventory or fixed assets whose current values may differ sharply from their recorded values.

Current value is also of use when there has been a prolonged period of excessive inflation. Under these conditions, the historical values at which assets and liabilities were recorded will likely be much lower than their current values.

Both GAAP and IFRS have been moving in the direction of requiring more current value accounting, so that fewer assets and liabilities are still recorded on the balance sheet at their original costs.

Though current value accounting has been presented here as generally a good concept, it suffers from the following problems:

- *Accounting cost.* It takes time to accumulate current value information, which increases the cost and time associated with the production of financial statements.
- *Availability of information.* It can be difficult or impossible to obtain current value information about some assets and liabilities.
- *Accuracy of information.* Some current value information may be based less on facts and more on guesses or poorly-founded estimates, which impacts the reliability of the financial statements in which this information is included.

Illusory Profits

Illusory profits are generated when there is a difference between historical and current costs. These profits are largest when two circumstances are present:

- Costs are rising; and
- A business has a large asset base.

Under these circumstances, an organization may charge to expense older costs that have been on the books for some time, and which can only be replaced at higher current costs. Thus, the profits reported have only occurred because the firm had a large store of assets that were acquired at a lower cost. Once these assets are depleted, the illusory profits will vanish.

For example, a business has a cost layering system that requires it to retain in its records the costs of the earliest inventory items acquired, until these items are used. When these inventory items are eventually sold, their earlier (and lower) costs are charged to expense. If the company had not retained these extra units of inventory, the company would instead have been forced to acquire or produce goods at current costs, and then charge these costs to expense, which would have resulted in a lower reported profit.

Financial Statement Reporting Issues

A company may elect to issue financial results that are not strictly in accordance with the accounting standards, or which have been adjusted to yield better results than would normally be the case. This section describes several of these situations to be aware of when reviewing financial statements.

Headline Earnings

Headline earnings is a subset of the profits reported by a business. It only includes the following earnings:

- Profits or losses generated by operations
- Profits or losses generated by investment activities

Headline earnings does not include the following types of earnings:

- Profits or losses caused by the sale of assets
- Profits or losses caused by the termination of discontinued operations
- Profits or losses caused by write-downs in the value of assets
- Profits or losses caused by reductions in the number of employees

Headline earnings are useful for a financial analyst who wants to determine the earnings level of the core day-to-day operations of a business, without other ancillary transactions cluttering up the earnings information. It is also useful for comparing the results of the core operations of similar businesses. However, this presentation is not allowed under any accounting standards.

EXAMPLE

Fireball Flight Services reports $100,000 of earnings in its most recent quarter, which includes a $10,000 gain on the sale of fixed assets and a $30,000 impairment charge on other fixed assets. The headline earnings for Fireball would be $120,000, which factors out the two transactions just noted.

Pro Forma Earnings

Pro forma earnings are based on an alternative measure of performance that typically excludes various costs at the discretion of the reporting entity, allegedly to compensate for deficiencies in GAAP or IFRS.

Because the accounting frameworks require the inclusion of various non-cash charges and credits, as well as nonrecurring gains and losses, the argument in favor of pro forma earnings states that compliance with an accounting framework does not provide investors with a true picture of an entity's performance. Thus, the intent of pro forma earnings reporting is to reveal an entity's "normalized" earnings, which typically do not include such items as charges for layoffs, inventory obsolescence, or asset impairments.

Pro forma earnings tend to exclude supposedly one-time expense events, and so nearly always reveal earnings that are better than those reported under strict compliance with an accounting framework. However, one-time events are usually events that *are* recurring, just not very frequently, and so should be included in the calculation of earnings.

When a publicly held company wants to release a non-GAAP financial measurement, its ability to do so is governed by Regulation G of the Securities and Exchange Commission (SEC). The regulation requires that the issuance of a non-GAAP financial measurement be accompanied by the following information:

- The most comparable financial metric, both calculated and presented as per GAAP; and
- A reconciliation of the non-GAAP information to this most comparable financial metric.

The SEC considers a non-GAAP financial measurement to be one that includes either more or less information than is included in the most comparable GAAP financial metric.

In short, the analyst should consider any pro forma earnings released by a business to be excessively optimistic, and therefore to be viewed with suspicion. If there is an SEC-mandated reconciliation of pro forma earnings, use it to determine which items were stripped out of the reported earnings.

Window Dressing

Window dressing refers to actions taken by management to improve the appearance of a company's financial statements, usually shortly before the end of a reporting period. Window dressing is particularly common when a business has a large number of shareholders, so that management can give the appearance of a well-run company to investors who probably do not have much day-to-day contact with the business. It may also be used when a company wants to impress a lender in order to qualify for a loan. If a business is closely held, the owners are usually better informed about company results, so there is no reason for anyone to apply window dressing to the financial statements. Examples of window dressing are:

- *Cash.* Postpone paying suppliers, so that the period-end cash balance appears higher than it should be.
- *Accounts receivable.* Record an unusually low bad debt expense, so that the accounts receivable balance (and therefore the current ratio) looks better than is really the case.
- *Fixed assets.* Sell off those fixed assets with large amounts of accumulated depreciation associated with them, so the net book value of the remaining assets appears to indicate a relatively new cluster of assets.

- *Revenue*. Offer customers an early shipment discount, thereby accelerating revenues from a future period into the current period.
- *Depreciation*. Switch from accelerated to straight line depreciation in order to reduce the amount of depreciation charged to expense in the current period.
- *Expenses*. Withhold supplier expenses, so that they are recorded in a later period.

The entire concept of window dressing is clearly unethical, since it is misleading. Also, it merely robs results from a future period in order to make the current period look better, so it is extremely short-term in nature.

Auditor Certification

When reviewing the financial statements of a business, be sure to examine the level of auditor certification that accompanies the statements. Only a full audit gives reasonable assurance that an auditor has conducted an in-depth review of an entity's financial statements. Two other variations on the audit, the review and compilation, do not provide such a high level of assurance (if any). The types of certifications are:

- *Audit*. A financial statement audit is the examination of an entity's financial statements and accompanying disclosures by an auditor, resulting in a report by the auditor, attesting to the fairness of presentation of the financial statements and related disclosures. Lenders typically require an audit of the financial statements of any entity to which they lend funds. Audits are also required for all publicly-held companies.
- *Review*. A financial statement review is a service under which the auditor obtains limited assurance that there are no material modifications that need to be made to an entity's financial statements for them to be in conformity with the applicable accounting framework. A review does not require the auditor to obtain an understanding of internal controls, or to assess fraud risk, or to conduct several other audit procedures. Consequently, a review does not provide the analyst with assurance that the auditor has become aware of all the significant matters that would normally have been discovered and disclosed in an audit.
- *Compilation*. A financial statement compilation is a service to assist the management of a business in presenting its financial statements. This presentation involves no activities to obtain any assurance that there are no material modifications needed for the financial statements to be in conformity with the applicable accounting framework. Thus, a person engaged in a compilation does not use inquiries, analytical procedures, or review procedures, nor is there any requirement to understand internal controls, or engage in other audit procedures. In short, compilation activities are not designed to provide any assurance regarding a company's financial statements.

In summary, financial statements for which only review services were provided should be viewed with a certain amount of caution, while compilations have essentially not been audited, and so may be considered to contain the least reliable information of all. When these financial statements are encountered, the question for the analyst to pursue is why these services were used – in some cases, companies pay for reviews or compilations precisely because they *do not* want an in-depth investigation of their accounting records.

Summary

Most of the issues noted in this chapter impact either reported profits or the financial position of a business. They do not usually impact the statement of cash flows. Consequently, if there is ever an issue regarding whether an accounting policy is altering the financial statements, you can sidestep the concern by concentrating the bulk of the analysis efforts on the statement of cash flows.

While the issues covered here can skew financial statements, they are of somewhat less concern when applied by the issuing entity on a consistent basis, since the analyst can still track information on a trend line to spot anomalies. The effects of these issues are considerably worsened when the senior management of a company continually changes its accounting policies to manipulate reported results. When accounting policies are being manipulated, the analyst is faced with a veritable minefield of accounting issues that must be stripped away in order to obtain a true picture of a company's financial and operational situation.

Chapter 4
Interpretation of Financial Statements

Introduction

When reviewing the financial statements of a business, what interpretation can be extracted from these statements? In this chapter, we cover several types of financial statement analysis, mostly related to the ratio comparison of different line items in the statements. By comparing these results, and especially over multiple reporting periods, we can arrive at a reasonable estimation of the financial results and condition of a business. We also include a cautionary discussion of the limitations of ratio analysis.

Interpretation of Financial Statements

There are two key techniques for analyzing financial statements. The first is the use of horizontal and vertical analysis. Horizontal analysis is the comparison of financial information over a series of reporting periods, while vertical analysis is the proportional analysis of a financial statement, where each line item on a statement is listed as a percentage of another item. Typically, this means that every line item on an income statement is stated as a percentage of gross sales, while every line item on a balance sheet is stated as a percentage of total assets. Thus, horizontal analysis is the review of the results of multiple time periods, while vertical analysis is the review of the proportion of accounts to each other within a single period. Later sections describe horizontal and vertical analysis more fully.

Another heavily-used technique is ratio analysis. Ratios are used to calculate the relative size of one number in relation to another. After a ratio is calculated, compare it to the same ratio calculated for a prior period, or that is based on an industry average, to see if the target company is performing in accordance with expectations. In a typical financial statement analysis, most ratios will be within expectations, leaving a small number of outlier ratios that require additional detailed analysis.

There are several general categories of ratios, each designed to examine a different aspect of a company's performance. These categories are:

- *Liquidity ratios*. This is the most fundamentally important set of ratios, because they measure the ability of a company to remain in business. Samples of ratios in this category are:
    o *Cash coverage ratio*. Shows the amount of cash available to pay interest.
    o *Current ratio*. Measures the amount of liquidity available to pay for current liabilities.

- *Quick ratio.* The same as the current ratio, but does not include inventory.
- *Liquidity index.* Measures the amount of time required to convert assets into cash.

- *Activity ratios.* These ratios are a strong indicator of the quality of management, since they reveal how well management is utilizing company resources. Samples of ratios in this category are:
  - *Accounts payable turnover ratio.* Measures the speed with which a company pays its suppliers.
  - *Accounts receivable turnover ratio.* Measures a company's ability to collect accounts receivable.
  - *Inventory turnover ratio.* Measures the amount of inventory needed to support a given level of sales.
  - *Fixed asset turnover ratio.* Measures a company's ability to generate sales from a certain base of fixed assets.
  - *Sales to working capital ratio.* Shows the amount of working capital required to support a given amount of sales.

- *Leverage ratios.* These ratios reveal the extent to which a company is relying upon debt to fund its operations, and its ability to pay back the debt. Samples of ratios in the category are:
  - *Debt to equity ratio.* Shows the extent to which management is willing to fund operations with debt, rather than equity.
  - *Fixed charge coverage.* Shows the ability of a company to pay for its fixed costs.

- *Profitability ratios.* These ratios measure how well a company performs in generating a profit. Samples of ratios in this category are:
  - *Breakeven point.* Reveals the sales level at which a company breaks even.
  - *Gross profit ratio.* Shows revenues minus the cost of goods sold, as a proportion of sales.
  - *Net profit ratio.* Calculates the amount of profit after taxes and all expenses have been deducted from net sales.
  - *Return on net assets.* Shows company profits as a percentage of fixed assets and working capital.

Each of these ratios is described in more detail in the following sections. At the end of the chapter, we also note the use of EBITDA and NOPAT as additional techniques for the interpretation of financial statements.

Interpretation of Financial Statements

Horizontal Analysis

Horizontal analysis is the comparison of historical financial information over a series of reporting periods, or of the ratios derived from this information. The analysis is most commonly a simple grouping of information that is sorted by period, but the numbers in each succeeding period can also be expressed as a percentage of the amount in the baseline year, with the baseline amount being listed as 100%.

When conducting a horizontal analysis, it is useful to conduct the analysis for all of the financial statements at the same time, to see the complete impact of operational results on the company's financial condition over the review period. For example, as noted in the next two examples, the income statement analysis shows a company having an excellent second year, but the related balance sheet analysis shows that it is having trouble funding growth, given the decline in cash, increase in accounts payable, and increase in debt.

Horizontal analysis of the income statement is usually in a two-year format such as the one shown below, with a variance also reported that states the difference between the two years for each line item. An alternative format is to simply add as many years as will fit on the page, without showing a variance, in order to see general changes by account over multiple years.

	20X1	20X2	Variance
Sales	$1,000,000	$1,500,000	$500,000
Cost of goods sold	400,000	600,000	-200,000
Gross margin	600,000	900,000	300,000
Salaries and wages	250,000	375,000	-125,000
Office rent	50,000	80,000	-30,000
Supplies	10,000	20,000	-10,000
Utilities	20,000	30,000	-10,000
Other expenses	90,000	110,000	-20,000
Total expenses	420,000	615,000	-195,000
Net profit	$180,000	$285,000	$105,000

Horizontal analysis of the balance sheet is also usually in a two-year format, such as the one shown below, with a variance stating the difference between the two years for each line item. An alternative format is to add as many years as will fit on the page, without showing a variance, in order to see general changes by account over multiple years.

Interpretation of Financial Statements

	20X1	20X2	Variance
Cash	$100,000	$80,000	-$20,000
Accounts receivable	350,000	525,000	175,000
Inventory	150,000	275,000	125,000
Total current assets	600,000	880,000	280,000
Fixed assets	400,000	800,000	400,000
Total assets	$1,000,000	$1,680,000	$680,000
Accounts payable	$180,000	$300,000	$120,000
Accrued liabilities	70,000	120,000	50,000
Total current liabilities	250,000	420,000	170,000
Notes payable	300,000	525,000	225,000
Total liabilities	550,000	945,000	395,000
Capital stock	200,000	200,000	0
Retained earnings	250,000	535,000	285,000
Total equity	450,000	735,000	285,000
Total liabilities and equity	$1,000,000	$1,680,000	$680,000

Vertical Analysis

Vertical analysis is the proportional analysis of a financial statement, where each line item on a financial statement is listed as a percentage of another item. Typically, this means that every line item on an income statement is stated as a percentage of gross sales, while every line item on a balance sheet is stated as a percentage of total assets.

The most common use of vertical analysis is within a financial statement for a single time period, to see the relative proportions of account balances. Vertical analysis is also useful for timeline analysis, to see relative changes in accounts over time, such as on a comparative basis over a five-year period. For example, if the cost of goods sold has a history of being 40% of sales in each of the past four years, then a new percentage of 48% would be a cause for alarm. An example of vertical analysis for an income statement is shown in the far right column of the following condensed income statement:

Interpretation of Financial Statements

	$ Totals	Percent
Sales	$1,000,000	100%
Cost of goods sold	400,000	40%
Gross margin	600,000	60%
Salaries and wages	250,000	25%
Office rent	50,000	5%
Supplies	10,000	1%
Utilities	20,000	2%
Other expenses	90,000	9%
Total expenses	420,000	42%
Net profit	$180,000	18%

The information provided by this income statement format is primarily useful for spotting spikes in expenses.

The central issue when creating a vertical analysis of a balance sheet is what to use as the denominator in the percentage calculation. The usual denominator is the asset total, but the total of all liabilities can also be used when calculating all liability line item percentages, and the total of all equity accounts when calculating all equity line item percentages. An example of vertical analysis for a balance sheet is shown in the far right column of the following condensed balance sheet.

	20X1	Percent
Cash	$100,000	10%
Accounts receivable	350,000	35%
Inventory	150,000	15%
Total current assets	600,000	60%
Fixed assets	400,000	40%
Total assets	$1,000,000	100%
Accounts payable	$180,000	18%
Accrued liabilities	70,000	7%
Total current liabilities	250,000	25%
Notes payable	300,000	30%
Total liabilities	550,000	55%
Capital stock	200,000	20%
Retained earnings	250,000	25%
Total equity	450,000	45%
Total liabilities and equity	$1,000,000	100%

The information provided by this balance sheet format is useful for noting changes in a company's investment in working capital and fixed assets over time, which may indicate an altered business model that requires a different amount of ongoing funding.

We now turn to an explanation of the ratios that may be of use to a financial analyst. Each explanation is accompanied by an example to illustrate how the ratio can be employed.

Cash Coverage Ratio

The cash coverage ratio is useful for determining the amount of cash available to pay for interest, and is expressed as a ratio of the cash available to the amount of interest to be paid. This is a useful ratio when the entity evaluating a company is a prospective lender. The ratio should be substantially greater than 1:1. To calculate this ratio, take the earnings before interest and taxes (EBIT) from the income statement, add back to it all non-cash expenses included in EBIT (such as depreciation and amortization), and divide by the interest expense. The formula is:

$$\frac{\text{Earnings before interest and taxes} + \text{Non-cash expenses}}{\text{Interest expense}}$$

There may be a number of additional non-cash items to subtract in the numerator of the formula. For example, there may have been charges in a period to increase reserves for sales allowances, product returns, bad debts, or inventory obsolescence. If these non-cash items are substantial, be sure to include them in the calculation. Also, the interest expense in the denominator should only include the actual interest expense to be paid – if there is a premium or discount to the amount being paid, it is not a cash payment, and so should not be included in the denominator.

EXAMPLE

The controller of Currency Bank is concerned that a borrower has recently taken on a great deal of debt to pay for a leveraged buyout, and wants to ensure that there is sufficient cash to pay for its new interest burden. The borrower is generating earnings before interest and taxes of $1,200,000 and it records annual depreciation of $800,000. The borrower is scheduled to pay $1,500,000 in interest expenses in the coming year. Based on this information, the borrower has the following cash coverage ratio:

$$\frac{\$1{,}200{,}000 \text{ EBIT} + \$800{,}000 \text{ Depreciation}}{\$1{,}500{,}000 \text{ Interest expense}}$$

$$= 1.33 \text{ cash coverage ratio}$$

The calculation reveals that the borrower can pay for its interest expense, but has very little cash left for any other payments.

Interpretation of Financial Statements

Current Ratio

One of the first ratios that a lender or supplier reviews when examining a company is its current ratio. The current ratio measures the short-term liquidity of a business; that is, it gives an indication of the ability of a business to pay its bills. A ratio of 2:1 is preferred, with a lower proportion indicating a reduced ability to pay in a timely manner. Since the ratio is current assets divided by current liabilities, the ratio essentially implies that current assets can be liquidated to pay for current liabilities.

To calculate the current ratio, divide the total of all current assets by the total of all current liabilities. The formula is:

$$\frac{\text{Current assets}}{\text{Current liabilities}}$$

The current ratio can yield misleading results under the following circumstances:

- *Inventory component.* When the current assets figure includes a large proportion of inventory assets, since these assets can be difficult to liquidate. This can be a particular problem if management is using aggressive accounting techniques to apply an unusually large amount of overhead costs to inventory, which further inflates the recorded amount of inventory.
- *Paying from debt.* When a company is drawing upon its line of credit to pay bills as they come due, which means that the cash balance is near zero. In this case, the current ratio could be fairly low, and yet the presence of a line of credit still allows the business to pay in a timely manner.

EXAMPLE

A supplier wants to learn about the financial condition of Lowry Locomotion. The supplier calculates the current ratio of Lowry for the past three years:

	Year 1	Year 2	Year 3
Current assets	$8,000,000	$16,400,000	$23,400,000
Current liabilities	$4,000,000	$9,650,000	$18,000,000
Current ratio	2:1	1.7:1	1.3:1

The sudden rise in current assets over the past two years indicates that Lowry has undergone a rapid expansion of its operations. Of particular concern is the increase in accounts payable in Year 3, which indicates a rapidly deteriorating ability to pay suppliers. Based on this information, the supplier elects to restrict the extension of credit to Lowry.

Quick Ratio

The quick ratio formula matches the most easily liquidated portions of current assets with current liabilities. The intent of this ratio is to see if a business has sufficient assets that are immediately convertible to cash to pay its bills. The key elements of current assets that are included in the quick ratio are cash, marketable securities, and accounts receivable. Inventory is not included in the quick ratio, since it can be quite difficult to sell off in the short term. Because of the exclusion of inventory from the formula, the quick ratio is a better indicator than the current ratio of the ability of a company to pay its obligations.

To calculate the quick ratio, summarize cash, marketable securities and trade receivables, and divide by current liabilities. Do not include in the numerator any excessively old receivables that are unlikely to be paid. The formula is:

$$\frac{\text{Cash + Marketable securities + Accounts receivable}}{\text{Current liabilities}}$$

Despite the absence of inventory from the calculation, the quick ratio may still not yield a good view of immediate liquidity if current liabilities are payable right now, while receipts from receivables are not expected for several more weeks.

EXAMPLE

Rapunzel Hair Products appears to have a respectable current ratio of 4:1. The breakdown of the ratio components is:

Item	Amount
Cash	$100,000
Marketable securities	50,000
Accounts receivable	420,000
Inventory	3,430,000
Current liabilities	1,000,000
Current ratio	4:1
Quick ratio	0.57:1

The component breakdown reveals that nearly all of Rapunzel's current assets are in the inventory area, where short-term liquidity is questionable. This issue is only visible when the quick ratio is substituted for the current ratio.

Liquidity Index

The liquidity index calculates the days required to convert a company's trade receivables and inventory into cash. The index is used to estimate the ability of a business to generate the cash needed to meet current liabilities. Use the following steps to calculate the liquidity index:

1. Multiply the ending trade receivables balance by the average collection period.
2. Multiply the ending inventory balance by the average inventory liquidation period. This includes the average days to sell inventory and to collect the resulting receivables.
3. Summarize the first two items and divide by the total of all trade receivables and inventory.

The liquidity index formula is:

$$\frac{(\text{Trade receivables} \times \text{Days to liquidate}) + (\text{Inventory} \times \text{Days to liquidate})}{\text{Trade receivables} + \text{Inventory}}$$

The liquidation days information in the formula is based on historical averages, which may not translate well to the receivables and inventory currently on hand. Actual cash flows may vary substantially around the averages indicated by the formula.

EXAMPLE

A financial analyst wants to understand the ability of a customer, Hassle Corporation, to convert its receivables and inventory into cash. Hassle has $400,000 of trade receivables on hand, which can normally be converted to cash within 50 days. Hassle also has $650,000 of inventory, which can be liquidated in an average of 90 days. When combined with the receivable collection period, this means it takes 140 days to fully liquidate inventory *and* collect the proceeds. Based on this information, the liquidity index is:

$$\frac{(\$400{,}000 \text{ Receivables} \times 50 \text{ Days to liquidate}) + (\$650{,}000 \text{ Inventory} \times \text{Days to liquidate})}{\$400{,}000 \text{ Receivables} + \$650{,}000 \text{ Inventory}}$$

$$= 106 \text{ Days to convert assets to cash}$$

The larger proportion of inventory in this calculation tends to skew the number of days well past the liquidation days for trade receivables. In short, Hassle will require a lengthy period to convert several current assets to cash, which may impact its ability to pay bills in the short term.

It may appear difficult for a financial analyst to obtain the liquidation days information required for this formula. However, using industry averages can yield a reasonable estimate of the liquidity index for a business.

Accounts Payable Turnover Ratio

Accounts payable turnover measures the speed with which a company pays its suppliers. If the turnover ratio declines from one period to the next, this indicates that the business is paying its suppliers more slowly, and may be an indicator of worsening financial condition. A change in the turnover ratio can also indicate altered payment terms with suppliers, though this rarely has more than a slight impact on the overall outcome of the ratio. If a company is paying its suppliers very quickly, it may mean that the suppliers are demanding fast payment terms.

To calculate the ratio, summarize all purchases from suppliers during the measurement period, and divide by the average amount of accounts payable during that period. The formula is:

$$\frac{\text{Total supplier purchases}}{(\text{Beginning accounts payable} + \text{Ending accounts payable}) \div 2}$$

The formula can be modified to exclude cash payments to suppliers, since the numerator should include only purchases on credit from suppliers. However, the amount of up-front cash payments to suppliers is normally so small that this modification is not necessary.

EXAMPLE

An analyst is reviewing Mulligan Imports, and wants to determine the company's accounts payable turnover for the past year. In the beginning of this period, the accounts payable balance was $800,000, and the ending balance was $884,000. Purchases for the last 12 months were $7,500,000. Based on this information, the analyst calculates the accounts payable turnover as:

$$\frac{\$7,500,000 \text{ Purchases}}{(\$800,000 \text{ Beginning payables} + \$884,000 \text{ Ending payables}) \div 2}$$

$$= 8.9 \text{ Accounts payable turns per year}$$

To calculate the accounts payable turnover in days, the analyst divides the 8.9 turns into 365 days, which yields:

$$365 \text{ Days} \div 8.9 \text{ Turns} = 41 \text{ Days}$$

Accounts Receivable Turnover Ratio

Accounts receivable turnover measures the ability of a company to efficiently issue credit to its customers and collect it back in a timely manner. A high turnover ratio indicates a combination of a conservative credit policy and an aggressive collections department, while a low turnover ratio represents an opportunity to collect excessively old receivables that are tying up working capital. This is useful information for a financial analyst, since a customer with its own collection problems is less likely to pay its suppliers on time.

To calculate accounts receivable turnover, add together the beginning and ending accounts receivable to arrive at the average accounts receivable for the measurement period, and divide this amount into the net credit sales for the year. The formula is:

$$\frac{\text{Net annual credit sales}}{(\text{Beginning accounts receivable} + \text{Ending accounts receivable}) \div 2}$$

If the receivables balance is quite variable over the measurement period, the use of just the beginning and ending receivable balances in the denominator may skew the measurement. In this case, consider using a larger number of data points to derive the average.

EXAMPLE

A financial analyst is investigating the credit application of Norrona Software, and wants to see if it is experiencing any of its own collection problems. In the beginning of the measurement period, the beginning receivable balance was $316,000, and the ending balance was $384,000. Net credit sales for the last 12 months were $3,500,000. Based on this information, the analyst calculates the accounts receivable turnover as:

$$\frac{\$3,500,000 \text{ Net credit sales}}{(\$316,000 \text{ Beginning receivables} + \$384,000 \text{ Ending receivables}) \div 2}$$

$$= 10 \text{ Accounts receivable turns}$$

To calculate the accounts receivable turnover in days, the analyst divides the 10 turns into 365 days, which yields:

$$365 \text{ Days} \div 10 \text{ Turns} = 36.5 \text{ Days}$$

Inventory Turnover Ratio

The inventory turnover ratio is the rate at which inventory is used over a measurement period. This is an important measurement, for many businesses are burdened by an excessively large investment in inventory, which can consume available cash.

When there is a low rate of inventory turnover, this implies that a business may have a flawed purchasing system that bought too many goods, or that stocks were increased in anticipation of sales that did not occur. In both cases, there is a high risk of inventory aging, in which case it becomes obsolete and has little residual value.

When there is a high rate of inventory turnover, this implies that the purchasing function is tightly managed. However, it may also mean that a business does not have the cash reserves to maintain normal inventory levels, and so is turning away prospective sales. The latter scenario is most likely when the amount of debt is unusually high and there are minimal cash reserves.

To calculate inventory turnover, divide the ending inventory figure into the annualized cost of sales. If the ending inventory figure is not a representative number, then use an average figure instead. The formula is:

$$\frac{\text{Annual cost of goods sold}}{\text{Inventory}}$$

The result of this calculation can also be divided into 365 days to arrive at days of inventory on hand. Thus, a turnover rate of 4.0 becomes 91 days of inventory.

EXAMPLE

An analyst is reviewing the inventory situation of the Hegemony Toy Company. The business incurred $8,150,000 of cost of goods sold in the past year, and has ending inventory of $1,630,000. Total inventory turnover is calculated as:

$$\frac{\$8,150,000 \text{ Cost of goods sold}}{\$1,630,000 \text{ Inventory}}$$

$$= 5 \text{ Turns per year}$$

The five turns figure is then divided into 365 days to arrive at 73 days of inventory on hand.

Fixed Asset Turnover Ratio

The fixed asset turnover ratio is the ratio of net sales to net fixed assets. A high ratio indicates that a company is doing an effective job of generating sales with a relatively small amount of fixed assets. Conversely, if the ratio is declining over time, the company has either overinvested in fixed assets or it needs to issue new products to revive its sales. Another possible effect is for a company to make a large investment in fixed assets, with a time delay of several months to a year before the new assets start generating revenues. Finally, a lack of ongoing investment in fixed assets will yield an apparently high turnover ratio over time, as depreciation reduces the reported amount of net fixed assets; this issue can be spotted by reviewing the cash expenditures for fixed assets that are reported in the statement of cash flows.

To derive fixed asset turnover, subtract accumulated depreciation from gross fixed assets, and divide into net annual sales. It may be necessary to obtain an average fixed asset figure, if the amount varies significantly over time. Do not include intangible assets in the denominator, since it can skew the results. The formula is:

$$\frac{\text{Net annual sales}}{\text{Gross fixed assets} - \text{Accumulated depreciation}}$$

This ratio is of most use in a "heavy industry," such as manufacturing, where a large capital investment is required. It is less useful in a services or knowledge-intensive industry, where the amount of fixed assets may be quite small.

If accelerated depreciation is used, it can rapidly reduce the amount of net fixed assets in the denominator, which makes the turnover figure look higher than is really the case.

EXAMPLE

Latham Lumber has gross fixed assets of $5,000,000 and accumulated depreciation of $2,000,000. Sales over the last 12 months totaled $9,000,000. The calculation of Latham's fixed asset turnover ratio is:

$$\frac{\$9,000,000 \text{ Net sales}}{\$5,000,000 \text{ Gross fixed assets} - \$2,000,000 \text{ Accumulated depreciation}}$$

$$= 3.0 \text{ Fixed asset turns per year}$$

Sales to Working Capital Ratio

It usually takes a certain amount of invested cash to maintain sales. There must be an investment in accounts receivable and inventory, against which accounts payable are offset. Thus, there is typically a ratio of working capital to sales that remains fairly constant in a business, even as sales levels change. This relationship can be measured with the sales to working capital ratio, which should be reported on a trend line to more easily spot spikes or dips. A spike in the ratio could be caused by a decision to grant more credit to customers in order to encourage more sales, while a dip could signal the reverse. A spike might also be triggered by a decision to keep more inventory on hand in order to more easily fulfill customer orders.

The ratio is calculated by dividing annualized net sales by average working capital. The formula is:

$$\frac{\text{Annualized net sales}}{\text{Accounts receivable} + \text{Inventory} - \text{Accounts payable}}$$

EXAMPLE

An analyst is reviewing the sales to working capital ratio of Milford Sound, which has applied for credit. Milford has been adjusting its inventory levels over the past few quarters, with the intent of doubling inventory turnover from its current level. The result is shown in the following table:

Interpretation of Financial Statements

	Quarter 1	Quarter 2	Quarter 3	Quarter 4
Revenue	$640,000	$620,000	$580,000	$460,000
Accounts receivable	214,000	206,000	194,000	186,000
Inventory	1,280,000	640,000	640,000	640,000
Accounts payable	106,000	104,000	96,000	94,000
Total working capital	1,388,000	742,000	738,000	732,000
Sales to working capital ratio	1.8:1	3.3:1	3.1:1	3.1:1

The table includes a quarterly ratio calculation that is based on annualized sales. The table reveals that Milford achieved its goal of reducing inventory, but at the cost of a significant sales reduction, probably caused by customers turning to competitors that offered a larger selection of inventory.

Debt to Equity Ratio

The debt to equity ratio of a business is closely monitored by the lenders and creditors of the company, since it can provide early warning that an organization is so overwhelmed by debt that it is unable to meet its payment obligations. This may also be triggered by a funding issue. For example, the owners of a business may not want to contribute any more cash to the company, so they acquire more debt to address the cash shortfall. Or, a company may use debt to buy back shares, thereby increasing the return on investment to the remaining shareholders.

Whatever the reason for debt usage, the outcome can be catastrophic, if corporate cash flows are not sufficient to make ongoing debt payments. This is a concern to lenders, whose loans may not be paid back. Suppliers are also concerned about the ratio for the same reason. A lender can protect its interests by imposing collateral requirements or restrictive covenants; suppliers usually offer credit with less restrictive terms, and so can suffer more if a company is unable to meet its payment obligations to them.

To calculate the debt to equity ratio, simply divide total debt by total equity. In this calculation, the debt figure should also include all lease obligations. The formula is:

$$\frac{\text{Long-term debt} + \text{Short-term debt} + \text{Leases}}{\text{Equity}}$$

EXAMPLE

An analyst is reviewing the credit application of New Centurion Corporation. The company reports a $500,000 line of credit, $1,700,000 in long-term debt, and a $200,000 operating lease. The company has $800,000 of equity. Based on this information, New Centurion's debt to equity ratio is:

Interpretation of Financial Statements

$$\frac{\$500,000 \text{ Line of credit} + \$1,700,000 \text{ Debt} + \$200,000 \text{ Lease}}{\$800,000 \text{ Equity}}$$

$$= 3:1 \text{ Debt to equity ratio}$$

The debt to equity ratio exceeds the 2:1 ratio threshold above which the analyst is not allowed to grant credit. Consequently, New Centurion is kept on cash in advance payment terms.

Fixed Charge Coverage

A business may incur so many fixed costs that its cash flow is mostly consumed by payments for these costs. The problem is particularly common when a company has incurred a large amount of debt, and must make ongoing interest payments. In this situation, use the fixed charge coverage ratio to determine the extent of the problem. If the resulting ratio is low, it is a strong indicator that any subsequent drop in the profits of a business may bring about its failure.

To calculate the fixed charge coverage ratio, combine earnings before interest and taxes (EBIT) with any lease expense, and then divide by the combined total of interest expense and lease expense. The formula is:

$$\frac{\text{Earnings before interest and taxes} + \text{Lease expense}}{\text{Interest expense} + \text{Lease expense}}$$

EXAMPLE

Luminescence Corporation recorded earnings before interest and taxes of $800,000 in the preceding year. The company also recorded $200,000 of lease expense and $50,000 of interest expense. Based on this information, its fixed charge coverage is:

$$\frac{\$800,000 \text{ EBIT} + \$200,000 \text{ Lease expense}}{\$50,000 \text{ Interest expense} + \$200,000 \text{ Lease expense}}$$

$$= 4:1 \text{ Fixed charge coverage ratio}$$

Breakeven Point

The breakeven point is the sales volume at which a business earns exactly no money. It is mostly used for internal analysis purposes, but it is also useful for a credit analyst, who can use it to determine the amount of losses that could be sustained if a credit applicant were to suffer a sales downturn.

To calculate the breakeven point, divide total fixed expenses by the contribution margin. Contribution margin is sales minus all variable expenses, divided by sales. The formula is:

$$\frac{\text{Total fixed expenses}}{\text{Contribution margin percentage}}$$

A more refined approach is to eliminate all non-cash expenses (such as depreciation) from the numerator, so that the calculation focuses on the breakeven cash flow level.

EXAMPLE

A credit analyst is reviewing the financial statements of a customer that has a large amount of fixed costs. The industry is highly cyclical, so the analyst wants to know what a large downturn in sales will do to the customer. The customer has total fixed expenses of $3,000,000, sales of $8,000,000, and variable expenses of $4,000,000. Based on this information, the customer's contribution margin is 50%. The breakeven calculation is:

$$\frac{\$3,000,000 \text{ Total fixed costs}}{50\% \text{ Contribution margin}}$$

$$= \$6,000,000 \text{ Breakeven sales level}$$

Thus, the customer's sales can decline by $2,000,000 from their current level before the customer will begin to lose money.

Gross Profit Ratio

The gross profit ratio shows the proportion of profits generated by the sale of goods or services, before selling and administrative expenses. In essence, it reveals the ability of a business to create sellable products in a cost-effective manner. The ratio is of some importance from an analysis perspective, especially when tracked on a trend line, to see if a business is continuing to provide products to the marketplace for which customers are willing to pay.

The gross margin ratio is calculated as sales minus the cost of goods sold, divided by sales. The formula is:

$$\frac{\text{Sales} - \text{Cost of goods sold}}{\text{Sales}}$$

The ratio can vary over time as sales volumes change, since the cost of goods sold contains some fixed cost elements that will not vary with sales volume.

EXAMPLE

An analyst is reviewing a credit application from Quest Adventure Gear, which includes financial statements for the past three years. The analyst extracts the following information from the financial statements of Quest:

Interpretation of Financial Statements

	20X1	20X2	20X3
Sales	$12,000,000	$13,500,000	$14,800,000
Cost of goods sold	$5,000,000	$5,100,000	$4,700,000
Gross profit ratio	58%	62%	68%

The analysis reveals that Quest is suffering from an ongoing decline in its gross profits, which should certainly be a concern from the perspective of allowing credit.

Net Profit Ratio

The net profit ratio is a comparison of after-tax profits to net sales. It reveals the remaining profit after all costs of production and administration have been deducted from sales, and income taxes recognized. As such, it is one of the best measures of the overall results of a firm, especially when combined with an evaluation of how well it is using its working capital. The measure is commonly reported on a trend line, to judge performance over time. It is also used to compare the results of a business with its competitors.

The net profit ratio is really a short-term measurement, because it does not reveal a company's actions to maintain profitability over the long term, as may be indicated by the level of capital investment or research and development expenditures. Also, a company may delay a variety of discretionary expenses, such as maintenance or training, to make its net profit ratio look better than it normally is. Consequently, evaluate this ratio alongside an array of other metrics to gain a full picture of a company's ability to continue as a going concern.

Another issue with the net profit ratio is that a company may intentionally keep it low through a variety of expense recognition strategies in order to avoid paying taxes. If so, review the statement of cash flows to determine the real cash-generating ability of the business.

To calculate the net profit ratio, divide net profits by net sales and then multiply by 100. The formula is:

$$(\text{Net profit} \div \text{Net sales}) \times 100$$

EXAMPLE

Kelvin Corporation has $1,000,000 of sales in its most recent month, as well as sales returns of $40,000, a cost of goods sold of $550,000, and administrative expenses of $360,000. The income tax rate is 35%. The calculation of its net profit percentage is:

$1,000,000 Sales - $40,000 Sales returns = $960,000 Net sales

$960,000 Net sales - $550,000 Cost of goods - $360,000 Administrative expenses

= $50,000 Income before tax

Interpretation of Financial Statements

$50,000 Income before tax × (1 − 0.35) = $32,500 Profit after tax

($32,500 Profit after tax ÷ $960,000 Net Sales) × 100

= 3.4% Net profit ratio

Return on Net Assets

The return on net assets measurement compares net profits to net assets to see how well a company is able to utilize its asset base to create profits. A high ratio is an indicator of excellent management performance.

To calculate the return on net assets, add together fixed assets and net working capital, and divide the result into net after-tax profits. Net working capital is defined as current assets minus current liabilities. It is best to eliminate unusual items from the calculation, since they can skew the results. The calculation is:

$$\frac{\text{Net profit}}{\text{Fixed assets + Net working capital}}$$

The fixed asset figure in the calculation can be net of depreciation, but the type of depreciation calculation used can skew the net amount significantly, since some accelerated depreciation methods can eliminate as much as 40% of an asset's value in its first full year of usage.

EXAMPLE

Quality Cabinets, an old maker of fine mahogany cabinets, has net income of $2,000,000, which includes an unusual, one-time expense of $500,000. It also has fixed assets of $4,000,000 and net working capital of $1,000,000. For the purposes of the return on net assets calculation, the unusual one-time expense item is eliminated, which increases the net income figure to $2,500,000. The calculation of return on net assets is:

$$\frac{\$2,500,000 \text{ Net income}}{\$4,000,000 \text{ Fixed assets} + \$1,000,000 \text{ Net working capital}}$$

= 50% Return on net assets

EBITDA

EBITDA is a contraction of the term Earnings Before Interest, Taxes, Depreciation, and Amortization. It is a commonly-used formula designed to reveal the approximate operational results of a business on a cash flow basis. The following calculation for EBITDA is a simple one, since it exactly follows the acronym:

Net income + Interest expense + Taxes + Depreciation + Amortization = EBITDA

Interpretation of Financial Statements

In essence, the calculation adds back all non-cash and non-operational expenses to the net income figure. The interest and tax line items that are excluded from the measure are not directly related to company operations, while the depreciation and amortization line items are non-cash items.

Of the four items that are excluded from the EBITDA measure, the two most critical are depreciation and amortization, since these can be extremely large numbers in capital-intensive industries, or in cases where a company has acquired a large amount of intangible assets and must amortize them. The interest line item is usually a considerably smaller figure, except in debt-heavy situations. All of the preceding information is derived from the income statement of the business under review.

EBITDA is a subset of the net income information presented in a company's income statement, and is designed for three purposes:

- To yield a rough estimate of a company's cash flow from operations
- To provide a basis for comparison between different companies that strip away financing and non-cash items
- To provide an estimate of the funds available to pay for debt

Unfortunately, it has also been used by companies experiencing net losses, so that they can point toward a different performance figure that shows a positive gain.

The EBITDA measure is only an approximation of company cash flow, since it incorporates revenue and expense accruals that do not reflect actual cash flows, and does not factor in any fixed asset expenditures. For a more precise view of cash flow, instead use the statement of cash flows, which defines the sources and uses of funds in some detail.

The EBITDA measure should only be used in conjunction with the net income figure, since EBITDA can give the impression that a company is highly profitable, when in fact the net income figure may be a loss.

In short, EBITDA is a moderately useful, quick-and-easy measure that is a general indicator of a company's operational results. However, only use it in conjunction with a company's full set of financial statements.

NOPAT

NOPAT is an acronym that stands for Net Operating Profit After Tax. The measurement is a good way to understand the underlying profitability of a business by stripping away the effects of financing, since its primary focus is on earnings generated by operations.

NOPAT is particularly effective when comparing the results of several companies in the same industry that employ different financing structures, since the results will exclude the effects of financing. Otherwise, the results of a highly leveraged company would likely be seen to spike or drop in relation to the results of other companies with more conventional financing structures.

However, NOPAT should not be used to compare companies in different industries, since the operations of these organizations will still have essentially different cost structures.

If a company has no financing costs or interest income, then NOPAT is the same as net income. Thus, NOPAT is not especially useful for a company that has little or no debt. In this situation, a simple net income calculation should be sufficient for interpreting the results of the organization.

The formula for NOPAT is as follows:

$$\text{Net operating income} \times (1 - \text{Tax rate})$$

For example, a business has revenues of $1,000,000, cost of goods sold of $650,000, administrative costs of $250,000, and interest expense (on a heavy debt load) of $100,000. Its tax rate is 35%. The company's income statement reveals net profits of $0, which seems to imply that the organization is not capable of generating a profit. However, when the interest expense is stripped away and the tax rate is applied to the remaining profit, it is apparent that the company has an after-tax operating profit of $65,000.

Limitations of Ratio Analysis

Ratio analysis is a useful tool, especially for an outsider such as a credit analyst or stock analyst, who needs to create a picture of the financial results and position of a business just from its financial statements. However, there are a number of limitations of ratio analysis to be aware of. They are:

- *Historical.* All of the information used in ratio analysis is derived from actual historical results. This does not mean that the same results will carry forward into the future. However, you can use ratio analysis on pro forma information and compare it to historical results for consistency.
- *Historical versus current cost.* The information on the income statement is stated in current costs (or close to it), whereas some elements of the balance sheet may be stated at historical cost (which could vary substantially from current costs). This disparity can result in unusual ratio results.
- *Aggregation.* The information in a financial statement line item being used for a ratio analysis may have been aggregated differently in the past, so that running the ratio analysis on a trend line does not compare the same information through the entire trend period.
- *Operational changes.* A company may change its underlying operational structure to such an extent that a ratio calculated several years ago and compared to the same ratio today would yield a misleading conclusion. For example, if a constraint analysis system was implemented, this might lead to a reduced investment in fixed assets, whereas a ratio analysis might conclude that the company is letting its fixed asset base become too old.
- *Accounting policies.* Different companies may have different policies for recording the same accounting transaction. This means that comparing the

ratio results of different companies may be like comparing apples and oranges. For example, one company might use accelerated depreciation while another company uses straight line depreciation, or one company records a sale at gross while the other company does so at net.
- *Business conditions.* Place ratio analysis in the context of the general business environment. For example, 60 days of sales outstanding might be considered poor in a period of rapidly growing sales, but might be excellent during an economic contraction when customers are in severe financial condition and unable to pay their bills.
- *Interpretation.* It can be quite difficult to ascertain the reason for the results of a ratio. For example, a current ratio of 2:1 might appear to be excellent, until you realize that the company just sold a large amount of its stock to bolster its cash position. A more detailed analysis might reveal that the current ratio will only temporarily be at that level, and will probably decline in the near future.
- *Company strategy.* It can be dangerous to conduct a ratio analysis comparison between two firms that are pursuing different strategies. For example, one company may be following a low-cost strategy, and so is willing to accept a lower gross margin in exchange for more market share. Conversely, a company in the same industry is focusing on a high customer service strategy where its prices are higher and gross margins are higher, but it will never attain the revenue levels of the first company.
- *Point in time.* Some ratios extract information from the balance sheet. Be aware that the information on the balance sheet is only as of the last day of the reporting period. If there was an unusual spike or decline in the account balance on the last day of the reporting period, this can impact the outcome of the ratio analysis.

In short, ratio analysis has a variety of limitations. However, as long as you are aware of these problems and use alternative and supplemental methods to collect and interpret information, ratio analysis is still useful.

Summary

Which of the preceding review methods are most critical from the perspective of an analyst, and which merely provide useful additional information? The answer depends upon the reason for the analysis. If the analysis is intended to determine the basic viability of a business, then consider using the following tranches of analysis activities to obtain layers of information about a business:
- *Essential information.* The core requirement is to understand the short-term viability of a business. To find this information, use a combination of the quick ratio, accounts payable turnover ratio, and the net profit ratio.
- *Expanded information.* Supplement the first layer of analysis with the liquidity index, sales to working capital ratio, and fixed charge coverage analysis.

- *Long-term viability.* To understand the long-term viability of a business, add to the preceding analyses all asset turnover ratios, the debt to equity ratio, and the breakeven point.

When using these layers of analysis, always do so using trend line (horizontal) analysis. By doing so, any declines in profitability or financial position are much more apparent.

Chapter 5
Cost-Volume-Profit Analysis

Introduction

A business may incur fixed costs that do not vary with activity volume, or variable costs that *do* change in relation to activity volume. In this chapter, we integrate fixed and variable costs into several tools that can be used to review the results and projections of a business. The concept of contribution margin is examined first, as well as how it can be employed in a different income statement format. We then use contribution margin to derive the breakeven point of a business, and discuss the uses to which breakeven analysis can be put. The breakeven concept is then extended to calculate the margin of safety. These issues are all components of cost-volume-profit analysis, for which we provide a number of examples. Finally, we address sales mix, which impacts the results of a cost-volume-profit analysis. In total, this chapter is intended to provide the reader with a view of how sales volumes interact with the cost structure of a business to achieve profitability.

Contribution Margin

The contribution margin is a product's price minus its variable costs, resulting in the incremental profit earned for each unit sold. The total contribution margin generated by an entity represents the total earnings available to pay for fixed expenses and generate a profit. The contribution margin concept can be applied throughout a business, for individual products, product lines, profit centers, subsidiaries, and for an entire organization.

The measure is useful for determining whether to allow a lower price in special pricing situations. If the contribution margin is excessively low or negative, it would be unwise to continue selling a product at that price point. It is also useful for determining the profits that will arise from various sales levels (see the next example). Further, the concept can be used to decide which of several products to sell if they use a common bottleneck resource, so that the product with the highest contribution margin is sold.

To determine the amount of contribution margin for a product, subtract all variable costs of a product from its revenues, and divide by its revenue. The calculation is:

$$\frac{\text{Product revenue} - \text{Product variable costs}}{\text{Product revenue}}$$

Cost-Volume-Profit Analysis

EXAMPLE

The Iverson Drum Company sells drum sets to high schools. In the most recent period, it sold $1,000,000 of drum sets that had related variable costs of $400,000. Iverson had $660,000 of fixed costs during the period, resulting in a loss of $60,000.

Revenue	$1,000,000
Variable expenses	400,000
Contribution margin	600,000
Fixed expenses	$660,000
Net loss	-$60,000

Iverson's contribution margin is 60%, so if it wants to break even, the company needs to either reduce its fixed expenses by $60,000 or increase its sales by $100,000 (calculated as the $60,000 loss divided by the 60% contribution margin).

EXAMPLE

The president of Giro Cabinetry is examining the gross margins on the five products that his company sells. A summary of this information is:

Product	Sales Price	Variable Cost	Fixed Cost	Gross Margin	Contribution Margin
A	$100	$60	$30	10%	40%
B	200	100	60	20%	50%
C	75	25	23	36%	67%
D	400	300	120	-5%	25%
E	325	230	98	-1%	29%

Fixed costs are comprised of factory overhead, which are assigned to products based on their prices. Thus, a high-priced product will be assigned more fixed cost than a lower-priced product. However, there is no linkage between price and fixed cost, so the fixed cost allocations are artificial.

Based on the information in the table, the president might be tempted to cancel products D and E, since both have negative gross margins. However, if he were to do so, the factory overhead would still remain, and would now be allocated among the smaller number of remaining products, which would reduce their gross margins. Only by examining the contribution margin is it obvious that *all* of the products are profitable, and should be retained in order to generate sufficient profits to offset the total amount of fixed costs incurred by the company.

Cost-Volume-Profit Analysis

Breakeven Point

The breakeven point is the sales volume at which a business earns exactly no money, where all contribution margin earned is needed to pay for the company's fixed costs. The concept is most easily illustrated in the following chart, where fixed costs occupy a block of expense at the bottom of the table, irrespective of any sales being generated. Variable costs are incurred in concert with the sales level. Once the contribution margin on each sale cumulatively matches the total amount of fixed costs, the breakeven point has been reached. All sales above that level directly contribute to profits.

Breakeven Table

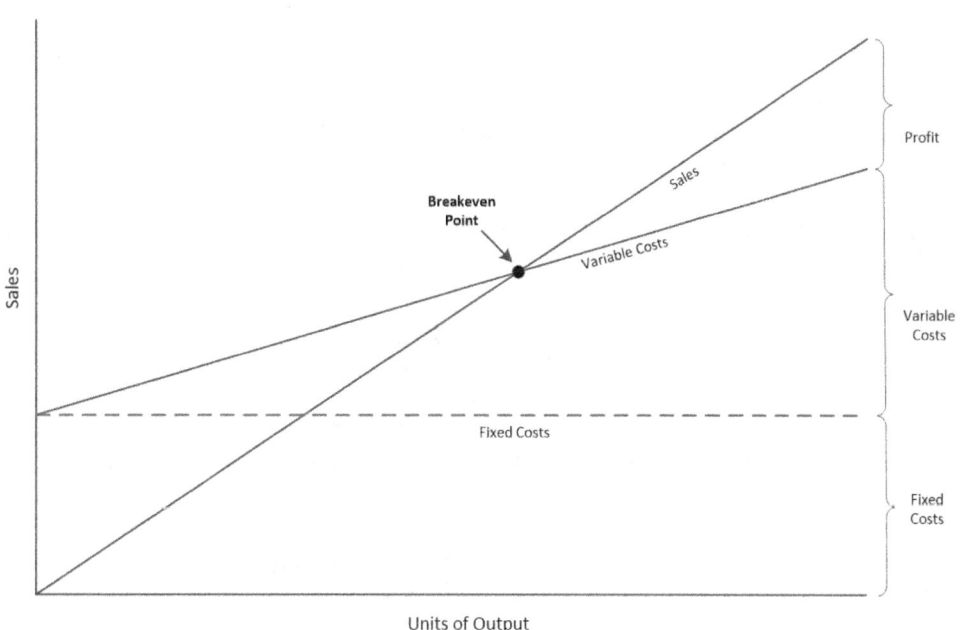

Knowledge of the breakeven point is useful for the following reasons:

- Determining the amount of remaining capacity after the breakeven point is reached, which reveals the maximum amount of profit that can be generated.
- Determining the impact on profit if automation (a fixed cost) replaces labor (a variable cost).
- Determining the change in profits if product prices are altered.
- Determining the amount of losses that could be sustained if the business suffers a sales downturn.

In addition, the breakeven concept is useful for establishing the overall ability of a company to generate a profit. When the breakeven point is near the maximum sales level of a business, this means it is nearly impossible for the company to earn a profit even under the best of circumstances.

Management should constantly monitor the breakeven point, particularly in regard to the last item noted, in order to reduce the breakeven point whenever possible. Ways to do this include:

- *Cost analysis.* Continually review all fixed costs, to see if any can be eliminated. Also review variable costs to see if they can be eliminated, since doing so increases margins and reduces the breakeven point.
- *Margin analysis.* Pay close attention to product margins, and push sales of the highest-margin items, thereby reducing the breakeven point.
- *Outsourcing.* If an activity involves a fixed cost, consider outsourcing it in order to turn it into a per-unit variable cost, which reduces the breakeven point.
- *Pricing.* Reduce or eliminate the use of coupons or other price reductions, since they increase the breakeven point.
- *Technologies.* Implement any technologies that can improve the efficiency of the business, thereby increasing capacity with no increase in cost.

To calculate the breakeven point, divide total fixed expenses by the contribution margin (which was described in an earlier section). The formula is:

$$\frac{\text{Total fixed expenses}}{\text{Contribution margin percentage}}$$

A more refined approach is to eliminate all non-cash expenses (such as depreciation) from the numerator, so that the calculation focuses on the breakeven cash flow level. The formula is:

$$\frac{\text{Total fixed expenses} - \text{Depreciation} - \text{Amortization}}{\text{Contribution margin percentage}}$$

Another variation on the formula is to focus instead on the number of units that must be sold in order to break even, rather than the sales level in dollars. This formula is:

$$\frac{\text{Total fixed expenses}}{\text{Average contribution margin per unit}}$$

EXAMPLE

The management of Ninja Cutlery is interested in buying a competitor that makes ceramic knives. The company's due diligence team wants to know if the competitor's breakeven point is too high to allow for a reasonable profit, and if there are any overhead cost opportunities that may reduce the breakeven point. The following information is available:

Cost-Volume-Profit Analysis

Maximum sales capacity	$5,000,000
Current average sales	$4,750,000
Contribution margin percentage	35%
Total operating expenses	$1,750,000
Breakeven point	$5,000,000
Operating expense reductions	$375,000
Revised breakeven level	$3,929,000
Maximum profits with revised breakeven point	$375,000

The analysis shows that the competitor has an inordinately high breakeven point that allows for little profit, if any. However, there are several operating expense reductions that can trigger a steep decline in the breakeven point. The management of Ninja Cutlery makes an offer to the owners of the competitor, based on the cash flows that can be gained from the reduced breakeven level.

A potential problem with the breakeven concept is that it assumes the contribution margin in the future will remain the same as the current level, which may not be the case. The breakeven analysis can be modeled using a range of contribution margins to gain a better understanding of possible future profits and losses at different unit sales levels. See the Sales Mix section for a discussion of variations in contribution margin.

EXAMPLE

Milford Sound sells a broad range of audio products. The financial analyst is concerned that the average contribution margin of these products has been slipping over the past few years, as customers have been switching to personal audio devices. The current average contribution margin is 38%, but the declining trend indicates that the margin could be 30% within two years. The analyst uses this information to construct the following breakeven analysis for the company:

	Current Case	Projected Case
Total fixed costs	$20,000,000	$20,000,000
÷ Contribution margin	38%	30%
= Breakeven sales	$52,632,000	$66,667,000

The calculation shows that the breakeven point will increase by $14 million over the next two years. Since Milford's current sales level is $58,000,000, this means that the company faces the alternatives of driving a massive sales increase, fixed cost reductions, or margin improvements in order to remain profitable.

Margin of Safety

The margin of safety is the reduction in sales that can occur before the breakeven point of a business is reached. The amount of this buffer is expressed as a percentage.

The margin of safety concept is especially useful when a significant proportion of sales are at risk of decline or elimination, as may be the case when a sales contract is coming to an end. By knowing the amount of the margin of safety, management can gain a better understanding of the risk of loss to which a business is subjected by changes in sales. The opposite situation may also arise, where the margin of safety is so large that a business is well-protected from sales variations.

To calculate the margin of safety, subtract the current breakeven point from sales, and divide the result by sales. The breakeven point is calculated by dividing the contribution margin into total fixed expenses. The formula is:

$$\frac{\text{Total current sales} - \text{Breakeven point}}{\text{Total current sales}}$$

To translate the margin of safety into the number of units sold, use the following formula instead:

$$\frac{\text{Total current sales} - \text{Breakeven point}}{\text{Selling price per unit}}$$

If the margin of safety is expressed as the number of units sold, the result works best if a company only sells one type of product. Otherwise, it can be difficult to translate the result into a range of products that have different price points and contribution margins.

EXAMPLE

Lowry Locomotion is considering the purchase of new equipment to expand the production capacity of its toy tractor product line. The addition will increase Lowry's operating costs by $100,000 per year, though sales will also be increased. Relevant information is noted in the following table.

Cost-Volume-Profit Analysis

	Before Machinery Purchase	After Machinery Purchase
Sales	$4,000,000	$4,200,000
Contribution margin percentage	48%	48%
Fixed expenses	$1,800,000	$1,900,000
Breakeven point	$3,750,000	$3,958,000
Profits	$120,000	$116,000
Margin of safety	6.3%	5.8%

The table reveals that both the margin of safety and profits worsen slightly as a result of the equipment purchase, so expanding production capacity is probably not a good idea.

Cost-Volume-Profit Analysis

Cost-volume-profit (CVP) analysis is designed to show how changes in product margins, prices, and unit volumes impact the profitability of a business. It is one of the fundamental financial analysis tools for ascertaining the underlying profitability of a business. The components of cost-volume-profit analysis are:

- *Activity level.* This is the total number of units sold in the measurement period.
- *Price per unit.* This is the average price per unit sold, including any sales discounts and allowances. The price per unit can vary substantially from period to period, based on changes in the mix of products and services, which may be caused by old product terminations, new product introductions, and the seasonality of sales.
- *Variable cost per unit.* This is the totally variable cost per unit sold, which is usually just the amount of direct materials and the sales commission associated with a unit sale. Nearly all other expenses do not vary with sales volume, and so are considered fixed costs.
- *Total fixed cost.* This is the total fixed cost of the business within the measurement period. This figure tends to be relatively steady from period to period, unless there is a step cost transition where the company has elected to incur an entirely new cost in response to a change in activity level (such as adding a production line).

These components can be mixed and matched in a variety of ways to arrive at different analyses. For example:

- What is the breakeven unit volume of a business? We divide the total fixed cost of the company by its contribution margin per unit. Thus, if a business has $50,000 of fixed costs per month, and the average contribution margin

of a product is $50, then the necessary unit volume to reach a breakeven sales level is 1,000 units.
- What unit quantity is needed to achieve $__ in profits? We add the target profit level to the total fixed cost of the company, and divide by its contribution margin per unit. Thus, if the CEO of the business in the last example wants to earn $20,000 per month, we add that amount to the $50,000 of fixed costs, and divide by the average contribution margin of $50 to arrive at a required unit sales level of 1,400 units.
- If I add a fixed cost, what sales are needed to maintain profits of $__? We add the new fixed cost to the target profit level and original fixed cost of the business, and divide by the unit contribution margin. To continue with the last example, the company is planning to add $10,000 of fixed costs per month. We add that to the $70,000 baseline fixed costs and profit and divide by the $50 average contribution margin to arrive at a new required sales level of 1,600 units per month.
- If I cut unit prices by $__, how many additional units must be sold to maintain profit levels? To continue with the last example, the baseline fixed costs are $60,000, profits are $20,000, and the contribution margin is $50 per unit. The plan is to reduce the unit price by $10 in an attempt to increase sales. Doing so will decrease the contribution margin to $40. To calculate the total number of unit sales required, we divide the $40 contribution margin per unit into the combined fixed costs and profits to arrive at total unit sales of 2,000. Thus, if prices are cut by $10, unit sales must increase by 400 units from the last example in order to maintain profit levels.

In short, the various components of CVP analysis can be used to uncover the financial results arising from many possible scenarios.

EXAMPLE

The president of Micron Metallic is working through the annual budgeting process, and wants to know how many stamping machines the company must produce in the upcoming year in order to earn a target before-tax profit of $3,000,000. The business has $24,000,000 of fixed costs, and its contribution margin per unit is $20,000. The calculation of units to sell is:

$$\frac{\$24{,}000{,}000 \text{ Fixed costs} + \$3{,}000{,}000 \text{ Target profit}}{\$20{,}000 \text{ Contribution margin per unit}}$$

$$= 1{,}350 \text{ Units}$$

The analysis can be refined to include the impact of income taxes, so that the formula for establishing a target after-tax profit for a certain number of units sold becomes:

Cost-Volume-Profit Analysis

$$\frac{\text{Fixed costs} + (\text{Target profit} \div (1 - \text{Tax \%}))}{\text{Contribution margin per unit}}$$

EXAMPLE

To continue with the last example, the president of Micron Metallic wants to determine the number of stamping machines that must be sold in order to achieve an *after-tax* profit of $3,000,000, using the same information. The tax rate is 35%. The calculation is:

$$\frac{\$24{,}000{,}000 \text{ Fixed costs} + (\$3{,}000{,}000 \text{ Target profit} \div (1 - 35\%))}{\$20{,}000 \text{ Contribution margin per unit}}$$

$$= 1{,}431 \text{ Units}$$

We do not present a single cost-volume-profit formula, for there is no single formula that applies to all situations. Instead, the basic concept must be revised to meet the requirements of each financial analysis topic as it arises.

Sales Mix

Sales mix refers to the proportions of different products and services that comprise the total sales of a company. In most cases, each product or service that a company provides has a different contribution margin, so changes in sales mix (even if the total sales level remains the same) usually result in differing amounts of profit.

EXAMPLE

The financial analyst of Creekside Industrial is examining the sales and profit figures for the past two months, and is having difficulty understanding why sales were identical, but profits were radically different in the two months. He creates the following analysis of sales of the company's two types of batteries:

	January			February		
	Product A	Product B	Total	Product A	Product B	Total
Sales	$2,000,000	$3,500,000	$5,500,000	$4,000,000	$1,500,000	$5,500,000
Variable costs	1,600,000	1,400,000	3,000,000	3,200,000	600,000	3,800,000
Variable cost %	80%	40%	55%	80%	40%	69%
Contribution	400,000	2,100,000	2,500,000	800,000	900,000	1,700,000
Fixed costs			2,000,000			2,000,000
Profit (loss)			$500,000			-$300,000

Because sales have shifted between the two products, which have radically different contribution margins, the profit level is heavily impacted by the sales mix.

Cost-Volume-Profit Analysis

If a company introduces a new product that has a low profit, and which it sells aggressively, it is quite possible that profits will decline even as sales increase. Conversely, if a company elects to drop a low-profit product line and instead push sales of a higher-profit product line, total profits can increase even as total sales decline.

> **Tip:** Sales managers must be aware of sales mix when they devise commission plans for the sales staff, since the intent should be to incentivize the sales staff to sell high-profit items. Otherwise, a poorly-constructed commission plan could push the sales staff in the direction of selling the wrong products, which alters the sales mix and results in lower profits.

A cost accounting variance called the *sales mix variance* is used to measure the difference in unit volumes in the actual sales mix from the planned sales mix. Follow these steps to calculate it at the individual product level:

1. Subtract budgeted unit volume from actual unit volume and multiply by the standard contribution margin.
2. Do the same for each of the products sold.
3. Aggregate this information to arrive at the sales mix variance for the company.

The formula is:

(Actual unit sales − Budgeted unit sales) × Budgeted contribution margin

---

EXAMPLE

Oberlin Acoustics expects to sell 100 platinum harmonicas, which have a contribution margin of $12 per unit, but actually sells only 80 units. Also, Oberlin expects to sell 400 stainless steel harmonicas, which have a contribution margin of $6, but actually sells 500 units. The sales mix variance is:

Platinum harmonica: (80 actual units − 100 budgeted units) × $12 contribution margin = -$240

Stainless steel harmonica: (500 actual units − 400 budgeted units) × $6 contribution margin = $600

Thus, the aggregated sales mix variance is $360, which reflects a large increase in the sales volume of a product having a lower contribution margin, combined with a decline in sales for a product that has a higher contribution margin.

Summary

The interaction of unit costs, fixed costs, sales volumes, and contribution margins is critical to an understanding of how a business earns a profit. By altering the inputs to a cost-volume-profit model, it is possible to estimate how the results of a business will change, which affects management's decisions to invest in fixed assets, withdraw products, cut back business units, hire staff, and so forth.

A note of caution must be inserted into this discussion. Cost-volume-profit analysis assumptions are not entirely under the control of an organization. It may be possible to adhere to planned changes in costs, but unit sales and product price points may not be accepted by customers, rendering a financial model invalid. Consequently, it may be necessary to revise these models frequently in response to pilot tests in the market; alternatively, incorporate worst-case scenarios for unit sales and price points, in case customer acceptance of a new company initiative is indifferent.

Chapter 6
Pricing Decisions

Introduction

Ultimately, the likelihood of long-term business profitability is based on its revenues. Management traditionally reviews total sales and unit volumes, and so has knowledge of the sources of revenue at an aggregate level. However, a deeper understanding of revenue requires an understanding of how a business develops prices. In this chapter, we delve into the different types of pricing strategies, which tend to fall into the following categories:

- *Cost based pricing.* Prices are derived from the costs of the underlying products.
- *Strategic pricing.* Pricing is set to drive away competitors or position the business within a market.
- *Teaser pricing.* Prices on a few items are kept low to attract customers.
- *Value based pricing.* Prices are based on customer perceptions of the value of products.

We discuss the more important pricing concepts in separate sections, along with the advantages and disadvantages of each one. We also provide summary descriptions of several additional pricing strategies, and introduce the concepts of price elasticity of demand and cross price elasticity of demand.

Psychological Pricing

We begin the discussion of pricing with the concept of psychological pricing, which is a general pricing concept that can be applied to many of the following strategies as a pricing adjustment. Psychological pricing is the practice of setting prices slightly lower than rounded numbers, in the expectation that customers do not round up these prices, and so will treat them as lower prices than they really are. This practice is based on the belief that customers tend to process a price from the left-most digit to the right, and so will tend to ignore the last few digits of a price. This effect appears to be accentuated when the fractional portion of a price is printed in smaller font than the rest of a price.

An example of psychological pricing is setting the price of an automobile at $19,999, rather than $20,000. This type of pricing is extremely common for consumer goods.

EXAMPLE

Hammer Industries has created an all-electric miniature backhoe. Upon investigation of competing price points, Hammer finds that there is a cluster of similar vehicles priced at $29,999. Also, many backhoe buyers use on-line price shopping services to evaluate backhoes, and those services present choices to buyers in $10,000 pricing bands. Thus, Hammer decides to price the backhoe at $29,999, not only to match the competition, but also to position itself within the $20,001 - $30,000 pricing band.

The following are advantages of using the psychological pricing method:

- *Control.* It is much more difficult for an employee to create a fraudulent sales transaction and remove cash when product prices are set at fractional levels, since it is more difficult to calculate the amount of cash to steal.
- *Discount pricing.* If a company is having a sale on selected goods, it can alter the ending digits of product prices to identify them as being on sale. Thus, any product ending with a ".98" price will receive a 20% discount at the checkout counter.
- *Non-rational pricing.* If customers are swayed by the incremental price reductions advocated under psychological pricing (which is a debatable premise) then sales should increase.
- *Price bands.* If a customer is accessing information about product prices that are segregated into bands, the use of fractional pricing can shift the price of a product into a lower price band, where customers may be more likely to make a purchase. For example, if a customer only wants to consider automobiles that cost less than $20,000, pricing a vehicle at $19,999 will drop it into the lower price band and potentially increase its sales.

The following are disadvantages of using the psychological pricing method:

- *Calculation.* It can be difficult for cashiers to calculate the total amount owed when fractional prices are used, as well as to make change for such purchases. This is less of a problem when credit card and other types of electronic payments are used.
- *Rational pricing.* If customers are more rational than psychological pricing gives them credit for, they will ignore fractional pricing and instead base their purchases on the value of the underlying products.

The overwhelming use of psychological pricing makes it clear that, whether or not the underlying concept is flawed, businesses are setting prices in this manner in order to compete with each other. Thus, to use the earlier example, setting a price a fraction higher than the prices charged by competitors might indeed lead to an incremental drop in unit sales volume, so a company probably has to use psychological pricing in order to remain competitive.

Cost Plus Pricing

Cost plus pricing is a price-setting method under which you add together the direct material cost, direct labor cost, and overhead cost for a product, and add to it a markup percentage in order to derive the price of the product. It can also be used under a contract with a customer, where the customer reimburses the seller for all costs incurred and also pays a negotiated profit in addition to the costs incurred.

EXAMPLE

Hammer Industries has designed a product that contains the following costs:

- Direct material costs = $20.00
- Direct labor costs = $5.50
- Allocated overhead = $8.25

The company applies a standard 30% markup to all of its products. To derive the price of this product, Hammer adds together the stated costs to arrive at a total cost of $33.75, and then multiplies this amount by (1 + 0.30) to arrive at the product price of $43.88.

The following are advantages to using the cost plus pricing method:

- *Assured contract profits*. Any contractor is willing to accept this method for a contractual agreement with a customer, since it is assured of having its costs reimbursed and of making a profit. There is no risk of loss on such a contract.
- *Justifiable*. In cases where the supplier must persuade its customers of the need for a price increase, the supplier can point to an increase in its costs as the reason for the price increase.
- *Simple*. It is quite easy to derive a product price using this method, though the overhead allocation method should be defined in order to be consistent in calculating the prices of multiple products.

The following are disadvantages of using the cost plus method:

- *Contract cost overruns*. From the perspective of any government entity that hires a supplier under a cost plus pricing arrangement, the supplier has no incentive to curtail its expenditures - on the contrary, it will likely include as many costs as possible in the contract so that it can be reimbursed. Thus, a contractual arrangement should include cost-reduction incentives for the supplier.
- *Ignores competition*. A company may set a product price based on the cost plus formula and then be surprised when it finds that competitors are charging substantially different prices. This has a huge impact on the market share and profits that a company can expect to achieve. The company either ends

up pricing too low and giving away potential profits, or pricing too high and achieving minor revenues.
- *Product cost overruns.* Under this method, the engineering department has no incentive to prudently design a product that has the appropriate feature set and design characteristics for its target market. Instead, the department simply designs what it wants and launches the product.

This method is not acceptable for deriving the price of a product that is to be sold in a competitive market, primarily because it does not factor in the prices charged by competitors. Thus, this method is likely to result in a seriously overpriced product. Further, prices should be set based on what the market is willing to pay - which could result in a substantially different margin than the standard margin typically assigned to a product.

Cost plus pricing is a more valuable tool in a contractual situation, since the supplier has no downside risk. However, be sure to review which costs are allowable for reimbursement under the contract; it is possible that the terms of the contract are so restrictive that the supplier must exclude many costs from reimbursement, and can potentially incur a loss.

Dynamic Pricing

Dynamic pricing is a partially technology-based pricing system under which prices are altered to different customers, depending upon their willingness to pay. Several examples of dynamic pricing are:

- *Airlines.* The airline industry alters the price of its seats based on the type of seat, the number of seats remaining, and the amount of time before the flight departs. Thus, many different prices may be charged for seats on a single flight.
- *Electricity.* Utilities may charge higher prices during peak usage periods.
- *Hotels.* The hotel industry alters its prices depending on the size and configuration of its rooms, as well as the time of year. Thus, ski resorts increase their room rates over the Christmas holiday, while Vermont inns increase their prices during the fall foliage season, and Caribbean resorts reduce their prices during the hurricane season.

Some industries, such as airlines, use heavily computerized systems to alter prices constantly, while other industries institute pricing changes at longer intervals. Thus, dynamic pricing can be adopted along a broad continuum, ranging from constant to infrequent pricing changes.

Dynamic pricing works best in the following situations:

- When it is used in concert by all of the major players in an industry. Thus, if a single hotel were to keep its prices low during the peak tourist season, it could likely steal business away from competitors.

- When demand fluctuates considerably in comparison to a relatively fixed amount of supply. In this situation, sellers reduce prices as demand falls and increase it as demand increases.

The following are advantages of using the dynamic pricing method:
- *Profit maximization.* If a seller constantly updates its prices with dynamic pricing, it will likely maximize its potential profits.
- *Clear out slow-moving inventory.* Dynamic pricing involves a large amount of inventory monitoring, with price reductions in response to higher inventory levels. This approach tends to eliminate excess inventory quickly.

The following are disadvantages of using the dynamic pricing method:
- *Competitor monitoring.* If the entire industry adopts dynamic pricing, then a company must invest in competitor price monitoring systems, to see if its prices are similar to those offered by competitors.
- *Customer confusion.* If prices change constantly, customers can become confused by the situation and be attracted to those sellers who do not use dynamic pricing. Thus, it can result in a loss of market share.
- *Increased marketing activity.* An expanded marketing presence may be required to communicate pricing changes to customers.
- *Inventory management.* Sudden changes in price can alter the demand for goods, which makes it difficult to plan for inventory replenishment.
- *Printed price changes.* If used in a retail environment, it requires considerable activity to physically update prices on products as soon as the computer system alters prices.

This approach can be an annoying one for customers, but its proven ability to maximize profits means that it will likely continue to be used in many markets.

Freemium Pricing

Freemium pricing is the practice of offering a basic set of services for free, and enhanced features and/or content for a fee. This approach has had notable success on the Internet, where services can be provided by the seller at close to a zero variable cost. Thus, a company can scale its customer base rapidly with little or no incremental cost for each additional customer gained (assuming no incremental marketing expenses), and then charge for additional services. This approach will result in a larger proportion of customers using the company's offerings for free, and a smaller proportion paying for additional services.

A key point with freemium pricing is that the initial "free" price in essence is the marketing that the provider uses, since word of the zero price point will likely spread quickly among users.

Freemium pricing can be applied to the following circumstances:

- Customers can use a service for a certain amount of time for free, after which they will be charged for any continuing provision of services.
- Customers have access to a version of the service that has few features, and can scale to an expanded version by paying a price.
- Only students are allowed the free service, with corporations paying the full price. This approach assumes that students will become addicted to the service, and later demand that companies they work for buy it.
- Only allow a certain amount of usage per time period, such as one download per month, without paying extra.

The following are advantages of using the freemium pricing method:

- *Low marketing cost.* The absence of a price becomes the key marketing tool of the company, which relies upon word of mouth to spread news about the company.
- *Potential paying customer base.* There will likely be a large pool of users of the free service at all times, any of whom represent the obvious sales funnel for additional paid customers.

The following are disadvantages of using the freemium pricing method:

- *Competition.* The freemium model is one that any number of competitors can also use, which may increase price competition for the premium version of the service provided.
- *Fixed cost coverage.* Any business has a certain amount of fixed costs, and if the premium-priced packages do not generate enough revenue to offset the fixed costs, the business will fail.
- *Value perception.* Since the basic package offered by the seller is free, customers might get the perception that all versions offered by the seller are worth very little.

This approach is extremely common on the Internet, where customers can be attracted to a website at zero incremental cost per person. The approach is much less economical elsewhere, where a seller must incur a cost when a customer uses its free services. Also, if you use this model, be careful to price the premium services to offset all fixed costs and generate sufficient cash for continued growth.

High-Low Pricing

High-low pricing is the practice of setting the price of most products higher than the market rate, while offering a small number of products at below-market prices. By doing so, a retail or web store location hopes to attract customers with its low-price offerings, at which point they will also buy some of the high-price items.

The low-price items are not usually set permanently at a lower price. Instead, coupons and other promotions are used to reduce prices to low levels for short periods of time. By doing so, management can shift low pricing among different products, which may attract different customers or attract the same customers to shop at the store multiple times. Thus, the use of low prices is an ongoing marketing technique that should be in continual use.

Grocery stores routinely issue a continuing stream of advertisements that feature low prices for specific items. The advertised items are usually located far back in the stores, so that shoppers must pass an array of other products before finding the low-priced items that are on sale. Since most grocery shoppers need to buy a large number of items every time they enter the store, the business is nearly guaranteed to sell a number of high-priced items along with the low-priced item(s).

The following are advantages of using the high-low pricing method:

- *Marketing.* The high-low method essentially becomes the marketing method for the business, since it must constantly advertise a selection of low-price items.
- *Profit increase.* When properly implemented, the high-low technique can yield substantial profits; but only if customers buy multiple additional items that are fully priced.

The following are disadvantages of using the high-low pricing method:

- *Customer loyalty.* If customers become aware that the bulk of the products offered by a business are higher than the market rate, they will be more likely to shift their spending loyalties elsewhere.
- *Marketing cost.* It can be expensive to run a perpetual series of marketing campaigns to tout the latest low prices.
- *Risk of loss.* If a business does not place its low-price items properly, or is dealing with price-sensitive shoppers, it may find that it loses money on its low-price promotions.

In short, the high-low pricing method is widely used, but discerning shoppers in the Internet era are more capable of spotting lower-priced items elsewhere, and so will only buy the low-price items and will avoid the high-price items. Also, a business that persistently offers high prices on the bulk of its products will not garner much customer loyalty.

Premium Pricing

Premium pricing is the practice of setting a price higher than the market price, in the expectation that customers will purchase it due to the perception that it must have unusually high quality or reputation. In some cases, the product quality is not better, but the seller has invested heavily in the marketing needed to give the impression of high quality. Premium pricing works best in the following circumstances:

- There is a perception among consumers that the product is a "luxury" product, or has unusually high quality or product design.
- There are strong barriers to entry. These barriers may include such factors as a large marketing expenditure to gain notice among consumers, a large field service operation to support the product, a reputation for product durability, a reputation for being "fashion forward," and/or a strong replacement warranty policy.
- The seller can restrict the amount of product sold, thereby giving its products an aura of exclusivity.
- There are no substitutes for the product. The company can create this situation by taking aggressive legal action against anyone attempting to copy its products.
- The product is protected by a patent, and the company is aggressively maintaining its rights under that patent.

EXAMPLE

Hammer Industries has developed a patented titanium pen that stores ink at high pressure, thereby allowing it to store four times the normal amount of ink. The company uses metal etching craftsmen to etch custom designs into the metal of the pens. Because of the customized nature of the product and its unique ink storage system, as well as the legal protection provided by its patent, Hammer elects to price each pen at $2,000, which is substantially greater than its $200 cost. To enhance the image of the product, Hammer invests heroically in advertising the pen in premium magazines, and also supports it with a lifetime warranty.

The following are advantages of using the premium pricing method:

- *Entry barrier.* If a company invests heavily in its premium brands, it can be extremely difficult for a competitor to offer a competing product at the same price point without also investing a large amount in marketing.
- *High profit margin.* There can be an unusually high gross margin associated with premium pricing. However, a company engaging in this strategy must attain sufficient volume to offset the hefty marketing costs associated with it.

The following are disadvantages of using the premium pricing method:

- *Branding cost.* The costs required to establish and maintain a premium pricing strategy are massive, and must be maintained for as long as this strategy is followed. Otherwise, the premium brand recognition by consumers will falter, and the company will have difficulty maintaining its price points.
- *Competition.* There will be a continual stream of competitors challenging the top tier pricing category with lower-priced offerings. This can cause a

problem, because it increases the perception in the minds of consumers that the entire product category is worth less than it used to be.
- *High unit costs.* Because the company using this strategy is restricting itself to low sales volume, it can never generate the cost reductions that a high-volume producer would be able to achieve.
- *Sales volume.* If a company chooses to follow a premium pricing strategy, it will have to confine its selling efforts to the top tier of the market, which limits its overall sales volume. This makes it difficult for a company to pursue aggressive sales growth and premium pricing at the same time. The strategy can be followed as long as the company is expanding into new geographic regions, since it is still pursuing the top tier in these new markets.

This approach is a difficult one to create and maintain, requiring an organization experienced in creating, presenting, and supporting products that give the user a premium experience. Companies aspiring to enter the top pricing tier may flounder in this market and lose a great deal of money while they try to establish themselves. For those entities already succeeding with premium pricing, they must be aware that a continual, daily emphasis on the premium strategy is the only way to continually charge the highest prices for what they offer.

Time and Materials Pricing

Time and materials pricing is used in service industries to bill customers for a standard labor rate per hour used, plus the actual cost of materials used. The standard labor rate per hour being billed does not necessarily relate to the underlying cost of the labor; instead, it may be based on the market rate for the services of someone having a certain skill set. Thus, a computer technician may bill out at $100 per hour, while costing $30 per hour, while a cable television mechanic may only bill out at $80 per hour, despite costing the same amount per hour. The cost of materials charged to the customer is for any materials actually used during the performance of services for the customer. This cost may be at the supplier's actual cost, or it may be a marked-up cost that includes a fee for the overhead cost associated with ordering, handling, and holding the materials in stock.

Under the time and materials pricing methodology, a single hourly rate may be charged irrespective of the experience level of the person performing the services, but usually there are different rates for different experience levels within the company. Thus, an associate consultant will have a lower billing rate than a consulting manager, who in turn has a lower billing rate than a consulting partner.

Industries in which time and materials pricing are used include:

- Accounting, auditing, and tax services
- Consulting services
- Legal work
- Medical services
- Vehicle repair

If a company chooses to base its labor rate under time and materials pricing on its underlying costs, rather than the market rate, it can do so by adding together the following:

- The cost of compensation, payroll taxes, and benefits per hour for the employee providing billable services
- An allocation of general overhead costs
- An additional factor to account for the proportion of expected unbillable time

---

EXAMPLE

Hammer Industries has an equipment repair group that charges out its staff at a level that covers the cost of labor, plus a profit factor. In the past year, Hammer incurred $2,000,000 of salary expenses, plus $140,000 of payroll taxes, $300,000 of employee benefits, and $500,000 of office expenses; this totaled $2,940,000 of expenses for the year. In the past year, the company had 30,000 billable hours, which is roughly what it expects to bill out in the near future. Hammer wants the division to earn a 20% profit. Based on this information, the division charges $122.50 per hour for each of its repair personnel. The calculation of the labor price per hour is:

$2,940,000 annual costs ÷ (1 - 20% profit percentage) = $3,675,000 revenue needed
$3,675,000 revenue needed ÷ 30,000 billable hours = $122.50 billing rate

---

The following are advantages to using the time and materials pricing method:

- *Assured profits.* If a company can keep its employees billable, this pricing structure makes it difficult *not* to earn a profit. However, the reverse situation can arise if the proportion of billable hours declines (see below).
- *High risk situations.* This pricing method is excellent in situations where the outcome of the work is in such doubt that the supplier will only take on the work if it can be properly reimbursed.

The following are disadvantages of using the time and materials pricing method:

- *Cost basis ignores market prices.* If a company sets its time and materials prices based on its internal cost structure, it may be setting prices lower than the market rate, thereby potentially losing profits. The reverse situation may also occur, where market prices are lower than internally-compiled prices. If so, an organization will find itself unable to generate much business.
- *Customers will not allow.* This pricing format allows a company to potentially run up its hours billed and charge more than the customer expects. Thus, customers prefer a fixed price to time and materials pricing.
- *Lost profits.* A company that provides highly value-added services could potentially use value based pricing, where prices are set based on the per-

ceived value delivered to the customer. Not using this approach could result in lost profits.
- *Low billable hours situations.* The basis of the time and materials pricing system is that a company will be able to bill enough hours to offset its fixed costs (usually the salaries of its employees). If the number of billable hours declines and headcount does not decline in proportion, then the company will lose money.
- *Price negotiations.* More sophisticated customers will negotiate reductions in the billable rate per hour, eliminate any mark-up on materials, and impose a "not to exceed" clause in any time and materials contract, thereby limiting profits.

Time and materials pricing is a standard practice in many services businesses, and works well, as long as you set sufficiently competitive prices and maintain a high rate of billable hours. Otherwise, the amount of revenue generated will not offset the fixed costs of the business, resulting in losses.

Value Based Pricing

Value based pricing is the practice of setting the price of a product or service at the perceived value to the customer. This approach does not take into account the cost of the product or service, nor market prices. Value based pricing tends to result in very high prices and correspondingly high profits for those companies that can convince their customers to agree to it.

Value based pricing is usually applied to very specialized services. For example, an attorney experienced in defense against criminal charges can charge a very high price to his or her clients, since the value to them of not being incarcerated is presumably quite high. Similarly, an attorney skilled in initial public offerings can use value pricing, since clients might not otherwise raise millions of dollars without their services. Other areas where value based pricing may be possible include:

- Bankruptcy work outs
- Cost reduction analysis
- Lawsuit defense
- Pharmaceuticals
- Product design

Value based pricing is also more applicable to situations where customer approval is made at the executive level, rather than by the procurement department. The purchasing staff is more skilled in evaluating supplier prices, and so would be less likely to allow such pricing.

EXAMPLE

Hammer Industries has built up a tool design service that assists its clients with the creation of tunnel boring equipment. The internal cost for Hammer to provide this service is usually about 1,000 hours of staff time at a cost of $100 per hour, or $100,000 in total. The typical consulting charge is $500,000. There is no relationship between the fee charged and the cost incurred by Hammer. Thus, Hammer earns $400,000 on $100,000 of internal costs. The company's clients do not complain, because they are passing through this fee to the governments commissioning the tunnel bores.

The following are advantages to using the value based pricing method:

- *Customer loyalty.* Despite the high prices charged, extremely high customer loyalty can be achieved for repeat business and referrals, but only if the service or product provided justifies the high price. This advantage tends to also derive from the nature of the sales relationship, which needs to be both close and trusting before value based pricing can even be contemplated.
- *Increases profits.* This method results in the highest possible price that can be charged, and so maximizes profits.

The following are disadvantages of using the value based pricing method:

- *Competition.* Any company that persistently engages in value based pricing is leaving a great deal of room for competitors to offer lower prices and take away market share.
- *Labor costs.* Assuming that a service is being provided, the business is likely offering such a high-end skill set that the employees needed to provide the service will be quite expensive. There is also a risk that they may leave to start competing firms.
- *Niche market.* The very high prices to be expected under this method will only be acceptable to a small number of customers. It may even alienate some prospective customers.
- *Not scalable.* This method tends to work best for smaller organizations that are highly specialized. It is difficult to apply to larger businesses where employee skill levels may not be so high.

This method is exceptionally profitable in those niche areas where a company can offer premium services that are highly valued by their customers. Many attorneys and investment bankers have engaged in value based pricing for decades, so it is clearly a viable method. However, it is not applicable in most businesses, where normal competitive pressures make it impossible to use value based pricing.

Other Pricing Strategies

We have thus far analyzed the most common pricing strategies, but have by no means exhausted the full range of pricing alternatives. The following bullet points make note of additional pricing strategies that can be of use in more limited circumstances:

- *Breakeven pricing* is the practice of setting a price point at which a business will earn zero profits on a sale. The intention behind the use of breakeven pricing is to gain market share and drive competitors from the marketplace. By doing so, a company may be able to increase its production volumes to such an extent that it can reduce costs and then earn a profit at what had been the breakeven price. Alternatively, once it has driven out competitors, the company can raise its prices sufficiently to earn a profit, but not so high that the increased price is tempting for new market entrants.
- *Limit pricing* is the practice by a competitor engaging in monopolistic behavior of setting a product or service price at a level just low enough to deter potential market entrants from competing in the market. This limit price may not be the price point at which the existing competitor earns the largest profit, but it does keep other companies out of the market.
- *Marginal cost pricing* is the practice of setting the price of a product at or slightly above the variable cost to produce it. This may be done when a company has a small amount of remaining unused production capacity available that it wishes to use to maximize its profits, or when it is unable to sell at a higher price. In either case, the sales are intended to be on an incremental basis; this is not intended to be a long-term pricing strategy.
- *Predatory pricing* is the practice of deliberately setting prices so low that competitors are driven from the marketplace. Predatory pricing can also act as a strong barrier to entry, since potential competitors will steer clear of any company sending such a strong competitive signal. A predatory price is considered to be one that is lower than the incremental marginal cost of manufacturing a product.
- *Price leadership* is a situation where one company, usually the dominant one in its industry, sets prices which are closely followed by its competitors. This firm is usually the one having the lowest production costs, and so is in a position to undercut the prices charged by any competitor who attempts to set its prices lower than the price point of the price leader. Competitors could charge higher prices than the price leader, but this would likely result in reduced market share, unless competitors could sufficiently differentiate their products.
- *Price skimming* is the practice of selling a product at a high price, usually during the introduction of a new product when the demand for it is relatively inelastic. This approach is used to generate substantial profits during the first months of the release of a product, usually so that a company can recoup its investment in the product. However, by engaging in price skimming, a company is potentially sacrificing much higher sales than it could garner at a lower price point. Eventually, a company that engages in price skimming must drop its prices, as competitors enter the market and undercut its prices. Thus, price skimming tends to be a short-term strategy.

When to Review Pricing

There are several situations in which it may be worthwhile to review company pricing, presented as follows in order of advance warning:

1. *When the results of competitors begin to decline.* The business itself may not be experiencing any changes in its rates of unit or profit growth, but companies operating on the periphery of the market may begin to report declines. Conversely, it may mean that a competitor has a pricing problem which the company can exploit to take away customers.
2. *When the order backlog begins to decline.* When the company's production capabilities catch up with the number of orders not yet processed, the backlog of orders will decline.
3. *When the growth in unit volume begins to decline.* This can happen quite suddenly, once the order backlog approaches zero. It can be triggered by an influx of low-cost competitors or the saturation of the market, where there are no incremental increases in total sales occurring.
4. *When net profits decline.* This situation can arise earlier, if management is excessively willing to cut deals with customers to obtain more unit volume.

When these scenarios begin to appear, it is time to examine the system by which prices are generated and offered to customers. The following analyses may be of use:

- *Customer margin analysis.* Calculate the total contribution margin being earned from each customer, net of all sales discounts and other credits from the gross prices at which goods and services are sold. This will likely uncover a few larger customers that are using their large ordering volumes to force the company into offering large volume discounts. If these deals result in negative contribution margins, then renegotiate the pricing deals or terminate relations with these customers.
- *Examine customer characteristics.* Review the size, location, business model, and other characteristics of those customers from which the company earns the highest contribution margins. This information can be used to alter the company's marketing efforts to attract more of this type of customer.
- *Salesperson analysis.* Review the contribution margins generated by each salesperson. It is entirely possible that the customers of some salespeople may be demanding unusually large discounts, requiring rebates, returning damaged goods and so forth, all of which could be indicative of poor customer management by the salesperson.
- *Discounting analysis.* Review the reasons why discounts are being taken by customers. Deep discounting should only be granted to those customers for whom the company wants to develop long-term relationships for significant sales volume in strategically-important market segments. If this is not the case, then customers merely feel that they are entitled to discounts, rather than having discounts influence their purchasing behavior.

- *Price elasticity analysis.* In some markets, a reduction in prices can yield an outsized increase in customer orders. If so, a price reduction may be in order. However, there are also many markets in which such a strategy will not generate any additional sales, so that a price decline merely cuts into profits. In the latter case, it may make more sense to increase prices, if doing so will only trigger the departure of a small number of customers. Price elasticity is discussed in the following two sections.

Price Elasticity of Demand

Price elasticity is the degree to which changes in price impact the unit sales of a product or service. The demand for a product is considered to be *inelastic* if changes in price have minimal impact on unit sales volume. Conversely, the demand for a product is considered to be *elastic* if changes in price have a large impact on unit sales volume. This concept can be a key determinant of the underlying profitability of a business. In particular, a high level of price elasticity can directly correlate with low profit margins.

A product is more likely to have inelastic demand if customers buy it for reasons other than price. This typically involves high-end luxury goods, or the "latest and greatest" products that are impacted by style considerations, where there are no obvious substitutes for the product. Thus, altering the price of a custom-made watch may not appreciably alter the amount of unit sales volume, since roughly the same number of potential customers will still be interested in buying it, irrespective of the price.

A product is more likely to have elastic demand when it is a commodity that is offered by many suppliers. In this situation, there is no way to differentiate the product, so customers only buy it based on price. Thus, if prices were to be raised on a product that has elastic demand, unit volume would likely plummet as customers go elsewhere to find a better deal. Examples of products having elastic demand are gasoline and many of its byproducts, corn, wheat, and cement.

The key considerations in whether a product will have elastic or inelastic demand are:

- *Duration.* Over time, consumers will alter their behavior to avoid excessively expensive goods. This means that the price for a product may be inelastic in the short term, and increasingly elastic over the long term. For example, the owner of a fuel-inefficient vehicle will be forced to pay for higher gasoline prices in the short term, but may switch to a more fuel-efficient vehicle over the long term in order to buy less fuel.
- *Necessity.* If something must be purchased (such as a drug for a specific medical condition), then the consumer will buy it, irrespective of price.
- *Payer.* People who can have their purchases reimbursed by someone else (such as the company they work for) are more likely to exhibit price inelastic behavior. For example, an employee is more likely to stay at an expensive hotel if the company is paying for it.

- *Percent of income*. If something involves a significant proportion of the income of the consumer, the consumer is more likely to look for substitute products, which makes a product more price elastic.
- *Uniqueness*. If there is no ready substitute for the product, it will be more price inelastic. This is particularly true where intensive marketing is used to make the product appear indispensable in the minds of consumers.

The elasticity or inelasticity of demand is a consideration in the pricing of products. Clearly, inelastic demand permits a great deal of room in price setting, whereas elastic demand means that the appropriate price is already defined by the market. Products having inelastic demand tend to have smaller markets, whereas products with elastic demand can involve much larger sales volume. Thus, a company pursuing a strategy of only selling products with inelastic demand may be limiting its potential sales growth.

From a practical perspective, companies are most likely to set prices based on what competitors are charging for their products, modified by the perceived value of certain product features. Price elasticity can also be used to fine-tune prices, but it is still more of a theoretical concept than one that has practical applicability.

The formula for the price elasticity of demand is the percent change in unit demand as a result of a one percent change in price. The calculation is:

$$\frac{\% \text{ Change in unit demand}}{\% \text{ Change in price}}$$

A product is said to be price inelastic if this ratio is less than 1, and price elastic if the ratio is greater than 1. Revenue should be maximized when the price can be set to have an elasticity of exactly 1.

EXAMPLE

Hammer Industries wants to test the price elasticity of demand for two of its products. It alters the price of its steel construction hammer by 3%, which generates a reduction in unit volume of 2%. This indicates some inelasticity of demand, since the company can raise prices and experience a smaller offsetting reduction in sales.

Hammer then tests the price inelasticity of its home screwdriver set by altering its price by 2%. This results in a reduction in unit volume of 4%. The result indicates significant elasticity of demand, since unit sales drop twice as fast as the increase in price.

Cross Price Elasticity of Demand

Cross price elasticity of demand is the percentage change in the demand for one product when the price of a different product changes. This concept is useful for many companies that sell a multitude of products and services, since what at first may appear to be an isolated price change can have a ripple effect on other parts of the business. The analyst should be aware of these interrelationships, and how they can impact profits. The cross price elasticity formula is:

Percentage change in demand of one product
Percentage change in price of a different product

If there is no relationship between the two products, then this ratio will be zero. However, if a product is a valid *substitute* for the product whose price has changed, there will be a positive ratio - that is, a price increase in one product will yield an increase in demand for another product. Conversely, if two products are typically purchased together (known as *complementary* products), then a price change will result in a negative ratio - that is, a price increase in one product will yield a decrease in demand for the other product.

Here are examples of different ratio results for the cross price elasticity of demand:

- *Positive ratio*. When the admission price at a movie theater increases, the demand for downloaded movies increases, because downloaded movies are a substitute for a movie theater.
- *Negative ratio*. When the admission price at a movie theater increases, the demand at the nearby parking garage also declines, because fewer people are parking there to go to the movie theater. These are complementary products.
- *Zero ratio*. When the admission price at a movie theater increases, the demand at a nearby furniture store is unchanged, because the two are unrelated.

A company can use the concept of cross price elasticity of demand in its pricing strategies. For example, the food served in a movie theater has a strong complementary relationship with the number of theater tickets sold, so it may make sense to drop ticket prices in order to attract more movie viewers, which in turn generates more food sales. Thus, the net effect of lowering ticket prices may be more total profit for the theater owner.

A business can also use heavy branding of its product line to mitigate the substitution effect. Thus, by spending money on advertising, a business can make customers want to buy its products so much that a price increase will not send them out to buy substitute products (at least not within a certain price range).

Non-Price Determinants of Demand

We have spent this entire chapter describing a variety of pricing strategies and theories. But what if customers have other reasons for buying products or services? The following list enumerates several non-price determinants of demand. These factors are important, because they can change the number of units sold, irrespective of their prices. As such, they can provide great value to a company, and so should be a factor in ongoing company planning and pricing discussions. The determinants are:

- *Available income.* If the amount of available buyer income changes, it alters their propensity to purchase. Thus, if there is an economic boom, someone is more likely to buy, irrespective of price.
- *Branding.* Sellers can use advertising, product differentiation, customer service, and so forth to create such strong brand images that buyers have a strong preference for their goods.
- *Complementary goods.* If there is a price change in a complementary item, it can impact the demand for a product. Thus, a change in the price of popcorn in a movie theatre could impact the demand for movies.
- *Demographics.* A change in the proportions of the population in different age ranges can alter demand in favor of those groups increasing in size (and vice versa). Thus, an aging population will increase the demand for arthritis drugs.
- *Future expectations.* If buyers believe that the market will change in the future, such as may happen with an anticipated constriction of supplies, this may alter their purchasing behavior now. Thus, an expected constriction in the supply of rubber might increase the demand for tires now.
- *Market size.* If the market is expanding rapidly, customers may be compelled to purchase based on other factors than price, simply because the supply of goods is not keeping up with demand.
- *Seasonality.* The need for goods varies by time of year; for example, there is a strong demand for lawn mowers in the spring, but not in the fall.

These determinants will alter the demand for goods and services, but only within certain price ranges. For example, if non-price determinants are driving increased demand, but prices are very high, it is likely that buyers will be driven to look at substitute products.

Summary

Clearly, there are a multitude of methods available for pricing products. Of the pricing strategies noted here, there is no "best" method. Instead, the overall positioning of a business in the marketplace will likely dictate the type of pricing to be employed. Thus, a business that is positioned to provide high-end luxury goods that are well differentiated would almost certainly use value based pricing – no other pricing method would maximize profits. Conversely, a company deadlocked in a price war over the sale of commodity-level products would be completely unable to follow the same strategy.

The analyst should therefore be aware of the overall company strategy, and how product pricing dovetails into that strategy. In particular, be aware of instances where proposed pricing diverges from the normal pricing strategy. These situations may represent pricing flaws that should be corrected at once, or they could signal a new strategic direction for the company, or just for a particular subsidiary or product line.

Chapter 7
Cost Object Analysis

Introduction

A cost object is any item for which costs are separately measured. It may be necessary to track a cost object in order to derive pricing from a baseline cost, or to see if costs are reasonable, or to derive the full cost of a relationship with another entity. Here are several types of cost objects:

- *Output.* The most common cost objects are a company's products and services, since it wants to know the cost of its output for profitability analysis and price setting.
- *Operational.* A cost object can be within a company, such as a department, machining operation, or process. Examples are the design of a new product, a customer service call, or the reworking of a returned product.
- *Business relationship.* A cost object could be a business partner, such as a supplier or customer.

In this chapter, we address which costs to assign to a cost object that are relevant to decisions concerning that cost object. A number of the more common cost objects are described.

Factors in Cost Object Analysis

From a cost management perspective, why review cost objects? The main point is that there are vast differences in the amount of cost accumulated by each cost object, and your intent is to spotlight those cost objects that are soaking up more costs than their counterparts. The intent is not to spotlight slight differences in the costs of cost objects, since these could just as easily be caused by measurement problems as by actual differences in costs. Instead, the focus is on major spikes in cost that are causing significant profitability issues.

When reviewing cost objects, any of the following factors can be causing unusually high costs:

- *High complexity.* Any extremely complex cost object attracts more costs. This can include a higher initial investment, as well as more maintenance and training costs. For example, a large piece of automated equipment will attract more costs than a simpler device that can be manually operated.
- *High investment.* A high initial investment immediately applies a significant cost to a cost object, even if no additional costs accrue over time.
- *High support levels.* This concept applies specifically to customers, and refers to the greatly increased level of customer support that some customers

require. This concept can also involve the cost of bad debts, product returns, and warranties.
- *Low volume.* A cost object may attract a large amount of costs because there are so few units of it. Any costs incurred cannot be allocated across a large number of units, so the cost per cost object tends to be quite high.
- *Small lot size.* This concept mostly applies to production lines. When a significant amount of time is required to retool a production line, a small lot size will accumulate more setup costs on a per-unit basis than a larger lot size.

An unusually high cost in a cost object is not necessarily to be avoided, as long as a sufficient amount of profit can still be derived from the object. A business may intentionally invest in extremely expensive cost objects, with the intent of charging premium prices on products relating to these objects. For example:

- *Employees.* A company hires only the best programmers and rewards them with high-end compensation and a rich benefits package. The company then charges premium prices to customers for their services.
- *Machinery.* A company invests in a massively expensive automated factory that allows it to alter the production schedule on a moment's notice. The company then charges far more than the usual price for its products, based on its ability to customize orders and ship to customers on the same day.
- *Products.* A watchmaker manufactures very short production runs of premium watches and sells them to collectors at inordinately high prices.

However, all of these examples highlight the fact that only a premium pricing strategy can be used when cost objects collect unusually large costs. If a business pursues any other type of strategy, it must pay close attention to its cost objects.

The Assignability of Costs

The bulk of this chapter is concerned with the accumulation of costs for specific cost objects. When doing so, a key issue is which costs to include or exclude. The concept is not a minor one, for the resulting report may trigger a management decision to eliminate the cost object – which may be, for example, an employee, a store, a product, or a customer. Consequently, assigning the correct costs is crucial.

When assigning costs to cost objects, the rule is to do so if the elimination of the cost object in question would also eliminate the cost. Thus, the termination of employment for a single individual will certainly eliminate that person's compensation, but will not affect the additional costs of the payroll or human resources departments. However, the situation changes considerably when the scope of the cost object expands. Thus, if an entire production facility is considered a cost object, then it is entirely likely that the payroll and human resources departments of that facility should be included in the cost, since those departments would be eliminated if the facility were to be eliminated.

Cost Object Analysis

Overhead costs should never be allocated to cost objects. The reason is that the most common management decision related to a cost object is whether to retain or eliminate it, so only costs that will verifiably be eliminated should be attached to a cost object. Since overhead is, by its nature, not associated with a cost object, it should not be assigned to a cost object.

EXAMPLE

The president of Grubstake Brothers is concerned that the cost reports for the company's new Trench Demon digger machine indicate that it is losing money. A close examination of the cost report reveals that one cost assigned to this cost object is not actually closely related to the product, and so should be stripped away. The revised report is noted in the following table.

	Assignable Cost or Revenue	Costs not Assignable	Notes
Revenue	$1,000,000		
Direct materials	350,000		
Direct labor	120,000		All direct labor staff work on this product, and so should be included
Corporate overhead		$150,000	No corporate costs would be terminated if the product were cancelled
Facility overhead	450,000		The facility would be shut down if the product were cancelled, and so should be included
Warranty costs	35,000		
Net profit/loss	$45,000	-$150,000	

Because the production facility would be shut down if the product were terminated, it is acceptable to assign all costs of the facility to the product. This is not the case for the corporate overhead costs, which should therefore not be allocated to the product. In short, once the corporate overhead cost has been excluded from the cost object, there is a discernible profit.

In summary, the assignability of cost will vary, depending on the nature of the cost object, and should always be restricted to the variable costs incurred by a cost object.

The Customer Cost Object

A major cost object is the customer, since the primary purpose of a business is to expend funds specifically to serve its customers. Unfortunately, the cost accounting system is not designed to track costs for individual customers, so new systems will be needed to track the customer service time devoted to each customer, salesperson time by customer, and the cost of returned goods. Consider the assignable costs in the following table.

Costs to Assign to a Customer

+/-	Assignable Cost	Commentary
+	Customer service	Only include the cost of customer service if there would be a reduction in this cost if a customer were to be terminated
+	Salesperson	Only include the cost of the sales staff if salespeople would be terminated along with a customer
+	Returned goods	Include the out-of-pocket cost to handle returned goods, which may include freight, repackaging, and the profit lost from reselling these goods at a reduced price
+	Credits	Include the cost of all credits claimed by a customer, which may include volume discounts, damaged goods claims, and so forth
+	Early payment discounts	All early payment discounts taken by a customer are a cost of doing business with that specific customer, and so should be included

When a customer demands a great deal of attention, management is most likely to hear complaints from all over the company regarding how much staff time this customer requires. However, the issue is irrelevant unless the termination of the customer would directly trigger a reduction in company support staff. If not, and despite all the complaining, there is no incremental staff cost associated with a demanding customer.

EXAMPLE

Dude Skis sells to Stuffy Skis, which is a high-end retailer of the most expensive all-mountain skis, as well as Warehouse Sports, which retails the lowest-cost skis through many outlets to beginner skiers. The skis that Dude sells to Stuffy have the highest margins, and Stuffy requires little administrative support. Warehouse buys in massive volume, but only buys low-margin items, and returns 20% of its purchases under various pretexts in order to clear out its inventory at the end of the season. Dude's management wants to know how much it earns from each customer, and whether it should drop either one. Dude's financial analyst constructs the following table:

Cost Object Analysis

	Stuffy Customer	Warehouse Customer
Revenue	$520,000	$2,780,000
Direct costs		
Materials	210,000	1,390,000
Direct labor	100,000	550,000
Customer service cost	0	130,000
Sales returns cost	0	600,000
Total direct costs	310,000	2,670,000
Contribution margin ($)	$210,000	$110,000
Contribution margin (%)	40%	4%

In the table, there is no customer service cost at all for Stuffy Skis, since no customer service positions would be eliminated if Dude were to drop Stuffy as a customer. On the other hand, there are four customer service employees assigned to the Warehouse Sports account who would be laid off if Dude were to drop that account.

The analysis reveals that Stuffy Skis produces far more contribution margin than Warehouse Sports, despite much lower revenues. However, this does not mean that Dude should eliminate Warehouse as a customer, since it still produces $110,000 of contribution margin. If Dude has a large amount of overhead to cover, it may be quite necessary to continue dealing with Warehouse Sports in order to retain the associated amount of contribution margin.

Customer Acquisition Costs

Thus far, we have only addressed the cost of *maintaining* a relationship with a customer. In addition, there is the cost of *acquiring* a customer, which can be extraordinarily high. There may be a marketing campaign that triggers a few expressions of interest from potential customers, followed by salesperson visits that further reduce the pool of prospects, followed by product demonstrations that finally yield a small number of actual customers. If the total cost of this acquisition process were to be spread across the few resulting customers, it would be apparent that an existing customer relationship is extremely valuable. Knowledge of this acquisition cost might trigger additional actions, such as:

- *More analysis of acquisition methods.* The profits garnered from newly-acquired customers may not justify the cost of their acquisition, resulting in the testing of alternative acquisition methods.
- *More initial analysis of customers.* Management is likely to spend more time reviewing the incremental cost of acquiring a new customer. It may pay to be picky about acquiring new customers in order to avoid those that will soak up an excessive amount of company resources.

- *More customer service*. Since it is less expensive to maintain an existing relationship than to acquire a new relationship, management could commit to spend more money on existing customers in order to improve the relationship, such as faster customer service response times or paying for faster shipping to customers.

Customer Lifetime Value

The typical analysis of the value represented by an individual customer is based on the identifiable profits generated from sales to a customer within a measurement period, typically a month, quarter, or year. This measurement approach does not result in a complete view of a customer relationship, however, for it fails to consider the initial investment in acquiring the customer. This could be a substantial amount, which may call for a long-term relationship before a notable return on that investment is achieved.

When valuing a customer based on its lifetime value to the company (or CLV), it may not be possible to simply extrapolate current buying patterns into the future. A customer's buying needs may change over time, resulting in different types of sales or changes in the level of effort required to complete a sale. For example:

- Since the relationship is already established, additional sales can be made with less selling effort, such as not being forced to engage in a bidding process.
- The customer may be amenable to the company's effort to cross-sell other types of products and services to it.
- A change in the size of the customer over time may require it to ask for alternative products from the company that are different in size, complexity, or features.

If so, these changes in buying patterns may be predictable, and can be incorporated into an analysis of lifetime value. The following example illustrates the concept:

EXAMPLE

AirLife Turbines competes in the wind turbine market, where it sells turbines to power generation companies. The industry is fiercely competitive, with initial sales margins of only 3% being the average on turbine sales. However, once a sales relationship is established, Airlife can reliably achieve after-market servicing margins of 25% per customer over the remaining 30-year life of a turbine.

A new financial analyst is hired, examines the company's margins for new sales, and promptly recommends an immediate 10% increase in turbine prices to increase the margins on initial sales. However, the vastly more experienced CFO points out that, when a full customer lifetime value analysis is made, the actual profitability of every customer is really quite high. In effect, the low initial product prices are needed to lock customers into long-term service agreements.

A likely outcome of CLV analysis is an enhanced emphasis on customer turnover rates. If there is a high rate of customer turnover, then the initial cost of customer acquisition must be correspondingly low, so that the CLV remains profitable. Conversely, if the turnover rate is extremely low, it makes more sense to spend what might otherwise be considered an inordinate amount of money to acquire new customers, since these customers are more likely to generate profits over a long period of time.

A company can also take a variety of steps to keep customer turnover from occurring, thereby expanding the average customer lifetime. Ways to reduce customer turnover include:

- *Enhanced product quality.* Create a feedback loop from the customer service department to the engineering staff, to ensure that all customer complaints regarding products result in product design changes or materials upgrades.
- *Enhanced customer experience.* Improve the response time for customer calls, and increase the speed with which field service calls are made.
- *Enhanced customer relations.* Assign customer relations officers to the most profitable customers, and ask customers to serve on customer advisory boards.

The Employee Cost Object

One of the most commonly-reviewed cost objects is the employee, particularly in regard to those administrative positions that can be more easily culled in the event of a downturn in business. However, the typical analysis only includes base-level compensation and the related payroll taxes, which does not yield a complete picture of the situation. Instead, a more comprehensive view should be assembled. Consider the assignable costs in the following table:

Costs to Assign to an Employee

+/-	Assignable Cost	Commentary
+	Base compensation	Base compensation is always included in the cost of an employee
+	Historical overtime	If a person has a history of incurring overtime, then include the average amount of this overtime, plus applicable payroll taxes
+	Bonuses	Only include the amount of bonuses that are likely to be earned, plus applicable payroll taxes
-	Increased compensation elsewhere	If an employee is to be let go, consider the cost of increased overtime for those employees remaining, as well as the payroll taxes associated with that overtime
+	Payroll taxes	This includes the social security, Medicare, and federal unemployment taxes paid by the employer
+	Benefits	This is the net cost of benefits paid by the company, after employee payroll deductions are subtracted
+	Travel and entertainment	This includes the historical average cost of travel and entertainment incurred by the employee

Several costs should not be included in an employee cost analysis, since they would still remain if an employee were to be let go. Consider the following costs:

- *Cell phones.* If a cell phone is considered common property that is simply passed along to a different person when one individual leaves the company, then its cost should not be assigned to a specific individual.
- *Commissions.* In many cases, a customer will be assigned to a different salesperson if the original salesperson is let go, so the company continues to incur a commission. However, if each sale is unique and there is no transfer of customers to a replacement salesperson, then the cost of commissions could be assigned to an employee.
- *Depreciation.* The depreciation on computer equipment and furniture used by an employee will remain if the position is eliminated, so do not assign the cost to an employee.
- *Profit sharing.* If an employee were to be laid off, profits would simply be shared with someone else who remains on the staff.
- *Square footage allocation.* The department to which an employee is assigned may be charged for the square footage occupied by an employee. Since this cost would remain even if an employee were not on staff, it should not be considered an employee-specific cost.

A particularly large point that is frequently missed is to assign the *actual* net cost of benefits to employees, rather than the *average* net cost per employee. For example, it is entirely likely that an employee taking family medical insurance is much more expensive than one taking single coverage, since there is such a large disparity in the costs of these two variations on medical insurance.

The Product Cost Object

A common analysis is to accumulate costs for a product, and use this as the basis for a decision to cancel the product. In this case, the analysis should be entirely based on the variable cost of the product, and nothing else. Since most costs in the production area are fixed, this means that comparatively few costs should be assigned to a product. Consider the assignable costs in the following table.

Cost Object Analysis

Costs to Assign to a Product

+/-	Assignable Cost	Commentary
+	Direct materials	Always assigned as a product cost
+	Packaging costs	Always assigned as a product cost
+	Commissions	Only assigned to a product if the commission specifically relates to the sale of that product
+	Piece rate pay	Add the cost of labor and related payroll taxes when employees are being paid for the incremental production of each individual unit, as occurs under a piece rate pay plan
+	Outside processing charges	If a third party is being paid for some or all of the processing work on a product, include this cost
+	Licensing fees	When the company is paying a third party a licensing fee for each unit sold, include this cost

Several costs should not be included in a product cost analysis, since they would still remain if the product were to be eliminated. Consider the following costs:

- *Non-product commissions.* Do not assign to a product any commissions paid for other reasons than a product sale, such as a quarterly override or a bonus for managing a new sales region.
- *Direct labor.* Most direct labor is incurred to provide minimum staffing for a product line, rather than to produce an individual unit. Theoretically, direct labor costs could be incurred even if there is *no* production. Thus, this cost should be considered part of factory overhead.

The cost of many purchased components varies considerably, based on the quantities in which they are purchased. For example, if you buy a widget in a standard supplier's economy pack of 100 units, the supplier charges $5.00 per unit. However, if a smaller quantity is needed, which requires the supplier to break its normal packaging and ship the widget in a custom-sized shipping container, the price increases to $15.00. Further, if there is a need to buy in massive quantities, such as a truckload, the supplier can reduce the price further, to $3.50 per unit. Thus, the cost of a purchased component can vary substantially, depending upon the quantities in which it is purchased. It may be necessary to include this concept in the derivation of costs for a product.

EXAMPLE

Blitz Communications is considering developing a new desktop phone. The marketing department estimates that there is a 25% chance that the phone will sell 20,000 units or less, a 60% chance that it will sell between 20,000 and 50,000 units, and a 15% chance that it will sell more than 50,000 units. The phone is to be constructed almost entirely from purchased parts, with final assembly at the Blitz factory. The cost analysis is:

Cost Object Analysis

Component	(25% Probability) 20,000 Units or Less	(60% Probability) 20,001 – 50,000 Units	(15% Probability) 50,000+ Units
Price/Unit	$25.00	$25.00	$25.00
Base	3.00	2.50	2.00
Keypad	0.54	0.45	0.36
Microphone	0.78	0.65	0.52
Cord	0.96	0.80	0.64
Shell	4.50	3.75	3.00
Speaker	1.38	1.15	0.92
Direct labor	3.75	3.75	3.75
Overhead	8.00	4.20	2.00
Cost Total	$22.91	$17.25	$13.19
Profit	$2.09	$7.75	$11.81
Profit %	8%	31%	47%

The analysis uses the 20,001 to 50,000 unit range as the baseline. If product sales fall below the 20,001 unit level, the analysis shows that purchased component costs will increase by 20%, and that costs will decrease by 20% if the product sells more than 50,000 units. Further, the amount of fixed overhead costs must be spread over fewer units if the product sells 20,000 units or less, with the reverse effect if it sells more than 50,000 units.

The preceding example reveals the problem that management faces when evaluating product costs that could change with purchasing volumes; there is a possibility that profits could severely underperform. When this situation arises, management needs to decide if it should take the risk of releasing a product into the market, or of setting a lower price to attract more sales, or of reengineering the product to reduce its cost.

The Product Line Cost Object

It may be necessary to reach a decision regarding the termination of an entire product line. If so, the number of costs to include in the decision skyrockets, as compared to the meager cost listing for a single product. There may also be issues in the reverse direction, when costs must be added in order to expand a product line.

An entire facility may be used to create all of the products in a product family. If so, all of the costs of that facility are now considered variable when deciding whether to retain the product line. Consider the assignable costs in the following table, which are in addition to those listed in the last section for a product.

Cost Object Analysis

Additional Costs to Assign to a Product Line

+/-	Assignable Cost	Commentary
+	Direct labor	Direct labor is a fixed cost of the production line, and would be eliminated if the product line is terminated
+	Factory overhead	If the entire factory only produced that production line, then all factory overhead is associated with the production line
+	Marketing costs	There is usually a separate budget for marketing the product line, which therefore varies with the product line
+	Sales costs	If the sales staff only sells the product line, they are a variable cost of the line. If they sell other items as well, then do not include their cost.
+	Factory administration costs	All of the administrative costs associated with running the factory are associated with the product line, if the factory only produces the product line

A sample product line margin report follows.

Sample Product Line Margin Report

Product Line	Revenue	Direct Materials	Engineering	Overhead	Sales and Marketing	Margin
Home products	$800,000	$320,000	$65,000	$165,000	$130,000	$120,000
Restaurant products	390,000	156,000	82,000	80,000	40,000	32,000
School products	640,000	320,000	39,000	128,000	90,000	63,000
Totals	$1,830,000	$796,000	$186,000	$373,000	$260,000	$215,000

It is quite likely that the only cost *not* assigned to a product line will be the allocation of corporate overhead to the facility that produces these goods, since that would not necessarily be impacted by the termination of the product line.

Costs related to a product line can vary whenever they reach a step cost boundary. For example, a production manager finds that his facility can produce a maximum of 3,000 widgets per week if he uses one shift, but that he needs to start a second shift in order to meet any additional demand. When he adds the shift, the company will have to incur certain additional fixed costs, such as the salary of a supervisor for that shift.

When a company exceeds a step cost boundary and incurs a new step cost, how does this impact the cost of an individual unit of production? For incremental costing decisions, it does nothing at all, since the variable cost of producing a single unit has not changed. It has, however, increased the total overhead cost of the production system, as well as (presumably) the ability of the system to produce more units. The only way to see if a step cost has improved or reduced the ability of a production system to produce a profit is to subject it to constraint analysis, which we deal with in the Constraint Analysis chapter.

For the purposes of analyzing the impact of a step cost on a product line, the main consideration for the analyst is to point out to management the existence of any impending step costs, their amount, and how they impact the production system. Management then needs to decide if it has a long-term need for the additional production capacity that the step cost represents, or whether it makes more sense to avoid the step cost by either turning away additional business or outsourcing the work.

The Sales Channel Cost Object

Management may need to consider the cost of its various sales channels, to see if they are being operated in a cost-effective manner that produces profits. If so, the analysis should certainly include the costs of all goods and services generated by that sales channel, as well as the support costs required to maintain the channel, which could involve any separate distribution infrastructure. Consider the assignable costs in the following table:

Additional Costs to Assign to a Product Line

+/-	Assignable Cost	Commentary
+	Product cost objects	This is the cost of any products sold through the sales channel
+	Marketing costs	If there is a separate budget for marketing through the sales channel, consider it a variable cost of the sales channel
+	Sales costs	If the sales staff is assigned solely to a sales channel, then they are a variable cost of that channel. If they sell through multiple sales channels, then do not assign their cost to this cost object.
+	Logistics costs	If the storage and distribution of goods is separate for the sales channel, consider logistics a variable cost of the sales channel

This is not a minor topic, for a chain of retail stores can be considered a sales channel cost object. It is not uncommon for management to evaluate an entire cluster of retail stores and their supporting regional warehouse and marketing budget to see if the cluster should be retained or shut down. The same analysis can be applied to Internet stores, distributors, and other sales channels. Thus, the proper analysis of sales channels can result in some of the largest decisions that a business can make – and those decisions must be supported by the correct information.

Cost Object Termination Issues

Much of the discussion surrounding cost objects tends to involve their termination. If it is considered necessary to actually terminate a cost object, there are several additional issues to be considered regarding how that termination is conducted. Consider the following issues:

- *Inventory reduction.* When a product or an entire product line is being terminated, the remaining inventory of raw materials and work-in-process should be converted into finished goods, and the finished goods completely sold off. Otherwise, the company will end up holding inventory that it will only be able to liquidate with difficulty. Thus, detailed planning regarding residual inventory levels must take place, which can impact the timing of a product or product line termination.
- *Inventory for warranties.* If a product is to be terminated and there is a warranty period associated with it, estimate the number of units to be held in reserve for warranty replacement purposes, and set them aside. Otherwise, production may have to be restarted at a later date to fulfill the company's warranty obligations.
- *Fixed asset maintenance.* If an entire production line is to be terminated, be sure to include fixed asset acquisition proposals in this decision. Ideally, maintenance of existing equipment should be enhanced during the final months of scheduled production, rather than spending funds on equipment that replaces worn-out machinery. This may mean that some production must be outsourced in order to sidestep production equipment that is no longer functional.
- *Severance costs.* If a product line or sales channel is being terminated, there will be associated severance costs for those employees impacted by the decision. Also, various laws may require that employees be given a certain amount of advance warning, which can delay the effective date of the shutdown.

These issues do not impact the decision to eliminate a cost object, but they can have an impact on the timing of the cancellation. Consequently, review these points on a regular basis as the termination date for a cost object approaches.

Which Cost Objects to Track

It is not necessary to track the cost of every conceivable cost object in a business. Some attract such a small amount of cost that there is no point in doing so, while there are no decisions that can be made in regard to other cost objects. The following table illustrates how to sort through the various cost objects in a business.

Cost Object Analysis

Tracking Concepts for Cost Objects

Cost Object	When to Track	When not to Track
Customers	When significant sales volume is concentrated with a small number of customers	When sales volume is widely dispersed among a large number of accounts
Employees	When specific sales can be traced back to an individual, or where pay levels are unusually high (examples: salespeople and engineers)	When there are a large number of employees whose pay is relatively low (example: retail clerks)
Products	When there is considerable pricing pressure that may drive product margins to zero	When product profitability is uniformly high
Product lines	When a product line is the sole focus of an entire production facility	When the product line has dispersed production and minimal targeted marketing or sales
Sales channels	When there is a large amount of supporting infrastructure, such as warehouses and a dedicated sales force	When the channel is incidental, with minimal ongoing costs

Summary

In essence, the study of cost objects is designed to focus attention on those aspects of a business that accumulate costs, and which therefore can interfere with profitability. This does not mean that the cost of all cost objects will be continually ground down over time to the bare minimum. On the contrary, management may conclude that *increased* spending on a cost object is needed in order to fulfill the corporate mission. However, these cases should be in the minority. In most situations, management should be made aware on a regular basis of how costs are concentrated throughout the business, and of any material changes in these costs over time.

Chapter 8
Constraint Analysis

Introduction

In financial analysis, the mindset is usually that a decision is to be based on a specific cost object. The decision does not take into account the greater corporate structure within which it takes place. For example, you may be called upon to judge whether a product should be cancelled because of an excessively low margin, or to choose between two possible capital investments based on their cash flows. However, the impacts of these decisions are rarely considered in relation to a company's *entire* capability, as an integrated unit, to earn a profit.

Constraint analysis does the reverse – its starting point is determining which company operation is constraining the entire company from earning a greater profit, and then focuses all decision-making upon how they impact this constraint (or "bottleneck"). To use the previous two examples, it may not be judicious to cancel a product that generates *any* amount of profit, since that profit helps to pay for the overhead cost of the entire system. Further, it may not be necessary to invest in any fixed assets unless it improves the capacity of the bottleneck operation.

This chapter gives an overview of constraint analysis, and then delves into a number of management decisions where using it can alter your perception of how to manage various aspects of a company.

> **Related Podcast Episodes:** Episodes 43 through 47 of the Accounting Best Practices Podcast discuss many aspects of constraint analysis. They are available at: **accountingtools.com/podcasts** or **iTunes**

Constraint Analysis Operational Terminology

Constraint analysis makes use of several unique terms, so we will begin with a set of definitions before proceeding to an overview of constraint analysis. The key operational terms are:

- *Drum*. This is a third variation of the *constraint* term, along with *bottleneck*. It is the operation, person, or (occasionally) the materials within a company that prevent it from generating additional sales. Since the ultimate profitability of the company depends on this one item, it sets the pace for how the company operates. Picture the drum beating on a rowed galley, and you can see why it is called a *drum*.
- *Buffer*. The drum operation should operate at as close to 100% of capacity as possible, but this is impossible when the flow of materials from upstream operations is unreliable. The buffer is inventory that is positioned in front of

the drum operation, and which protects the drum from any stoppage in materials coming from upstream operations. The buffer may need to be quite large if there is considerable variability in the inflow of materials, or it may be of more modest proportions if the inflow is more stable.
- *Rope*. The rope represents the date and time when jobs must be released into the production process in order to have inventory arrive at the buffer just when it is needed by the drum; thus, it is really the total time duration needed to bring work-in-process to the drum.

These three terms are sometimes strung together in a single phrase, and are called the *drum-buffer-rope* system. As a group, they describe the essential operational components of constraint analysis.

Overview of Constraint Analysis

The key points in understanding constraint analysis are the following two concepts:
1. A company is an integrated set of processes that function together to generate a profit; and
2. There is a chokepoint somewhere in a company that absolutely controls its ability to earn a profit.

The chokepoint is also known as the drum operation (as defined above, or the bottleneck, or the constrained resource). We will refer to it as bottleneck, since the word most clearly describes its impact on an organization.

The first concept, that of a company being an integrated set of processes, applies very strongly at the product line level, but less so at the corporate parent level. At the product line level, there is almost certainly a bottleneck that restricts the ability to generate more profit. At the corporate parent level, there may be multiple subsidiaries, each with a multitude of product lines. Thus, from the perspective of the corporate parent, there are still bottlenecks, but there may be a number of them scattered throughout the operations of the subsidiaries.

The second concept, that of the bottleneck, is most typically characterized by a machine that can only process a certain number of units per day. To improve profits, a company must focus all of its attention on that machine by taking such steps as:

- Adding supplemental staff to cover any employee breaks or downtime during shift changes
- Reviewing the quality of work-in-process going into the operation, so that it does not waste any time processing items that are already defective
- Positioning extra maintenance personnel near it to ensure that service intervals are short
- Reducing the amount of processing time per unit, so that more units can be run through the machine
- Adding more capacity to the machine
- Outsourcing work to suppliers

It is also possible that the bottleneck is not in the production area at all. It may be caused by a materials shortage, or by a lack of sales staff. In those rare cases where there is simply no bottleneck to be found, then the company has excess capacity, and can choose to either reduce its capacity (and the related cost) or try to sell more volume, possibly at a lower price.

EXAMPLE

Hammer Industries produces construction equipment. Its products are large, complex, and mostly sold through a request for proposals process. Its financial analyst has reviewed all production operations in detail and concluded that there is no bottleneck operation to be found. Instead, the real chokepoint appears to be in the sales department.

Hammer has a multi-tiered sales process, where one group makes initial contacts with prospective customers, another group of technical writers responds to requests for proposal (RFP), yet another group conducts sales presentations, and a final group conducts final contract negotiations. A brief analysis shows that the technical writers are completely overwhelmed with writing RFP responses, and have missed several RFP filing deadlines. The sales staff positioned ahead of them in the process flow, those making contacts with prospective customers, are aware of the problem and have scaled back their activities to meet with new customers, since they know the company is not capable of making timely RFP responses. Thus, it is evident that the sales department is the true company bottleneck.

The analyst reports this issue to management, and recommends a combination of additional technical writer hiring and the purchase of RFP response software to simplify the writing task.

It is usually easy to tell where the bottleneck is located, because it has a large amount of work piled up in front of it, while the work operation immediately downstream from it is starved for work.

A major part of the management of the bottleneck operation is the inventory buffer located immediately in front of it. Constraint analysis holds that there will always be flaws in the production process that result in variability in the flow of materials to the bottleneck, so a buffer must be built up to insulate the bottleneck from these issues. The buffer should be quite large if there are lots of upstream production problems, or much smaller if the production flow is relatively placid.

If production problems start to eat into the size of the inventory buffer, then the bottleneck is in danger of having a stock-out condition, which may cause it to run out of work. To avoid this, there should be a large *sprint capacity* in selected upstream production operations. Sprint capacity is essentially excess production capacity. There should be a sufficient amount of this capacity available to rapidly rebuild the inventory buffer. If there has been an investment in significant sprint capacity, then there is also less need for a large inventory buffer.

Finally, there is the concept of the *rope* that was mentioned earlier as a key definition. It is very important to only release new jobs into the production queue so that they arrive at the inventory buffer just in time to be used. The natural inclination of a production scheduler would be to release jobs too soon, to ensure that there is always a healthy flow of jobs arriving at the inventory buffer. However, doing so represents an excessive inventory investment, and also confuses the production staff, which does not know which of the plethora of jobs to process next. Thus, the rope concept represents a fine balance between overloading the system and starving it of work.

In summary, the bottleneck operation is the most important operation in a company. The management team needs to know where it is located, and spend a great deal of time figuring out how to maximize its operation so that it hardly ever stops.

The Cost of the Bottleneck

How expensive is it when a bottleneck operation is not running? The traditional financial analysis approach would be to calculate the foregone gross margin on any products that would otherwise have been produced if it had been operational. Under constraint analysis, the calculation is the entire operating cost of the facility, divided by the bottleneck's operating hours. We use the entire cost of the facility, because the bottleneck drives the profitability of the entire facility.

For example, a bottleneck operation is running 160 hours a week, which is three shifts, less eight hours for maintenance downtime. The facility has operating expenses of $1,600,000 per week. Therefore, the cost of *not* running the bottleneck operation is $10,000 per hour. When viewed from this perspective, it very expensive indeed to stop a bottleneck operation.

EXAMPLE

Mole Industries incurs $250,000 of operational expenses per week for its Digger equipment line. The bottleneck work center is operational 150 hours per week, with the remaining 18 hours of the week being used for necessary maintenance. Thus, the cost of not running the bottleneck is $1,667 per hour ($250,000 operational expenses ÷ 150 hours per week).

The shift supervisor has received a demand from the union to give a one-hour lunch break to the three people working in the bottleneck operation, in each of the three shifts. The shift supervisor has the choice of shutting down the operation for 21 hours per week to accede to this request (7 days × 3 shifts × 1 hour per shift), or of bringing in additional staff at an astronomical $100 per hour per person to run the operation in their absence. Which is the better alternative?

Option 1, Stop the Bottleneck: The cost of not running the bottleneck is $1,667 per hour, so the total cost over 21 hours would be $35,000 per week.

Option 2, Use Supplemental Staff: The cost of using supplemental staff is $6,300 (21 hours × 3 staff × $100 per person).

Though the use of supplemental staff initially appears excessive, the cost is still far lower than shutting down the bottleneck operation.

The example makes it quite clear that a bottleneck operation should never be shut down. It is always less expensive to add staff to it, or do whatever else is necessary, to ensure that it keeps running.

An ancillary question is, what is the cost of running an operation that is not the bottleneck operation? It is zero. Since company operations do not hinge on any other operation, it is usually acceptable to shut them down for short periods. The only exception is when doing so may impact the bottleneck operation.

Local Optimization

The concept of the constraint is very much at odds with the traditional concept of local optimization, where you work to improve the efficiency of every operation throughout a company. In many cases, these improvements do nothing to increase overall company profits, because the primary driver of profits is still the bottleneck operation. Consequently, if investments are made in local optimization projects, profits do not improve, but the investment in the company increases, so the only logical outcome is that the return on investment declines. Here are several examples of how constraint analysis alters the view of local optimization:

Situation	Local Optimization Solution	Constraint Analysis Solution
Overtime is 10% of payroll	Restrict all overtime	Do not restrict overtime if it is being spent on the bottleneck operation, or on any operations feeding the bottleneck
A machine is not being utilized	Sell the machine	Keep the machine if it provides sprint capacity for the bottleneck operation
A product can be redesigned	Only do so if the product is at the end of its normal life cycle	Do so if the redesign reduces the product processing time at the bottleneck operation
The production staff is not fully utilized	Cut back on operations and lay off staff	If there is no bottleneck operation, then lower prices to attract more sales
A machine is reaching its maximum utilization	Buy an additional machine	Only buy an additional unit if it will provide more sprint capacity. Do not buy if it is located downstream from the bottleneck operation
A supplier is asking us to outsource production	Do so if it passes a cost-benefit analysis	Do so if it reduces the load on the bottleneck operation

In all of the cases noted in the table, it is useful to step back from the individual decision and see what the impact will be on the entire company before determining the correct course of action. In particular, be aware of two problems that are caused by local optimization:

1. *Excess inventory.* If a production operation is optimized that is not the bottleneck operation, then all you have done is give it the ability to churn out even more inventory than was previously the case, and which the bottleneck will be unable to process. Thus, you have not only needlessly invested in the operation, but also needlessly invested in additional inventory that must now wait to be processed.
2. *Overly efficient labor.* When a good manufacturing process was considered to be one with very long production runs, there was a strong emphasis on highly efficient labor. If the focus is instead on maximizing the amount of production passing through the bottleneck – and nowhere else – then grossly overstaff the bottleneck operation to make sure that it is always operating, and pay much less attention to labor efficiencies elsewhere. Employees should only work if inventory is actually needed. In short, it is better to have employees be underutilized and produce less inventory than to be more efficient and produce inventory that is not needed.

In summary, a company does not even have to be especially efficient in production areas located away from the bottleneck operation. Instead, the one and only focus is on maximizing the efficiency of the bottleneck. This change in focus alters most of the decisions that would be reached if you only focused on local optimization.

Constraint Analysis Financial Terminology

By now it should be apparent that constraint analysis is quite a valuable tool from an operational perspective. But what about from a financial perspective? How is the concept used to make decisions? There is a model for using constraint analysis in this role, but first we need to define the terms in the model. They are:

- *Throughput.* This is the margin left after subtracting totally variable costs from revenue. This tends to be a large proportion of revenues, since all overhead costs are excluded from the calculation.
- *Totally variable costs.* This is usually just the cost of materials, since it is only those costs that vary when one incremental unit of a product is manufactured. This does not normally include the cost of labor, since employees are not usually paid based on one incremental unit of output. There are a few other possible costs that may be totally variable, such as commissions, subcontractor fees, customs duties, and freight costs.
- *Operating expenses.* This is all company expenses other than totally variable costs. There is no differentiation between overhead costs, administrative costs or financing costs – quite simply, *all* other company expenses are lumped into this category.
- *Investment.* This is the amount invested in assets. "Investment" includes changes in the level of working capital resulting from a management decision.
- *Net profit.* This is throughput, less operating expenses.

Constraint Analysis from a Financial Perspective

When you look at a company from the perspective of constraints, it no longer makes sense to evaluate individual products, because overhead costs do not vary at the individual product level. In reality, most companies spend a great deal of money to maintain a production infrastructure, and that infrastructure is what really generates a profit – the trick is making that infrastructure produce the maximum profit with the best mix of products having the highest possible throughput. Under the constraint analysis model, there are three ways to improve the financial position of the entire production infrastructure. They are:

- *Increase throughput.* This is by either increasing revenues or reducing the amount of totally variable costs.
- *Reduce operating expenses.* This is by reducing some element of overhead expenses.
- *Improve the return on investment.* This is by either improving profits in conjunction with the lowest possible investment, or by reducing profits slightly along with a correspondingly larger decline in investment.

Note that only the increase in throughput is related in any way to decisions made at the product level. The other two improvement methods may be concerned with changes anywhere in the production system.

The Constraint Analysis Model

An excellent constraint analysis model was developed by Thomas Corbett, which is outlined here. The basic thrust of the model is to give priority in the bottleneck operation to those products that generate the highest throughput per minute of bottleneck time. After these products are manufactured, give priority to the product having the next highest throughput per minute, and so on. Eventually, the production queue is filled, and the operation can accept no additional work.

The key element in the model is the use of throughput per minute, because the key limiting factor in a bottleneck operation is time – hence, maximizing throughput within the shortest possible time frame is paramount. Note that throughput *per minute* is much more important than total throughput *per unit*. The following example illustrates the point.

Constraint Analysis

EXAMPLE

Mole Industries manufacturers trench digging equipment. It has two products with different amounts of throughput and processing times at the bottleneck operation. The key information about these products is:

Product	Total Throughput	Bottleneck Processing Time	Throughput per Minute
Mole Hole Digger	$400	2 minutes	$200
Mole Driver Deluxe	800	8 minutes	100

Of the two products, the Mole Driver Deluxe creates the most overall throughput, but the Mole Hole Digger creates more throughput per minute of bottleneck processing time. To determine which one is more valuable to Mole Industries, consider what would happen if the company had an unlimited order quantity of each product, and could run the bottleneck operation nonstop, all day (which equates to 1,440 minutes). The operating results would be:

Product	Throughput per Minute		Total Processing Time Available		Total Throughput
Mole Hole Digger	$200	×	1,440 minutes	=	$288,000
Mole Driver Deluxe	100	×	1,440 minutes	=	144,000

Clearly, the Mole Hole Digger, with its higher throughput per minute, is much more valuable to Mole Industries than its Mole Driver Deluxe product. Consequently, the company should push sales of the Mole Hole Digger product whenever possible.

The constraint analysis model is essentially a production plan that itemizes the amount of throughput that can be generated, as well as the total amount of operating expenses and investment. In the model, we use four different products, each requiring some processing time in the bottleneck operation. The columns in the model are as follows:

- *Throughput per minute.* This is the total amount of throughput that a product generates, divided by the amount of processing time at the bottleneck operation.
- *Bottleneck usage.* This is the number of minutes of processing time required by a product at the bottleneck operation.
- *Units scheduled.* This is the number of units scheduled to be processed at the bottleneck operation.
- *Total bottleneck time.* This is the total number of minutes of processing time required by a product, multiplied by the number of units to be processed.
- *Total throughput.* This is the throughput per minute multiplied by the number of units processed at the bottleneck operation.

This grid produces a total amount of throughput to be generated if production proceeds according to plan. Below the grid of planned production, there is a subtotal of the total amount of throughput, from which the total amount of operating expenses are subtracted to arrive at the amount of profit. Finally, the total amount of investment in assets is divided into the profit to calculate the return on investment. Thus, the model provides a complete analysis of all three ways in which one can improve the results of a company – increase throughput, decrease operating expenses, or increase the return on investment. An example of the model follows:

Sample Constraint Analysis Model

Product	Throughput per Minute	Bottleneck Usage (minutes)	Units Scheduled	Total Bottleneck Time	Total Throughput
1. Hedgehog Deluxe	$80	14	1,000	14,000	$1,120,000
2. Hedgehog Mini	70	20	500	10,000	700,000
3. Hedgehog Classic	65	40	200	8,000	520,000
4. Hedgehog Digger	42	10	688	6,880	288,960
		Total bottleneck scheduled time		38,880	
		Total bottleneck time available*		38,880	
				Total throughput	$2,628,960
				Total operating expenses	2,400,000
				Profit	$228,960
				Profit percentage	8.7%
				Investment	$23,000,000
				Annualized return on investment	11.9%

* Minutes per month (30 days × 24 hours × 60 minutes × (1 – 0.10 maintenance time)

In the example, the Hedgehog Deluxe product has the largest throughput per minute, and so is scheduled to be first priority for production. The Hedgehog Digger has the lowest throughput per minute, so it is given last priority in the production schedule. If there is less time available on the bottleneck operation, the company should reduce the number of the Hedgehog Digger product manufactured in order to maximize overall profits.

In the middle of the model, the "Total bottleneck scheduled time" row contains the total number of minutes of scheduled production. The row below it, labeled "Total bottleneck time available," represents the total estimate of time that the bottleneck should have available for production purposes during the scheduling period. Since the time scheduled and available are identical, this means that the production schedule has completely maximized the availability of the bottleneck operation.

One calculation anomaly in the model is that the profit percentage is normally calculated as profit divided by revenues. However, since revenues are not included in the model, we instead use profits divided by throughput. Since throughput is less than revenue, we are overstating the profit percentage as compared to the traditional profit percentage calculation.

Use the constraint analysis model in a before-and-after mode, to see what effect a proposed change will have on profitability or the return on investment. If the model improves as a result of a change, then implement the change. In the next few sections, we will examine how the constraint analysis model is used to arrive at several management decisions.

The Decision to Sell at a Lower Price

A common scenario is for a customer to promise a large order, but only if the company agrees to a substantial price drop. The sales department may favor such deals, because they bolster the company backlog, earn commissions, and increase market share. The trouble is that these deals also elbow out other jobs that may have higher throughput per minute. If so, the special deal drops overall throughput and may lead to a loss. The following example, which uses the basic constraint model as a baseline, illustrates the problem.

EXAMPLE

Mole Industries has received an offer from a customer to buy 2,000 units of its highly profitable Hedgehog Deluxe, but only if the company reduces the price. The new price will shrink the Deluxe's throughput per minute to $60. The analysis is:

Product	Throughput per Minute	Bottleneck Usage (minutes)	Units Scheduled	Total Bottleneck Time	Total Throughput
1. Hedgehog Deluxe	$60	14	2,000	28,000	$1,680,000
2. Hedgehog Mini	70	20	500	10,000	700,000
3. Hedgehog Classic	65	40	22	880	57,200
4. Hedgehog Digger	42	10	0	0	0
		Total bottleneck scheduled time		38,880	
		Total bottleneck time available*		38,880	
			Total throughput		$2,437,200
			Total operating expenses		2,400,000
			Profit		$37,200
			Profit percentage		1.5%
			Investment		$23,000,000
			Annualized return on investment		1.9%

* Minutes per month (30 days × 24 hours × 60 minutes × (1 − 0.10 maintenance time)

The baseline production configuration generated a profit of $228,960, while this new situation creates a profit of only $37,200. The profit decline was caused by a combination of lower throughput per minute for the Hedgehog Deluxe and the increased production capacity assigned to this lower-throughput product, which displaced other, more profitable products.

Note that there was no production capacity available at all for the Hedgehog Digger product. Clearly, the company should reject the customer's offer.

The Decision to Outsource Production

One way to manage the bottleneck operation is to outsource work to keep some of the production burden away from the bottleneck. This option is always acceptable if the throughput generated by the outsourced products exceeds the price charged to the company by the supplier, *and* the company can replace the throughput per minute that was taken away from the bottleneck operation. The following example, which uses the basic constraint model as a baseline, illustrates the concept.

EXAMPLE

Mole Industries receives an offer from a supplier to outsource the Hedgehog Classic to it. The supplier will even drop ship the product to customers, so the product would no longer impact Mole's production process in any way. The downside of the offer is that the supplier's price is higher than the cost at which Mole can produce the Classic internally, so the total monthly throughput attributable to the Classic would decline by $300,000, from $520,000 to $220,000. However, there is a large customer order backlog for the Hedgehog Digger, so Mole could give increased production priority to the Digger instead. The analysis is:

Product	Throughput per Minute	Bottleneck Usage (minutes)	Units Scheduled	Total Bottleneck Time	Total Throughput
1. Hedgehog Deluxe	$80	14	1,000	14,000	$1,120,000
2. Hedgehog Mini	70	20	500	10,000	700,000
3. Hedgehog Classic	65	40	200	N/A	220,000
4. Hedgehog Digger	42	10	1,488	14,880	624,960
		Total bottleneck scheduled time		38,880	
		Total bottleneck time available*		38,880	
			Total throughput		$2,664,960
			Total operating expenses		2,400,000
			Profit		$264,960
			Profit percentage		9.9%
			Investment		$23,000,000
			Annualized return on investment		13.8%

* Minutes per month (30 days × 24 hours × 60 minutes × (1 – 0.10 maintenance time)

Despite a large decline in throughput caused by the outsourcing deal, the company actually earns $36,000 more profit overall, because the Hedgehog Classic uses more of the bottleneck time per unit (40 minutes) than any other product; this allows the company to fill the available bottleneck time with 800 more Hedgehog Digger products, which require the smallest amount of bottleneck time per unit (10 minutes), and which generate sufficient additional throughput to easily offset the throughput decline caused by outsourcing. Mole Industries should accept the supplier's offer to outsource.

The Capital Investment Decision

In a large production environment, there are constant requests to invest more funds in various areas in order to increase efficiencies. However, it rarely makes sense to invest in areas that do not favorably impact the bottleneck operation in some way. In particular, investments in the capacity of operations located downstream from the bottleneck operation rarely yield a return, since improving them does nothing for the overall profitability of the entire system. The issue is addressed in the following example, which uses the basic constraint model as a baseline.

EXAMPLE

The industrial engineering manager of Mole Industries examines the entire production line, and concludes that he can double the speed of the paint shop for an investment of $250,000. This operation is located at the very end of the production line, and so is located downstream from the bottleneck operation. The analysis is:

Product	Throughput per Minute	Bottleneck Usage (minutes)	Units Scheduled	Total Bottleneck Time	Total Throughput
1. Hedgehog Deluxe	$80	14	1,000	14,000	$1,120,000
2. Hedgehog Mini	70	20	500	10,000	700,000
3. Hedgehog Classic	65	40	200	8,000	520,000
4. Hedgehog Digger	42	10	688	6,880	288,960
		Total bottleneck scheduled time		38,880	
		Total bottleneck time available*		38,880	
			Total throughput		$2,628,960
			Total operating expenses		2,400,000
			Profit		$228,960
			Profit percentage		8.7%
			Investment		$23,250,000
			Annualized return on investment		11.8%

* Minutes per month (30 days × 24 hours × 60 minutes × (1 − 0.10 maintenance time)

The only item that changes in the analysis is the amount of the investment, which increases by $250,000 and results in a reduced return on investment. Improving the capacity of the paint shop has no effect on throughput, since the entire production line can still only run at the maximum pace of the bottleneck operation.

Constraint Analysis

There are some types of investment that can make sense, even if they are not associated with the bottleneck operation. In particular, if an investment can reduce the cost of an operation, then the investment is acceptable, as long as the return on investment percentage increases as a result of the change. The concept is illustrated in the following example.

EXAMPLE

Rather than proposing a capacity increase in the paint shop (as was the case in the last example), the industrial engineering manager of Mole Industries proposes to invest $250,000 in the paint shop, but only to add sufficient automation to reduce operating expenses by $5,000 per month. The analysis is:

Product	Throughput per Minute	Bottleneck Usage (minutes)	Units Scheduled	Total Bottleneck Time	Total Throughput
1. Hedgehog Deluxe	$80	14	1,000	14,000	$1,120,000
2. Hedgehog Mini	70	20	500	10,000	700,000
3. Hedgehog Classic	65	40	200	8,000	520,000
4. Hedgehog Digger	42	10	688	6,880	288,960
		Total bottleneck scheduled time		38,880	
		Total bottleneck time available*		38,880	
			Total throughput		$2,628,960
			Total operating expenses		2,395,000
			Profit		$233,960
			Profit percentage		8.7%
			Investment		$23,250,000
			Annualized return on investment		12.1%

* Minutes per month (30 days × 24 hours × 60 minutes × (1 − 0.10 maintenance time)

The investment creates a sufficient decline in total operating expenses to yield an increase in the annualized rate of return, to 12.1%. Consequently, this is a worthwhile investment opportunity.

The Decision to Cancel a Product

A common practice is to review all products issued by a company, carefully allocating costs to each one, to see if any are losing money. If so, management may agree to cancel them. However, when products are reviewed from the perspective of constraint analysis, they are almost never cancelled. The reason is that the basis of measurement should be throughput, which is revenues minus totally variable expenses, and since the cost of materials is really the only variable expense, there is *always* throughput. A company rarely prices its products at or below the cost of its materials, since that would result in catastrophic losses.

Constraint Analysis

Since all products are likely to have throughput, the real question is not which products have the lowest throughput, but rather which ones have the highest throughput. By focusing on these high-throughput products, management can readily see which items to bring most forcibly to the attention of customers. If the result is an increased volume of production of products having high throughput, then the low throughput products may be forced out of the production mix, simply because there is no production capacity left to manufacture them.

If you were to follow the more traditional approach of assigning overhead to products and then deciding if they are unprofitable, the result would be the ongoing elimination of products, as overhead costs are gradually shifted to fewer and fewer remaining products, driving up the cost of each one in turn and forcing management to conclude that each one should be cancelled. The following example illustrates the concept.

EXAMPLE

Mole Industries has three versions of a trench digging tool. The company has $4,000,000 of overhead that it allocates to the three products. The company allocates the overhead based on revenue. The cost characteristics of the products are:

Product	Revenue	Variable Costs	Overhead Costs	Margin
Hedgehog Classic	$2,000,000	$1,300,000	$800,000	-$100,000
Hedgehog Mini	3,000,000	1,600,000	1,200,000	200,000
Hedgehog Deluxe	5,000,000	2,400,000	2,000,000	600,000
Totals	$10,000,000	$5,300,000	$4,000,000	$700,000

Hedgehog's president decides that, since the full cost of the Hedgehog Classic results in a loss, he should cancel that product. This results in the next table, where the same overhead is now being allocated (based on revenue) between the two remaining products.

Product	Revenue	Variable Costs	Overhead Costs	Margin
Hedgehog Mini	$3,000,000	$1,600,000	$1,500,000	-$100,000
Hedgehog Deluxe	5,000,000	2,400,000	2,500,000	100,000
Totals	$8,000,000	$4,000,000	$4,000,000	$0

Hedgehog's president now sees that the Hedgehog mini is losing money! Not knowing what else to do, he cancels that product, too. The result is shown in the next table:

Product	Revenue	Variable Costs	Overhead Costs	Margin
Hedgehog Deluxe	$5,000,000	$2,400,000	$4,000,000	-$1,400,000
Totals	$5,000,000	$2,400,000	$4,000,000	-$1,400,000

Hedgehog's president gives up, closes down the company, and takes a financial analysis class to figure out what happened. He later learns that all three products were contributing toward the pool of overhead that needed to be paid for. As he successively stripped away each product, that left the remaining products to shoulder more of the overhead load. Eventually, the Hedgehog Deluxe was left, and it did not generate enough of a margin to pay for all of the overhead.

Summary

Constraint analysis is one of the primary tools available for the financial analysis of operational decisions. It makes quite clear where the bottleneck operation is located, the extreme expense associated with not maximizing it, and how to manage operations to maximize profits.

However, it can be a foreign concept to many managers, who have spent their careers working on local optimization issues, allocating overhead, and improving the efficiency of labor – all of which are concepts that constraint analysis teaches do not improve overall profitability. Accordingly, we suggest training the financial analyst in constraint analysis, and having this person use constraint concepts to render opinions on whether certain decisions should be made.

Chapter 9
Credit Decisions

Introduction

A key element of financial analysis within a business is the daily decision of whether to extend credit to the company's customers. The initial granting of credit should be driven by a standardized analysis system, such as credit ratings. The ongoing monitoring of customer credit is typically triggered by a number of customer performance indicators. In this chapter, we address the nature of credit ratings, how to create an internal rating system, the availability of third party systems, and how to evaluate the results of a credit rating system. We then describe payment delinquency indicators, credit monitoring activities, and related topics.

The discussion in this chapter is from the perspective of the credit department, not the financial analyst, since the credit group has primary responsibility for extending credit to customers.

> **Related Podcast Episode:** Episode 86 of the Accounting Best Practices Podcast discusses credit best practices. The episode is available at: **accounting-tools.com/podcasts** or **iTunes**

The Credit Rating

It is possible to individually judge the merits of each customer's ability to pay for a sale made on credit, based on such information as credit applications, financial statements, and payment history. However, doing so on an individual basis introduces inconsistency into the granting of credit to all customers. It is entirely likely that a credit manager will grant more credit to a customer because he or she likes the customer, or less credit because their accounts payable person is annoying – hardly quantitative reasons, but all too common.

A better approach is to develop a standardized method for granting credit that is based on hard facts, such as customer payment history and liquidity. Doing so results in considerable consistency in how much credit is granted across the entire spectrum of customers, and should also reduce the incidence of bad debt losses. Such a system should ideally reject a request for credit when a customer is likely to default, as well as extend credit when a customer is not likely to default. Though the concept seems obvious, it can be quite difficult for a standardized system to differentiate between acceptable and unacceptable customers. A high-quality credit rating system does the best job of sorting through the credit applications of *marginal* customers; the applications of substantially better and worse customers can be more easily sorted through by even the more pedestrian credit rating systems.

Internal Credit Rating Systems

It is possible to develop an internal credit rating system, since the credit department has access to a large amount of information about customers, especially those that have been doing business with the company for a long time. However, a credit rating system will only be useful if a company has well over a thousand customers, since statistical analysis yields better results across large populations. Trying to develop a credit rating system based on the information from a smaller pool of customers will not yield an accurate credit scoring system.

An internal credit rating system should be based on any factors that a company finds to be important in determining the credit quality of customers in its specific industry. It is entirely possible that a credit determinant of ability to pay in one industry is a relatively minor one in another industry. Thus, the mix and weightings given to factors in the home improvement industry for contractor customers may differ wildly from those used by a sporting goods manufacturer for its retailer customers. Despite the broad potential range of variability in factors, the following are considered to be among the more reliable indicators of creditworthiness:

- *Bankruptcy*. There should not have been a recent bankruptcy filing, or the prospect of one.
- *Legal proceedings*. There should be no tax liens or other judgments against the customer.
- *Liquidity*. The customer's current assets greatly exceed its current liabilities, as measured by the current ratio or quick ratio.
- *Payment history*. The customer should have a track record of reliably paying on time.
- *Profitability*. The customer has a recent history of achieving a profit over the past few years, preferably close to the median profit level for the industry.
- *Stability*. The longer the customer has been in business, the better.
- *Third party credit score*. The credit score assigned to the customer by a credit scoring business should indicate that it is a reliable payer to *all* of its suppliers.

To construct an internal credit rating system, itemize the factors you intend to use for the system, and assign a range of scores to each of the factors that are either added to or subtracted from a customer's score. The following table illustrates the concept:

Point Assignment for Credit Scoring

Credit Scoring Factor	Excellent	Average	Neutral	Poor
Liquidity	+10	+5	-5	-10
Profitability	+15	+5	-5	-15
Payment history	+20	+5	0	-10
Stability	+5	0	-10	-20
Adverse judgments	0	0	0	-20
Third party credit score	+10	0	-5	-10
Bankruptcy	0	0	0	-100

The scores assigned in the preceding table can vary substantially, depending on the company's experience with how a particular factor appears to impact the ability of a customer to pay in a timely manner. For example, the credit manager may decide that payment history is the most important factor, and so assigns a large number of points to an excellent rating for that factor.

Also, note how some scores in the point assignment table are only activated if there is a negative result. Thus, there are only large negative scores related to bankruptcy or adverse judgments; a customer is not awarded points for the absence of these factors.

The point scoring system should be designed to keep a large cluster of customers from inhabiting the high and low ends of the scoring range. It is not useful when the assigned scores indicate that all customers should be granted maximum credit, or that none of them deserve credit, since this does not provide useful information.

The points assigned under a credit scoring system can be used as thresholds for a variety of actions by the credit department. For example, a score of 60 or more may allow for the automatic granting of credit, while a score between 40 and 50 calls for an escalated review, and scores between 30 and 40 indicate the need for a personal guarantee.

EXAMPLE

The credit manager of Kelvin Corporation is evaluating the credit application of a prospective new customer, which has submitted a complete set of audited financial statements. Further investigation reveals that the applicant has a 3:1 quick ratio, has been solidly profitable for the past five years, and has no adverse judgments against it. The business has been assigned an average credit score by a third party scoring firm. Based on this information, the credit manager assigns the following score to the applicant:

Credit Decisions

Factor	Issues	Score
Liquidity	High liquidity level	+10
Profitability	High historical profitability	+15
Stability	Five year history	+5
Adverse judgments	None detected	0
Third party credit score	Average ranking	0
	Score	+30

In essence, the ranking indicates that the applicant is an ideal prospective customer. According to Kelvin's credit policy, the applicant should be offered a $10,000 initial maximum credit, with re-evaluation to occur once a payment history has been compiled over the next six months. If the payment history is acceptable, the applicant can then be assigned an additional ten points, which will give it a total credit score of 40 and allow the credit manager to increase its maximum credit to $25,000.

A number of additional features can be applied to an internal credit scoring system that may enhance its usefulness. Consider the following features:

- Adjust credit scores based on the economic environment, where (for example) a contracting economy results in an automatic 5% reduction in all credit scores, thereby contracting the total amount of credit offered.
- Adjust the credit score based on the average or trending number of days past terms that a customer pays, either with the company or according to a third party credit report.
- Cap the amount of credit granted at a certain percentage of the reported net worth of the applicant.
- Cap the amount of credit granted at the amount of credit granted by anyone else to that customer, as stated on the third party credit report.
- Reduce the credit score of a customer located in a country that is perceived to have a high level of political risk.
- Reduce a credit score an increasing amount based on how long the applicant has been unable to report a profit.
- Reduce the number of points assigned to an applicant if its financial statements have not been audited, thereby reflecting the increased unreliability of the underlying information.

A company may conclude that having an internal credit rating system is a competitive advantage, since the in-house system may give a superior ability to grant credit to those customers whose credit fundamentals might lead competitors to reject their requests for credit. The result may be increased sales and profits, but only if the internal system continues to generate high-quality information. It is quite possible that the accuracy of the system will decline over time unless the company continues to compare actual results to what was indicated by the scoring system, and adjusts the system accordingly. If it appears too difficult to maintain an in-house scoring system, then an alternative is to use a third party credit rating system, as described in the following section.

Third Party Credit Ratings

A business may find that it has too few customers to develop a sufficient pool of information for its own in-house credit rating system. Also, it may not compile enough information about its customers to develop a rating system. If so, a common option is to subscribe to a third party credit rating service. Even a business that has an internal credit rating system may buy such a subscription in order to supplement its own system.

A credit rating organization, such as Experian or Dun & Bradstreet, collects information from many customers about their credit experiences with other entities, and also collects public information about liens, bankruptcies, and so forth, and aggregates this information into a credit report. These credit reports can be purchased with varying amounts of information, such as a credit rating, payment performance trend, legal filings, corporate officers, and much more.

The credit rating assigned to a business is based on the credit scoring methodology developed by the credit rating organization, which uses certain types of information and applies weightings that may differ from what a company would use if it were to develop its own credit scores. Nonetheless, these third party credit scores can provide a valuable view of how outside scoring analysts calculate credit scores.

> **Tip:** If a credit reporting subscription is purchased, be sure to include automatic updates of major changes in customer status, so that notifications of large credit downgrades or bankruptcies are received by e-mail as soon as possible.

The range of inputs that a credit rating agency may employ for the scoring of individuals is well beyond what a company could compile on its own. For example, here is a sample of some of the inputs that are reportedly used to derive the FICO score that comprises a large part of the credit rating for an individual:

FICO Score Components

Age of non-mortgage balance information	Number of accounts with delinquency
Amount of recent installment loan information	Number of bank revolving accounts
Amount owed on accounts	Number of other revolving accounts
Amount owed on revolving accounts	Number of consumer finance accounts
Amount past due on accounts	Number of established accounts
Delinquency on accounts	Number of inquiries in last 12 months
Length of credit history	Number of revolving accounts
Length of revolving credit history	Proportion of balances to credit limits
Number of accounts currently paid	Serious delinquencies
Number of accounts opened in last 12 months	Time since delinquencies recorded
Number of accounts with balances	

In short, a credit rating organization has access to much more information than a business could possibly find on its own, and uses this information to construct comprehensive credit reports about most larger businesses currently in existence, as well as for individuals.

Evaluating Credit Scores

Is it possible to tell which credit scoring methodology issues the highest-quality credit scores? Most companies avoid the issue and subscribe to the most reputable service (a subjective approach at best), or the one with the lowest prices, but either approach may not yield the best results – and results can vary substantially, since the scoring companies input different types of data into their models, as well as assign different weights to the data.

A good way to quantitatively evaluate scoring systems is to conduct a credit score comparison test, with the objective of identifying the scoring model that most clearly polarizes good and bad credit risks. This level of polarization can be measured with the Kolmogorov-Smirnov test, which evaluates the ability of a model to separate data. More information about this test can be found on Wikipedia under the "Kolmogorov-Smirnov Test" topic.

To conduct the comparison test, extract a statistically significant proportion of the account file for the past twelve months and compare its results to the credit scores issued by each credit scoring company. Look in particular for situations where the credit scores differ substantially, and where those differences would have resulted in a credit request being rejected that has subsequently resulted in a bad debt write-off. In addition, look for consistent results by a scoring model over a multi-month period.

If this test results in the decision to change to a new credit scoring methodology, also be sure to conduct a retrospective validation of the results, using both credit scores again, just to ensure that the original analysis held up over time. In addition, this subsequent analysis will allow the company to test which customers have been accepted under the new credit model that would have been rejected under the old model, and whether those additional credit acceptances turned out to be good credit risks. By weighing the benefits of reduced bad debt write-offs against any potential change in the cost of the credit scoring service, you can now arrive at a rational evaluation of which credit scoring methodology works best for the company.

Use of Credit Ratings

Credit ratings are valuable tools, and should be a mandated part of the credit management function. The corporate credit policy should require that a credit rating be developed or purchased for every credit application where doing so is cost-effective. Nonetheless, management may sometimes override the use of credit ratings when it wants to make a sale or to increase profits. For example, if the intent is to gain market share, one approach is to acquire higher-risk customers by granting credit that competitors are not willing to issue. Conversely, management can increase the profit percentage (not necessarily total profits) by contracting the use of credit and thereby avoiding bad debt losses.

When management intends to increase or decrease the use of credit, credit ratings should still be used. If credit is to be increased, then the credit manager simply authorizes the extension of credit to customers whose credit scores are further down the continuum of credit ratings, rather than granting extra credit on a spot basis. Conversely, if credit is to be contracted, the reduction occurs at the low end of the current range of approved credit ratings, leaving the credit to higher-scoring customers relatively untouched.

Credit Rating Errors

Credit ratings are developed from historical information, and so cannot be expected to perfectly predict the future. For example, a corporate customer with a sterling payment history may suddenly lose its warehouse due to flooding or an earthquake, and no longer be able to pay its bills. Or, an individual with a high credit rating may lose his job, and immediately begin delaying payments. And in general, an escalation or decline in general economic conditions will create a corresponding change in the proportion of bad debts experienced.

Another issue with credit ratings is the information upon which they are based. The information collected about a customer may not be perfect. It could be outdated or incorrect, or may contain fraudulent information (such as false financial statements). Also, key information may be missing, such as the existence of a loan. Consequently, credit ratings are only as accurate as the information upon which they are based.

For both of the preceding reasons, credit ratings will generate misleading results from time to time, which means that bad debts will be incurred. The built-in errors associated with credit rating systems will likely result in an average rate of bad debt losses that is relatively consistent over time, barring the effects of such major systemic changes as a recession.

Indicators of Future Payment Delinquency

When conducting ongoing credit monitoring activities, look for several flags that can indicate future payment difficulties with a debtor. These flags include the following:

- *Bankruptcy.* Once a customer declares bankruptcy, the odds of the seller being paid decline rapidly. Consequently, subscribe to a bankruptcy notification service, under which a credit reporting agency provides immediate notice of bankruptcy filings.
- *Change from proprietorship.* A customer may have originally been granted credit in part because the business was a sole proprietorship, which means that the owner is personally responsible for the debts of the business. If the customer later converts the structure of the business into some form of corporation, this means that the owner is no longer liable for the debts of the business. When this change happens, it may be necessary to reduce the amount of credit to reflect the reduced amount of assets that are now available to the company for collection purposes. A change in the form of legal organization can be detected on a credit report.
- *Credit report results.* It may be that a customer is paying within terms, but is paying everyone else late, perhaps because your business is more important to the customer. If so, a declining payment history on a credit report will reveal this issue, as reported by the other suppliers of the customer.
- *Days to pay.* The main indicator of future delinquency is simply a lengthening of the number of days that a customer takes to pay an invoice. The number of days to pay is most easily monitored with a report that states the trend line of days to pay for each customer. However, since this report may be generated only once a month, there are other more immediate indicators. For example, a check payment may be rejected by the bank on the grounds that there are not sufficient funds in the bank account of the customer. Or, a customer may avoid paying the largest outstanding invoice while still paying a number of smaller invoices on time. Another possibility is that the number of deductions taken will suddenly rise.
- *Decline in financial indicators.* If there is a noticeable decline in the financial condition or results of a customer, the decline will eventually be felt in their accounts payable area, which will not have sufficient cash with which to make timely payments. Of course, it is only possible to notice such issues if the credit staff has arranged for the ongoing receipt of financial statements from its customers.
- *Failed payment promises.* Whenever a debtor states that a payment will be made as of a certain date and in a certain amount, and that payment fails to appear, this represents a significant indicator of severe cash flow difficulties

by the debtor. Such an event should be a clear trigger to shut down all credit to a customer.
- *Missing credit application information.* When a customer fills out a credit application, every field on the form should be completed. When this is not the case, it is entirely possible that the customer is attempting to hide information from the credit staff. It is particularly important to delve into this missing information to identify why no information was provided.
- *Order decline.* If a customer is facing financial hardship or a decline in its core business, it should cut back on the volume of its orders to the company. If the credit staff is monitoring the trend of these orders, it should cut back on the amount of credit granted to be more in line with actual order volume. This is not necessarily a case where entirely cutting off credit is warranted – instead, the amount of credit granted should merely be scaled back to meet the needs of the customer.
- *Ownership changes.* Whenever the ownership of a business changes hands, this indicates that the payment history associated with that account becomes much less reliable, since it is now based on the payment habits of the new owner. In essence, a change in ownership could trigger a resetting of credit to that of a new business. This issue is particularly important for a smaller business, where a new owner is more likely to directly impose his or her payment practices on the accounts payable department. It can be difficult to spot a change in ownership. It may be noted on a credit report, or indicated when a collection person's call is routed to a new person at a debtor.
- *Triggering events.* An event may occur that is considered critical to the operations of a customer, such as an armed insurrection in a country where it generates most of its sales, or an earthquake that destroys its facilities. The credit staff needs to monitor news reports to be aware of these events. While rare, they can have a major impact on the credit terms extended to a customer.

The occurrence of any one of these items should certainly trigger a more detailed review by the credit staff, while a cluster of them should be considered a major warning sign that the amount of credit granted should be reduced forthwith.

The real issue with delinquency indicators is formulating a system for bringing them to the attention of the credit staff and ensuring that some action is taken, as described in the next section.

Ongoing Credit Monitoring Actions

The credit staff should decide upon the frequency and type of monitoring that it wants to impose upon its customers, which will be driven by many of the factors described in the preceding section. The *frequency* and *type* of monitoring are two different issues, and can be modified at the individual customer level, based on the circumstances. For example, a new customer that has reported shaky financial results could warrant a full quarterly review, as well as a requirement to issue its financial statements to the company as part of these quarterly reviews, on the grounds that the seller is at substantial risk of loss. Conversely, a cursory annual review may be sufficient for a small but well-established customer with a long history of on-time payments, since the track record is excellent and the amount of receivables at risk is small. In addition, it may be necessary to conduct a review whenever new customer orders result in a customer exceeding its allowed credit limit. This issue is dealt with in more detail in the next section, Requests for Credit Increases.

In addition to formal credit reviews, the credit staff's other main form of credit monitoring activity is centered on the accounts receivable aging report. This is a standard report generated by any accounting system, which classifies the age of unpaid accounts receivable by time bucket (such as for invoices that are 0-30 days old, 31-60 days old, and so forth). The credit staff can skim through this report each day to determine which customer receivables are trending longer than usual before being paid, which can trigger a more active and thorough credit investigation.

An alternative to the accounts receivable aging report is to review the days sales outstanding (DSO) for each customer, tracked on a trend line. If the DSO suddenly trends or spikes upward, this is a strong indicator of customer payment problems that should trigger a credit review. The calculation of DSO is:

$$\frac{\text{Accounts receivable}}{\text{Total credit sales}} \times \text{Number of days}$$

For example, if the credit sales to a customer for the past quarter were $100,000 and the accounts receivable due from that customer were $40,000 at the end of the period, then its DSO would be:

$$\frac{\$40,000 \text{ Accounts receivable}}{\$100,000 \text{ Total credit sales}} \times 90 \text{ Days} = 36 \text{ Days sales outstanding}$$

There is an issue with calculating DSO information over too short a period, such as the last 30 days, since the measurement will likely contain receivables from a prior period that should not be compared to the total credit sales shown in the denominator of the equation. To avoid this comparability problem, consider using a DSO calculation period of no less than 90 days, calculated on a rolling basis for the past 90 days. Thus, DSO could be calculated on a weekly basis for each customer, for the 90 days immediately preceding each calculation date.

The main forms of credit monitoring for many credit departments stop at the use of scheduled credit reviews and DSO analysis. However, there are other types of monitoring available that come from a variety of sources within and outside of the company, all of which provide useful clues regarding the financial condition of customers. Consider using the following additional types and sources of information:

- *Credit report updates.* Subscribe to the credit report updating service of a credit reporting agency. The agency will issue updates whenever there is a significant change in the status of a customer, including a bankruptcy filing.
- *Credit uptake.* A customer typically operates at a level where it does not use all of the credit allowed to it by the credit department. The difference between the amount of credit used and available tends to be fairly steady, except for seasonal industries. When there is a sudden surge from the normal amount of credit taken to a level close to the maximum allowed, this is known as *credit uptake*. A company's computer system can spot these sudden increases and bring them to the attention of the credit department, which can contact the indicated customers to learn more about the reason for the ordering change.
- *Customer service conversations.* Customers may contact the company for a variety of reasons, some of which may provide clues to their financial condition or willingness to pay for a specific invoice. For example, a call about an improper installation of equipment could result in a delayed payment by a customer. The customer service staff should record a summary of all such calls in a database, which the credit staff can peruse for clues regarding credit issues.
- *Data mining.* In some industries, analysis firms can be hired to sift through all available information about an individual or corporate customer, resulting in improved estimates about which customers are more likely to be delinquent in their payments, as well as the appropriate level of credit to extend. This service is most prevalent when customers are individuals.
- *Discounts not taken.* A customer may have been in the habit of taking all early payment discounts offered by the company, and suddenly stops doing so, which can indicate cash flow problems. This is an extremely difficult item to detect, since accounting systems do not monitor it. A possible option is to develop a list of customers that have historically taken early payment discounts, and periodically compare that list to the most recent payments made by customers.
- *Exception payments.* A notable sign of impending cash flow trouble is when a customer pays smaller invoice amounts on time, but not the larger invoices. This issue is most easily discernible by the cash application staff, which can readily see that invoices are not being paid at the point of cash application. They should note these situations in an e-mail to the credit department. This approach gives the credit staff faster notification of a problem than if they simply reviewed the accounts receivable aging report on a periodic basis and gradually became aware that certain invoices were not being paid.
- *Industry rumors.* The sales department is the best-networked group in the company, and so has the best information about any rumors in the industry concerning specific customers. When these rumors could impact customer credit, the information should be forwarded to the credit department. This type of information can be extremely difficult to extract from the sales staff,

so consider having the credit manager and sales manager meet on a scheduled basis to discuss and interpret this information.
- *Inquiry rate.* When someone wants to engage in fraud, one of the more clever ways is to establish a shell company that is then kept inactive for a number of years, thereby establishing a historical basis upon which credit requests can be made. It is possible to spot this type of fraud by looking for a sudden spike in the inquiry rate for credit reports on that company, since the operators of the shell will likely begin requesting credit from several companies at once.
- *Not sufficient funds checks.* Someone within the accounting department is responsible for reviewing all notifications from the bank at which the company deposits its checks. These notifications can include a notice that a customer check was rejected, due to insufficient funds in the customer's bank account. Whenever such a notice is received, the credit department should be notified at once, preferably with complete information about the specific check that was rejected.
- *Public filings.* If a customer is publicly-held, it must submit regular filings to the Securities and Exchange Commission (SEC). These filings contain the complete financial statements of the business on the Forms 10-K and 10-Q. In addition, Form 8-K filings contain descriptions of significant events impacting the filing company. The Form 8-K disclosures can be particularly relevant to the credit department, since they reflect the current circumstances of the filing entity. SEC filings are available for public viewing at the www.sec.gov website.
- *Site visits.* The credit department should schedule an ongoing series of site visits with those customers having the most credit with the company, or for those situations where other information indicates that there may be a problem. The credit staff can look for a number of physical indicators of financial difficulty, as well as establish relations with their counterparts that may create better access to credit information.

If the company has installed a comprehensive enterprise resources planning system, it may be possible to collect some of the preceding information from the system, since an ERP system collects every possible scrap of information. If such a system is not available, a separate arrangement will have to be made with each person providing information to send it to the credit department by whatever means is most efficient and foolproof.

Requests for Credit Increases

Customers continually ask for increases in the amount of credit granted to them. There are several ways to deal with these requests, depending upon the perceived duration of the need for credit, and the amount of additional credit requested. Several possible credit-granting scenarios are:

- *One-time small order increase.* A customer may request a small credit increase, perhaps to allow for the acceptance of one incremental order. If so, an option is to grant additional credit just for that order, and then drop the credit level back to its pre-existing level once the order has been paid for by the customer. This approach calls for a small amount of additional monitoring by the credit staff, to reduce the credit level at a later date.
- *Permanent small order increase.* A customer may request a relatively small and permanent increase in its level of credit. If so, this likely results from a gradual, trending increase in the order volume from that customer. This common occurrence calls for a modest review by a credit staff person with a minimal request for additional information by the customer, and probably does not call for an excessive amount of approval escalation within the department.
- *Large increase by old customer.* An existing customer with a lengthy payment history may ask for a large increase in credit. In this case, the credit staff should move the customer to a higher reporting level, such as quarterly financial statements, quarterly credit reports, and oversight by a senior credit employee. Also, the additional amount approved should be escalated to a high level within the organization.
- *Large request by new customer.* The riskiest credit request is a large one from a new customer with which the company has no experience. In this case, the level of investigation is similar to what a lender would impose on a prospective borrower, including financial statements for the past few years, a credit report, an on-site meeting, and approval by the credit manager. Every possible risk mitigation strategy should be considered in this situation.

Thus, the information requested and the amount of additional analysis and management oversight required will increase in stages, based on the type of credit request. For the largest credit requests from the newest customers, the sheer volume of information required and analysis to be conducted will require a fair amount of time; this may present a problem when a customer wants a quick decision on a credit increase.

The Riskiest Customers

A prior section described a number of indicators of payment delinquency, which can be used for ongoing credit monitoring purposes. In addition, there are several types of businesses that are worthy of particularly detailed examination on an ongoing basis. These are:

- *New businesses.* Most new businesses fail within a few years. This is an established fact, so be aware that any new business requesting credit is several times more likely to default on its trade receivables than a more established business.

- *Distributors and retailers with newly-granted credit increases.* Whenever a large increase in credit is granted to a customer, the customer is presumably banking on a ramp-up in its own business in order to sell the goods that have been sold to the customer. However, an increase in business by the distributor or retailer may call for a presumed increase in market share, or extra distribution or marketing efforts that will not be realized. If so, the customer will not sell the goods, and so cannot pay the company.
- *Transitional businesses.* Whenever a customer is transitioning out of one line of business and into another, it is essentially encountering the same conditions that an entirely new business must deal with. In these cases, the risk of default is high. Unfortunately, it can be quite difficult to ascertain when such a change is occurring, since a business may give the appearance of having been in operation for years, and give no indication that it is abandoning one line of business and shifting to another.

Whenever a customer falls into this "riskiest" category, the credit staff must monitor every possible indicator of their condition and performance on a very frequent basis. This high level of hands-on monitoring requires a great deal of credit staff time, which brings up the issue of whether it is cost-effective to have such customers. In those cases where the company is not doing much business with a "riskiest" customer and there are few prospects for more revenue, it makes sense to shut down the relationship entirely. Only in cases where sales to such a customer are expected to increase, and the customer will eventually progress beyond the "riskiest" classification does it make sense to extend credit to this class of customer.

The Demanding Customer

There are usually a few customers who constantly demand attention in many areas, such as customized products, overnight delivery, and – yes, additional credit on short notice. In these cases, it is useful to examine the situation from a high level to understand the complete picture. In essence, the customer is treating your business as an extension of its own business, in order to obtain a sale that benefits the customer. In addition, your business is funding the customer's operations through the extension of credit to it. Thus, you are relying upon the business sense of the customer's management to continually conclude business deals with *its* customers that allow your customer to pay in a timely manner.

This scenario is a bad one from several perspectives, and can result in both increased costs and the prospect of substantial losses. Here are several examples:

- A distributor is about to close a deal with a large retail chain, and asks Seller Company for $5,000,000 of additional credit on 30-day terms in order to have sufficient goods on hand to sell to the retail chain. At the last minute, the retailer's purchasing manager negotiates 60-day payment terms from the retail chain to the distributor. The distributor does not have the resources to still pay Seller Company within terms, and so asks for 60-day terms. In es-

sence, Seller is financing the distributor's sale to the retailer. If the retailer fails to pay the distributor, Seller will sustain a large loss.
- A retailer wants Seller Company to repackage one of its mainstream products in time for the Christmas selling season. In order to do so, Seller must pay its employees overtime to design the revised packaging and repackage the product, as well as ship the products by overnight delivery service to the retailer's many locations. In this case, if the products do not sell, Seller can take back the goods and repackage them for shipment elsewhere. However, it has incurred the costs of employee overtime, packaging, and shipping for this special deal, and will not be compensated for these expenses. In this case, the retailer benefits from any sales, while the seller incurs greater losses than usual if the promotion fails.

These scenarios might tempt the credit manager to always avoid deals with demanding customers. How to handle these customers depends upon the circumstances, since it is also possible to earn a large profit by doing business with them. The following two factors are paramount in making a decision to extend credit:

- *Track record.* If a customer is very demanding but always pays on time, this is a strong indicator that the customer may be an acceptable risk for the ongoing extension of credit. It is entirely possible that the customer's management team simply treats all of its suppliers in a demanding manner, but is also quite successful in its own business dealings, and so is capable of earning sufficient profits to pay its suppliers in a timely manner.
- *Product margins.* If the products being sold have razor-thin margins, the seller stands to lose more than when its products carry substantial margins. In the first case, the credit manager is much less inclined to take a chance on a demanding customer, since the business is built around the standardized sale of goods in the most cost-efficient manner; there is no margin for error if a customer proves to be *too* demanding. In the latter case, margins are so comfortable for the seller that it can afford to take on a number of demanding customers, meet their special needs, and still earn a respectable profit.

In short, the decision to deal with a demanding customer is driven by both an analysis of the capabilities of the customer's management team and the profitability of a company's own products. The first factor is knowledge that can only be gained over time, which calls for the gradual extension of credit. The second factor is based on a simple profit calculation, of which the credit manager should be well aware at all times.

Effects of Industry Credit Practices

A certain set of credit terms will likely have become widespread within an industry over time. For example, payment terms may be extremely short in one industry (such as overnight delivery services) or quite long in others (such as durable goods).

It is very difficult to improve upon these terms (from the perspective of the seller) if the goods and services being offered cannot be easily differentiated from those of competitors.

The dominance of standard industry terms is a particular concern in an industry being severely impacted by a downturn, since industry practice may continue to require relatively generous credit terms. The credit manager may want to tighten credit terms in a variety of ways, but cannot do so, since the seller's offerings are so undifferentiated that customers simply shift their business to competitors.

The best way to deal with rigid industry credit practices is to reformulate the company's offerings to make them more unique. By doing so, customers are more willing to accept more conservative credit terms than would normally be the case, and will continue to do business with the company. Having unique products can have a particularly favorable impact during an industry downturn, since the credit manager can more readily retract credit and still expect customers to do business with the company.

Summary

When a business first decides to use credit ratings, it is easiest to purchase a subscription from a third party credit rating agency. Once the company has built up its own database of information about customers, which may take several years, it can then consider the option of developing its own credit scoring system, which can supplement or completely replace the information being provided by the credit rating agency. The decision to use an in-house system may be driven by the need to develop a competitive advantage in ascertaining which riskier customers should be granted or denied credit.

The use of credit scoring does not completely mechanize the credit granting function, but it does introduce a high level of consistency in the credit granting process that is probably sufficient for 80% of all customers. The unique circumstances of the remaining customers will likely require more hands-on analysis that may result in adjustments to the baseline credit scores, and therefore to the credit terms offered.

Once credit has been granted, the credit staff cannot possibly conduct detailed credit reviews of all customers on a continuous basis. Instead, they must use the tools and concepts presented here to focus the attention of the department on those customers most likely to have payment problems; all other customers can be subjected to considerably less credit oversight.

Chapter 10
Financing Choices

Introduction

The financial results, growth rate, or capital investment needs of a business may require it to obtain financing. If so, the analyst must be aware of the types of financing available, as well as their costs, terms and impact on the capital structure of the business. In this chapter, we review the types of debt and equity financing that are commonly available, ranging from early payment discounting to the issuance of warrants. We also address a number of issues closely related to debt, including the borrowing base and deleveraging.

> **Related Podcast Episodes:** Episodes 93, 124, 125, and 242 of the Accounting Best Practices Podcast discuss stock registrations, lender relations, refinancing debt, and crowdfunding, respectively. The episodes are available at: **accountingtools.com/podcasts** or **iTunes**

Overview of Debt Funding

A large part of the cash management task of a business is to ensure that there is sufficient cash on hand to fund company operations. While some of this cash may come from company sales and maturing investments, it is also entirely possible that cash must be raised from outside parties. A major source of funding is debt financing, which falls into these categories:

- *Asset-based financing.* Company assets are used as collateral for this type of debt. Examples are the line of credit, invoice discounting, factoring, inventory financing, and leases.
- *Unsecured financing.* No company assets are used as collateral. Instead, lenders rely upon the cash flows of the business to obtain repayment. Examples are long-term loans, bonds, and floating-rate notes.
- *Guaranteed financing.* A third party guarantees debt payments by the company. Government entities, such as the Export-Import Bank, usually provide these guarantees.

Examples of these types of debt financing are noted through the remainder of this chapter.

If a company obtains financing, it must pay interest on the amount borrowed. The interest percentage may be variable, with the rate adjusting in accordance with a benchmark rate at regular intervals. If the rate is variable and may rise suddenly, a company is at some risk of incurring much higher interest expenses. These costs are mitigated by the tax deductibility of interest expense. For example, if a company incurs $100,000 of interest expense and is in the 35% incremental income tax bracket, it can use the $100,000 interest deduction to reduce its income tax liability (if any) by $35,000.

There may also be a fee for an annual audit of the company's books by a bank-designated auditor, as well as an annual facility fee for keeping open a line of credit.

When reviewing the following types of debt, take note of any administrative charges that may also be billed to the company. This is a particularly large issue for financings involving accounts receivable or inventory as collateral, and can noticeably increase the total borrowing cost.

The Line of Credit

A line of credit is a commitment from a lender to pay a company whenever it needs cash, up to a pre-set maximum limit. A line of credit is generally secured by company assets, which the lender can take if the company is unable to pay back the line of credit. The lender will not allow a drawdown against a line of credit if the total amount lent will then exceed the amount of assets pledged as collateral against the line (known as the *borrowing base*). Any debt made available under a line of credit can be accessed multiple times over the course of the debt agreement. The lender may also block out a portion of a line of credit for letter of credit transactions where the borrower is committing to pay a supplier a predetermined amount on a future date. A line of credit is a highly useful form of financing for a business that does not have sufficient cash reserves to fund its day-to-day needs.

A larger and more credit-worthy business may be able to avoid any collateral; if so, the lender is relying on the general credit quality of the company. The usual agreement under which a line of credit is granted requires the company to pay an annual fee in exchange for the lender's commitment to keep a certain amount of debt available for the company's use; this is called a *committed* line of credit. It is also possible to have a less formal arrangement at a lower cost, where the lender is not obligated to make funds available to the company. This latter arrangement is called an *uncommitted* line of credit, and is useful for rare lending needs when a company has several sources of funds from which to choose.

When a bank offers a line of credit, it is typically under the agreement that the bank will also handle the company's other banking business, such as its checking accounts and lockboxes. This arrangement can be useful, since the staff can monitor cash balances and routinely transfer borrowed funds back to the bank through an inexpensive intrabank transfer transaction. Doing so on a frequent basis minimizes the interest cost of the line of credit.

When entering into a line of credit arrangement, be sure to also obtain separate debt funding to handle all of the company's long-term debt needs. The reason is that a line of credit is intended to be a source of short-term funding *only*, which means that the line of credit balance is expected to drop to zero at some point each year. Otherwise, it will appear that the company is using the line as part of its long-term borrowing arrangements.

The Borrowing Base

A borrowing base is the total amount of collateral against which a lender will lend funds to a business. This typically involves multiplying a discount factor by each type of asset used as collateral. For example:

- *Accounts receivable*. 60% to 80% of accounts receivable less than 90 days old may be accepted as a borrowing base. Receivables from related parties and foreign entities are excluded.
- *Inventory*. A smaller percentage of finished goods inventory may be accepted as a borrowing base. Raw materials and work-in-process, as well as custom-made goods and slow-moving finished goods are usually not allowed, since they are more difficult to liquidate.

It is also common for a lender to only use the accounts receivable of a borrower as collateral - it may not accept *any* inventory as part of the borrowing base.

If the business is a small one, the lender issuing a line of credit will probably also want a personal guarantee from the owner of the business, in addition to the underlying collateral.

EXAMPLE

Hammer Industries enters into a line of credit arrangement that has a maximum lending limit of $6 million. The amount of the accounts receivable to be used in the borrowing base is limited to 80% of all trade receivables less than 90 days old. The amount of the inventory to be used is limited to finished goods. The amount of finished goods to be used in the borrowing base is limited to 65%.

At the end of March, there are $4.8 million of accounts receivable outstanding, of which $200,000 are more than 90 days old. Hammer also has $6.5 million of inventory on hand, of which $3.5 million is finished goods. The amount of debt that has been drawn down on the line of credit is $5 million. Based on this information, the financial analyst of Hammer constructs the following borrowing base certificate.

Hammer Industries	
Borrowing Base Certificate	as of 3/31/20x3
Total accounts receivable	$4,800,000
Less: Receivables > 90 days old	-200,000
Eligible accounts receivable	$4,600,000
× Advance rate	80%
= Collateral value of accounts receivable	$3,680,000
Total finished goods inventory	$3,500,000
× Advance rate	65%
= Collateral value of finished goods inventory	$2,275,000
Total collateral	$5,955,000
Total debt outstanding	5,000,000
Excess collateral	$955,000

A business that borrows money under a borrowing base arrangement usually fills out a *borrowing base certificate* at regular intervals, in which it calculates the applicable borrowing base. A company officer signs the certificate and submits it to the lender, which retains it as proof of the available amount of collateral. If the borrowing base stated on the certificate is less than the amount that the company is currently borrowing from the lender, then the company must pay the difference to the lender at once.

A lender may want to protect its borrowing base by requiring the borrower to obtain credit insurance for all of its outstanding accounts receivable. The cost of this insurance is essentially an additional borrowing cost for the borrower.

Careful monitoring of the borrowing base is of particular importance in seasonal businesses, since the inventory portion of the base gradually builds prior to the selling season, followed by a sharp increase in the receivable asset during the selling season, and then a rapid decline in all assets immediately after the season has been completed. It is necessary to balance loan drawdowns and repayments against these rapid changes in the borrowing base to ensure that a company does not violate its loan agreement.

Early Payment Discounting

A key question for the analyst is whether to offer early payment terms to customers in order to accelerate the flow of inbound cash. This is a common ploy if the company is cash-strapped, or where there is no backup line of credit with the local bank to absorb any cash shortfalls.

The early payment terms offered to customers need to be sufficiently lucrative for them to want to pay their invoices early, but not have such egregious terms that the company is effectively paying an inordinately high interest rate for access to the funds that it is receiving early.

The term structure used for credit terms is to first state the number of days being given to customers from the invoice date in which to take advantage of the early payment credit terms. For example, if a customer is supposed to pay within 10 days without a discount, the terms are "net 10 days," whereas if the customer must pay within 10 days to qualify for a 2% discount, the terms are "2/10." Or, if the customer must pay within 10 days to obtain a 2% discount or can make a normal payment in 30 days, then the terms are stated as "2/10 net 30."

The table below shows some of the more common credit terms, explains what they mean, and also notes the effective interest rate being offered to customers with each one.

Credit Terms	Explanation	Effective Interest
Net 10	Pay in 10 days	None
Net 30	Pay in 30 days	None
Net EOM 10	Pay within 10 days of month-end	None
1/10 net 30	Take a 1% discount if pay in 10 days, otherwise pay in 30 days	18.2%
2/10 net 30	Take a 2% discount if pay in 10 days, otherwise pay in 30 days	36.7%
1/10 net 60	Take a 1% discount if pay in 10 days, otherwise pay in 60 days	7.3%
2/10 net 60	Take a 2% discount if pay in 10 days, otherwise pay in 60 days	14.7%

In case you are dealing with terms different from those shown in the preceding table, be aware of the formula for calculating the effective interest rate associated with early payment discount terms. The calculation steps are:

1. Calculate the difference between the payment date for those taking the early payment discount and the date when payment is normally due, and divide it into 360 days. For example, under "2/10 net 30" terms, you would divide 20 days into 360 to arrive at 18. Use this number to annualize the interest rate calculated in the next step.
2. Subtract the discount percentage from 100% and divide the result into the discount percentage. For example, under "2/10 net 30" terms, you would divide 2% by 98% to arrive at 0.0204. This is the interest rate being offered through the credit terms.
3. Multiply the result of both calculations together to obtain the annualized interest rate. To conclude the example, you would multiply 18 by 0.0204 to arrive at an effective annualized interest rate of 36.72%.

Thus, the full calculation for the cost of credit is:

(Discount % ÷ (1 − Discount %)) × (360 ÷ (Allowed payment days − Discount days))

> **Tip:** It usually takes a hefty discount to persuade customers to pay early. Consequently, unless the company has a desperate need for cash, it is generally not worthwhile to offer a temptingly-high discount. However, consider offering a discount with a low effective interest rate on an ongoing basis; this might trigger a few early payments at little cost to the company.

Invoice Discounting

Invoice discounting is the practice of using a company's unpaid accounts receivable as collateral for a loan, which is issued by a finance company. Invoice discounting essentially accelerates cash flow from customers, so that instead of waiting for customers to pay within their normal credit terms, cash is received almost as soon as the invoice is issued.

This is an extremely short-term form of borrowing, since the finance company can alter the amount of debt outstanding as soon as the amount of accounts receivable collateral changes. The amount of debt issued by the finance company is less than the total amount of outstanding receivables (typically 80% of all invoices less than 90 days old).

The finance company earns money both from the interest rate it charges on the loan (which is well above the prime rate), and a monthly fee to maintain the arrangement. The amount of interest that it charges the borrower is based on the amount of funds loaned, not the amount of funds available to be loaned.

Invoice discounting is impossible if another lender already has blanket title to all company assets as collateral on a different loan. In such cases, the other lender needs to waive its right to the accounts receivable collateral, and instead take a junior position behind the finance company.

From an operational perspective, the borrower sends an accounts receivable report to the finance company at least once a month, aggregating receivables into the categories required by the finance company. The finance company uses this information to adjust the amount of debt that it is willing to loan the borrower. The borrower retains control over the accounts receivable, which means that it is responsible for extending credit to customers, invoicing them, and collecting from them. There is no need to notify customers of the discounting arrangement.

Invoice discounting works best for companies with relatively high profit margins, since they can readily absorb the higher interest charges associated with this form of financing. It is especially common in high-profit businesses that are growing at a rapid rate, and need the cash flow to fund additional growth. Conversely, this is not a good form of financing for low-margin businesses, since the interest on the debt may eliminate any prospect of earning a profit.

Invoice discounting tends to be a financing source of last resort, because of the substantial fees associated with it. You would normally use it only after most other forms of financing have been attempted.

Factoring

Another type of asset-based lending is *factoring*. A company that engages in factoring sells its accounts receivable to a third party, known as the *factor*. As was the case with invoice discounting, factoring is only an option if a company has not allowed other parties to attach its receivables as collateral on other loans.

The pricing arrangement for a factoring deal includes the following components:

- *Advance*. This is a proportion of the face amount of the invoices that the factor pays to the company at the point of sale.
- *Reserve*. This is the remaining proportion of the face amount of the invoices, which the factor retains until collections have been completed.
- *Fee*. This is the cost of the factoring arrangement, which is deducted from the reserve payment.

Once the factor owns a company's receivables, customers are notified to send their payments to a lockbox controlled by the factor. Payments made into the lockbox are retained by the factor. If the factoring arrangement is *with recourse*, the factor can pursue the company for any unpaid customer invoices. If the arrangement is *without recourse*, the factor absorbs any bad debt losses. A without recourse arrangement is more expensive, to compensate the factor for bad debt losses.

The total amount of fees associated with a factoring arrangement can be substantial, so this is generally considered a fund-raising arrangement of last resort.

Inventory Financing

The preceding two sections discussed how to use accounts receivable as collateral for different types of loan arrangements. The same approach can be applied to inventory. To make this arrangement work to the satisfaction of the lender, the inventory being used as collateral is placed in a controlled area and under the supervision of a third party that only releases inventory with the approval of the lender. The lender is paid from the proceeds of inventory sales. Under a less controlled environment, the lender may agree to periodic inventory reports by the borrower, with occasional inspections of the inventory to ensure that the counted amounts match the borrower's reports.

There must be a sufficient amount of insurance in place to ensure that the lender will be paid back if the inventory is destroyed or damaged. Also, depending on state laws, it may be necessary to post notices around the collateralized inventory, stating that a lien has been imposed on the inventory. Further, the inventory cannot be used as collateral on any other loans, unless they are subordinate to the arrangement with the inventory financing company.

If the amount of inventory being used as collateral drops below the amount of the loan associated with it, the borrower must immediately pay the lender the difference.

Because of the cost of third party monitoring, inventory financing is one of the more expensive forms of financing available and can also be quite intrusive, so it is used only after less-expensive alternatives have been explored. The sole advantage of this form of financing is that the lender relies exclusively on the inventory asset to ensure that it is repaid; it does not impose covenants on the borrower.

Purchase Order Financing

Purchase order financing is applicable when a company receives an order from a customer that it cannot process with its existing working capital. A lender accepts the purchase order as collateral, which allows the borrower to obtain sufficient funds to buy the materials and labor required to complete the order. This arrangement is risky for the lender, since the borrower must perform under the contract in order to receive payment from the customer. Given the extra risk, the borrowing cost is higher for purchase order financing.

Leases

When cash is needed to acquire a fixed asset, an excellent choice is to do so with a lease, rather than using cash from other sources. A lease is an agreement under which the lessee makes a number of incremental payments to the lessor, rather than a lump sum payment, while the lessor owns the asset associated with the lease. A lease can be structured so that the lessee owns the asset at the end of the lease term, which is called a *capital lease*. If the lessor continues to own the asset at the end of the lease, then the lease is called an *operating lease*.

Leases are especially useful under the following circumstances:

- *Cash flow*. Lease payments are spread out over the term of a lease, thereby keeping a business from having to deal with large one-time cash outflows to purchase assets.
- *Covenants*. A lessor does not impose any covenants on a company as a whole, since it is only concerned with the specific asset it is leasing to the company. Thus, a company wanting to avoid covenants should consider leases.
- *Specific collateralization*. When a company has pledged its other assets under a blanket collateralization agreement for another loan, a lease essentially segregates a single asset as collateral for a new loan (the lease).

There are two problems with leases. First, the company is committing to a minimum set of lease payments, which can be quite expensive to terminate early. Second, it can be difficult to ascertain the interest rate used to compile lease payments, so be sure to manually derive the interest rate before agreeing to a lease.

The Long-Term Loan

When a company finds that it is unable to draw its line of credit down to zero at any point during the year, this means that its funding needs have become more long-term. If so, it should apply to a lender for a long-term loan that will be paid off over a number of years.

The following points may clarify whether it is even possible to obtain such a loan, and whether you would want to do so:

- *Banking services.* The provider of a long-term loan may insist on providing a complete package of banking services, to maximize its profits. If so, expect to shift all bank accounts, lines of credit, lockboxes, and other services to the lender.
- *Cash flow.* The lender is particularly sensitive to the historical and projected performance of the business, since the loan must be repaid from continuing cash flows. If positive cash flows have been a rare event, it will be very difficult to obtain a long-term loan. The lender may also want to see a budget for at least the next year.
- *Covenants.* The lender will probably impose covenants on the company that are designed to keep it from disbursing cash outside of the normal course of business. In particular, dividends may be restricted.
- *Creditor positioning.* A lender willing to commit to a long-term loan will certainly want to be designated as having the senior position among all creditors of the company, so that it will be more likely to be paid back in the event of a loan default by the company. This positioning is necessary, because the lender is committing a large amount of funds to the company over a long period of time, during which the company's financial results may change dramatically.
- *Personal guarantee.* In a smaller business where there are few owners, and especially where historical cash flow has been uncertain, the lender may insist on personal guarantees that allow the lender to pursue the owners for repayment.

A long-term loan can be configured as a series of fixed payments, or as interest-only payments with a large balloon payment due at the end of the loan. While the balloon payment option may appear tempting from a short-term cash flow perspective, it introduces the risk that credit conditions may have changed by the time it is due for payment, making it difficult to refinance.

The conditions associated with a long-term loan might leave management less inclined to pursue this option. However, a long-term loan allows a business to lock in debt for an extended period of time, without having to worry about the vagaries of the short-term credit markets. Thus, it can make sense to assign a portion of a company's debt to longer-term loans.

Bonds

When a business sells a fixed obligation to investors, this is generally described as a *bond*. The typical bond has a face value of $1,000, which means that the issuer is obligated to pay the investor $1,000 on the maturity date of the bond. If investors feel that the stated interest rate on a bond is too low, they will only agree to buy the bond at a price lower than its stated amount, thereby increasing the effective interest rate that they will earn on the investment. Conversely, a high stated interest rate can lead investors to pay a premium for a bond.

When a bond is registered, the issuer is maintaining a list of which investors own its bonds. The issuer then sends periodic interest payments directly to these investors. When the issuer does not maintain a list of investors who own its bonds, the bonds are considered to be *coupon bonds*. A coupon bond contains attached coupons that investors send to the issuer; these coupons obligate the company to issue interest payments to the holders of the bonds. A coupon bond is easier to transfer between investors, but it is also more difficult to establish ownership of the bonds.

There are many types of bonds. The following list represents a sampling of the more common types:

- *Collateral trust bond.* This bond includes the investment holdings of the issuer as collateral.
- *Convertible bond.* This bond can be converted into the common stock of the issuer at a predetermined conversion ratio.
- *Debenture.* This bond has no collateral associated with it. A variation is the subordinated debenture, which has junior rights to collateral.
- *Deferred interest bond.* This bond offers little or no interest at the start of the bond term, and more interest near the end. The format is useful for businesses currently having little cash with which to pay interest.
- *Guaranteed bond.* The payments associated with this bond are guaranteed by a third party, which can result in a lower effective interest rate for the issuer.
- *Income bond.* The issuer is only obligated to make interest payments to bond holders if the issuer or a specific project earns a profit. If the bond terms allow for cumulative interest, then the unpaid interest will accumulate until such time as there is sufficient income to pay the amounts owed.
- *Mortgage bond.* This bond is backed by real estate or equipment owned by the issuer.
- *Serial bond.* This bond is gradually paid off in each successive year, so the total amount of debt outstanding is gradually reduced.
- *Variable rate bond.* The interest rate paid on this bond varies with a baseline indicator, such as LIBOR.
- *Zero coupon bond.* No interest is paid on this type of bond. Instead, investors buy the bonds at large discounts to their face values in order to earn an effective interest rate.

- *Zero coupon convertible bond.* This variation on the zero coupon bond allows investors to convert their bond holdings into the common stock of the issuer. This allows investors to take advantage of a run-up in the price of a company's stock. The conversion option can increase the price that investors are willing to pay for this type of bond.

Additional features can be added to a bond to make it easier to sell to investors at a higher price. These features can include:

- *Sinking fund.* The issuer creates a sinking fund to which cash is periodically added, and which is used to ensure that bonds are eventually paid off.
- *Conversion feature.* Bond holders have the option to convert their bonds into the stock of the issuer at a predetermined conversion rate.
- *Guarantees.* The repayment of a bond may be guaranteed by a third party.

The following additional bond features favor the issuer, and so may reduce the price at which investors are willing to purchase bonds:

- *Call feature.* The issuer has the right to buy back bonds earlier than the stated maturity date.
- *Subordination.* Bond holders are positioned after more senior debt holders to be paid back from issuer assets in the event of a default.

Agency Financing

When a company needs to finance the export or import of goods, this can constitute a large surge in borrowings that cannot be supported by its line of credit. A good alternative is to use agency-backed financing for these transactions. An "agency" is a government-sponsored export credit agency, such as the Export-Import Bank (Ex-Im Bank) of the United States. These agencies provide financial packages for the export or import of goods. A typical financing arrangement is for a commercial bank to supply credit to the borrowing entity, with the agency providing a credit guarantee to the bank. Alternatively, an agency may directly provide credit, thereby eliminating the need for an intermediary bank.

Agencies are not in the business of losing money on their financing packages, so minimum standards apply to all applications. For example, a first-time applicant to the Ex-Im Bank of the United States must meet the following criteria:

- Has been in the same line of business for at least three years
- Has at least one year of exporting experience
- Had an operating profit in the most recent fiscal year
- Has a Dun & Bradstreet Paydex score of at least 50, as well as no derogatory information
- Has signed financial statements for the last fiscal year that shows positive net worth
- Has no material adverse issues

In addition, the Ex-Im Bank may require corporate guarantees, personal guarantees, and/or collateral. Thus, agencies do not gratuitously give away funds; a company must qualify for financing under specific standards, and may be turned down. Nonetheless, this is a viable alternative when other sources of funds are not available.

Deleveraging

If a company has accumulated a large amount of cash, does it make sense to use some portion of this cash to pay down any remaining debt? The key decision factors are:

- *Cost of debt.* Itemize the debt by interest cost, and pay down the debt having the highest interest cost. Convertible debt may also be ranked for immediate pay down, if the company wants to avoid the conversion of debt into stock.
- *Use of cash.* If cash is simply being invested at the best possible interest rate, rather than being employed for operational purposes, it may be better to use it to pay down debt.
- *Differential cost.* If the interest rate on invested cash is lower than the interest rate on debt, pay down the debt.

Even if the preceding criteria point strongly in the direction of deleveraging, also consider the benefits of retaining a cash hoard for downturns in the economic cycle. It is entirely possible that the company can snap up assets or competitors at bargain-basement prices during a downturn – but that is only possible if there is sufficient cash on hand to do so.

Overview of Equity Funding

The first source of funding that most organizations turn to is debt financing, since interest expense is tax deductible and it does not change the ownership of a business. However, lenders are risk-averse, and will only lend a certain amount of cash. When that point is reached, the main alternative for fund raising is to sell shares in the business.

Though there is no legal obligation for a company to make regular payments to its investors, there is an expectation by investors of substantial returns, which they can achieve either through dividend payments or the appreciation in value of the company's stock. This expectation for returns is higher than the interest cost associated with debt, which is why the average company manager is reluctant to advocate the sale of stock when there are still opportunities for other types of fund raising.

When the decision is made to issue stock, a privately-held business may find that there are few investors willing to buy its shares, on the grounds that the shares cannot be easily resold to other investors. Also, since there is no market for its stock, there is no easy way to determine the value of the shares. As just noted, stock appreciation is one of the primary means by which an investor gains a return on shares held – but with no way to value the shares, appreciation cannot occur. Given these issues, a privately-held company has three options for selling equity:

- *Sell shares at a discount.* Investors may be interested in buying shares if the shares are being sold at a substantial discount, and especially if warrants are attached to the shares that give the right to buy additional shares at a certain strike price. Of course, this means that the ownership percentages of existing shareholders could decline dramatically.
- *Sell preferred shares.* More sophisticated investors will want to purchase preferred shares, which may carry a variety of features, such as dividends, conversion privileges to common stock, liquidation rights ahead of common stockholders, and/or the right to approve the sale of the business.
- *Go public.* Many stock sale agreements include a provision that requires the company to register the shares with the Securities and Exchange Commission (SEC) within a certain period of time. This means that the business must go public specifically so that the shareholders can be placed in a position to more easily sell their shares.

In addition to the issues associated with each alternative for selling equity, there is also the problem that shares bought by more sophisticated investors may come with the additional price of a board seat, monthly reporting packages, and possibly even control over the management of the business. In short, fund raising with equity is particularly unpalatable for privately-held businesses.

The situation is less dire for larger publicly-held companies, which can have new shares registered for sale within a short period of time and sell them on a stock exchange. Smaller publicly-held companies may face a considerably more prolonged review period before their shares can be registered for sale; further, the trading market for their stock may be so small that it takes some time to sell new shares.

In short, only larger public companies can easily sell shares within a reasonable time period and at a reasonable price. Most other entities must offer discounts or some sort of preference rights to convince investors to buy their shares. These issues should make it clear why so many smaller businesses actively avoid fund raising with equity.

Restricted Stock

Restricted stock carries a restriction statement on the face or back of the certificate, stating that there are restrictions on its transfer, purchase, or resale. This restriction is usually because the issuing company has not yet registered the shares with the SEC. It can be quite difficult for the holder of restricted shares to move the shares to a different owner. An example of the restriction verbiage shown on a stock certificate is:

> "These securities may not be sold, offered for sale, or pledged in the absence of a registration statement."

Unrestricted stock does not contain a restriction legend, and so can be sold or transferred. Because of the issues with restricted stock, the typical investor is much more interested in buying unrestricted stock from a company.

Unrestricted Stock

Investors are always the most interested in buying unrestricted stock, which is also known as registered stock. A company that wants to sell registered stock must file a Form S-1 registration statement with the SEC. The Form S-1 is an extremely detailed document that describes a company's financial and operational condition, as well as other matters. Among the more important categories of information in the form are:

- *Risk factors*. States the risks that may impact the company.
- *Use of proceeds*. Notes how the cash garnered from sale of the stock will be used.
- *Selling security holders*. Lists any current shareholders whose shares in the company are being sold.
- *Registrant information*. Describes the company, its financial results, management's discussion and analysis of the company, legal proceedings, and many other matters.

Completing the form properly requires the services of the company's auditors and attorneys, as well as their assistance when the SEC sends back several iterations of questions about the information in the form. It is likely that a number of months will pass before the SEC declares the form effective, which means that the stock listed in the form is now registered, and can be sold without restriction.

Once a Form S-1 has been declared effective, the company having made the filing is now considered a publicly held company, which means that it must file regular reports with the SEC about its financial results and material changes in its business.

If a company is already publicly held, it can use a *shelf registration* to pre-register stock that it does not necessarily plan to sell immediately. This still involves the difficult registration process, but the company is in less of a rush to complete it, since there is not an immediate need to sell shares. Under SEC rules, shelf registration requirements are eased for larger public companies.

In general, a privately held company will want to stay that way, since the costs of registering stock and making subsequent filings with the SEC as a public company are substantial.

Warrants

A warrant is a call option issued by a company on its own shares. The recipient has the right, but not the obligation, to buy the company's shares at a certain price during a specific period of time, which is usually at least five years. It may be tempting to issue warrants as part of a package deal under which investors buy company stock and warrants. The value of a warrant to an investor is that any future uptick in the price of the company's stock can be converted into an immediate profit by exercising the warrant at the price stated in the warrant agreement, and then selling the shares for a profit at the market price.

The value of the arrangement is not so clear from the perspective of the company, since it will be forced to sell its shares at a reduced price if warrants are eventually exercised. Because of this possible watering down of the shareholder base in exchange for a relatively small cash inflow, it is better to negotiate hard for the issuance of a reduced number of warrants. The worst-case scenario is *100% coverage*, where one warrant is issued for every share sold. A *50% coverage* scenario is better, since only one warrant is issued for every two shares sold. It is certainly worthwhile to negotiate even lower warrant coverage if the circumstances allow for it.

EXAMPLE

Hammer Industries sells 10,000 shares of its common stock for $10.00, along with 10,000 warrants to buy additional shares of the company for the next three years at $10.00 per share. The price of the company's stock later rises to $17.00, at which point the investor uses his warrant privileges to buy an additional 10,000 shares at $10.00 each. If he can then have the shares registered and sells them at the $17.00 market price, he will pocket a profit of $70,000 on his exercise of the warrants.

The best way to consider the impact of warrants is that they allow warrant holders to profit from any upside in the stock price, at the expense of existing shareholders whose percentage of ownership will decline if the warrants are exercised.

Angel Investors and Venture Capital

When a business is in its startup phase and the owners want to grow it quickly, they may initially turn to an angel investor for funding. An angel investor is a wealthy individual who usually invests between $25,000 and $1,000,000 in a business, in exchange for a significant minority ownership position. This is an extremely risky investment for the investor, since the business is unproven and could quite possibly fail. Given the high risk, expect to issue a disproportionate number of shares for this investment.

After a business has developed a proof of concept, or has perhaps issued its first products or services, it may again be in need of cash to ramp up its rate of growth. The cash requirement at this point will be larger, so funding from angel investors will no longer be sufficient. Instead, a venture capital fund (VC) is a possible source of capital. A VC is a corporate entity that pools the cash contributions of multiple investors and institutions for investments in startup companies. Typical investments made by a VC are in the range of $500,000 to $5,000,000.

It can be quite difficult to obtain funding from VCs, since they are looking for those few companies that have the potential for an extremely high rate of growth.

Their basic business model is to invest in a number of companies that have superstar potential, knowing that most will fail or become substandard investments, while a few will have stratospheric returns that offset the losses in the rest of their portfolios.

To obtain funding from a VC, create a short presentation and business plan, and present it to a VC partner. This presentation is critical, since venture funds see an enormous number of proposals every year, and only select a few for investment. If the VC partner is interested, expect a detailed due diligence investigation before any funding offer is made.

Venture firms want a certain amount of control over their investments. This may call for majority ownership, perhaps the issuance of preferred stock, a change in key management positions, and/or board seats. They want this level of control in order to be closely involved in how the company is managed. This can mean that company founders are pushed out or relegated to non-critical management positions.

A strong case can be made that most businesses should not even attempt to gain VC funding. A VC firm will push a company to expand extremely rapidly in order to increase its valuation as quickly as possible. An excessively rapid pace of growth can severely damage a company and increase its long-term risk of failure. Instead, it may make more sense to adopt a slower-growth stance with more traditional forms of equity and debt funding.

Crowdfunding

Crowdfunding involves raising funds from a large number of people, usually via the Internet. Selling shares through crowdfunding is regulated by the Securities and Exchange Commission's Regulation Crowdfunding. This regulation imposes several conditions on a company's fundraising efforts, of which the most important are as follows:

- *Funding cap.* The firm can raise a maximum of $1,000,000 in a one-year period (inflation adjusted). This cap effectively restricts crowdfunding to small startup businesses, since larger firms need more capital.
- *Investment cap.* Investors are limited to quite small investments, which means that a large number of investors will be needed to attain the maximum amount of annual funding.
- *Reporting.* The firm must file an initial Form C report with the Commission, as well as interim reports and what will likely be three subsequent annual Form C-AR reports, totaling about 200 hours of reporting effort.

In addition, the firm will need to register these shares with the SEC if its asset total ever exceeds $25 million. Given these restrictions, crowdfunding might initially appear to be a poor financing option. However, the SEC has also presented a better option, which is Rule 506(c) of its Regulation D. This Rule allows for unlimited fund raising, as long as funds are raised only from accredited investors (who are high net worth, high income investors) and the fund raising event is routed through a fundraising portal, which is a registered website that handles these events on a recurring basis.

Private Investment in Public Equity

When a publicly held company's equity is sold to accredited private investors, this is referred to as a *private investment in public equity* (PIPE). Private investors are usually willing to engage in such a transaction when they are offered a discount from the market price of a company's stock, typically in the range of a 10% to 25% discount.

A major advantage of a PIPE is that it is considered a private investment by the SEC, so the shares do not have to be registered with the SEC. Since no registration is required, the offering can be completed quickly and with minimal administrative hassles. A further advantage for the issuing company is that shares are typically sold in large blocks under a PIPE transaction to longer-term and more knowledgeable investors.

However, there are some disadvantages to entering into a PIPE transaction, from the perspective of the issuer. The concerns are:

- *Additional shares*. The company may have to guarantee the issuance of additional shares to PIPE investors if the market price of the shares subsequently falls below a threshold amount.
- *Warrants*. Investors may demand that they also be granted warrants, so that they can participate in any upside growth in the price of the company's stock. Typical terms are to grant warrants for anywhere from 50% to 100% of the shares sold.
- *Rapid sell-off*. Unless the company is careful about which investors are allowed to buy shares in a PIPE deal, it may find that the investors sell off their shares as soon as possible, thereby driving down the market price of the stock.
- *Short seller manipulation*. If the company is obligated to issue more shares to investors if the stock price declines, short sellers could take advantage of the situation by continually driving down the stock price, which triggers the issuance of more and more shares. This *death spiral PIPE* can even result in majority ownership of the company by the PIPE investors. The scenario can be avoided by specifying a minimum stock price below which no additional compensatory shares will be issued.

Debt for Equity Swaps

In some cases, it may be possible to swap company shares for outstanding company debt securities. This is most common when a company issues convertible bonds that allow bond holders to convert their bonds into company stock at certain predefined exchange ratios. This option is only available to publicly-held companies.

In a privately-held company, a debt for equity swap usually occurs only when a company is in such dire financial straits that it is unable to repay its debt. If so, taking an equity interest in the company may be the only option remaining to the lender, other than writing off the debt as being uncollectible. This conversion to equity is more likely when the lender is an individual, rather than a bank, since banks may be constrained by their own lending rules from engaging in debt for equity swaps. A company that succeeds in converting debt to equity under these difficult financial circumstances may find that it can issue stock at such a low valuation that it is required by the accounting standards to book a profit on the conversion of debt to equity.

When a large public company issues convertible debt, any resulting conversions to equity are unlikely to be large enough to alter the debt-equity ratio of the business to a significant extent. The reverse is the case when a private company succeeds in converting debt to equity; it may be eliminating much of its debt, and had such little equity to begin with that it switches from having a dangerously unbalanced debt-equity ratio to one that gives the appearance of being solidly well-funded. Of course, the operational profitability of such a company is still questionable, but the debt for equity swap can repair its balance sheet.

Summary

Most of the forms of debt financing noted in this chapter can only be accessed in limited amounts that are defined by the amount of collateral, after which lenders will be extremely unwilling to advance additional funds. For really high debt levels, it will be necessary to obtain personal guarantees from the company owners, or the sale of stock to increase the amount of equity on hand.

If a business has extremely variable earnings, it may not make sense to have *any* debt, since it may be difficult to pay back the lender. In such a situation, it makes more sense to stockpile cash during periods when the company is flush with cash, or to rely primarily on the sale of stock to raise cash.

It can be quite difficult to obtain equity funding in a privately-held company, since an investor's prospects for reselling the shares are not especially good. In order to obtain such investments, expect a negotiating battle with prospective investors, who will want a variety of extremely favorable terms. If the company needs successive rounds of equity funding, expect the terms to change for each round, depending upon relative changes in the negotiating power of the company and its investors. The result may well be a tangle of different types of preferred stock, each with different rights. If such a company is ever in a position to go public, it will then be necessary to clean up these different classes of stock by converting them to common stock at whatever conversion ratios were built into the original stock agreements. The situation is substantially different for a large public company, which can routinely issue new common stock whenever the market price is reasonable. Thus, the decision to raise funds through the sale of stock is substantially different for a private company and a public company.

Chapter 11
Financial Leverage

Introduction

In the preceding chapter, we noted that the cost of debt financing is substantially lower than the cost of equity financing. In addition, using debt for funding requirements results in a reduced need for additional equity, which can result in outsized gains in the return on equity measurement. This cost differential and potential to improve a key metric might lead management to load up on debt. However, these benefits are offset by serious risks. In this chapter, we address how financial leverage works, how it can be used in a prudent manner, and the serious downside of debt overuse.

The Financial Leverage Concept

The essential concept behind financial leverage is that the return on equity of a business can be increased by funding new projects with debt, rather than equity. Doing so freezes the equity portion of the return on equity calculation, so that any incremental profits generated by the debt-funded activities will automatically increase the return to shareholders. This is called *positive leverage*. If profits decline as a result of debt financing, it is known as *negative leverage*.

In short, when used properly, debt financing allows a business to increase the numerator in the following return on equity measurement, while freezing the denominator:

Return on Equity Formula		Effect of Funding with Debt
Net income	=	Increases when leverage is positive
Equity	=	No impact on equity

The concept is best illustrated with an example, as follows.

EXAMPLE

The management team of Grissom Granaries wants to invest in five barges and a tugboat, which it will use to transport grain down the Mississippi River. The cost of these assets is $10,000,000. The company expects to generate an annual $2,000,000 profit by operating the barges and tugboat. The company can elect to fund the purchases either by selling shares or issuing bonds at an interest rate of 8%. The current amount of equity held by the company is

Financial Leverage

$50,000,000, and it typically earns $5,000,000 per year for an average return on equity of 10%. The results of the alternative forms of financing appear in the following table.

	Equity Funding	Debt Funding
Current equity	$50,000,000	$50,000,000
Additional equity	10,000,000	
Total equity	$60,000,000	$50,000,000
Existing profit	$5,000,000	$5,000,000
Profit from invested funds	2,000,000	2,000,000
Less: debt cost		-800,000
Total profit	$7,000,000	$6,200,000
Return on equity	11.7%	12.4%

Based on the information in the table, Grissom's shareholders can earn a greater return on equity by directing the company to fund the fixed asset purchase with debt. By doing so, the denominator in the return on equity calculation (i.e., equity) is held constant, thereby boosting the return on equity with profits from the new venture.

The preceding example illustrates the benefits of financial leverage at the simplest possible level, without also factoring in the beneficial effects of income taxes on debt funding. When a company borrows money, the related interest expense is tax deductible in most taxing jurisdictions, so the net amount of profit generated is actually higher than was indicated in the example. In the following example, we adjust the calculation to reveal the effects of taxation.

EXAMPLE

Grissom Granaries is subject to a 35% incremental income tax rate. The return on equity table from the preceding example is adjusted below for the beneficial effects of this tax rate:

	Equity Funding	Debt Funding
Current equity	$50,000,000	$50,000,000
Additional equity	10,000,000	
Total equity	$60,000,000	$50,000,000
Existing profit	$5,000,000	$5,000,000
Profit from invested funds	2,000,000	2,000,000
Less: debt cost		**-520,000**
Total profit	$7,000,000	$6,480,000
Return on equity	11.7%	13.0%

Financial Leverage

Once the effects of taxes are included in the return on equity calculation, Grissom's management sees that the return on equity has now increased from 12.4% to 13.0%, which makes the use of debt an even more attractive option.

If a company is not currently earning a profit, then the tax-deductible status of interest expense is a moot point, and should not be included in the calculation of earnings to be achieved through the use of leverage. However, it may be possible to include the tax effect if the current lack of income is expected to be of short duration, since tax losses can be rolled forward and applied as net operating loss carryforwards against future earnings.

In short, we have established that financial leverage can be a substantially beneficial alternative. However, there is also a downside to the use of debt. If the borrower cannot generate a net positive return on the borrowed funds, then the result can be a major decline in overall profitability, as well as some risk that the company cannot pay back the borrowed funds. The issue is illustrated in the following example.

EXAMPLE

The financial analyst of Grissom Granaries hears about the prospective sale of $10,000,000 in bonds (from the earlier examples) to pay for barges and a tugboat, and is concerned that the profits from this operation will be too variable to support payment of the related interest expense. As proof, she notes a recent study that the depth of the Mississippi River has been too low in four of the past 10 years in the area where Grissom intends to use the barges to support the draft of the barges. This results in a binary situation – either the company can operate the barges fully or it cannot operate them at all. In the latter case, there will be no income from the invested funds, while the company must still pay the $520,000 after-tax cost of the debt. If this situation were to arise, the result would be as noted in the following table:

	Debt Funding
Total equity	$50,000,000
Existing profit	$5,000,000
Less: debt cost	**-520,000**
Total profit	$4,480,000
Return on equity	9.0%

The table indicates that a combination of debt financing and a low-water season on the Mississippi will result in a net decline in Grissom's net income, to a point below the 10% that the company was earning prior to its contemplated investment in the barges and tugboat.

The result of this preliminary analysis should be a detailed review of the odds of low-water conditions on the Mississippi during the period when the related debt is outstanding, whether management wants to sustain reduced earnings during these periods, and also whether lower-draft barges can be obtained that would make the fleet usable even in low-water seasons. If management is risk averse, it may choose to avoid these problems by either using additional equity to fund the asset purchases, or by not investing in the assets at all.

Stated another way, financial leverage increases the fixed cost base of a business by adding interest expense. This means that the breakeven point of a business rises, so that additional sales must be generated in order to provide sufficient additional contribution margin to pay for the added interest expense.

In short, financial leverage can provide a boost to the return on equity by providing funding for the generation of additional earnings, but at the risk of incurring a debt load that may prove to be unmanageable if incremental earnings cannot be created.

> **Tip:** If the company's debt agreements with lenders include covenants that will trigger the recall of loans, model the earnings scenarios under which the covenants will be triggered, and discuss with management the probability of occurrence of these scenarios under a leveraged financing situation.

Issues Impacting Leverage

The preceding examples describing leverage assumed that a business would have access to both debt and equity funding, and would be willing to use either one. In reality, this may not be the case, resulting in the ability to only use one option, irrespective of the effects of leverage. For example:

- *Availability of debt.* There may be a credit crunch, under which banks are calling loans in order to preserve their capital, and will only lend under very low-risk situations where the borrower will accept a high rate of interest.
- *Bankruptcy risk.* A family-held business may be less inclined to employ financial leverage, since the result could be the bankruptcy of the business that provides income to the family.
- *Business partner perceptions.* The suppliers and customers of a business may react adversely if there is even a hint of a negative leverage situation. If so, and management values these relationships, it may avoid using any significant amount of debt.
- *Dilution.* The owners of a business may not want to sell an ownership percentage to outside investors, thereby giving up some control over the entity.
- *Future financing options.* The company may want to keep its future financing options open, which may call for a specific financing strategy over the near term. For example, if it appears that the credit markets are poised to collapse in the near future, it may be necessary to load up on debt while it is still possible to do so, even if not all of the funds are needed right now, or if equity would normally have been the better financing alternative.

- *Stock price*. A business may not be able to find any investors willing to buy its stock at a price that the company considers acceptable. Also, the sale of stock can be viewed as a not sufficiently aggressive financing choice by the investment community, which may signal its disapproval by driving down the market price of the stock.

For these and similar reasons, the debate regarding the most appropriate amount of leverage to maintain could be a short one – there may be so few options available that the company must accept a certain type of financing, irrespective of the resulting amount of leverage.

Leverage Risk

The downside of funding a business with a large amount of debt is that positive leverage can turn negative under the following circumstances:

- Lenders will only issue funds at a variable rate of interest, and the short-term after-tax interest rate increases to the point where it exceeds the incremental profitability of the business; or
- Lenders reduce the amount of debt they are willing to extend, requiring a business to replace the funds with more expensive financing; or
- The company's incremental earnings rate drops below the after-tax tax rate charged by lenders.

Some of these circumstances may be combined during an economic contraction, where banks routinely cut back on the amount of funds they are willing to loan, while company profits plunge. These combined effects routinely lead to the bankruptcy of those firms that employed leverage too much during the good times, without regard to what would happen under more adverse circumstances.

Examples of situations under which financial leverage can be best employed or where it should be avoided are noted in the following table.

Condition	Favorable for Leverage	Unfavorable for Leverage
Barriers to entry	When it is difficult for new competitors to enter a market, there is less downward pressure on prices, so it is easier to earn a profit on additional funds invested	When there are low barriers to entry in a market, there is a risk that a new competitor will enter at a low price point, driving down profits for all existing companies in that market, and turning their positive leverage into negative leverage
Competition	A near-monopoly situation is favorable for leverage, since a business can more easily maintain prices	It is unwise to maintain much leverage when there is a large amount of competition, since it is more likely that profits will be driven down over time, impacting the ability to pay back debt

Condition	Favorable for Leverage	Unfavorable for Leverage
Interest rates	If money can be borrowed at a fixed interest rate, the company has no risk of a rate increase over the term of the loan, and so can borrow more funds as long as the invested cash can yield a return greater than the fixed interest rate	If money can only be borrowed at a variable interest rate, then there is a risk of a rate increase eliminating all positive leverage
Lending environment	If there is a credit crunch where bankers are retracting credit, it may not be possible to obtain funds at any reasonable interest rate	When the lending environment allows for easy credit terms and low interest rates, this is an ideal time to engage in leverage, especially if the funds can be obtained at a fixed interest rate
Product life cycles	When product life cycles are long, it is easier to reliably forecast profits into the future, so there is a low risk of an unanticipated profit decline	When there are short product life cycles, a company may find that its newest products are not catching on in the market, so it can no longer support the debt payments associated with its financial leverage

The senior managers of a company may elect to engage in a large amount of financial leverage, even knowing that the preceding factors will put their companies at risk of negative leverage. The reason may be an excessive degree of optimism, where they assign a lower probability of occurrence to the preceding factors. In such cases, it is useful to keep management informed of changes in the various factors that can contribute to negative leverage. By doing so, it may be possible to take early action to reduce debt levels enough to mitigate the effects of negative leverage before the business is imperiled.

Impact of Compensation on Leverage

The management team of a business is typically given a compensation package that issues bonuses if the company can achieve a higher level of profitability. This can yield an unfortunate side effect, which is that managers can increase their bonuses by expanding the financial leverage of the firm. This is most likely to occur when bonus plans cover short periods of time, and do not address the financial *position* of a business. In this case, a manager is not penalized for loading large amounts of debt onto the company's balance sheet, and so has no incentive *not* to employ leverage.

This unfortunate situation can be mitigated by altering the type of bonus compensation paid, so that rewards are based on the long-term market value of a business. For example, consider offering stock options or stock grants that vest over a number of years. By doing so, managers are less likely to place the company at risk during the period when they expect to have an equity stake in the business.

Summary

A business usually makes money by creating products and services, and marketing them aggressively – not through financial wizardry. Consequently, we do not suggest that management engage in an excessive amount of incremental financial leverage analysis, continually maximizing the amount of debt outstanding. Instead, conduct an occasional analysis of the mechanics of the business, as well as the comfort level of management and the owners with the amount of the debt that the business should support, and adjust the corporate lending policy accordingly. The policy should control the amount of debt acquired on an ongoing basis. With a policy in place, the choice of debt or equity financing is a simple one – if the current debt level is below the target level, then the next round of financing should involve more debt; if not, then the next round should be targeted at acquiring more equity.

Chapter 12
Capital Structure Analysis

Introduction

The capital structure of a business is the mix of long-term funds that it employs, which involves both equity and debt. In all likelihood, the average business has a capital structure that was not planned. Instead, the company has taken whatever types of funding were available. The resulting capital structure may not be one that best meets the needs of the company or its shareholders. In this chapter, we address a number of issues that should be considered in regard to capital structure, and which may lead to a different mix of funding sources.

Optimal Capital Structure

The optimal capital structure can be defined as the point where the cost of any additional incremental funds will be too high to generate a positive net present value on any additional projects that require the expenditure of capital. The concept is best viewed through an example.

EXAMPLE

The management of Grissom Granaries believes that there is a large market for its grain storage facilities throughout the Midwest region of the United States. Each of these facilities costs $20,000,000, and Grissom can potentially construct over a hundred of the facilities. The net present value of these facilities is greater than zero, as long as the discount rate used does not exceed 14%. The company is closely held, and the shareholders have not expressed any willingness for the company to raise funds through the sale of additional equity.

Grissom's CFO meets with lenders to see how much additional debt the company can obtain, and summarizes her findings as follows:

Funding Tranches	Cost of Funds
1st $100,000,000	10.0%
2nd $100,000,000	13.5%
Additional funding	18.0%

Based on this information, the company can elect to acquire an additional $200,000,000 of debt, which will allow it to generate a positive return on ten more grain storage facilities. If the company wants additional funding beyond the initial $200,000,000, lenders will assign a much higher risk premium to the associated debt, which will render all additional projects unprofitable on a net present value basis.

Capital Structure Analysis

It may initially appear that the derivation of the optimal capital structure is a simple quantitative calculation. This is not the case. There are a number of additional issues to be considered, none of which involve a formula. Instead, company management must integrate into the capital structure analysis the points raised in the next section.

> **Note:** we just referred to the discount rate. This is the rate used to discount a stream of cash flows to their present value. The baseline rate is a firm's cost of capital (see the Cost of Capital chapter for more information). This rate may be adjusted upward if the future cash flows being discounted are expected to be risky in nature.

Capital Structure Analysis

Capital structure analysis is a periodic evaluation of all components of the debt and equity financing used by a business. The intent of the analysis is to evaluate what combination of debt and equity a business should have, which varies over time based on the costs of debt and equity and the risks to which the business is subjected. The analysis may be on a regularly scheduled basis, or it could be triggered by one of the following events:

- The upcoming maturity of a debt instrument
- The need to find funding for the acquisition of a fixed asset
- The need to fund an acquisition
- A demand by a key investor to have the business buy back shares
- A demand by investors for a larger dividend
- An expected change in the market interest rate

When engaging in a capital structure analysis, it may be worth considering the following questions, and how they impact the mix of debt and equity that a company has obtained:

- How much financial leverage is the company currently employing, and is it safe to increase the level of debt to further extend the amount of leverage? See the Financial Leverage chapter and the following section in this chapter.
- Does the business generate a sufficient amount of income to offset the tax deductions generated by interest expense? If the organization is not able to do so, then the cost of its debt will increase. See the Tax Shield Effects section.
- Does management want to maintain additional flexibility in its ability to obtain additional debt financing in the future? See the Future Financing Flexibility section.
- Does the company have trouble paying off its line of credit each year? See the Line of Credit Issues section.
- How does the current or projected capital structure impact any loan covenants, such as the debt to equity ratio? If the effect is negative, it may

not be possible to acquire any additional debt, or existing debt may need to be paid down. See the Loan Covenant Issues section.
- What is the maturity structure of the company's debt? Ideally, company operations should always have sufficient cash flow to pay off debt as it comes due for payment. See the Maturity Structure of Debt section.
- Are shareholders sensitive about allowing creditors a claim on company assets in the event of a corporate liquidation? If so, the amount of debt that can be obtained may be severely limited. See the Creditor Position Considerations section.
- Are there any expensive tranches of debt that can be paid down? This involves a discussion of alternative uses for any available cash, which could be more profitably employed elsewhere. See the Debt Paydown section.
- Can the company's cost of capital be reduced by altering the capital structure? This can be of some importance when a large investment is needed in the business. See the Cost of Capital Reduction section.
- Are the uses for cash within the company's business beginning to decline? If so, does it make more sense to return cash to investors by buying back shares or issuing more dividends? See the Dividend Analysis chapter.
- Does the investor relations officer want to establish a floor for the company's stock price? This can be achieved by engaging in an ongoing stock repurchase program that is triggered whenever the stock price falls below a certain amount. See the Stock Buyback Option section in the Dividend Analysis chapter.
- Does the company want to achieve a certain rating for its bonds? If so, it may need to restructure its financing mix to be more conservative, thereby improving the odds of investors being repaid by the company for their purchases of the company's bonds. See the Planning for a Bond Rating section.

The following sections expand upon these questions.

Line of Credit Issues

A line of credit is a commitment from a lender to lend funds to a company as needed, up to a predetermined maximum amount. The intent of a line of credit is to fund the short-term cash shortfalls of a business, not its long-term funding requirements. To reinforce this point, lenders generally require that a line of credit balance be dropped to zero at least once a year. If you find that the business is unable to pay off the line of credit, then it is likely that long-term funding needs are being mixed with the short-term cash requirements of the business. If so, arrange for a longer-term loan that offloads some of the cash requirements currently being fulfilled by the line of credit. If the lender providing the line of credit has senior rights to the company's assets, then the provider of the longer-term loan may require a higher interest rate in exchange for accepting a junior rights position.

Capital Structure Analysis

Tax Shield Effects

When a company takes on debt, the related interest expense will be tax deductible in most government jurisdictions, thereby reducing the after-tax cost of the debt. This reduction in taxable income is referred to as a tax shield. However, the tax shield only operates if a business has taxable earnings from which interest expense can be deducted.

A common scenario for a growing business is that it needs to incur debt in order to build operations that will eventually generate taxable income – but there may be little or no taxable income during this growth stage. If so, the net cost of debt will be the full amount of the debt, with no tax shield effect, until such time as enough taxable income is being generated to offset the interest expense.

One could make the case that any tax losses in the current period can be rolled forward and applied against future taxable income as a tax loss carryforward. However, if a company is expanding into new lines of business, there is no certainty that this taxable income will ever appear. If so, it makes sense to assume that the capital structure will result in interest expense that has not been reduced by the effect of the tax shield. A possible outcome of this situation is that management elects not to take on any additional debt.

Tip: If a company does not have a sufficiently large amount of taxable income to take advantage of the interest expense deduction, consider acquiring assets with an operating lease, where the lessor takes the tax deduction instead, and passes the resulting savings through to the lessee in the form of lower lease payments.

Future Financing Flexibility

If a business acquires a large amount of debt, this may close off debt financing in the future, because lenders may then feel that the company is too highly leveraged to take on additional debt. This is particularly likely to be the case if the current lender has encumbered the bulk of the company's assets, leaving few assets available as collateral for additional rounds of financing.

To maintain flexibility in the capital structure, management might want to emphasize equity financing, or only entering into debt agreements that do not require collateral or overly restrictive covenants. This is an especially common issue in tight credit markets where debt can only be acquired at a high cost, and with tight restrictions.

Loan Covenant Issues

When a company takes on new debt, the associated debt agreement may contain any number of loan covenants that the company must meet over the period of the loan. If the company cannot do so, then the lender can force the immediate repayment of the loan. Typical covenants include:

- Maintaining a certain minimum profit amount or profit percentage

- Keeping the current ratio higher than a certain percentage
- Keeping the interest coverage ratio higher than a certain percentage
- Not issuing dividends to investors
- Freezing or limiting compensation levels for senior managers

Covenants are designed to protect the assets of the lender. For example, limiting dividends and compensation keep the borrower from shifting borrowed funds outside of the company, where the lender cannot recover the funds. Similarly, if certain performance or financial position ratios decline, the lender is in a better position to reclaim loaned funds at once, before the company's finances decline further.

In situations where restrictive loan covenants are in place or will be imposed, a company may conclude that the negative effects of the covenants supersede the benefits of having additional debt. If so, management may conclude that no additional debt should be obtained, or that existing debt should be paid off – thereby freeing the company from loan covenants. Doing so means that the optimal capital structure of a business may involve no debt at all.

Maturity Structure of Debt

A key element of the capital structure is the mix of maturity dates linked to corporate debt. Ideally, debt should mature shortly after the company is scheduled to liquidate a sufficient amount of assets to pay off the debt. This means that the company has the capability to liquidate debts through internal cash flows, rather than having to rely upon third parties to roll over the debt to a later period. Here are several examples of maturity structure issues:

- A company borrows $20,000,000 in order to purchase an office building. The payoff structure of the loan should approximately match the cash flows that the company earns from the building's tenant rental payments.
- A company borrows $500,000 to buy a machine that should produce goods for the next five years at an even rate. The payoff structure of the loan should be matched to the cash flows generated by the machine.
- A company borrows $50,000,000 to acquire a competitor, using a bond issuance. If it is not possible to estimate the timing and amounts of cash flows resulting from the acquisition, it may be best to design an attractive conversion feature into the bond, thereby encouraging bond holders to convert their bonds into the company's common stock.
- A company engages in separate borrowing transactions to fund several different projects. The analyst recommends adjusting the terms of these debt instruments so that their maturity dates are staggered. Doing so keeps the company from being dependent on lenders for a large amount of debt repayment within a short period of time.

The maturity structure of debt may be of less concern to a large, well-capitalized and publicly held business that routinely raises funds in the capital markets. However, even in these cases, economic downturns can increase the cost of funds dramatically from time to time. To avoid these situations, it may sometimes make sense to take advantage of times when credit is cheap, and the business can refinance existing debt at these lower rates.

When designing an appropriate maturity structure for corporate debt, plan for a gradual build-up of cash prior to debt repayment dates, so that the company is not suddenly faced with a large cash shortfall that is difficult to roll over.

A major trap that many treasurers fall into is the belief that interest rates will decline in the future. This belief leads them to continually finance company operations with short term debt, since they are always waiting for a decline in interest rates. A common result is that interest rates do *not* decline; instead, the company is subjected to short-term swings in interest rates, as well as the availability of short-term debt, which can lead to significant funding problems. Consequently, a prudent treasurer should arrange for a large portion of company debt to have a longer maturity. If interest rates eventually decline, then this longer-term debt can be refinanced at the new, lower rate.

Creditor Position Considerations

If a company is liquidated, the proceeds from sale of its remaining assets are paid to those creditors having the most senior claim on those assets. These creditors usually include lenders who have required that collateral be included in their debt agreements. If the claims of these senior creditors are fully paid off, then the claims of junior creditors are paid. Only after all of these claims have been settled can any residual funds be distributed to shareholders. Because of this positioning at the bottom of the creditor pecking order, shareholders may not be interested in the acquisition of debt, and may instead opt for growth that is only fueled by internally-generated cash flows.

Concern about the rights of creditors is of more importance to shareholders in organizations that have such shaky financial structures and earnings that the right to residual funds is a real concern. It may also be an issue in a family-controlled business where the assets of the organization represent the primary source of wealth of the family.

Debt Paydown

A business could have locked itself into an expensive cost of debt when it acquired debt at some earlier point in time. Management may have an interest in paying off this higher-cost debt under a variety of circumstances. Doing so will alter the capital structure of the business, as well as its weighted-average cost of capital. Here are several issues to consider when engaging in a debt paydown:

- *Bank relationship.* The bank issuing debt to the company may require unusually oppressive loan covenants, as well as require that all of the com-

pany's bank accounts be shifted to it. If so, the benefit of paying down high-cost debt may be enhanced by management's need to sever the banking relationship. If so, the nature of the lending relationship may drive the decision to accelerate the pay down of debt.
- *Alternative uses.* The company may not have adequate internal uses for its excess funds, so the pay down of expensive debt becomes the most economical use of the funds.
- *Balance sheet clean up.* The company may be preparing its financial statements for viewing by outside parties, and wants to reduce the amount of expensive debt listed on its balance sheet. This situation may arise when a company is applying for credit with a key supplier, going public, or is considering being acquired.

Cost of Capital Reduction

As noted in the Cost of Capital chapter, the cost of the funds employed by a business is derived from the weighted average cost of equity and debt. The cost of equity is much more expensive than debt in most cases, so a business wanting to reduce the weighted average cost of its capital would logically want to use as much debt as possible. With a lower cost of funds, it is then possible to invest in projects that have lower returns on investment.

As an example of this concept, a company that leases copier machines can offer its customers lease rates at lower prices than a competitor, if the company's cost of capital is lower than the competitor's cost of capital. As long as the company can continue to obtain debt funding at a lower cost than the competitor, it will have a definitive pricing advantage that may translate into additional sales.

A reduction in the cost of capital is of much less concern in a business that requires little capital investment. In this situation, there are few projects requiring capital investment, so the cost of funds is irrelevant.

Planning for a Bond Rating

A credit rating agency is an entity that assigns credit ratings to either the issuers of certain kinds of debt, or directly to their debt instruments. There are three major credit rating agencies that provide ratings for the bulk of all debt issuances. They are authorized for ratings work as Nationally Recognized Statistical Rating Organizations (NRSROs) by the SEC. The three agencies that collectively control most of the market are:

- Moody's Investor Service
- Standard & Poor's
- Fitch Ratings

The ratings issued by these agencies are used by investors to determine the price at which to buy debt (usually bonds). In addition, the investment policies of many entities require them to limit their investments to debt issuances having certain minimum credit ratings. It is difficult to issue debt without a credit rating, since the issuance may be undersubscribed or can only be sold at a high effective interest rate.

The rating classifications used by the agencies vary from each other to some extent. The following table presents a comparison of the credit rating classifications of the three largest agencies. Debt issuances rated as investment grade in the table are considered suitable for investment purposes. The ratings classified as speculative are generally avoided by those entities looking for safe investments.

Credit Rating Comparison

Risk Level	Moody's	Standard & Poor's	Fitch
Investment grade:			
(highest investment grade)	Aaa	AAA	AAA
	Aa1	AA+	AA+
	Aa2	AA	AA
	Aa3	AA-	AA-
	A1	A+	A+
	A2	A	A
	A3	A-	A-
	Baa1	BBB+	BBB+
	Baa2	BBB	BBB
(lowest investment grade)	Baa3	BBB-	BBB-
Speculative grade:			
(highest speculative grade)	Ba1	BB+	BB+
	Ba2	BB	BB
	Ba3	BB-	BB-
	B1	B+	B+
	B2	B	B
	B3	B-	B-
	Caa1	CCC+	CCC+

Note: There are additional lower speculative grades than those listed in this table.

Only a large company with a stable business model and conservative financial practices can hope to qualify for one of the top-tier investment grades. Indeed, so few AAA ratings are issued that the recipients tend to use them as marketing tools to impress customers, suppliers, and employees. Since the AAA rating is well out of reach for most companies, the primary goal is simply to obtain a mid-level investment grade rating. By doing so, investors will not demand an excessively high interest rate on bond issuances. Companies certainly do not want their debt instruments to be classified as speculative, since investors will not buy them unless the company is willing to pay a very high interest rate.

A debt issuer may find that the credit rating agencies assign different credit ratings to different bond issuances, even though the bonds are all being issued by the same entity. This variation is caused by differences in the amount of collateral (if any) assigned to the debt, the level of subordination to other debt instruments of the issuer, and other debt terms.

Credit ratings and the objectives of a business are intertwined. If senior management wants to achieve rapid growth, it may need to issue more debt than a rating agency might consider prudent, resulting in a lower credit rating. Conversely, if it is considered more important to maintain a high credit rating, doing so will mandate a level of fiscal prudence that cannot support a rapid rate of growth. In short, it is difficult to obtain both a high growth rate and a stratospheric credit rating – management has to choose which objective is more important.

If the management team is interested in altering the capital structure of the business by adding debt, it may make sense to pay a consulting firm or one of the credit rating agencies to advise the company on the amount of additional debt that can be added to the business before its credit rating will probably be reduced. This information is useful for determining when to balance the corporate debt burden with the issuance of additional equity.

Capital Structure Measurements

When estimating the correct capital structure, it is useful to measure the ability of the business to pay its fixed costs, which include interest expenses. The following measurements can be employed, beginning with the narrowly-focused interest coverage ratio and then expanding the focus of the measurement in the debt service coverage ratio to include principal.

Interest Coverage Ratio

The interest coverage ratio measures the ability of a company to pay the interest on its outstanding debt. A high interest coverage ratio indicates that a business can pay for its interest expense several times over, while a low ratio is a strong indicator that an organization may default on its loan payments.

It is useful to track the interest coverage ratio on a trend line, in order to spot situations where a company's results or debt burden are yielding a downward trend in the ratio. An investor would want to sell the equity holdings in a company showing such a downward trend, especially if the ratio drops below 1.5:1.

To calculate the interest coverage ratio, divide earnings before interest and taxes (EBIT) by the interest expense for the measurement period. The formula is:

$$\frac{\text{Earnings before interest and taxes}}{\text{Interest expense}}$$

Capital Structure Analysis

EXAMPLE

Carpenter Holdings generates $5,000,000 of earnings before interest and taxes in its most recent reporting period. Its interest expense in that period is $2,500,000. Therefore, the company's interest coverage ratio is calculated as:

$$\frac{\$5,000,000 \text{ EBIT}}{\$2,500,000 \text{ Interest expense}}$$

$$= 2:1 \text{ Interest coverage ratio}$$

The ratio indicates that Carpenter's earnings should be sufficient to enable it to pay the interest expense.

A company may be accruing an interest expense that is not actually due for payment yet, so the ratio can indicate a debt default that will not really occur, or at least until such time as the interest is due for payment.

Debt Service Coverage Ratio

The debt service coverage ratio measures the ability of a revenue-producing property to generate sufficient cash to pay for the cost of all related mortgage payments. A positive debt service ratio indicates that a property's cash outflows can cover all offsetting loan payments, whereas a negative ratio indicates that the owner must contribute additional funds to pay for the annual loan payments. A very high debt service coverage ratio gives the property owner a substantial cushion to pay for unexpected or unplanned expenditures related to the property, or if market conditions result in a significant decline in future rental rates.

To calculate the ratio, divide the net annual operating income of the property by all annual loan payments for the same property. The formula is:

$$\frac{\text{Net annual operating income}}{\text{Total of annual loan payments}}$$

EXAMPLE

A rental property generates $400,000 of cash flow per year, and the total annual loan payments of the property are $360,000. This yields a debt service ratio of 1.11, meaning that the property generates 11% more cash than the property owner needs to pay for the annual loan payments.

A negative debt service coverage ratio may result when a property is transitioning to new tenants, so that it is generating sufficient cash by the end of the measurement period, but was not doing so during the beginning or middle of the measurement period. Thus, the metric can yield inaccurate results during transition periods.

Recapitalization

Recapitalization occurs when the debt and equity structure of a business is significantly altered. This usually means converting outstanding debt to a firm's equity in order to put the business on a more solid financial footing. This process is typically not beneficial to creditors, who are swapping the security of debt repayments for the insecurity of equity ownership. A recapitalization can also occur when a significant offering of new shares is issued. The intent behind the offering is to use the resulting cash to pay down debt. This has the same effect as the debt for equity swap just noted.

A recapitalization can also be used in the reverse direction, taking on debt in order to buy back shares. Doing so places the company in a riskier financial position, which makes it less attractive to a hostile acquirer.

Timing of Changes to the Capital Structure

If an analysis of the capital structure reveals that a change is in order, this does not mean that such a change should be enacted at once. It is entirely possible that current market conditions are not optimal for the acquisition of new equity or debt funding. For example, there may be a bear market in which the price of equity securities are depressed, or a tight credit market in which the cost of debt is well above the historical average. If so, the most sensible approach may be to wait for conditions to improve, rather than taking any action that is not cost-effective for the business.

Summary

The capital structure of a business can be modeled using pro forma financial statements that show how changes in the amounts and relative proportions of debt and equity can impact a company's earnings, financial position, and risk. However, the large amount of qualitative decision making noted throughout this chapter should make it clear that the opinions of senior management and investors regarding the risk profile of the business should have a large bearing on the development of capital structure, rather than just using a rigid calculation that balances the cost of capital against the available use of funds.

The decision options explored in this chapter will likely result in a range of possible capital structure alternatives, all of which are acceptable ways to fund a business. As long as the actual capital structure does not stray beyond the boundaries of these alternatives, the structure can be considered satisfactory.

Chapter 13
Dividend Analysis

Introduction

An area that may draw the attention of the financial analyst is whether to pay out dividends, and if so, the appropriate amount to pay. This decision tends to be based on an understanding of what investors want and the alternative uses to which cash can be put, rather than a specific formula. In this chapter, we address the payment of dividends from the perspectives of both the investor and the company, and how these viewpoints drive the payment of dividends. In addition, we address related courses of action, which are the stock buyback option and the stock dividend.

The Investor Viewpoint

The financial performance and dividend payout policy of a company will attract a certain type of investor. If the company has a history of consistently issuing a certain amount of dividends, then it will attract investors who want this steady stream of income. Conversely, if a business chooses to instead plow its earnings back into operations, then it will attract a different set of investors that wants to profit from presumed increases in the company's share price. In the latter case, an increase in share price may be taxed at the capital gains rate, which results in more after-tax income to the investor.

In the former case, investors who want a dividend will evaluate a company based on its *dividend payout ratio*. This ratio is the percentage of a company's earnings paid out to its shareholders in the form of dividends. There are two ways to calculate the dividend payout ratio; each one results in the same outcome. One version is to divide total dividends paid by net income. The calculation is:

$$\frac{\text{Total dividends paid}}{\text{Net income}}$$

The alternative version essentially calculates the same information, but at the individual share level. The formula is to divide total dividend payments over the course of a year on a per-share basis by earnings per share for the same period. The calculation is:

$$\frac{\text{Annual dividend paid per share}}{\text{Earnings per share}}$$

EXAMPLE

The Conemaugh Cell Phone Company paid out $1,000,000 in dividends to its common shareholders in the last year. In the same time period, the company earned $2,500,000 in net income. The dividend payout ratio is:

$$\frac{\$1,000,000 \text{ Dividends paid}}{\$2,500,000 \text{ Net income}}$$

$$= 40\% \text{ Dividend payout ratio}$$

Investors interested in the long-term viability of a series of dividend payments will likely track the dividend payout ratio on a trend line, to see if a business is generating enough income to support its dividend payments over a number of years. If not, they may sell off their shares, thereby driving down the stock price. If an investor sees that the payout ratio is nearly 100% or greater than that amount, then the current dividend level is probably not sustainable. Conversely, if the ratio is quite low, investors will consider the risk of a dividend cutback to also be low, and so will be more inclined to buy the stock, thereby driving up its price.

Investors may also look at the reverse of the dividend payout ratio to see how much of earnings are being retained within a business. If the retention amount is declining, this indicates that the company does not see a sufficient return on investment to be worthy of plowing additional cash back into the business. From this perspective, a declining retention rate will drive away those growth-oriented investors who rely on an increasing share price.

In short, investors rely on ratio analysis on a trend line to determine whether a business is issuing an appropriate amount of dividends, and may alter their stock holdings based on the outcome of this analysis.

The Company Viewpoint

A company typically issues dividends under three circumstances, which are:

- Certain shareholders have sufficiently large stock holdings to force the company to pay out dividends; or
- There are not sufficient profitable internal uses for the cash being spun off by operations, so the excess amount is returned to investors in the form of a dividend; or
- Management believes it can bolster the company's stock price by issuing dividends.

In the first case, dividends being forcibly extracted from a company tend to be one-time events, and so require little financial analysis.

The second case is by far the most common reason for issuing dividends. Typically, a business needs to employ all of its cash internally during its initial growth stage, and so is not capable of issuing a dividend. Once the business matures, it may begin to spin off more cash than it needs to maintain its market position, which can be returned to investors in the form of a dividend.

The third case is a misguided one, for (as noted in the last section), investors are already holding company stock based on expectations regarding how the company is employing its cash. If the company suddenly pays a dividend, the stock price may initially decline, because the dividend is a signal to the existing group of growth-oriented investors that management no longer feels there are enough growth opportunities for the company. The stock price should eventually recover as income-oriented investors take the place of growth investors, so there may be no net change in the price of the stock over time.

The change in the type of investor is neither good nor bad, but it does mean that there will be an increased amount of turnover among shareholders for a period of time. During this transition period, it is possible that the share price will be somewhat more volatile than usual.

If the board of directors wants to find a use for excess cash, but does not want to turn away its growth-oriented investors, then some alternative uses for the cash are making acquisitions, paying off liabilities in advance of their scheduled payment dates, or buying back shares (see the next section).

If the board of directors elects to go forward with an initial dividend payment, it is important to signal to the marketplace that the company intends to continue to issue dividends at regular intervals. Otherwise, a one-time distribution to shareholders via a dividend will merely send growth-oriented investors to the exits without creating an incentive for income-oriented investors to take their place, thereby creating downward pressure on the stock price.

> **Tip:** When initially announcing a dividend, point out the timing and expected size of future dividends, so that the investment community can properly value the shares on which dividends are being paid.

When embarking on a strategy of issuing ongoing dividends, it is of some importance to begin with a small dividend that the company can easily support from its current resources and expected cash flows. By doing so, the board of directors can comfortably establish a gradual increase in the size of the dividend that the investment community can rely upon, which should result in a slow increase in the price of the company's stock. Conversely, the worst type of dividend is one that is so large that the company has a difficult time scraping together the cash needed to pay it, which can endanger its ability to operate on an ongoing basis.

It is also useful for the board of directors to consider the negative implications of not having sufficient cash to continue paying a dividend. If this were to happen, the income-oriented investors who are holding the stock precisely because of those dividends will sell their shares; this will trigger a supply and demand imbalance that will lower the price of the stock. Eventually, value-oriented investors will buy the stock when it has dropped by a sufficient amount, in hopes of a recovery in the stock price. Nonetheless, a dividend cancellation almost always triggers a steep stock price decline.

In short, the decision to issue dividends should be considered in light of the message being sent to the investment community, as well as the long-term ability of a business to continue paying dividends.

The Stock Buyback Option

Companies sometimes engage in stock buybacks, where the board of directors authorizes that a certain amount of cash be set aside for a repurchase program. The stock buyback can be considered an alternative to issuing dividends. There are three reasons why a company may engage in a buyback:

- To reduce the number of shares outstanding, which should increase the amount of earnings per share, and therefore provide pressure to increase the share price.
- Because management believes that the share price is currently too low, and does not adequately reflect the true market value of the business. Thus, if a buyback plan is announced that the company will buy back shares whenever the share price falls below a certain price point, there will be a tendency for the stock price to stay above that trigger point.
- To mop up excess shares that have been created through the issuance of stock options and warrants.

EXAMPLE

The Hegemony Toy Company has 5,000,000 shares of its common stock outstanding. These shares currently trade at $20. In the fiscal year just ended, Hegemony reported net profits of $2,000,000, which results in reported earnings per share of $0.40 (calculated as $2,000,000 profits ÷ 5,000,000 shares).

Hegemony's board of directors approves a $10,000,000 stock buyback. At the current $20 market price, this means the company can acquire 500,000 shares. By doing so, there will now be 4,500,000 shares outstanding. The altered share total changes the earnings per share figure to $0.444.

There are some problems with a stock buyback. One is that there will be fewer shares in circulation after the buyback has been completed, which reduces the liquidity of the stock. If a company already suffers from an excessively small number of shares outstanding, this is a valid objection to a buyback.

Another problem is that companies have a strong tendency to acquire shares when they are flush with cash, which is usually at a point in their life cycles when they have a very high stock price. Thus, they are converting a relatively small number of shares to treasury stock in exchange for a large amount of cash, which does little to boost the earnings per share for the remaining shares outstanding. This is the reverse of what would be considered prudent behavior for an investor, who attempts to buy low and sell high. If a company were as prudent as an investor, it would only buy back shares when its stock price was very low.

When a company has excess cash, it should consider a stock buyback to be one of the last uses for that cash. Instead, the sequence of possible uses should roughly follow this series of decision options:

1. *Invest in company operations.* This is assumed to be the best profit generator.
2. *Acquire related companies.* This approach is riskier than internal growth, but still focuses the company on its primary markets.
3. *Pay down debt.* This reduces the risk of not paying back loans. The approach can be extended to paying off leases and even reducing the amount of accounts payable.
4. *Build a reserve.* There is nothing wrong with building a large cash reserve to guard against a downturn in the company's fortunes.
5. *Buy back stock.* If all of the preceding steps have been taken, only then is a buyback warranted, and only if the stock is trading at a reasonably low price.

The Stock Dividend

A stock dividend is the issuance by a company of its common stock to its common shareholders without any consideration. For example, when a company declares a 15% stock dividend, this means that every shareholder receives an additional 15 shares for every 100 shares he already owns.

A company usually issues a stock dividend when it does not have the cash available to issue a normal cash dividend, but still wants to give the appearance of having issued a payment to investors.

In reality, the total market value of a company does not change just because a company has issued more shares, so the same market value is simply spread over more shares, which likely reduces the value of individual shares to compensate for the increased number of shares. For example, if a company has a total market value of $10 million and it has one million shares outstanding, then each share should sell on the open market for $10. If the company then issues a 15% stock dividend, there are now 1,150,000 shares outstanding, but the market value of the entire firm has not changed. Thus, the market value per share after the stock dividend is now $10,000,000 ÷ 1,150,000 shares, or $8.70.

If a company's shares are selling for such a large amount on a per-share basis that it appears to be keeping investors from buying the stock, a large stock dividend might sufficiently dilute the market value per share that more investors would be interested in buying the stock. This might result in a small net increase in the market value per share, and so would be useful for investors. However, a high stock price is rarely an impediment to an investor who wants to buy stock.

A problem with a stock dividend is that it may use up the remaining amount of authorized shares. For example, the board of directors may have initially authorized

15 million shares, and 10 million shares are outstanding. If the company issues a 50% stock dividend, this increases the number of shares outstanding to 15 million shares. The board will now have to authorize more shares before the company can issue any additional stock.

In short, any advantages of using a stock dividend are minor, and so its use is not recommended in most cases.

Summary

The board of directors should think long and hard about the decision to begin issuing dividends. Dividends work best when followed consistently over a long period of time, but doing so requires rock-solid cash flows. Any inability to meet a dividend obligation will trigger a rapid stock price decline. Thus, always consider a decision to issue dividends as a long-term strategic issue, not just a short-term payout. From a financial analysis perspective, it is useful to model for the board of directors a series of worst-case scenarios that reveal the company's ability to pay dividends even in the face of serious revenue declines; doing so may keep the board from committing to excessively large dividend payments.

Chapter 14
Foreign Exchange Risk Analysis

Introduction

A business may engage in transactions with customers and suppliers located in other countries. If so, the company will likely need to either pay out or accept foreign exchange as part of these transactions. When there is a delay in the payment or receipt dates of these transactions, the company is subject to some risk of loss if the exchange rate were to shift during the delay period. In this chapter, we describe the different types of foreign exchange risk, as well as the tools for mitigating this risk.

Foreign Exchange Risk Overview

When a business enters into transactions that involve foreign currencies, there is a risk that changes in the exchange rate can cause significant losses for the business. In this section, we describe the types of foreign exchange risks to which an organization can be subjected.

A company may incur *transaction exposure*, which is derived from changes in foreign exchange rates between the dates when a transaction is booked and when it is settled. For example, a company in the United States may sell goods to a company in the United Kingdom, to be paid in pounds having a value at the booking date of $100,000. Later, when the customer pays the company, the exchange rate has changed, resulting in a payment in pounds that translates to a $95,000 sale. Thus, the foreign exchange rate change related to a transaction has created a $5,000 loss for the seller. The following table shows the impact of transaction exposure on different scenarios.

Risk When Transactions Denominated in Foreign Currency

	Import Goods	Export Goods
Home currency weakens	Loss	Gain
Home currency strengthens	Gain	Loss

When a company has foreign subsidiaries, it denominates the recorded amount of their assets and liabilities in the currency of the country in which the subsidiaries generate and expend cash. This *functional currency* is typically the local currency of the country in which a subsidiary operates. When the company reports its consolidated results, it converts these valuations to the home currency of the parent company, which may suffer a loss if exchange rates have declined from the last time when the financial statements were consolidated. This type of risk is known as *translation exposure*.

EXAMPLE

Hammer Industries has a subsidiary located in England, which has its net assets denominated in pounds. The home currency of Hammer is U.S. dollars. At year-end, when the parent company consolidates the financial statements of its subsidiaries, the U.S. dollar has depreciated in comparison to the pound, resulting in a decline in the value of the subsidiary's net assets.

The following table shows the impact of translation exposure on different scenarios.

Risk When Net Assets Denominated in Foreign Currency

	Assets	Liabilities
Home currency weakens	Gain	Loss
Home currency strengthens	Loss	Gain

There are also several types of economic risk related to the specific country within which a company chooses to do business. These risks include:

- *Political risk* is based on the actions of a foreign government that can impact a company, such as the expropriation of assets. Political risk can also encompass the violence that may accompany a change in government. There can be a significant risk of expropriation when a company has a large asset base within a country.
- *Convertibility risk* is the inability to convert a local currency into a foreign currency, because of a shortage of hard currencies. This tends to be a short-term problem.
- *Transfer risk* is the inability to transfer funds across a national border, due to local-country regulatory restrictions on the movement of hard currencies out of the country. Thus, a company may find that a local subsidiary is extremely profitable, but the parent company cannot extract the profits from the country.

Country-specific risks call for strategic-level decisions in the executive suite, not in the accounting or treasury departments. The senior management team must decide if it is willing to accept the risks of expropriation or of not being able to extract cash from a country. If not, the risk is eliminated by refusing to do business within the country.

Please note that the *type* of risk has an impact on the time period over which a company is at risk. For example, transactional risk spans a relatively short period, from the signing date of the contract that initiates a sale, until the final payment date. The total interval may be only one or two months. However, translation risk and the various types of economic risks can extend over many years. There tends to be an inordinate focus in many companies on the short-term transactional risk, when more emphasis should be placed on hedging against these other risks that can result in substantial losses over the long term.

Foreign Exchange Risk Management

As noted in the last section, a company is at risk of incurring a loss due to fluctuations in any exchange rates that it must buy or sell as part of its business transactions. What can be done? Valid steps can range from no action at all to the active use of several types of hedges. In this section, we address the multitude of options available to mitigate foreign exchange-related risks. As you peruse these options, keep in mind that the most sophisticated response is not necessarily the best response. In many cases, the circumstances may make it quite acceptable to take on some degree of risk, rather than engaging in a hedging strategy that is not only expensive, but also difficult to understand.

Take No Action

There are many situations where a company rarely engages in transactions that involve foreign exchange, and so does not want to spend time investigating how to reduce risk. There are other situations where the amounts of foreign exchange involved are so small that the risk level is immaterial. In either case, a company will be tempted to take no action, which may be a reasonable course of action. The question to consider is, at what level of foreign exchange activity should a business begin to consider risk management alternatives?

The question cannot be answered without having an understanding of a company's *risk capacity*. Risk capacity is the maximum amount of a loss that a business can sustain before a financial crisis is triggered. The following are examples of maximum losses:

- A loss that would require the tapping of all remaining borrowing capacity
- A loss that would breach one or more debt covenants
- A loss that would reduce capital levels below those mandated by regulatory authorities

The preceding examples provide hard quantitative numbers for a firm's total risk capacity, all of which threaten the company's existence. This does not mean that management should routinely expose a business to threat levels that could destroy it. Instead, it is necessary to arrive at a much less quantitative number, which is the maximum risk tolerance that management is willing to operate under on an ongoing basis before it will take steps to reduce risk. The risk tolerance figure is likely to be far lower than total risk capacity – perhaps just 5% or 10% of a firm's risk capacity. The exact amount of risk tolerance will depend upon the willingness of managers to accept risk. A more entrepreneurially inclined group may be willing to bet the company on risky situations, while professional managers will probably begin managing risk at lower tolerance levels.

Avoid Risk

A company can avoid some types of risk by altering its strategy to completely sidestep the risk. Complete avoidance of a specific product, geographic region, or business line is an entirely reasonable alternative under the following circumstances:

- The potential loss from a risk condition is very high
- The probability of loss from a risk condition is very high
- It is difficult to develop a hedge against a risk
- The offsetting potential for profit does not offset the risk that will be incurred

For example, a company located in the United States buys the bulk of its supplies in China, and is required under its purchasing contracts to pay suppliers in yuan. If the company does not want to undertake the risk of exchange rate fluctuations in the yuan, it can consider altering its supply chain, so that it purchases within its home country, rather than in China. This alignment of sales and purchases within the same country to avoid foreign currency transactions is known as an *operational hedge*.

As another example, a company wants to sell products into a market where the government has just imposed severe restrictions on the cross-border transfer of funds out of the country. The government also has a history of nationalizing industries that had been privately-owned. Under these circumstances, it makes little sense for the company to sell into the new market if it cannot extract its profits, and if its assets in the country are subject to expropriation.

Shift Risk

When a company is either required to pay or receive payment in a foreign currency, it is taking on the risk associated with changes in the foreign currency exchange rate. This risk can be completely eliminated by requiring customers to pay in the company's home currency, or suppliers to accept payment in the company's home currency. This is a valid option when the company is a large one that can force this system of payment onto its suppliers, or when it sells a unique product that forces customers to accept the company's terms.

> **Tip:** Never give customers a choice of currency in which to pay the company, since they will likely pay with their home currency, leaving the company to bear the risk of exchange rate changes.

Another possibility is to charge business partners for any changes in the exchange rate between the date of order placement and the shipment date. This is an extremely difficult business practice to enforce, for the following reasons:

- *Continual rebillings.* There will always be some degree of variation in exchange rates between the order date and shipment date, so it is probable that a company would have to issue an invoice related to exchange rate ad-

justments for every order, or at least include a line item for the change in every invoice.
- *Two-way rebillings.* If a company is going to insist on billing for its exchange rate losses, it is only fair that it pay back its business partners when exchange rates shift in its favor.
- *Purchase order limitations.* Customers routinely place orders using a purchase order than only authorizes a certain spending level. If the company later issues an incremental billing that exceeds the total amount authorized for a purchase, the customer will probably not pay the company.

To mitigate these issues, billing a business partner for a change in exchange rates should only be enacted if the change is sufficiently large to breach a contractually-agreed minimum level. The minimum level should be set so that this additional billing is a rare event.

> **Example:** An outsourcing company enters into long-term services contracts with its customers, and so is at considerable foreign exchange risk. It offers customers a fixed price contract within a 5% currency trading band, outside of which customers share the risk with the company. If the company gains from a currency shift outside of the trading band, it discounts the contract price.

The conditions under which currency risk can be shifted elsewhere are not common ones. Most companies will find that if they insist on only dealing in their home currencies, such behavior will either annoy suppliers or drive away customers. Thus, we will continue with other risk management actions that will be more palatable to a company's business partners.

Time Compression

Large variations in exchange rates are more likely to occur over longer periods of time than over shorter periods of time. Thus, it may be possible to reduce the risk of exchange rate fluctuations by reducing the contractually-mandated payment period. For example, 30 day payment terms could be compressed to 10 or 15 days. However, delays in shipping, customs inspections, and resistance from business partners can make it difficult to achieve a compressed payment schedule. Also, a customer being asked to accept a shorter payment schedule may attempt to push back with lower prices or other benefits, which increases the cost of this option.

The time compression concept can take the form of a company policy that does not allow standard credit terms to foreign customers that exceed a certain number of days. By doing so, a company can at least minimize the number of days during which exchange rates can fluctuate.

Payment Leading and Lagging

If there is a pronounced trend in exchange rates over the short term, the accounts payable manager can be encouraged to alter the timing normally associated with payables payments to take advantage of expected changes in exchange rates. For example, if a foreign currency is becoming more expensive, it may make sense to pay those payables denominated in it as soon as possible, rather than waiting until the normal payment date to pay in a more expensive currency. Similarly, if a foreign currency is declining in value, there may be an opportunity to delay payments by a few days to take advantage of the ongoing decline in the exchange rate. The latter case may be too much trouble, since suppliers do not appreciate late payments.

Build Reserves

If company management believes that there is just as great a risk of a gain as a loss on a currency fluctuation, it may be willing to accept the downside risk in hopes of attaining an upside profit. If so, it is possible to build cash and debt reserves greater than what would normally be needed, against the possibility of an outsized loss. This may entail investing a large amount of cash in very liquid investments, or retaining extra cash that might otherwise be paid out in dividends or used for capital expenditures. Other options are to obtain an unusually large line of credit that can be called upon in the event of a loss, or selling more stock than would typically be needed for operational purposes.

Building reserves will protect a business from foreign exchange risk, but the cost of acquiring and maintaining those reserves is substantial. Cash that is kept on hand could have earned an investment, while a commitment fee must be paid for a line of credit, even if the line is never used. Similarly, investors who buy a company's stock expect to earn a return. Thus, there is a noticeable cost associated with building reserves. A less expensive option is hedging, which we will address in the next section.

Maintain Local Reserves

If the company is routinely engaging in the purchase and sale of goods and services within another country, the answer may be to maintain a cash reserve within that country, which is denominated in the local currency. Doing so eliminates the cost of repeatedly buying and selling currencies and paying the related conversion commissions. The downside of maintaining local reserves is that a company is still subject to translation risk, where it must periodically translate its local cash reserves into its home currency for financial reporting purposes – which carries with it the risk of recording a translation loss.

Hedging

When all operational and strategic alternatives have been exhausted, it is time to consider buying hedging instruments that offset the risk posed by specific foreign exchange positions. Hedging is accomplished by purchasing an offsetting currency exposure. For example, if a company has a liability to deliver 1 million euros in six months, it can hedge this risk by entering into a contract to purchase 1 million euros on the same date, so that it can buy and sell in the same currency on the same date. The ideal outcome of a hedge is when the distribution of probable outcomes is reduced, so that the size of any potential loss is reduced. The following exhibit shows the effect of hedging on the range of possible outcomes.

Impact of Hedging on Risk Outcome

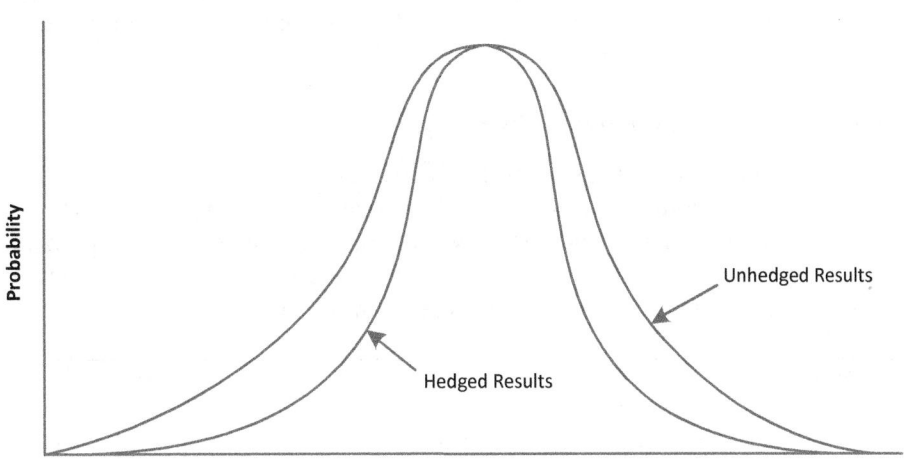

When a company has a multi-year contract with a customer, it may be necessary to create a long-term hedge to offset the related risk of currency fluctuations. If the customer subsequently terminates the contract early, the company may have to incur a significant cost to unwind the related hedge before its planned termination date. If this scenario appears possible, or if a business has experienced such events in the past, it may make sense to include in the contract a clause stating that the customer bears the cost of unwinding the hedge if there is an early contract termination.

> **Tip:** When entering into a long-term contract for which a hedge is anticipated, be sure to estimate the cost of the hedge in advance, and include it in the formulation of the price quoted to the customer.

Various types of hedges are described in the next section.

Summary

Clearly, there are many risk management alternatives available to a company that must deal with foreign exchange situations. We recommend avoiding active hedging strategies as long as possible, in favor of more passive methods that are easier to understand, implement, and monitor. If the risk situation is too extreme to be completely addressed by passive means, then an active hedging strategy is probably the answer. In the next section, we address several types of active hedging activities.

Types of Foreign Exchange Hedges

This section describes a number of methods for hedging foreign currency transactions. The first type of hedge, which is a loan denominated in a foreign currency, is designed to offset translation risk. The remaining hedges target the transaction risk related to the currency fluctuations associated with either specific or aggregated business transactions.

Loan Denominated in a Foreign Currency

When a company is at risk of recording a loss from the translation of assets and liabilities into its home currency, it can hedge the risk by obtaining a loan denominated in the functional currency in which the assets and liabilities are recorded. The effect of this hedge is to neutralize any loss on translation of the subsidiary's net assets with a gain on translation of the loan, or vice versa.

EXAMPLE

Hammer Industries has a subsidiary located in London, and which does business entirely within England. Accordingly, the subsidiary's net assets are denominated in pounds. The net assets of the subsidiary are currently recorded at £10 million. To hedge the translation risk associated with these assets, Hammer acquires a £10 million loan from a bank in London.

One month later, a change in the dollar/pound exchange rate results in a translation loss of $15,000 on the translation of the subsidiary's net assets into U.S. dollars. This amount is exactly offset by the translation gain of $15,000 on the liability associated with the £10 million loan.

> **Tip:** An ideal way to create an offsetting loan is to fund the purchase or expansion of a foreign subsidiary largely through the proceeds of a long-term loan obtained within the same country, so that the subsidiary's assets are approximately cancelled out by the amount of the loan.

There are two problems with this type of hedge. First, it can be difficult to obtain a loan in the country in which the net assets are located. Second, the company will incur an interest expense on a loan that it would otherwise not need, though the borrowed funds could be invested to offset the interest expense.

The Forward Contract

A forward contract is an agreement under which a business agrees to buy a certain amount of foreign currency on a specific future date, and at a predetermined exchange rate. Forward exchange rates can be obtained for twelve months into the future; quotes for major currency pairs can be obtained for as much as five to ten years in the future.

Foreign Exchange Risk Analysis

The exchange rate is comprised of the following elements:

- The spot price of the currency
- The bank's transaction fee
- An adjustment (up or down) for the interest rate differential between the two currencies. In essence, the currency of the country having a lower interest rate will trade at a premium, while the currency of the country having a higher interest rate will trade at a discount. For example, if the domestic interest rate is lower than the rate in the other country, the bank acting as the counterparty adds points to the spot rate, which increases the cost of the foreign currency in the forward contract.

The calculation of the number of discount or premium points to subtract from or add to a forward contract is based on the following formula:

$$\text{Exchange rate} \times \text{Interest rate differential} \times \frac{\text{Days in contract}}{360} = \text{Premium or discount}$$

Thus, if the spot price of pounds per dollar were 1.5459 and there were a premium of 15 points for a forward contract with a 360-day maturity, the forward rate (not including a transaction fee) would be 1.5474.

By entering into a forward contract, a company can ensure that a definite future liability can be settled at a specific exchange rate. Forward contracts are typically customized, and arranged between a company and its bank. The bank will require a partial payment to initiate a forward contract, as well as final payment shortly before the settlement date.

EXAMPLE

Hammer Industries has acquired equipment from a company in the United Kingdom, which Hammer must pay for in 60 days in the amount of £150,000. To hedge against the risk of an unfavorable change in exchange rates during the intervening 60 days, Hammer enters into a forward contract with its bank to buy £150,000 in 60 days, at the current exchange rate.

60 days later, the exchange rate has indeed taken a turn for the worse, but Hammer's treasurer is indifferent, since he obtains the £150,000 needed for the purchase transaction based on the exchange rate in existence when the contract with the supplier was originally signed.

A forward contract is designed to have a specific settlement date, but the business transaction to which it relates may not be so timely. For example, a business has a contract to sell £10,000 in 60 days, but may not be able to do so if it has not yet received funds from a customer. A *forward window contract* is designed to work around this variability in the timing of receipts from customers by incorporating a range of settlement dates. You can then wait for a cash receipt and trigger settlement of the forward contract immediately thereafter.

The primary difficulties with forward contracts relate to their being customized transactions that are designed specifically for two parties. Because of this level of customization, it is difficult for either party to offload the contract to a third party. Also, the level of customization makes it difficult to compare offerings from different banks, so there is a tendency for banks to build unusually large fees into these contracts. Finally, a company may find that the underlying transaction for which a forward contract was created has been cancelled, leaving the contract still to be settled. If so, one can enter into a second forward contract, whose net effect is to offset the first forward contract. Though the bank will charge fees for both contracts, this arrangement will settle the company's obligations.

The Futures Contract

A futures contract is similar in concept to a forward contract, in that a business can enter into a contract to buy or sell currency at a specific price on a future date. The difference is that futures contracts are traded on an exchange, so these contracts are for standard amounts and durations. An initial deposit into a margin account is required to initiate a futures contract. The contract is then repriced each day, and if cumulative losses drain the margin account, a company is required to add more funds to the margin account. If the company does not respond to a margin call, the exchange closes out the contract.

Given that futures contracts are standardized, they may not exactly match the timing and amounts of an underlying transaction that is being hedged, which can lead to over- or under-hedging. However, since these contracts are traded on an exchange, it is easier to trade them than forward contracts, which allows for the easy unwinding of a hedge position earlier than its normal settlement date.

In a forward contract, the bank includes a transaction fee in the contract. In a futures contract, a broker charges a commission to execute the deal.

The Currency Option

An option gives its owner the right, but not the obligation, to buy or sell an asset at a certain price (known as the *strike price*), either on or before a specific date. In exchange for this right, the buyer pays an up-front premium to the seller. The income earned by the seller is restricted to the premium payment received, while the buyer has a theoretically unlimited profit potential, depending upon the future direction of the relevant exchange rate.

Currency options are available for the purchase or sale of currencies within a certain future date range, with the following variations available for the option contract:

- *American option.* The option can be exercised on any date within the option period, so that delivery is two business days after the exercise date.

- *European option*. The option can only be exercised on the expiry date, which means that delivery will be two business days after the expiry date.
- *Burmudan option*. The option can only be exercised on certain predetermined dates.

The holder of an option will exercise it when the strike price is more favorable than the current market rate, which is called being *in-the-money*. If the strike price is less favorable than the current market rate, this is called being *out-of-the-money*, in which case the option holder will not exercise the option. If the option holder is inattentive, it is possible that an in-the-money option will not be exercised prior to its expiry date. Notice of option exercise must be given to the counterparty by the notification date stated in the option contract.

A currency option provides two key benefits:

- *Loss prevention*. An option can be exercised to hedge the risk of loss, while still leaving open the possibility of benefiting from a favorable change in exchange rates.
- *Date variability*. An option can be exercised within a predetermined date range, which is useful when there is uncertainty about the exact timing of the underlying exposure.

There are a number of factors that enter into the price of a currency option, which can make it difficult to ascertain whether a quoted option price is reasonable. These factors are:

- The difference between the designated strike price and the current spot price. The buyer of an option can choose a strike price that suits his specific circumstances. A strike price that is well away from the current spot price will cost less, since the likelihood of exercising the option is low. However, setting such a strike price means that the buyer is willing to absorb the loss associated with a significant change in the exchange rate before seeking cover behind an option.
- The current interest rates for the two currencies during the option period.
- The duration of the option.
- Volatility of the market. This is the expected amount by which the currency is expected to fluctuate during the option period, with higher volatility making it more likely that an option will be exercised. Volatility is a guesstimate, since there is no quantifiable way to predict it.
- The willingness of counterparties to issue options.

Banks generally allow an option exercise period of no more than three months. Multiple partial currency deliveries within a currency option can be arranged.

Exchange traded options for standard quantities are available. This type of option eliminates the risk of counterparty failure, since the clearing house operating the exchange guarantees the performance of all options traded on the exchange.

EXAMPLE

Hammer Industries has an obligation to buy £250,000 in three months. Currently, the forward rate for the British pound is 1.5000 U.S. dollars, so that it should require $375,000 to buy the £250,000 in 90 days. If the pound depreciates, Hammer will be able to buy pounds for less than the $375,000 that it currently anticipates spending, but if the pound appreciates, Hammer will have to spend more to acquire the £250,000.

Hammer's treasurer elects to buy an option, so that he can hedge against the appreciation of the pound, while leaving open the prospect of profits to be gained from any depreciation in the pound. The cost of an option with a strike price of 1.6000 U.S. dollars per pound is $3,000.

Three months later, the pound has appreciated against the dollar, with the price having changed to 1.75 U.S. dollars per pound. The treasurer exercises the option, and spends $400,000 for the requisite number of pounds (calculated as £250,000 × 1.6000). If he had not purchased the option, the purchase would instead have cost $437,500 (calculated as £250,000 × 1.7500). Thus, Hammer saved $34,500 by using a currency option (calculated as the savings of $37,500, less the $3,000 cost of the option).

Currency options are particularly valuable during periods of high currency price volatility. Unfortunately from the perspective of the buyer, high volatility equates to higher option prices, since there is a higher probability that the counterparty will have to make a payment to the option buyer.

The Cylinder Option

Two options can be combined to create a *cylinder option*. One option is priced above the current spot price of the target currency, while the other option is priced below the spot price. The gain from exercising one option is used to partially offset the cost of the other option, thereby reducing the overall cost of the hedge. In effect, the upside potential offered by one option is being sold for a premium payment in order to finance the protection afforded by the opposing option.

The cylinder option is configured so that a company can acquire the right to buy currency at a specified price (a call option) and sell an option to a counterparty to buy currency from the company at a specified price (a put option), usually as of the expiry date. The premium the company pays for the purchased call is partially offset by the premium payable to the company for the put option that it sold.

If the market exchange rate remains between the boundaries established by the two currency options, the company never uses its options and instead buys or sells currency on the open market to fulfill its currency needs. If the market price breaches the strike price of the call option, the company exercises the call option and buys currency at the designated strike price. Conversely, if the market price breaches the strike price of the put option, the counterparty exercises its option to sell the currency to the company.

A variation on the cylinder option is to construct call and put options that are very close together, so that the premium cost of the call is very close to the premium income generated by the put, resulting in a near-zero net hedging cost to the company. The two options have to be very close together for the zero cost option to work, which means that the effective currency price range being hedged is quite small.

Swaps

If a company has or expects to have an obligation to make a payment in a foreign currency, it can arrange to swap currency holdings with a third party that already has the required currency. The two entities engage in a swap transaction by agreeing upon an initial swap date, the date when the cash positions will be reversed back to their original positions, and an interest rate that reflects the comparative differences in interest rates between the two countries in which the entities are located.

Another use for a currency swap is when a forward exchange contract has been delayed. In this situation, you would normally sell to a counterparty the currency that it has just obtained through the receipt of an account receivable. If, however, the receivable has not yet been paid, the company can enter into a swap agreement to obtain the required currency and meet its immediate obligation under the forward exchange contract. Later, when the receivable is eventually paid, the company can reverse the swap, returning funds to the counterparty.

A swap arrangement may be for just a one-day period, or extend out for several years into the future. Swap transactions generally do not occur in amounts of less than $5 million, so this technique is not available to smaller businesses.

A potentially serious problem with swaps is the prospect of a default by the counterparty. If there is a default, the company once again assumes its foreign currency liability, and must now scramble to find an alternative hedge.

Netting

There are circumstances where a company has subsidiaries in multiple countries that actively trade with each other. If so, they should have accounts receivable and payable with each other, which could give rise to a flurry of foreign exchange transactions in multiple currencies that could trigger any number of hedging activities. It may be possible to reduce the amount of hedging activity through *payment netting*, where the corporate parent offsets all accounts receivable and payable against each other to determine the net amount of foreign exchange transactions that actually require hedges. A centralized netting function may be used, which means that each subsidiary either receives a single payment from the netting center, or makes a single payment to the netting center. Netting results in the following benefits:

- Foreign exchange exposure is no longer tracked at the subsidiary level
- The total amount of foreign exchange purchased and sold declines, which reduces the amount of foreign exchange commissions paid out

- The total amount of cash in transit (and therefore not available for investment) between subsidiaries declines

> **Tip:** It is easier to create an intracompany netting system when there is already a centralized accounts payable function for the entire business, which is called a *payment factory*.

The same concept can be applied to payables and receivables with outside entities, though a considerable amount of information sharing is needed to make the concept work. In some industries where there is a high level of trade between companies, industry-wide netting programs have been established that routinely offset a large proportion of the payables and receivables within the industry. The net result is that all offsetting obligations are reduced to a single payment per currency per value date between counterparties.

A related concept is *close-out netting*, where counterparties having forward contracts with each other can agree to net the obligations, rather than engaging in a large number of individual contract settlements. Before engaging in close-out netting, discuss the concept with corporate counsel. A case has been made in some jurisdictions that close-out netting runs counter to the interests of other creditors in the event of a bankruptcy by one of the counterparties.

The only downside of netting is that the accounting departments of the participating companies must sort out how their various transactions are settled. This requires a procedure for splitting a group of netted transactions into individual payments and receipts in the cash receipts and accounts payable modules of their accounting systems.

Summary

We have described a number of tools for dealing with foreign exchange risk, some of which require advanced knowledge of the underlying financial instruments. Since there is a risk of incorrectly setting up and unwinding these risk mitigation strategies, it always makes sense to give priority to the *least* complicated risk mitigation strategies. Once the organization is comfortable with these alternatives, it can move on to the various swaps, options, forward contracts, and futures contracts that can be tailored to the specific needs of the business and provide more comprehensive risk mitigation.

Chapter 15
Interest Rate Risk Analysis

Introduction

A business may borrow or invest funds. If so, the organization is at risk of loss from changes in the underlying interest rate. There could be an unexpected increase in the rate on borrowed funds, or a decline in the rate on invested funds. In this chapter, we describe the types of interest rate risk, as well as the tools for mitigating this risk.

Interest Risk Overview

Interest rate risk involves the risk of increases in interest rates on debt, as well as reductions in interest rates for investment instruments, with the attendant negative impact on profitability. This risk can take the following forms:

- *Absolute rate changes*. The market rate of interest will move up or down over time, resulting in immediate variances from the interest rates paid or earned by a company. This rate change is easily monitored.
- *Reinvestment risk*. Investments must be periodically re-invested and debt re-issued. If interest rates happen to be unfavorable during one of these rollover periods, a company will be forced to accept whatever interest rate is available.
- *Yield curve risk*. The yield curve shows the relationship between short-term and long-term interest rates, and typically slopes upward to indicate that long-term debt carries a higher interest rate to reflect the risk to the lender associated with such debt. If the yield curve steepens, flattens, or declines, these relationships change the debt duration that a company should use in its borrowing and investing strategies.

Interest risk is a particular concern for those businesses using large amounts of debt to fund their operations, since even a small increase in the interest rate could have a profound impact on profits, when multiplied by the volume of debt employed. Further, a sudden boost in interest expense could worsen a company's interest coverage ratio, which is a common covenant in loan agreements, and which could trigger a loan termination if the minimum ratio covenant is not met.

Interest Rate Risk Management

The primary objective of interest risk management is to keep fluctuations in interest rates from impacting company earnings. Management can respond to this objective in many ways, ranging from a conscious decision to take no action, passing through a number of relatively passive alternatives, and culminating in several active techniques for risk mitigation. We provide an overview of each option in this section.

Take No Action

There may be situations where a company has minimal investments that earn interest, or issues only minor amounts of debt. If so, it is certainly acceptable to not implement an aggressive risk management campaign related to interest rates. However, this state of affairs does not typically last for long, after which there will be some degree of risk related to interest rates. In anticipation of such an event, it is useful to model the amount of interest rate change that must occur before there will be a serious impact on company finances. Once that trigger point is known, you can begin to prepare any of the risk mitigation alternatives noted later in this section.

Avoid Risk

The risk associated with interest rates arises between external entities and a business; it does not arise between the subsidiaries of the same business. Thus, a company can act as its own bank to some extent, by providing intercompany lending arrangements at interest rates that are not subject to fluctuations. This is particularly useful in a multi-national corporation, where cash reserves in different currencies may be scattered throughout the business, and can be lent back and forth to cover immediate cash needs.

Another way to avoid risk is to operate the business in such a conservative manner that the company has no debt, thereby eliminating the risk associated with interest rates on debt. The same result can be achieved by using invested funds to pay off any outstanding debt. The main downside of the low-debt method is that a company may be constraining its growth by not taking advantage of a low-cost source of funds (i.e., debt).

Asset and Liability Matching

A key trigger for interest rate risk is when short-term debt is used to fund an asset that is expected to be held for a long period of time. In this situation, the short-term debt must be rolled over multiple times during the life span of the asset or until the debt is paid off, introducing the risk that each successive debt rollover will result in an increased interest rate. To avoid this risk, arrange for financing that approximately matches the useful life of the underlying asset. Thus, spending $1 million for a machine that is expected to have a useful life of 10 years should be funded with a loan that also has a 10-year life.

Hedging

Interest rate hedging is the practice of acquiring financial instruments whose effects offset those of the underlying scenario causing interest rate fluctuations, so that the net effect is minimized rate fluctuations. Hedges fall into two categories:

- *Forward rate agreements and futures.* These financial instruments are designed to lock in an interest rate, so that changes in the actual interest rate above or below the baseline interest rate do not impact a business. These instruments do not provide any flexibility for taking advantage of favorable changes in interest rates.
- *Options.* These financial instruments only lock in an interest rate if the holder wants to do so, thereby presenting the possibility of benefiting from a favorable change in an interest rate.

The various types of interest rate hedges are discussed next.

Types of Interest Rate Hedges

This section describes a number of methods for hedging the variability in interest rates. These options are mostly designed for high-value transactions, and so are not available to smaller companies.

The Forward Rate Agreement

A forward rate agreement (FRA) is an agreement between two parties to lock in a specific interest rate for a designated period of time, which usually spans just a few months. Under an FRA, the parties are protecting against opposing exposures: the FRA buyer wants to protect against an increase in the interest rate, while the FRA seller wants to protect against a decrease in the interest rate. Any payout under an FRA is based on a change in the reference interest rate from the interest rate stated in the contract (the FRA rate). An FRA is not related to a specific loan or investment – it simply provides interest rate protection.

The FRA rate is based on the yield curve, where interest rates usually increase for instruments having longer maturities. This means that the FRA rate typically increases for periods further in the future.

Several date-specific terms are referred to in a forward rate agreement, and are crucial to understanding how the FRA concept works. These terms are:

1. *Contract date.* The date on which the FRA begins.
2. *Expiry date.* The date on which any variance between the market rate and the reference rate is calculated.
3. *Settlement date.* The date on which the interest variance is paid by one counterparty to the other.
4. *Maturity date.* The final date of the date range that underlies the FRA contract.

In essence, these four dates anchor the two time periods covered by an FRA. The first period, which begins with the contract date and ends with the expiry date, spans the term of the contract. The second period begins with the settlement date and ends with the maturity date, and spans the period that underlies the contract. This date range is shown graphically in the following example.

Relevant FRA Dates

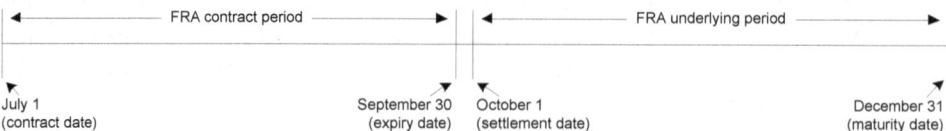

The FRA rate is based on a future period, such as the period starting in one month and ending in four months, which is said to have a "1 × 4" FRA term, and has an effective term of three months. Similarly, a contract starting in three months and ending in six months is said to have a "3 × 6" FRA term, and also has an effective term of three months.

At the *beginning* of the designated FRA period, the interest rate stated in the contract is compared to the reference rate. The reference rate is usually a well-known interest rate index, such as the London Interbank Offered Rate (LIBOR). If the reference rate is higher, the seller makes a payment to the FRA buyer, based on the incremental difference in interest rates and the notional amount of the contract. The payment calculation is shown in the following example. If the reference rate is lower than the interest rate stated in the contract, the buyer makes a payment to the FRA seller. The payment made between the counterparties must be discounted to its present value, since the payment is associated with the FRA underlying period that has not yet happened. Thus, the discount assumes that the money would actually be due on the maturity date, but is payable on the settlement date (which may be months before the maturity date). The calculation for discounting the payment between counterparties is:

$$\frac{\text{Settlement amount}}{1 + (\text{Days in FRA underlying period}/360 \text{ Days} \times \text{Reference rate})} = \frac{\text{Discounted}}{\text{Payment}}$$

The reason why the contract payment is calculated at the *beginning* of the designated FRA period is that the risk being hedged by the contract was from the initial contract date until the date on which the FRA buyer expects to borrow money and lock in an interest rate. For example, a company may enter into an FRA in January, because it is uncertain of what the market interest rate will be in April, when it intends to borrow funds; the period at risk is therefore from January through April. The following example illustrates the concept.

EXAMPLE

Hammer Industries has a legal commitment to borrow $50 million in two months, and for a period of three months. Hammer's treasurer is concerned that there may be an increase in the interest rate during the two-month period prior to borrowing the $50 million. The treasurer elects to hedge the risk of an increase in the interest rate by purchasing a three-month FRA, starting in two months. A broker quotes a rate of 5.50%. Hammer enters into an FRA at the 5.50% interest rate, with 3rd National Bank as the counterparty. The notional amount of the contract is for $50 million.

Interest Rate Risk Analysis

Two months later, the reference rate is 6.00%, so 3rd National pays Hammer the difference between the contract rate and reference rate, which is 0.50%. At the same time, Hammer borrows $50 million at the market rate (which happens to match the reference rate) of 6.00%. Because of the FRA, Hammer's effective borrowing rate is 5.50%.

The amount paid by 3rd National to Hammer is calculated as:

(Reference rate − FRA rate) × (FRA days/360 days) × Notional amount = Profit or loss

or

(6.00% − 5.50%) × (90 days/360 days) × $50 million = $62,500

Since the payment is made at the beginning of the borrowing period, rather than at its end, the $62,500 payment is discounted and its present value paid. The discounting calculation for the settlement amount is:

$$\frac{\$62,500}{1 + (90/360 \text{ Days} \times 6.00\%)} = \$61,576.35$$

What if the reference rate had fallen by 0.50%, instead of increasing? Then Hammer would have paid 3rd National the discounted amount of $62,500, rather than the reverse. Hammer would also end up borrowing the $50 million at the new market rate of 5.00%. When the payment to 3rd National is combined with the reduced 5.00% interest rate, Hammer will still be paying a 5.50% interest rate, which is what it wanted all along.

From the buyer's perspective, the result of an FRA is that it pays the expected interest rate – no higher, and no lower.

The Futures Contract

An interest rate futures contract is conceptually similar to a forward contract, except that it is traded on an exchange, which means that it is for a standard amount and duration. The standard size of a futures contract is $1 million, so multiple contracts may need to be purchased to create a hedge for a specific loan or investment amount. The pricing for futures contracts starts at a baseline figure of 100, and declines based on the implied interest rate in a contract. For example, if a futures contract has an implied interest rate of 5.00%, the price of that contract will be 95.00. The calculation of the profit or loss on a futures contract is derived as follows:

Notional contract amount × Contract duration/360 Days × (Ending price − Beginning price)

Most trading in interest rate futures is in Eurodollars (U.S. dollars held outside of the United States), and are traded on the Chicago Mercantile Exchange.

Hedging is not perfect, since the notional amount of a contract may vary from the actual amount of funding that a company wants to hedge, resulting in a modest amount of either over- or under-hedging. For example, hedging a $15.4 million position will require the purchase of either 15 or 16 $1 million contracts. There may also be differences between the time period required for a hedge and the actual hedge period as stated in a futures contract. For example, if there is a seven month exposure to be hedged, a treasurer could acquire two consecutive three-month contracts, and elect to have the seventh month be unhedged.

> **Tip:** If the buyer wants to protect against interest rate variability for a longer period, such as for the next year, it is possible to buy a series of futures contracts covering consecutive periods, so that coverage is achieved for the entire time period.

EXAMPLE

The treasurer of Hammer Industries wants to hedge an investment of $10 million. To do so, he sells 10 three-month futures contracts with contract terms of three months. The current three-month LIBOR is 3.50% and the 3 × 6 forward rate is 3.75%. These contracts are currently listed on the Chicago Mercantile Exchange at 96.25, which is calculated as 100 minus the 3.75% forward rate.

When the futures contracts expire, the forward rate has declined to 3.65%, so that the contracts are now listed at 96.35 (calculated as 100 − the 3.65 percent forward rate). By engaging in this hedge, Hammer has earned a profit of $2,500, which is calculated as follows:

$$\$10,000,000 \times (90/360) \times (0.9635 \text{ Ending price} - 0.9625 \text{ Beginning price}) = \$2,500$$

When the buyer purchases a futures contract, a minimum amount must initially be posted in a margin account to ensure performance under the contract terms. It may be necessary to fund the margin account with additional cash (a *margin call*) if the market value of the contract declines over time (margin accounts are revised daily, based on the market closing price). If the buyer cannot provide additional funding in the event of a contract decline, the futures exchange closes out the contract prior to its normal termination date. Conversely, if the market value of the contract increases, the net gain is credited to the buyer's margin account. On the last day of the contract, the exchange marks the contract to market and settles the accounts of the buyer and seller. Thus, transfers between buyers and sellers over the life of a contract are essentially a zero-sum game, where one party directly benefits at the expense of the other.

It is also possible to enter into a bond futures contract, which can be used to hedge interest rate risk. For example, a business that has borrowed funds can hedge against rising interest rates by selling a bond futures contract. Then, if interest rates do in fact rise, the resulting gain on the contract will offset the higher interest rate that the borrower is paying. Conversely, if interest rates subsequently fall, the borrower will experience a loss on the contract, which will offset the lower interest rate now being paid. Thus, the net effect of the contract is that the borrower locks in the beginning interest rate through the period of the contract.

> **Tip:** A bond futures contract is not a perfect hedge, for it is also impacted by changes in the credit rating of the bond issuer.

When a purchased futures contract expires, it is customary to settle it by selling a futures contract that has the same delivery date. Conversely, if the original contract was sold to a counterparty, then the seller can settle the contract by buying a futures contract that has the same delivery date.

The following table notes the key differences between forward rate agreements and futures contracts. Similarities between the two instruments are excluded from the table.

Differences between a Futures Contract and FRA

Feature	Futures Contract	Forward Rate Agreement
Trading platform	Exchange-based	Between two parties
Counterparty	The exchange	Single counterparty
Collateral	Margin account	None
Agreement	Standardized	Modified
Settlement	Daily mark to market	On expiry date

The preceding table reveals two key differences between a futures contract and an FRA. First, there can be significant counterparty risk in an FRA, since the contract period can be lengthy, and financial conditions can change markedly over that time. Second, a futures contract is settled every day, which can create pressure to fund a margin call if there are significant losses on the contract.

The Interest Rate Swap

An interest rate swap is a customized contract between two parties to swap two schedules of cash flows that could extend for anywhere from one to 25 years, and which represent interest payments. Only the interest rate obligations are swapped, not the underlying loans or investments from which the obligations are derived. The counterparties are usually a company and a bank. There are many types of rate swaps; we will confine this discussion to a swap arrangement where one schedule of cash flows is based on a floating interest rate, and the other is based on a fixed interest rate. For example, a five-year schedule of cash flows based on a fixed interest rate may be swapped for a five-year schedule of cash flows based on a floating interest rate that is tied to the LIBOR rate.

> **Tip:** To prevent confusion, replicate the same swap terms across all swap agreements. Replicated terms should include the reference rate, the interest calculation method, and the coupon frequency. Other terms, such as the notional amount and swap term, will probably vary by agreement.

The most common reason to engage in an interest rate swap is to exchange a variable-rate payment for a fixed-rate payment, or vice versa. Thus, a company that has only been able to obtain a floating-rate loan can effectively convert the loan to a fixed-rate loan through an interest rate swap. This approach is especially attractive when a borrower is only able to obtain a fixed-rate loan by paying a premium, but can combine a variable-rate loan and an interest rate swap to achieve a fixed-rate loan at a lower price.

A company may want to take the reverse approach and swap its fixed interest payments for floating payments. This situation arises when the treasurer believes that interest rates will decline during the swap period, and wants to take advantage of the lower rates.

A swap contract is settled through a multi-step process, which is:

1. Calculate the payment obligation of each party, typically once every six months through the life of the swap arrangement.
2. Determine the variance between the two amounts.
3. The party whose position is improved by the swap arrangement pays the variance to the party whose position is degraded by the swap arrangement.

Thus, a company continues to pay interest to its banker under the original lending agreement, while the company either accepts a payment from the rate swap counterparty, or issues a payment to the counterparty, with the result being that the net amount of interest paid by the company is the amount planned by the business when it entered into the swap agreement.

EXAMPLE

Hammer Industries has a $15 million variable-rate loan outstanding that matures in two years. The current interest rate on the loan is 6.5%. Hammer enters into an interest rate swap agreement with Big Regional Bank for a fixed-rate 7.0% loan with a $15 million notional amount. The first scheduled payment swap date is in six months. On that date, the variable rate on Hammer's loan has increased to 7.25%. Thus, the total interest payments on the swap date are $543,750 for Hammer and $525,000 for Big Regional. Since the two parties have agreed to swap payments, Big Regional pays Hammer the difference between the two payments, which is $18,750.

Hammer issues an interest payment of $543,750 to its bank. When netted with the cash inflow of $18,750 from Big Regional, this means that the net interest rate being paid by Hammer is 7.0%.

Several larger banks have active trading groups that routinely deal with interest rate swaps. Most swaps involve sums in the millions of dollars, but some banks are willing to engage in swap arrangements involving amounts of less than $1 million. There is a counterparty risk with interest rate swaps, since one party could fail to make a contractually-mandated payment to the other party. This risk is of particular concern when a swap arrangement covers multiple years, since the financial condition of a counterparty could change dramatically during that time.

If there is general agreement in the marketplace that interest rates are headed in a certain direction, it will be more expensive to obtain a swap that protects against interest rate changes in the anticipated direction.

Interest Rate Options

An option gives its owner the right, but not the obligation, to trigger a contract. The contract can be either a call option or a put option. A *call option* related to interest rates protects the option owner from rising interest rates, while a *put option* protects the option owner from declining interest rates. The party selling an option does so in exchange for a one-time premium payment. The party buying an option is doing so to mitigate its risk related to a change in interest rates.

An interest rate option can be relatively inexpensive if there has been or is expected to be little volatility in interest rates, since the option seller does not expect interest rates to move enough for the option to be exercised. Conversely, if there has been or is expected to be interest rate volatility, the option seller must assume that the option will be exercised, and so sets a higher price. Thus, periods of high interest rate volatility may make it cost-prohibitive to buy options.

> **Tip:** An interest rate hedge using an option may not be entirely successful if the reference rate used for the option is not the same one used for the underlying loan. For example, the reference rate for an option may be LIBOR, while the rate used for the underlying loan may be a bank's prime rate. The result is a hedging mismatch that can create an unplanned gain or loss.

An interest rate option sets a *strike price*, which is a specific interest rate at which the option buyer can borrow or lend money. The contract also states the amount of funds that the option buyer can borrow or lend (the *notional amount*). Rate increases and declines are measured using a *reference rate*, which is typically a well-known interest rate index, such as LIBOR. There is also an option expiration date, or *expiry date*, after which the option is cancelled. The buyer can specify the exact terms needed to hedge an interest rate position with a customized option.

If an option buyer wants to be protected from increases in interest rates, a *cap* (or ceiling) is created. A cap is a consecutive series of options, all having the same strike price. The buyer of a cap is paid whenever the reference rate exceeds the cap strike price on an option expiry date. For example, if a company wants to hedge its interest risk for one year with a strike price of 6.50%, beginning on January 1, it can buy the following options:

Interest Rate Risk Analysis

Desired Coverage Period	Option Number	Expiry Date	Option Term	Strike Price
January - March	--	Not applicable*	Not available*	N/A*
April - June	1	April 1	4 to 6 months	6.50%
July – September	2	July 1	7 to 9 months	6.50%
October - December	3	October 1	10 to 12 months	6.50%

* There is no option available for the first three-month period, since the expiry date is at the beginning of the contract period, so the expiry date will be reached immediately.

With a cap arrangement, the buyer is only subject to interest rate changes up to the cap, and is protected from rate changes above the cap if the reference rate exceeds the cap strike price on predetermined dates. If the reference interest rate is below the cap at the option expiration, the option buyer lets the option expire. However, if the reference rate is above the cap, the buyer exercises the option, which means that the option seller must reimburse the buyer for the difference between the reference rate and the cap rate, multiplied by the notional amount of the contract.

A cap may be included in a loan agreement, such that the borrower is guaranteed not to pay more than a designated maximum interest rate over the term of the loan, or for a predetermined portion of the loan. In this case, the lender has paid for the cap, and will probably include its cost in the interest rate or fees associated with the loan.

If a treasurer wants to be protected from decreases in interest rates (for invested funds), a *floor* is structured into an option, so that the option buyer is paid if the reference rate declines below the floor strike rate.

EXAMPLE

Hammer Industries has a $25 million 3-month loan that currently carries a fixed interest rate of 7.00%. Hammer's bank refuses to grant a fixed-rate loan for a longer time period, so Hammer plans to continually roll over the loan every three months. Recently, short-term interest rates have been spiking, so the treasurer decides to purchase an interest rate cap that is set at 7.50%, and which is comprised of two consecutive options, each with a three-month term.

At the expiry date of the first option, the reference rate is 7.25%, which is below the cap strike rate. The treasurer lets the option expire unused and rolls over the short-term loan at the new 7.25% rate.

Interest Rate Risk Analysis

At the next option expiry date, the reference rate has risen to 7.75%, which is 0.25% above the cap strike rate. The treasurer exercises the option, which forces the counterparty to pay Hammer for the difference between the cap strike rate and the reference rate. The calculation of the amount to be reimbursed is:

(Reference rate − Strike rate) × (Lending period/360 days) × Notional amount = Profit or loss

or

(7.75% − 7.50%) × (90/360) × $25 million = $15,625

Of course, the cost of the option reduces the benefits gained from an interest rate option, but still is useful for providing protection from outsized changes in interest rates.

> **Tip:** From an analysis perspective, it is useful to include the premium on an option with the amount of interest paid on a loan and any proceeds or payments associated with an exercised option, in order to derive the aggregate interest rate on any associated debt being hedged.

The cylinder option described in the last chapter for foreign exchange risk can also be applied to interest rates. Under this concept, a company purchases a cap and sells a floor, with the current reference rate located between the two strike rates. The gain from exercising one option is used to partially offset the cost of the other option, which reduces the overall cost of the hedge. The three possible outcomes of this *collar* arrangement are:

1. The reference rate remains between the cap and floor, so neither option is exercised.
2. The reference rate rises above the cap, so the company is paid for the difference between the reference rate and the cap strike rate, multiplied by the notional amount of the contract.
3. The reference rate falls below the floor, so the company pays the option counterparty for the difference between the reference rate and the floor strike rate, multiplied by the notional amount of the contract.

The functioning of a collar arrangement is shown in the following exhibit, where the cap is set at 5% and the floor is set at 3%. No option is triggered until the reference rate drops to 2% in one of the later quarters, and again when it rises to 6%. In the first case, the company pays the 1% difference between the 3% floor and the 2% reference rate. In the latter case, the company is paid the 1% difference between the 5% cap and the 6% reference rate.

The Operation of an Interest Rate Collar

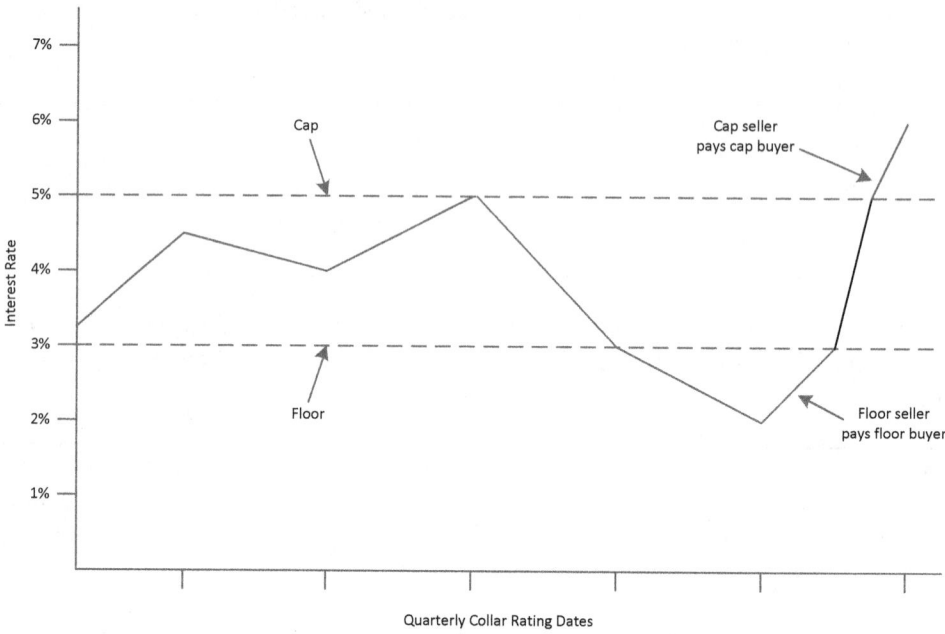

From the perspective of a company using a collar arrangement, the net effect is that interest rates will fluctuate only within the bounds set by the cap and floor strike rates.

A variation on the interest rate option concept is to include a call feature in a debt issuance. A call feature allows a company to buy back its debt from debt holders. The feature is quite useful in cases where the market interest rate has fallen since debt was issued, so a company can refinance its debt at a lower interest rate. However, the presence of the call option makes investors wary about buying it, which tends to increase the effective interest rate at which they will buy the debt. Investor concerns can be mitigated to some extent by providing for a fairly long time period before the issuing company can trigger the call option, and especially if the call price is set somewhat higher than the current market price.

Interest Rate Swaptions

A swaption is an option on an interest rate swap arrangement. The buyer of a swaption has the right, but not the obligation, to enter into an interest rate swap. In essence, a swaption presents the option of being able to lock in a fixed interest rate or a variable interest rate (depending on the terms of the underlying swap arrangement). Thus, a treasurer may suspect that interest rates will begin to rise in the near future, and so enters into a swaption to take over a fixed interest rate. If interest rates do indeed rise, the swaption holder can exercise the swaption. If interest rates hold steady or decline, the swaption is allowed to expire without being exercised.

The two types of swaption are the *payer swaption* and the *receiver swaption*, which are defined as follows:

- *Payer swaption*. The buyer can enter into a swap where it pays the fixed interest rate side of the transaction.
- *Receiver swaption*. The buyer can enter into a swap where it pays the floating interest rate side of the transaction.

There is no formal exchange for swaptions, so each agreement is between two counterparties. This means that each party is exposed to the potential failure of the counterparty to make scheduled payments on the underlying swap. Consequently, it is prudent to only enter into these arrangements with counterparties with high credit ratings or other evidence of financial stability.

Swaption market participants are primarily large corporations, banks, and hedge funds. The most likely counterparty for a corporation is a large bank that has a group specializing in swaption arrangements.

Summary

We have described a number of tools for dealing with interest rate risk, some of which require advanced knowledge of the underlying financial instruments. Since there is a risk of incorrectly setting up and unwinding these risk mitigation strategies, it always makes sense to give priority to the *least* complicated risk mitigation strategies. Once the organization is comfortable with these alternatives, it can move on to the various interest rate hedges that can be tailored to the specific needs of the business and provide more comprehensive risk mitigation. Also, note that many of the interest rate hedges are only available for significant cash balances, which restricts their use to organizations that maintain large debt or investment balances.

Chapter 16
Financial Forecasting

Introduction

The analyst is likely to be heavily involved in the development and ongoing maintenance of a company's financial forecasts. This information is used to plan company activities and related expenditures, as well as to anticipate changes in the level of business activity that may call for risk mitigation decisions. In addition, forecast information can be presented to outside parties, such as lenders and investors, as proof of a company's future plans. Further, it can be used to anticipate future cash balances, which drives the investment and borrowing activities of a business.

In this chapter, we describe the differences between a budget and a forecast, and then discuss the derivation of the revenue forecast, note the system of budgets that are largely driven *by* the revenue forecast, and then address the formulation and use of the cash forecast.

> **Related Podcast Episodes:** Episodes 71, 76, 130, and 131 of the Accounting Best Practices Podcast discuss budget model improvements, budgeting controls, problems with budgeting, and operating without a budget, respectively. These episodes are available at: **accountingtools.com/podcasts** or **iTunes**

The Differences between a Budget and a Forecast

There can be some confusion regarding the differences between a budget and a forecast. In essence, a budget is a quantified expectation for what a business wants to achieve. Its characteristics are:

- The budget is a detailed representation of the future results, financial position, and cash flows that management wants the business to achieve during a certain period of time.
- The budget may only be updated once a year, depending on how frequently senior management wants to revise information.
- The budget is compared to actual results to determine variances from expected performance.
- Management takes remedial steps to bring actual results back into line with the budget.
- The budget to actual comparison can trigger changes in performance-based compensation paid to employees.

Conversely, a forecast is an estimate of what will actually be achieved. Its characteristics are:

- The forecast is typically limited to major revenue and expense line items. There is usually no forecast for financial position, though cash flows may be forecasted.
- The forecast is updated at regular intervals, perhaps monthly or quarterly.
- The forecast may be used for short-term operational considerations, such as adjustments to staffing, inventory levels, and the production plan.
- There is no variance analysis that compares the forecast to actual results.
- Changes in the forecast do not impact performance-based compensation paid to employees.

Thus, the key difference between a budget and a forecast is that the budget is a plan for where a business wants to go, while a forecast is an indication of where it is actually going.

Realistically, the more useful of these tools is the forecast, for it gives a short-term representation of the actual circumstances in which a business finds itself. The information in a forecast can be used to take immediate action. A budget, on the other hand, may contain targets that are simply not achievable, or for which market circumstances have changed so much that it is not wise to attempt to achieve. If a budget is to be used, it should at least be updated more frequently than once a year, so that it bears some relationship to current market realities. The last point is of particular importance in a rapidly-changing market, where the assumptions used to create a budget may be rendered obsolete within a few months.

In this chapter, we place particular emphasis on the forecasting of revenues and cash, and the budgeting of expenditures. This is because revenues and (less directly) cash flows are subject to the actions of outside parties, and so are more variable over time than expenditures, which are under the direct control of the company.

The Run Rate Concept

The run rate concept refers to the extrapolation of financial results into future periods. For example, a company could report to its investors that its sales in the latest quarter were $5,000,000, which translates to an annual run rate of $20,000,000. Run rates can be used in a number of situations, including the following:

- The extrapolation of financial results by the seller of a business when attempting to obtain the highest possible price for the entity.
- The extrapolation of current results into future periods as part of the budgeting process.

There are several problems with the run rate concept that limit its ability to produce accurate projections. These issues are:

- *One-time sales*. A company may experience a large one-time sale and immediately extrapolate it into future periods to derive an unrealistically large revenue run rate. A more viable run rate would exclude the one-time sale.
- *Contractual limitations*. As was the case with one-time sales, there may be customer contracts set to expire during the extrapolated period, so the revenue associated with them will likely expire, as well. If so, a run rate based on these contracts would be excessively high.
- *Expense reductions*. A company engaged in a cost reduction effort (possibly occurring after an acquisition) initially achieves a large amount of expense reductions by focusing on the easiest savings, and uses this information to create an expense reduction run rate. This run rate is not likely to occur, since future expense reductions will be in areas that are more difficult to complete.
- *Seasonality*. A company's sales may be subject to a considerable amount of seasonality. If so, an annual run rate that is based on the peak part of the season will not be achievable. A better approach is to develop a run rate that is based on an entire year, so that the full span of the selling season is factored into the calculation.
- *Capacity constraints*. It is possible that the base period used to derive a run rate employed a very high level of capacity utilization within the business. If so, the run rate may not be sustainable, since some downtime will likely be required to maintain the overworked production equipment.

It is useful to keep the problems with the run rate in mind while perusing the remainder of this chapter, to keep from making overly optimistic extrapolations.

Sensitivity Analysis

Sensitivity analysis is the use of multiple what-if scenarios to model a range of possible outcomes. The technique is used to evaluate alternative business decisions or outcomes, employing different assumptions about variables. For example, a financial analyst could examine the potential revenue levels that may be achieved as a result of an investment in a new product line by altering the expected demand level, distribution channel alternatives, and types of competitor response.

A particularly useful aspect of sensitivity analysis is to locate those variables that can have an unusually large impact on the outcome of the analysis. The decision maker can then evaluate the probability of the variables experiencing significant changes. The outcome is a better understanding of the risks associated with an investment.

One way to create a sensitivity analysis is to aggregate variables into three scenarios, which are the worst case, most likely case, and best case. The probability of occurrence for the variables used in these three cases clusters the highest probability variables in the most likely case.

Revenue Forecasting

If there is any part of a company's financial results that should be forecasted, it is revenues. This information is critical for planning production, inventory, and staffing levels. Also, revenue results can change in the near term, and so must be constantly monitored to ensure that the company is adjusting its activity levels to forecasted results. This section describes how to compile revenue information for future periods.

The basic revenue forecast contains an itemization of a company's sales expectations for the forecast period, which may be in both units and dollars. If a company has a large number of products, it usually aggregates its expected sales into a smaller number of product categories; otherwise, the forecasting process becomes too unwieldy.

The basic calculation in the revenue forecast is to itemize the number of unit sales expected in one row of the forecast, and then list the average expected unit price in the next row, with the total revenues appearing in the third row. If any sales discounts or returns are anticipated, these items are also listed in the forecast.

The projected unit sales information in the revenue forecast feeds directly into the production budget, from which the direct materials and direct labor budgets are created. The revenue forecast is also used to give managers a general sense of the scale of operations, for when they create the manufacturing overhead budget, the sales and marketing budget, and the administration budget.

EXAMPLE

Quest Adventure Gear is a maker of rugged travel gear. One of its equipment lines is a propane-powered camp stove. Its revenue forecast is as follows:

	Quarter 1	Quarter 2	Quarter 3	Quarter 4	Total
Forecasted unit sales	5,500	6,000	7,000	8,000	26,500
× Price per unit	$35	$35	$38	$38	--
= Total gross sales	$192,500	$210,000	$266,000	$304,000	$972,500
- Sales discounts and allowances	-3,850	-$4,200	-$5,320	-6,080	-19,450
= Total net sales	$188,650	$205,800	$260,680	$297,920	$953,050

Quest's sales manager expects that increased demand in the second half of the year will allow it to increase its wholesale unit price from $35 to $38. Also, the sales manager expects that the company's historical sales discounts and allowances percentage of two percent of gross sales will continue through the forecast period.

This revenue forecast example only incorporates a single product, which results in a very simplistic forecast. Realistically, most companies sell many products and services, and must find a way to aggregate them into a forecast that strikes a balance between revealing a reasonable level of detail and not overwhelming the reader with a massive list of line-item projections. There are several ways to aggregate information to meet this goal.

One approach is to summarize revenue information by sales territory, as shown below. This approach is most useful when the primary source of information for the revenue forecast is the sales managers of the various territories, and is particularly important if the company is planning to close down or open up new sales territories; changes at the territory level may be the primary drivers of changes in sales. In the example, the Central Plains sales territory is expected to be launched midway through the forecast year and to contribute modestly to total sales volume by year end.

Sample Revenue Forecast by Territory

Territory	Quarter 1	Quarter 2	Quarter 3	Quarter 4	Total
Northeast	$135,000	$141,000	$145,000	$132,000	$553,000
Mid-Atlantic	200,000	210,000	208,000	195,000	813,000
Southeast	400,000	425,000	425,000	395,000	$1,645,000
Central Plains	0	0	100,000	175,000	275,000
Rocky Mountain	225,000	235,000	242,000	230,000	932,000
West Coast	500,000	560,000	585,000	525,000	2,170,000
Totals	$1,460,000	$1,571,000	$1,705,000	$1,652,000	$6,388,000

Another approach is to summarize revenue information by contract, as shown below. This is realistically the only viable way to structure the revenue forecast in situations where a company is heavily dependent upon a set of contracts that have definite ending dates. In this situation, divide the forecast into existing and projected contracts, with subtotals for each type of contract, in order to separately show firm revenues and less-likely revenues. This type of forecast is commonly used when a company is engaged in services or government work.

Financial Forecasting

Sample Revenue Forecast by Contract

Contract	Quarter 1	Quarter 2	Quarter 3	Quarter 4	Total
Existing Contracts:					
Air Force #01327	$175,000	$175,000	$25,000	$--	$375,000
Coast Guard #AC124	460,000	460,000	460,000	25,000	1,405,000
Marines #BG0047	260,000	280,000	280,000	260,000	1,080,000
Subtotal	$895,000	$915,000	$765,000	$285,000	$2,860,000
Projected Contracts:					
Air Force resupply	$--	$--	$150,000	$300,000	$450,000
Army training	--	210,000	600,000	550,000	1,360,000
Marines software	10,000	80,000	80,000	100,000	270,000
Subtotal	$10,000	$290,000	$830,000	$950,000	$2,080,000
Totals	$905,000	$1,205,000	$1,595,000	$1,235,000	$4,940,000

Yet another approach for a company having a large number of products is to aggregate them into product lines, and then create a summary-level forecast at the product line level. This approach is shown below. However, if a revenue forecast is created for product lines, also consider creating a supporting schedule of projected sales for each of the products within that product line, in order to properly account for the timing and revenue volumes associated with the ongoing introduction of new products and cancellation of old ones. An example of such a supporting schedule is also shown below, itemizing the "Alpha" line item in the product line revenue forecast. Note that this schedule provides detail about the launch of a new product (the Alpha Windmill) and the termination of another product (the Alpha Methane Converter) that are crucial to the formulation of the total revenue figure for the product line.

Sample Revenue Forecast by Product Line

Product Line	Quarter 1	Quarter 2	Quarter 3	Quarter 4	Total
Product line alpha	$450,000	$500,000	$625,000	$525,000	$2,100,000
Product line beta	100,000	110,000	150,000	125,000	485,000
Product line charlie	250,000	250,000	300,000	300,000	1,100,000
Product line delta	80,000	60,000	40,000	20,000	200,000
Totals	$880,000	$920,000	$1,115,000	$970,000	$3,885,000

Sample Supporting Schedule for the Revenue Forecast by Product Line

	Quarter 1	Quarter 2	Quarter 3	Quarter 4	Total
Alpha product line detail:					
Alpha Flywheel	$25,000	$35,000	$40,000	$20,000	$120,000
Alpha Generator	175,000	225,000	210,000	180,000	790,000
Alpha Windmill	--	--	200,000	250,000	450,000
Alpha Methane Converter	150,000	140,000	25,000	--	315,000
Alpha Nuclear Converter	100,000	100,000	150,000	75,000	425,000
Totals	$450,000	$500,000	$625,000	$525,000	$2,100,000

A danger in constructing a supporting schedule for a product line forecast is that you delve too deeply into all of the various manifestations of a product, resulting in an inordinately large and detailed schedule. This situation might arise when a product comes in many colors or options. In such cases, engage in as much aggregation at the individual product level as necessary to yield a schedule that is not *excessively* detailed. It is nearly impossible to forecast revenue at the level of the color or specific option mix associated with a product, so it makes little sense to create a schedule at that level of detail.

In summary, the layout of the revenue forecast is highly dependent upon the type of revenue that a company generates. We have described different formats for companies that are structured around products, contract-based services, and sales territories. If a company engages in more than one of these activities, then still create the revenue-specific formats shown in this section in order to provide insights into the sources of revenues, and then carry forward the totals of those schedules to a master revenue forecast that lists the totals in separate line items. Users of this master revenue forecast can then drill down to the underlying schedules to obtain additional information. An example of a master revenue forecast that is derived from the last two example forecasts is shown next.

Sample Master Revenue Forecast

	Quarter 1	Quarter 2	Quarter 3	Quarter 4	Total
Contract revenue	$905,000	$1,205,000	$1,595,000	$1,235,000	$4,940,000
Product revenue	880,000	920,000	1,115,000	970,000	3,885,000
Totals	$1,785,000	$2,125,000	$2,710,000	$2,205,000	$8,825,000

A common trap that companies fall into when forecasting rapid growth is to account for the delaying effect of pacing. From the perspective of forecasting, pacing is the rate at which an entity can ramp up an operational issue until it can handle a target revenue level. Here are several pacing scenarios to consider:

- *Sales staff.* A company sells a product that requires an intensive hands-on sale by an experienced salesperson. The company must delay forecasted revenues that are associated with new salespeople until such time as they are

capable of selling at the same success rate as more experienced salespeople. This is one of the most significant pacing issues.
- *Selling cycle.* In some industries, customers only buy products at a certain pace. This is particularly true for large capital products, where purchases are only considered once a year, and must go through a lengthy review process before a purchase order is issued. In such situations, a company may hire a group of excellent, well-trained sales people, and yet not earn a single new customer order for a long time.
- *Retail roll out.* A company has developed an excellent retail concept store, and can gain sales rapidly if it can roll out the concept into new locations as fast as possible. This is a major pacing issue, since the company likely has only a small number of people who are sufficiently skilled in store openings, and that group can only open a certain number of stores within a given period of time.
- *Production facilities.* If a company can only gain new sales after it builds new production facilities, it cannot forecast more sales until the facilities are complete and tested, and the new staff hired for the facility is capable of running it at the planned level of productivity. The variety of issues involved can mean that new sales cannot begin until a long time after a facility has been constructed.
- *Permits.* A company can only do business in a new sales region after it obtains all necessary government permits. This is a particular problem when a business is attempting to gain entry into a new country where it has few contacts or local partners.
- *New technology.* A company has created a product that has cutting-edge technology. Such products tend to have a higher failure rate until the engineering and production staffs can figure out the underlying issues. This process of working out the kinks can greatly delay revenue generation.

Pacing is an important topic that less seasoned managers tend to ignore. The result is a revenue forecast that initially appears reasonable, but which a company is not able to meet, due to a lack of attention to underlying factors that exert a natural slowing effect on revenue growth.

No matter how detailed and thorough the analysis of the underlying factors affecting revenue may be, the revenue forecast will inevitably depart from actual results after just a few months. This level of inherent variability can be massive if a company's sales cycle is quite short, and it has a small backlog of customer orders. In that situation, a company has to create new sales "from scratch" after just a few months, which makes it very difficult to forecast revenue. Conversely, if a company has a massive order backlog that extends beyond the entire forecast period, then the company can probably come fairly close to matching its revenue forecast. However, even in this latter case, there will inevitably be production constraints and delays that impact sales, as will cancelled customer orders – and these issues will build over time to cause an increasing level of variability.

There is no way to deal with the inherent variability of the revenue forecast, other than to tailor the period covered by the forecast to the time period over which a company can predict its revenues with a reasonable degree of certainty. Thus, the company in our first scenario may find that it can only create a budget for the next three months, while the company in the second scenario may be able to comfortably prepare a forecast that covers the next two years. An alternative is to intensively review and update the forecast over just the period when sales are relatively predictable, while maintaining a longer-term forecast for which little effort is made to compile a detailed operational budget. Doing so reduces the amount of work that goes into the forecast, while still presenting an approximate view of the company's revenue direction.

The System of Budgets

Thus far, we have only dealt with the generation of a revenue forecast. However, there is also an array of expenditures to be considered in the development of a complete financial forecast. These expenditures are typically derived through a system of budgets, many of which are tied to the revenue forecast. In this section, we present an overview of the system of budgets. For a comprehensive discussion of how to create these budgets, see the author's *Budgeting* book.

Once the revenue forecast is in place, a number of additional budgets are derived from it that relate to the production capabilities of the company. The following components are included in this cluster of budgets:

- *Ending inventory budget*. As its name implies, this budget sets the inventory level as of the end of each accounting period listed in the budget. Management uses this budget to force changes in the inventory level, which is usually driven by a policy to have more or less finished goods inventory on hand. Having more inventory presumably improves the speed with which a company can ship goods to customers, at the cost of an increased investment in working capital. A forced reduction in inventory may delay some shipments to customers due to stockout conditions, but requires less working capital to maintain. The ending inventory budget is used as an input to the production budget.
- *Production budget*. This budget shows expected production at an aggregated level. The production budget is based primarily on the sales estimates in the revenue budget, but it must also take into consideration existing inventory levels and the desired amount of ending inventory, as stated in the ending inventory budget. If management wants to increase inventory levels in order to provide more rapid shipments to customers, the required increase in production may trigger a need for more production equipment and direct labor staff. The production budget is needed in order to derive the direct labor budget, manufacturing overhead budget, and direct materials budget.
- *Direct labor budget*. This budget calculates the amount of direct labor staffing expected during the budget period, based on the production levels itemized in the production budget. This information can only be generally

estimated, given the vagaries of short-term changes in actual production scheduling. However, direct labor usually involves specific staffing levels to crew production lines, so the estimated amount of direct labor should not vary excessively over time, within certain production volume parameters. This budget should incorporate any planned changes in the cost of labor, which may be easy to do if there is a union contract that specifies pay increases as of specific dates. This budget provides rough estimates of the number of employees needed, and is of particular interest to the human resources staff in developing hiring plans. It is a key source document for the cost of goods sold budget.

- *Manufacturing overhead budget.* This budget includes all of the overhead costs expected to be incurred in the manufacturing area during the budget period. It is usually based on historical cost information, but can be adjusted for step cost situations, where a change in the structure or capacity level of a production facility strips away or adds large amounts of expenses at one time. Even if there are no changes in structure or capacity, the manufacturing overhead budget may change somewhat in the maintenance cost area if management plans to alter these expenditures as machines age or are replaced. It is particularly important to adjust this budget if management contemplates running a production facility at close to 100% utilization, since doing so requires an incremental increase in many types of expenditures. This budget is a source document for the cost of goods sold budget.

- *Direct materials budget.* This budget is derived from a combination of the manufacturing unit totals in the production budget and the bills of material for those units, and is used in the cost of goods sold budget. The bills of material must be precise if this budget is to be remotely accurate. If a company produces a large variety of products, this can become an excessively detailed and burdensome budget to create and maintain. Consequently, it is customary to estimate material costs in aggregate, such as at the product line level. It may also be necessary to state expected scrap and spoilage levels in this budget, especially if management plans to improve its production practices to reduce scrap and spoilage below their historical levels.

- *Cost of goods sold budget.* This budget contains a summarization of the expenses detailed in the direct material budget, manufacturing overhead budget, and direct materials budget. This budget usually contains such additional information as line items for revenue, the gross margin, and key production statistics. It is heavily used during budget iterations, since management can consult it to view the impact of various assumptions on gross margins and other aspects of the production process.

Once the revenue and production-related budgets have been completed, there are still several other budgets to assemble that relate to other functions of the company. They are:

- *Sales and marketing budget.* This budget is comprised of the compensation of the sales and marketing staff, sales travel costs, and expenditures related to various marketing programs. It is closely linked to the revenue budget, since the number of sales staff (in some industries) is the prime determinant of additional sales. Further, marketing campaigns can impact the timing of the sales shown in the revenue budget.
- *Administration budget.* This budget includes the expenses of the executive, accounting, treasury, human resources, and other administrative staff. These expenses are primarily comprised of compensation, followed by office expenses. A large proportion of these expenses are fixed, with some headcount changes driven by total revenues or other types of activity elsewhere in the company.

A budget that is not directly impacted by the revenue budget is the research and development budget. This budget is authorized by senior management, and is set at an amount that is deemed appropriate, given the projected level of new product introductions that management wants to achieve, and the company's competitive posture within the industry. The size of this budget is also influenced by the amount of available funding and an estimate of how many potentially profitable projects can be pursued.

Once these budgets have been completed, it is possible to determine the capital budgeting requirements of the company, as well as its financing needs. These two topics are addressed in the following capital budget and financing budget:

- *Capital budget.* This budget shows the cash flows associated with the acquisition of fixed assets during the budget period. Larger fixed assets are noted individually, while smaller purchases are noted in aggregate. The information in this budget is used to develop the budgeted balance sheet, depreciation expense, and cash requirements needed for the financing budget.
- *Financing budget.* This budget is the last of the component budgets developed, because it needs the cash inflow and outflow information from the other budgets. With this information in hand, the financing budget addresses how funds will be invested (if there are excess cash inflows) or obtained through debt or equity financing (if there is a need for additional cash). This budget also incorporates any additional cash usage information that is typically addressed by the board of directors, including dividends, stock repurchases, and repositioning of the company's debt to equity ratio. The interest expense or interest income resulting from this budget is incorporated into the budgeted income statement.

Once the capital budget and financing budget have been created, the information in all of the budgets is summarized into a master budget. This master budget is essentially an income statement. A more complex budget also includes a balance sheet that itemizes the major categories of assets, liabilities, and equity. There may also be a statement of cash flows that itemizes the sources and uses of funds.

The complete system of budgets is shown in the following exhibit.

Exhibit: The System of Budgets

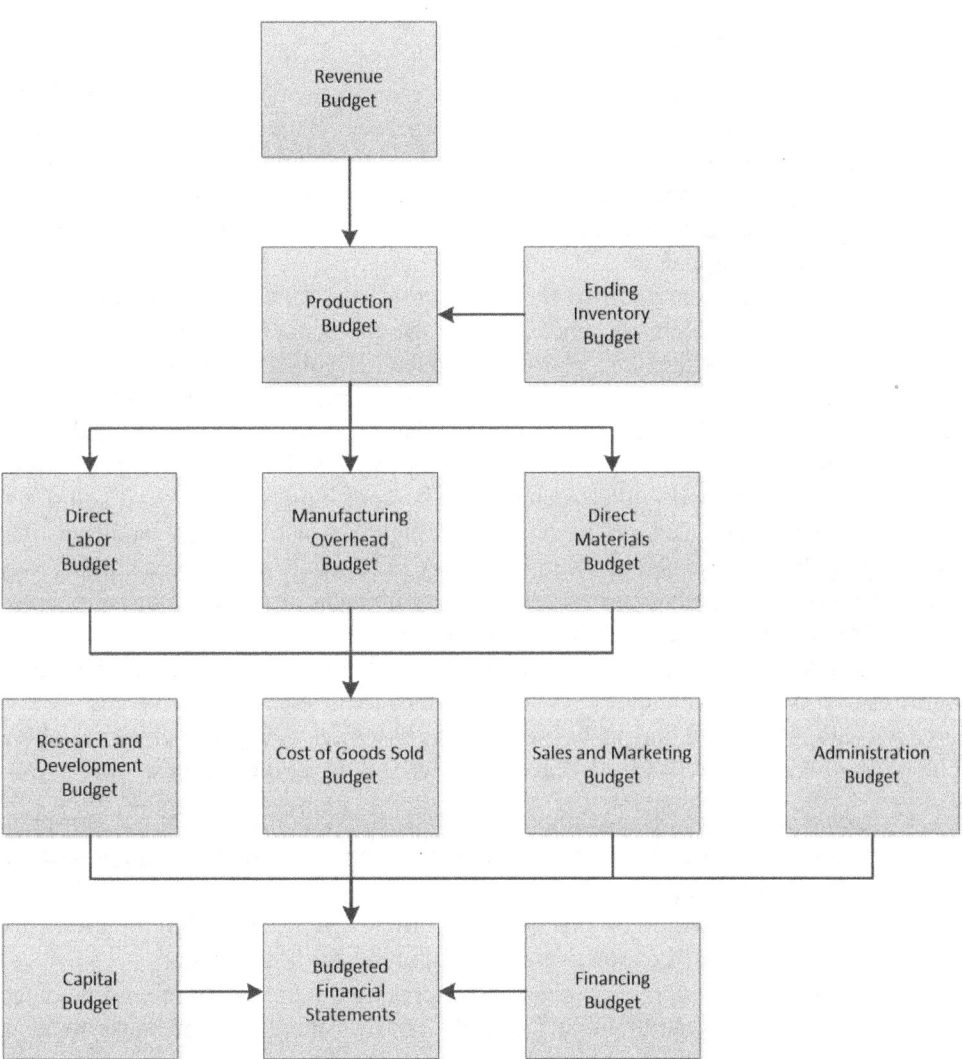

Employee staffing levels are usually included in each of the various budgets, so that employee compensation is fully integrated into the expenses in each budget. However, since compensation comprises a major proportion of all company expenses, it may be useful to also create a staffing budget that summarizes headcount and compensation for all areas of the business. This information is useful for determining whether there will be a sufficient number of employees to support planned revenue levels, as well as to provide guidance for the recruiting and layoff plans of the human resources department.

In summary, the system of budgets ultimately depends upon the revenue forecast and the amount of planned ending inventory. These two information sources directly or indirectly influence the amounts stated in many parts of the corporate budget.

The Number of Budget Scenarios

Most companies prepare a single budget scenario, which is their best guess regarding how the next year will turn out. This scenario is based upon a range of supporting assumptions, any one of which can lead to diverging results - and usually does. So, though a considerable amount of time may be spent on a "mainstream" budget scenario, just that one version will not be enough to prepare for what may - and probably will - happen.

It may make sense to add two more scenarios, one for the absolute worst case, where bankruptcy is looming, and one for the most phenomenal sales success. Sounds unlikely that either one will ever happen? If you don't plan for success, it never *will* happen, and bankruptcy scenarios are far more frequent than you might think. Consequently, it is useful to know what resources will be needed for a phenomenally successful year, and how deep you will have to cut to avoid bankruptcy. Of these two outlier scenarios, it is more important to spend additional time on the worst case scenario, perhaps matching the worst business conditions that the company has ever experienced in its history. The result should be a contingency plan for how the company can deal effectively with a catastrophic situation, coupled with a commitment to fast execution of the plan.

Is that a sufficient number of scenarios? No. There are key variables that could significantly skew the company's results if specific events arise, and you should have a rough, high-level budget in place that is based on changes in those variables. The types of variables will vary by business. Here are several examples:

- *Commodity costs*. For example, the price of aviation fuel is of extraordinary importance in the airline industry, since it comprises such a large proportion of an airline's expenses.
- *Credit availability*. For example, the fortunes of the home building industry rise and fall based on the availability of credit for home owners.
- *Government action*. For example, increases in the government-mandated capital reserve requirement for banks restricts the ability of banks to lend, and therefore reduces their ability to earn a profit.
- *Supplier availability*. For example, the combined earthquake and tsunami in Japan in 2011 interrupted the flow of automobiles and related parts to other markets.

Thus, there should be one thoroughly-constructed budget scenario, and two other budgets dealing with best-case and worst-case scenarios that require a lesser amount of detail, as well as other high-level budget models to deal with key variables.

All of this talk of multiple models does not mean that an equal amount of time should be spent on each one. The mainstream scenario requires the most work, because it is (presumably) the most likely, with less work needed for the less likely alternatives. Nonetheless, spend some time determining financial results at a high level for each scenario, and conceptualize what those situations will do to the company's operations and financial position.

The discussion of budget scenarios so far has been about constructing budget versions that are essentially based on probability of occurrence. Another possibility is to construct a top-down model and a bottom-up model, and reconcile the two. Under this approach, ask the senior management team to construct a budget based on their view of the business (the top-down model), while front-line managers and staff independently create a budget that is based on their street-level view of the company's business (the bottom-up model). The top-down model is largely derived from senior management's presumably better strategic view of the industry and general trends, while the bottom-up model is derived from the more immediate, short-term view of those people dealing directly with customers and products. Since these two budgets are derived from fundamentally different sources of information, there will inevitably be significant differences. Examining these differences can yield valuable insights into the business, and can lead to the creation of an integrated model that better represents the capabilities of the company and the industry within which it operates.

The Rolling Forecast

A rolling forecast is a recasting of a company's financial prospects on a frequent basis. The frequency of forecasting means that the forecast could potentially occupy a central role in a company's planning activities. In this section we address several aspects of that role – the timing of updates, the updating method, the time period covered, and the format of the forecast.

Ideally, a rolling forecast could be created as soon as a company issues its financial statements for the most recent reporting period. By doing so, management can update the existing forecast based in part on the information contained in the most recent financial statements. You may want to update the forecast on a monthly basis, but do so only if the resulting information is useful to management – which is usually only the case in a volatile market. In most situations, a quarterly update to the forecast is sufficient, and is not looked upon as quite so much of a chore by the management team. An alternative view of when to update a forecast is whenever there is a significant triggering event. This may be a change in the business environment, the release of a new product, the loss of a key employee, and so forth. If updates are only after a triggering event, the revision of a rolling forecast may be quite sporadic.

The rolling forecast is usually considered to be a much more frequent creation than the annual budget, so a revision process is needed that minimizes the amount of updating effort. Here are several ways to construct a rolling forecast, beginning with the simplest approach:

1. *Adjust recent results.* Copy forward the company's most recent actual financial results, and then adjust revenues and expenses based on any changed expectations for the forecasting period. This method is essentially based on historical results. It requires the input of very few people, and can be created very quickly.
2. *Block revision.* Only forecast at a very high level, where there is essentially a single line item block for the expenses of an entire department. There may be somewhat more detail for the revenue portion of the forecast, since this is the most critical area. This information will likely be extracted from the most recent historical results, but may be subject to more revision than the method just discussed. This approach can also be constructed quickly, with input from just a few people.
3. *Detailed revision.* Forecast every line item in the financial statements "from scratch." This approach takes substantially more time and requires broad-based input. Few companies are willing to expend the time needed for this level of forecasting.

Of the preceding methods, either the first or second should work well, because they require little time to create. When forecasting requires little time, it is more likely to be accepted on a long-term basis by employees. Ideally, it should take no more than one day to update a rolling forecast.

Another issue with the rolling forecast is the time period to be covered by it. There is no universally correct period. Instead, the time period covered depends on the nature of the business. Here are several examples of situations calling for different forecast periods:

- *Software development.* A business creates software and launches it through the Internet. Its investment in fixed assets is low. In this case, competing products can appear at any time, and the market can pivot in a new direction at a moment's notice. If so, management probably does not need a forecast that extends more than three months into the future.
- *Market leading manufacturer.* A business is the dominant low-cost provider of industrial goods in its market niche, thanks to its heavy investment in fixed assets and production technology. The market is probably steady and changes little, so management can get by with a quarterly forecast update that extends over a two-year period.
- *Government contractor.* A company has a backlog of long-term contracts with the federal government. Its cost structure is easily predicted, and revenues are based largely on contracts that are already in hand. Management probably only needs a quarterly forecast update, with particular emphasis on the revenues generated by specific contracts. The forecast duration should match the duration of key contracts.
- *Retail business.* A company sells fashion-oriented retail goods from multiple stores. Sales levels are highly variable, so management probably needs a

monthly forecast that has a particular emphasis on sales by product line and by store.

Another way to view the duration of the forecast period is whether extending it further into the future will alter any management decision making. If not, there is no point in creating the extended forecast. A good way to determine the correct duration is to start with a rolling 12-month forecast and adjust the duration after a few months to more closely fit the needs of management. It is quite common to have a forecast duration of at least one year, and rarely more than two years.

What should a rolling forecast look like? As just noted, keep it relatively short in order to make the updating task as easy as possible. However, this does not mean that the entire forecast should be encompassed within just a few lines. Instead, consider structuring the forecast to address the key variables in the business, so that managers focus on changes in just those areas that will make a difference.

The following sample format is designed for a manufacturing business that produces roughly the same items every year and in predictable quantities. There is a focus on the cost of commodities and managing the bottleneck operation, which leads to more detail on those specific items.

Sample Rolling Forecast for Manufacturing Operation

	Quarter 1	Quarter 2	Quarter 3	Quarter 4
Sales	$8,200,000	$8,225,000	$8,290,000	$8,320,000
Cost of goods sold	5,330,000	5,593,000	5,720,000	5,741,000
Gross margin	$2,870,000	$2,632,000	$2,570,000	$2,579,000
Gross margin percentage	35%	32%	31%	31%
Other expenses	2,510,000	2,535,000	2,550,000	2,565,000
Net profit or loss	$360,000	$97,000	$20,000	$14,000
Bottleneck utilization	92%	98%	105%	108%
Platinum cost/pound	$1,700	$1,750	$1,775	$1,775
Palladium cost/pound	$700	$705	$710	$715

The rolling forecast for the manufacturing operation reveals a decline in gross margins and net profits over time, which appears to be caused by an increase in the cost of platinum, which is listed on the report as a key commodity. Also, note that the forecast is in quarters, not months – the company has a sufficiently stable product line and marketplace that it does not need to update its forecast every month. Finally, the forecast reveals that there is a growing problem with the overutilization of the company's bottleneck operation, which management needs to address.

Financial Forecasting

What about if a company has minimal fixed costs and is located in a highly volatile marketplace – such as software development for smart phone apps? In this environment, a product may have a short life span or highly variable revenues, so the focus tends to be more on detailed revenue information and the rollout dates for new products. The following sample format could be applied to such a situation:

Sample Rolling Forecast for a Software Developer

	January	February	March	April
Revenue:				
App – Geolocator	$80,000	$75,000	$60,000	$45,000
App – Find my car	55,000	65,000	65,000	40,000
App – Family tracker	160,000	160,000	100,000	80,000
Total revenue	$295,000	$300,000	$225,000	$165,000
Expenses	165,000	175,000	175,000	180,000
Net profit or loss	$130,000	$125,000	$50,000	-$15,000
Product release dates:				
App – Backcountry locator	1/21/xx			
App – Wildlife tagger			3/5/xx	
App – Urban locator				4/4/xx

The rolling forecast for the software developer makes it clear that revenues decline rapidly, so revenues must be the key focus of the organization. There is also an emphasis on the release dates of new products, which will hopefully drive renewed revenue growth. Note that the preceding example format is expressed in months, rather than quarters. In a volatile marketplace, a quarterly update may be far too long an interval to show the rapid changes in sales that will likely occur.

What about a situation where a company relies upon a number of large contracts with its customers? In this case, the key focus must be on the revenue stream associated with each contract, as well as on the dates when contracts will terminate. The following sample format could be applied to such a situation.

Sample Rolling Forecast for a Contractor

	Quarter 1	Quarter 2	Quarter 3	Quarter 4
Revenue:				
Air Force contract	$1,700,000	$1,720,000	$1,690,000	$850,000
Marine Corp contract	2,400,000	2,350,000	130,000	0
USGS contract	850,000	875,000	430,000	0
Total revenue	$4,950,000	$4,945,000	$2,250,000	$850,000
Expenses	4,300,000	4,290,000	1,950,000	830,000
Net profit or loss	$650,000	$655,000	$300,000	$20,000
Contract terminations:				
Air Force contract				11/20/xx
Marine Corps contract			7/11/xx	
USGS contract			8/15/xx	

The rolling forecast for the contractor is driven entirely by revenues. The company can easily cut back on staffing when there is no work, so its expenses are not a concern. The non-financial information in the forecast keeps management aware of the truly critical item – when customer contracts are scheduled to expire.

The rolling forecast is an ideal way to give employees the best possible estimate of what will probably occur in the near future. The forecasting process is specifically designed not to be elaborate, on the grounds that a simple update is more likely to be accepted by a company than a lengthy, bureaucratic budgeting production. And by keeping the model simple, you can focus on the key drivers of success, rather than being bogged down in the details.

The Cash Forecast

Management needs to know the amount of cash that will probably be on hand in the near future, in order to make fund raising and investment decisions. This is accomplished with a cash forecast, which should be sufficiently detailed to inform management of projected cash shortfalls and excess funds on at least a weekly basis. This section covers the details of how to create and fine-tune a cash forecast.

The cash forecast can be divided into two parts: near-term cash flows that are highly predictable (typically covering a one-month period) and medium-term cash flows that are largely based on revenues that have not yet occurred and supplier invoices that have not yet arrived. The first part of the forecast can be quite accurate, while the second part yields increasingly tenuous results after not much more than a month has passed. It is also possible to create a long-term cash forecast that is essentially a modified version of the company budget, though its utility is relatively low. The following exhibit shows the severity of the decline in accuracy for short-term and medium-term forecasts. In particular, there is an immediate decline in accuracy as soon as the medium-term forecast replaces the short-term forecast, since less reliable information is used in the medium-term forecast.

> **Related Podcast Episode:** Episode 187 of the Accounting Best Practices Podcast discusses cash forecasting accuracy. The episode is available at: **accountingtools.com/podcasts** or **iTunes**

Variability of Actual from Forecasted Cash Flow Information

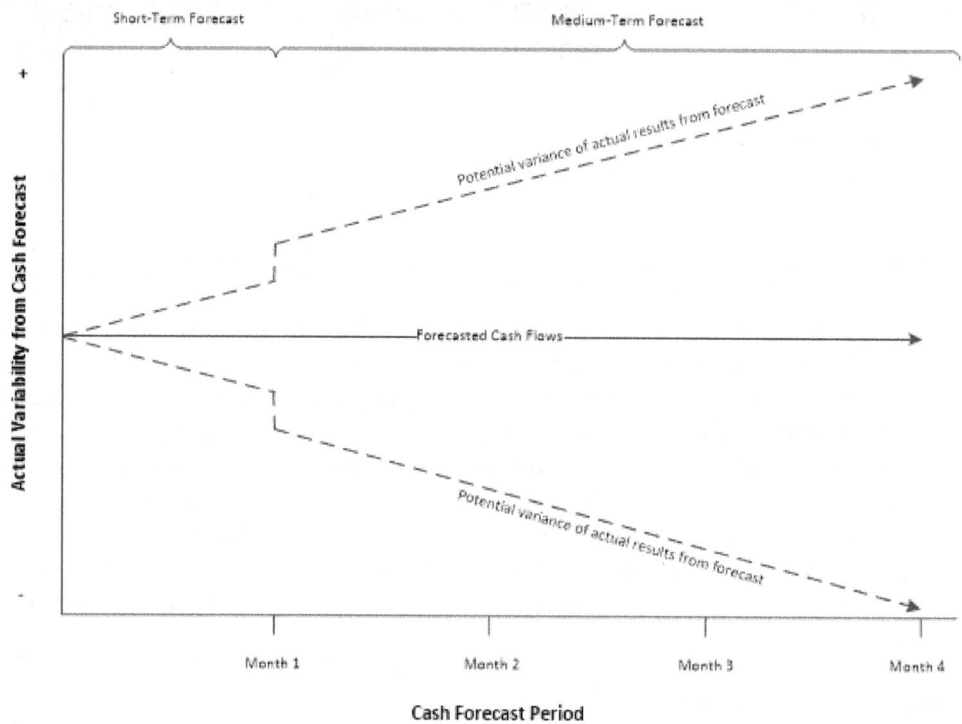

Through the remainder of this section, we will deal separately with how to construct the short-term and medium-term portions of the cash forecast, along with related topics.

The Short-Term Cash Forecast

The short-term cash forecast is based on a detailed accumulation of information from a variety of sources within the company. The bulk of this information comes from the accounts receivable, accounts payable, and payroll records, though other significant sources are the treasurer (for financing activities), the CFO (for acquisitions information) and even the corporate secretary (for scheduled dividend payments). Since this forecast is based on detailed itemizations of cash inflows and outflows, it is sometimes called the *receipts and disbursements method*.

Financial Forecasting

The forecast needs to be sufficiently detailed to create an accurate cash forecast, but not so detailed that it requires an inordinate amount of labor to update. Consequently, include a detailed analysis of only the *largest* receipts and expenditures, and aggregate all other items. The detailed analysis involves the manual prediction of selected cash receipts and expenditures, while the aggregated results are scheduled based on average dates of receipt and payment (see the comments at the end of this section about the use of averaging).

Tip: Use detailed analysis of cash items in the cash forecast for the 20% of items that comprise 80% of the cash flows, and use aggregation for the remaining 80% of items that comprise 20% of the cash flows.

The following table notes the treatment of the key line items in a cash forecast, including the level of detailed forecasting required.

+/-	Line Item	Discussion
+	Beginning cash	This is the current cash balance as of the creation date of the cash forecast, or, for subsequent weeks, it is the ending cash balance from the preceding week. Do not include restricted cash in this number, since you may not be able to use it to pay for expenditures.
+	Accounts receivable	Do not attempt to duplicate the detail of the aged accounts receivable report in this section of the forecast. However, itemize the largest receivables, stating the period in which cash receipt is most likely to occur. All other receivables can be listed in aggregate.
+	Other receivables	Only include this line item if there are significant amounts of other receivables (such as customer advances) for which you expect to receive cash within the forecast period.
-	Employee compensation	This is possibly the largest expense item, so be especially careful in estimating the amount. It is easiest to base the compensation expense on the amount paid in the preceding period, adjusted for any expected changes.
-	Payroll taxes	List this expense separately, since it is common to forget to include it when aggregated into the employee compensation line item.
-	Contractor compensation	If there are large payments to subcontractors, list them in one or more line items.
-	Key supplier payments	If there are large payments due to specific suppliers, itemize them separately. You may need to change the dates of these payments in the forecast in response to estimated cash positions.
-	Large recurring payments	There are usually large ongoing payments, such as rent and medical insurance, which can be itemized on separate lines of the forecast.

Financial Forecasting

+/-	Line Item	Discussion
-	Debt payments	If there are significant principal or interest payments coming due, itemize them in the report.
-	Dividend payments	If dividend payments are scheduled, itemize them in the forecast; this tends to be a large expenditure.
-	Expense reports	If there are a large number of expense reports in each month, they are probably clustered near month-end. You can usually estimate the amount likely to be submitted.
=	Net cash position	This is the total of all the preceding line items.
+/-	Financing activities	Add any new debt, which increases cash flow, or the reduction of debt, which decreases cash flow. Also add any investments that mature during the period.
	Ending cash	This is the sum of the net cash position line item and the financing activities line item.

The following example illustrates a cash forecast, using the line items described in the preceding table.

EXAMPLE

An analyst working for Suture Corporation constructs the following cash forecast for each week in the month of September.

+/-	Line Item	Sept. 1-7	Sept. 8-14	Sept. 15-22	Sept. 23-30
+	Beginning cash	$50,000	$30,000	$2,000	$0
+	Accounts receivable				
+	Alpha Pharmaceuticals	120,000		60,000	
+	St. Joseph's Burn Center		85,000		52,000
+	Third Degree Burn Center	29,000		109,000	
+	Other receivables	160,000	25,000	48,000	60,000
+	Other receivables	10,000		5,000	
-	Employee compensation	140,000		145,000	
-	Payroll taxes	10,000		11,000	
-	Contractor compensation				
-	Bryce Contractors	8,000		8,000	
-	Johnson Contractors	14,000		12,000	
-	Key supplier payments				
-	Chico Biomedical	100,000		35,000	
-	Stanford Research	20,000	80,000	29,000	14,000
-	Other suppliers	35,000	40,000	30,000	48,000

Financial Forecasting

+/-	Line Item	Sept. 1-7	Sept. 8-14	Sept. 15-22	Sept. 23-30
-	Large recurring payments				
-	Medical insurance				43,000
-	Rent				49,000
-	Debt payments		18,000		
-	Dividend payments			20,000	
-	Expense reports	12,000	0	0	21,000
=	Net cash position	$30,000	$2,000	-$66,000	-$63,000
+/-	Financing activities			66,000	63,000
=	Ending cash	$30,000	$2,000	$0	$0

The forecast reveals a cash shortfall beginning in the third week, which will require a cumulative total of $129,000 of additional financing if the company wants to meet its scheduled payment obligations.

The format is designed with the goal of giving sufficient visibility into cash flows to reveal the causes of unusual cash shortfalls or overages, without burying the reader in an excessive amount of detail. To meet this goal, note the use of the "Other receivables" and "Other suppliers" line items in the exhibit. They are used to aggregate smaller projected transactions that do not have a major impact on the forecast, but which would otherwise overwhelm the document with an excessive amount of detail if they were listed individually.

A possible addition to the cash forecast is the use of a *target balance*. This is essentially a "safety stock" of cash that is kept on hand to guard against unexpected cash requirements that were not planned for in the cash forecast. All excess cash above the target balance can be invested, while any shortfalls below the target balance should be funded. If a target balance had been incorporated into the preceding cash forecast example in the amount of $10,000, the amount would have been listed for the week of September 1-7 as a deduction from the ending cash position, leaving $20,000 of cash available for investment purposes.

The model we have outlined in this section requires a weekly update. It only covers a one-month period, so its contents become outdated very quickly. Ideally, block out time to complete the forecast at the same time, every week. Unless the cash flow environment is extremely tight, we do not recommend daily updates of cash forecasts – the time required to create these forecasts is excessive in comparison to the additional precision gained from the more frequent updates.

The very short-term portion of the cash forecast may be subject to some tweaking, usually to delay a few supplier payments to adjust for liquidity problems expected to arise over the next few days. To incorporate these changes into the forecast, use a preliminary draft of the forecast to coordinate changes in the timing of payments with the payables staff, and then record the delays in the forecast before issuing the final version.

The Medium-Term Cash Forecast

The medium-term cash forecast extends from the end of the short-term forecast through whatever time period is used to develop investment and funding strategies. Typically, this means that the medium-term forecast begins one month into the future.

The components of the medium-term forecast are largely comprised of formulas, rather than the specific data inputs used for a short-term forecast. For example, if the sales manager were to contribute estimated revenue figures for each forecasting period, then the model could derive the following additional information:

- *Cash paid for cost of goods sold items.* Can be estimated as a percentage of sales, with a time lag based on the average supplier payment terms.
- *Cash paid for payroll.* Sales activity can be used to estimate changes in production headcount, which in turn can be used to derive payroll payments.
- *Cash receipts from customers.* A standard time lag between the billing date and payment date can be incorporated into the estimation of when cash will be received from customers.

The concept of a formula-filled cash forecast that automatically generates cash balance information breaks down in some parts of the forecast. In the following areas, the staff will need to make manual updates to the forecast:

- *Fixed costs.* Some costs are entirely fixed, such as rent, and so will not vary with sales volume. Be aware of any contractually-mandated changes in these costs, and incorporate them into the forecast.
- *Step costs.* If revenues change significantly, the fixed costs just described may have to be altered by substantial amounts. For example, a certain sales level may mandate opening a new production facility. A more common step cost is having to hire an overhead staff position when certain sales levels are reached. Be aware of the activity levels at which these step costs will occur.
- *Seasonal / infrequent costs.* There may be expenditures that only arise at long intervals, such as for the company Christmas party. These amounts are manually added to the forecast.
- *Contractual items.* Both cash inflows and outflows may be linked to contract payments, as may be the case with service contracts. If so, the exact amount and timing of each periodic payment can be transferred from the contract directly into the cash forecast.

The methods used to construct a medium-term cash forecast are inherently less accurate than the much more precise information used to derive a short-term forecast. The problem is that much of the information is derived from the estimated revenue figure, which rapidly declines in accuracy just a few months into the future. Because of this inherent level of inaccuracy, do not extend the forecast over too long a time period. Instead, settle upon a time range that provides useful information for planning purposes. Any additional forecasting beyond that time period will waste staff time to create, and may yield misleading information.

The Long-Term Cash Forecast

There can also be a long-term cash forecast that extends for an additional one or two years past the end of the medium-term forecast. It can be extremely difficult and time-consuming to develop and maintain a sales forecast for this period, so the most common approach is to instead adapt information from the corporate budget, and update it regularly to coincide with management's best estimates of long-term results.

The cash flows indicated by a long-term cash forecast should be considered only approximate values, so management is probably justified in not using it as the basis for any investment activities having specific maturity dates. However, the long-term forecast may be of more use in dealing with projected cash shortfalls. For lack of any better information, use it to obtain approximations of how much cash may be needed, and to plan on acquiring debt or selling stock to meet the shortfall.

The Use of Averages

There can be a temptation to use averages for estimated cash flows in the cash forecast. For example, it may seem reasonable to divide the average cash collections for receivables in a month by four, and then enter the resulting average cash receipts figure in each week of the forecast. This is not a good idea in the short-term portion of the forecast, since there are a number of timing differences that will make actual results differ markedly from average results. The following bullets contain several cash flow issues that can have sharp spikes and declines in comparison to the average:

- The receipt of payment for an unusually large invoice
- The designation of a large invoice as a bad debt
- Once-a-month payments, such as rent and medical insurance
- Sporadic payments, such as for dividends and property taxes

It is particularly dangerous to use averaging to estimate accounts receivable. In many companies, there is a disproportionate amount of invoicing at the end of each month, which means that there is a correspondingly large amount of cash receipts one month later (assuming 30-day payment terms). In short, it is quite common to have billing surges cause payment surges that vary wildly from average cash receipt numbers.

If you were to rely upon an averages-based cash forecast, there would be a high risk of routinely having cash shortfalls and overages. After all, the company must have liquidity *every day*, not just on average. Thus, we strongly recommend against the use of averages when forecasting the larger items in a short-term cash forecast.

The situation is different in a medium-term forecast, since the time period is sufficiently far into the future to make it impossible to predict cash flows with any degree of precision. In this case, estimate based on averages, though with three enhancements:

- Insert specific cash flows that are very likely, such as contractually-mandated payments or receipts.
- Insert specific cash flows that have historically proven to be reliable. For example, if a customer has proven to be consistent in paying on a certain day of the month, assume that these payments will continue with the same timing.
- It may be possible to substitute actual cash flow information for averages in the least-distant time periods. This is particularly likely for cash outflows, such as payroll, where there is not a significant amount of change in the amount paid from period to period.

The Use of Clearing Dates in a Forecast

The overall intent of the cash forecast is to yield the best possible estimate of the amount of cash that is *available for use* on certain dates. This is an important issue, since a company may receive a check payment from a customer on one date, but not have use of the cash until several additional business days have passed. Similarly, the cash represented by an accounts payable check sent to a supplier may still be available to the company for a week or more, since there will be a delay associated with the transit time of the check to the supplier (mail float), as well as any in-house recordation delays at the supplier, and the time required for the check to clear the bank.

These delays in cash availability should be built into the cash forecast, but only if you can reliably predict the amount of cash that will be delayed and the duration of the delay. For example, it may be possible to predict the following distribution of checks expected to clear on the days following check issuance, where the distribution is built into the amount of cash disbursed through a check run:

Sample Forecast of Expected Check Clearing

Amount of Checks Issued	Business Days After Check Issuance	Percent Expected to Clear	Amount Expected to Clear	Day
$100,000				Monday
	1	5%	$5,000	Tuesday
	2	25%	25,000	Wednesday
	3	30%	30,000	Thursday
	4	20%	20,000	Friday
	5	15%	15,000	Monday
	6	5%	5,000	Tuesday
		100%	$100,000	

It is easiest to predict a standard number of days delay before deposited cash is made available. It is more difficult to predict the delay for accounts payable checks, since it involves the actions of the postal service and the payee; a conservative approach is to apply a minimum number of days delay to all payments issued.

The timing difference between the clearing date and recordation date is declining, since many companies have turned to electronic payments. In particular, the use of direct deposit for payroll payments means that there is essentially no delay in payments made to employees.

> **Tip:** If it is too complicated to incorporate clearing dates into the cash forecast, at least consider doing so for the largest individual cash inflows and outflows, so that a small amount of additional forecasting effort will still result in better timing accuracy for a significant part of the forecast.

Summary

The derivation of a revenue forecast, related budgets, and cash forecast are critical to the ongoing management of a business. However, these documents can also lead management to believe that future results and cash flows are likely to fall within a narrow range of possible outcomes. In all likelihood, actual results will routinely fall outside of this range, because of differences between planning assumptions and actual outcomes. You can prepare management for the possibility of these forecasting variations by routinely questioning planning assumptions and calculating a range of possible budget scenarios. With this more comprehensive set of outcomes in hand, management is better prepared to take action early to mitigate poor results or to take advantage of robust sales.

Chapter 17
Managing the Rate of Growth

Introduction

A common misconception among managers is that a high rate of growth is good for a business. In reality, excessive growth can trigger significant financial strains, which in turn can bankrupt a business. In this chapter, we address the factors that allow a company to increase its sales, a number of constraints on growth, the negative effects of growth on a business, and related topics.

The Funding of Growth

Whenever sales increase, it requires a certain amount of additional company resources to generate those sales. For example, increased sales may require the following:

- Additional fixed assets for a production line
- Additional production line workers
- Additional funding of accounts receivable for the additional sales
- Additional funding of inventory to support the additional sales

The following example illustrates just one element of the funding constraints that keep sales from growing.

EXAMPLE

Creekside Industrial is a new company that has patented a unique process that doubles the storage capacity of its batteries, which are designed for cell phones. Demand is strong, so the management team plans to double sales in the next year, from the current $6,000,000 level to $12,000,000. The industry's standard terms are net 45 days. In reality, Creekside is experiencing an average of 60 days for customers to pay their bills. The contribution margin on the batteries is 40%.

Creekside begins selling at the new $12,000,000 selling pace, which is a net increase of $500,000 per month. Creekside must invest an additional $300,000 in inventory (calculated as $500,000 of incremental sales per month × 60% cost of goods) to fund sales in each month. Since cash is not being received from customers for two months, this means that Creekside must come up with $600,000 of funding to support its inventory purchases for two months of sales at the new sales level.

If these added investments are needed to support sales, where will the cash come from? Some may come from the sale of existing products and services. However, this is only a large amount of cash if the contribution margin is quite high. Instead, a business may need to rely upon a significant amount of equity or debt funding in order to support additional sales. These and other funding concepts appear in the following table, which reveals the methods commonly used to generate the cash needed to expand sales.

Methods Used to Fund Growth

Action	Impact on Growth
Increase production efficiency	Increases the contribution margin per unit sold, which increases the amount of cash available to fund growth. This is a good option when producing in high volume, but tends to generate minimal margin increases when production volumes are low.
Increase inventory turnover	Reduces the investment in inventory, which increases the amount of cash available to fund growth. However, a reduction in finished goods inventory can *reduce* sales, if fast fulfillment is a key to customer satisfaction.
Increase receivable turnover	Reduces the investment in receivables, which makes more cash available for funding purposes. However, more active collection activities may turn away customers. Also, shortening payment terms may not be accepted by customers. If the seller requires cash in advance from its customers, this may prevent some sales from occurring.
Increase prices	Margins can be expanded by increasing the price of the product. However, this has the reverse effect of dampening additional sales, especially if customers are price-sensitive and there are competing products with similar features.
Eliminate cost objects	An excellent technique is to examine the contribution margins and related asset investments associated with each product, product line, and subsidiary to see if any of these cost objects are accumulating large amounts of cash investment without generating a corresponding amount of cash. If so, consider eliminating them and redirecting the resulting cash to fund more profitable products.
Outsource production	It may be possible to outsource production, in which case the company eliminates its investment in production facilities and staffing, though usually at the cost of an increased cost per unit. This option works best for those processes requiring large investments. However, the company will lose direct control over its production process.
Dividend payouts	Dividends can be eliminated or pared back in order to generate additional cash. However, this approach may run afoul of those investors who rely upon the dividends as a source of income. A possible result is a decline in the company's stock price, as income-targeted investors sell their shares.

Action	Impact on Growth
Debt to equity ratio	Management can agree to a higher proportion of debt to equity, so that the business can obtain more debt in relation to the amount of equity in the business. However, this decision assumes that lenders would be willing to lend additional funds at a reasonable rate of interest.

In a smaller business that does not actively plan its future financial position, it is likely that none of the preceding steps will be taken to support additional sales growth. Instead, the company will perpetually find itself short of cash, and will likely take more extreme short-term measures to support its growth, such as factoring, credit card debt, and greatly delayed payments to suppliers. If such a company does not eventually step back from its aggressive sales goals, it will eventually run completely out of cash, and may be forced into bankruptcy – despite impressive sales performance.

In short, the key to ongoing corporate growth is the ability to generate or procure a sufficient amount of cash to fund the growth. In the next section, we turn to the concept of the contribution margin, and how the cash generated by this margin directly relates to the rate of growth.

Contribution Margins and Sustainable Growth

A business may find that it cannot sell any additional equity or obtain debt at a reasonable price. If so, it must rely upon internal improvements to increase the amount of cash flow available to fund additional growth. If this is the case, a key concept is the contribution margin being earned on each product sold. Contribution margin is net sales, minus all costs directly associated with those sales. If the margin is low, then very little cash is being generated to fund additional growth. Conversely, if the margin is high, the resulting cash flows may be able to fund a significant rate of growth.

EXAMPLE

Laid Back Corporation sells business chairs. When the company first entered the market, it priced its chairs low in order to take market share away from competitors. As a result, Laid Back sells its chairs for $200 and earns an anemic $20 contribution margin on each sale, which is a 10% contribution margin. This means the direct cost of each chair sold is $180. If Laid Back wants to internally generate a sufficient amount of cash from operations to fund the materials for an additional chair, it must sell nine chairs (calculated as $20 contribution margin × nine units = $180).

If Laid Back instead earned a contribution margin of 30%, it would be generating $60 of cash per sale, which would require only one-third the number of unit sales to fund the production of an additional chair.

EXAMPLE

Norrona Software produces consumer-oriented software that it sells through a website. All purchases are downloaded, so no physical goods are sold. In this case, Norrona's contribution margin is 97%, where the 3% direct cost represents the credit card fee charged for each sale. Norrona's management can theoretically scale this company rapidly at little additional cost, since the contribution margin is astronomical, and the company only incurs a minor variable expense (the credit card fee) with each sale.

Organic Growth

Organic growth is the increase in sales of a business generated by those of its operations that were in existence at the beginning of the measurement period.

The concept is used to differentiate between sales generated from existing operations and those operations that were acquired during the measurement period. In particular, organic growth is used to determine whether existing operations are in a state of decline, neutral growth, or expansion. It is entirely possible that organic "growth" will actually be negative.

For example, a company may report 100% growth during a period, but further analysis may reveal that 95% of the growth was from sales attributable to an acquisition, and 5% to existing operations.

Organic growth can be caused by any of the following:

- An increase in prices
- An increase in units sold of existing products
- Sales of new products from existing operations
- Sales to new customers for products from existing operations
- Sales generated by new distribution channels

Organic growth nearly always refers to changes in revenue, but can be used in reference to changes in profitability or cash flows.

The organic growth concept is a solid growth strategy for many businesses. This approach depends on internally-generated growth, rather than through acquisitions, and is a particularly viable option for a business that does not have sufficient cash to acquire other entities. However, this type of growth tends to be rather slow, especially when compared to the massive sales gains that can be achieved through an acquisition strategy.

Step Costs and Sales Growth

When a business plans for growth, it should not assume that the cost of producing, marketing, selling, and servicing each additional unit will be the same as for the last unit sold. Instead, a business will likely address individual pockets of the market in turn, each of which requires some different expenditures that will impact the margins earned. If margins decline in some of these market segments, the internal cash flows needed to fund additional sales growth will also decline, thereby making it more difficult to expand as the overall sales level continues to rise.

The following bullet points reveal a number of instances where the actions required to obtain additional sales will require more costs that will reduce the profitability of a business:

- *Government sales.* A business currently sells in the business-to-business market, and elects to expand into the government market. Doing so requires that the company offer its best and lowest prices to the government at all times, which are lower than the average rates it charges in the B2B market. The company must also invest in a proposal writing department, as well as purchase bid bonds for each government contract.
- *Lower-credit customers.* A business currently sells to the most credit-worthy customers, and decides to obtain additional sales by also selling to those customers with weaker credit ratings. The bad debt expense associated with these additional sales will likely rise, so the company can expect fewer net profits from its sales into this new segment of the market.
- *Larger customers.* A company currently sells to a group of smaller customers, and wants to greatly expand its sales by selling to a large retail chain. However, this customer has the buying power to demand not only the lowest prices, but also the longest payment terms. The result can indeed be a sharp sales increase, but at the cost of much lower margins and a large investment in accounts receivable.
- *New territories.* A retail chain elects to expand beyond its original sales region. To do so, it must invest in a new warehousing system for the new region, a large increase in its delivery fleet, a regional director and her staff, and region-specific marketing. While these costs may eventually generate highly-profitable sales, the initial setup of the region will clearly involve a significant cash investment.
- *New sales channels.* If management wants to try selling through a new sales channel, it must hire the staff for that channel and invest in the related working capital and fixed assets. For example, a company that operates an Internet store might want to open up a chain of retail stores, which requires an investment in building leases, staff, inventory, and a supporting warehouse structure.
- *New products.* A company wants to offer a complete range of products to its customers, beyond the single product with which it originally began operations. Doing so requires an investment in design engineers, procurement staff, and a broader range of production equipment, as well as an investment in both raw materials and finished goods inventories.
- *Customization.* An organization finds that few competitors are willing to offer a customized solution to customers, and so begins providing a high level of customization. However, doing so means the company must maintain a staff of product designers. Also, the production process is rendered much more complex when every job is customized, so the company must

now invest in a job costing system and a large production planning staff. The production process also takes longer, so the investment in inventory increases.

Eventually, management may find that its only remaining choices for sales growth are in areas that yield minimal cash returns, and yet call for large asset investments. Also, management may feel that extending into new sales areas will make the business excessively unwieldy, with too much overhead and systems complexity. If so, it is time to discuss whether the business has reached the logical limit of its sales growth, and should now direct its cash flows toward the maintenance of existing margins, as well as returning cash to shareholders via stock repurchases or dividends.

Other Constraints on Growth

Thus far, we have implied that the primary factor restricting the rate of growth of a business is the availability of cash. If that were really the case, an aggressive management team could simply place a large stock offering, such as by going public or through a secondary offering, and then use this massive cash pile to obliterate the competition. Since we do not see such rapid expansion in the marketplace very often, there must be other reasons that prevent a business from adopting a high rate of growth.

One reason is staffing. If an organization provides services to customers, then it must employ a large number of people, each of which must be properly trained, or already have the requisite training. In addition, the business will experience a normal rate of employee turnover, so there must be an investment in additional recruiting activities just to maintain the current sales level. Staffing is a particular concern when highly specialized employees are needed, such as for a software development company. If the company cannot attract a sufficient number of employees who have a specific skill set, then it will not be able to sell their services to customers, and cannot grow.

EXAMPLE

Armadillo Industries sells body armor and metal plating for the protection of vehicles, which requires an intensive selling effort to the police departments and military entities that buy these items. Historically, Armadillo has noted that a salesperson can sell $1,000,000 of these items per year, so it budgets for the hiring of 10 more salespeople in order to increase its sales by $10,000,000. However, Armadillo's budgeting staff has not factored in the time required for new salespeople to be fully trained in the company's products, develop sales contacts, and work their way through customer purchasing processes. Also, three of the new recruits leave the company before their training is completed. The result is only $3,000,000 of new sales, with sales from this group increasing to $4,500,000 in the next year, and $7,000,000 in the following year.

Another constraint on growth is the marketing image that a company wants to convey. This is the primary growth restriction at the high end of the market, where a company intentionally imposes high prices in order to convey an image of exclusivity to its products. In this case, a business could even *reduce* its sales in order to maintain a proper balance of supply and demand at very high price points.

Yet another constraint can be the availability of raw materials or components. This is a particular problem when all available production is tied up in long-term supply contracts with competitors. In this case, a company may be forced to acquire what it needs on the open market at higher spot prices, which in turn drives down the contribution margin on goods sold. In this case, a common resolution is to redesign products that incorporate substitute materials that are in greater supply.

One of the more important constraints on growth is the concept of pacing. This is when there is a natural amount of time required to complete the rollout of a product, facility, or acquisition integration, which cannot be rushed. For example, if a bank acquires another bank, the acquirer may find that its integration team must always spend at least five days at each branch location of the acquiree, in order to complete a conversion of the computer systems to those of the acquirer. Similarly, the design process of a firm may mandate that only one new model is released per year. Though it may be possible to compress these pacing issues, they will likely still impact the growth rate of a business.

In short, there are a variety of reasons why a business will eventually find that it cannot grow any further, or that its rate of growth declines. Most organizations are perpetually constrained by the underlying reasons for reduced growth, and never return to their original rates of growth. If so, be sure to incorporate a realistic growth rate into the company's planning process that recognizes these constraints, so that the company is not perpetually pursuing a goal that it can never achieve.

Negative Effects of Excessive Growth

There are a number of reasons why an excessive rate of growth is not a good idea, and can even have a negative effect on the long-term prospects of a business. Consider the following issues:

- *Strain on employees.* When sales are growing at a high rate, it is difficult for employees to service customers and maintain systems properly, while also training new employees in their tasks. The result is usually an increased rate of employee turnover.
- *Product quality.* When management commits to a high rate of growth, there is ongoing pressure to meet new product release dates. A likely result is that some products are released with problems that may annoy customers, increase warranty costs, or even trigger product recalls.
- *Customer service.* The customer support function can be overwhelmed in a fast growth situation, especially when product quality has declined or the product manual is not clear about the functions of a product. This can be a particular concern when management attempts to save money by employing low-cost customer service people. Given the low rate of pay, these employ-

ees are less likely to remain with the company, and so have a reduced knowledge of its products.
- *Controls.* When a number of new locations are added to a growing business, it can be particularly difficult to consistently install a robust set of controls in all locations. The result can be fraud or just incorrect transaction processing, sometimes on such a scale that the viability of the entire entity is threatened.
- *Systems.* A smaller company can get away with relatively primitive systems to control its order entry, production, accounting, and shipping activities. As a business expands, all of these systems must be replaced with more robust enterprise-grade systems that are both expensive and difficult to install. The transition process to these systems can be painful, and may interrupt service to customers.
- *Culture.* The founders of a small business may go to great lengths to instill a certain culture among the employees. This culture may turn out to be the backbone of the business, engendering unusually high customer service levels and product innovation, as well as low employee turnover. If excessively rapid growth makes it difficult to maintain the culture, then the associated benefits will be lost.

For these reasons, a wise management team might consider setting its growth targets somewhat on the low side. By doing so, the day-to-day financial position of the business will be more tolerable, customer satisfaction will be higher, and employee turnover will be lower.

The Ideal Rate of Growth

There are formulas for determining the ideal rate of growth for a business which incorporate the amount of financial leverage, the profit margin, and the level of asset turnover. However, the result is extremely theoretical, and may lead management to believe that it can accomplish a higher rate of growth than is really practical. In particular, these formulas are based on the assumption that existing profit levels will continue into the future, which is rarely the case. Instead, profits are more likely to decline as management elects to sell into a broader array of markets, each of which requires additional expenditures.

Further, the level of asset turnover also changes as sales increase. For example, a company may begin by outsourcing its production to a supplier, and having the supplier drop ship goods directly to customers, resulting in no inventory investment for the seller. However, to increase sales, the company then elects to build a chain of retail stores, for which it must invest in inventory. Then the company also decides to sell to the federal government, which mandates that the company keep a large amount of goods on hand to meet warranty requirements – which calls for yet another investment in inventory. Consequently, asset turnover tends to change as a company enters into each new line of business in its pursuit of more sales.

For these reasons, we believe that the use of a formula to derive an average rate of growth is dangerous. A company's management may use such a growth rate to plan its sales for the next year, and find that any changes needed to obtain those sales make it more difficult to adhere to the historical growth rate. In short, an ideal long-term growth rate does not exist. Instead, focus on detailed financial modeling of the costs and adjusted inventory and receivable turnover rates that will be incurred as new sales are acquired, and also adjust the results for the many constraint issues noted earlier in this chapter.

Summary

Our key point of emphasis in this chapter has been reining in growth to a reasonable amount. It is only possible to adopt a modest rate of growth if management first realizes that there is a problem with accelerating growth beyond a certain level. This calls for ongoing modeling of what will happen to cash and debt levels at various growth rates, as well as an examination of what systemic and cultural issues will arise as growth continues over time. If management does not plan for a modest rate of growth, then it is likely that too-rapid expansion will engender a number of problems that may even threaten the continuing existence of the business.

Chapter 18
The Cost of Capital

Introduction

When a company makes a decision about how to invest its funds in various assets, part of the evaluation is based on the cost of those funds. This cost is known as the cost of capital. It is of some importance to be as precise as possible in deriving the cost of capital, since an incorrect measurement could lead to investments that yield excessively low returns, or foregone investments that would have generated returns in excess of the real cost of capital. In this chapter, we describe how the cost of capital is calculated and the ways in which the result can be skewed.

Cost of Capital Derivation

The cost of capital is the cost of funds for a business. Any investment of those funds must equal or exceed the cost of capital, or else investors in the business will experience a negative return on their investment, and the business may eventually fail.

The cost of capital is comprised of the cost of a company's debt, preferred stock, and common stock, which are then combined into a weighted average cost of capital. We will address the calculation of the cost of each of these components in this section at a simplified level, and then develop the concept in the following sections.

Cost of Debt

The cost of a company's debt is not just the average interest rate that it pays for all outstanding debt. Interest expense is tax-deductible, so reduce the interest rate by its tax impact. The calculation of the cost of debt is:

$$\frac{\text{Interest expense} \times (1 - \text{tax rate})}{\text{Amount of debt}} = \text{After-tax interest rate}$$

For example, if a company has $1,000,000 of outstanding debt at an interest rate of 6%, and its income tax rate is 35%, then its after-tax interest rate is:

$$\frac{\$60,000 \text{ interest expense} \times (1 - 35\% \text{ tax rate})}{\$1,000,000 \text{ of debt}} = 3.9\% \text{ after-tax interest rate}$$

The Cost of Capital

> **Tip:** If there are additional costs associated with debt, such as a placement fee, include this amount in the calculation of the interest rate being paid on the debt. The result will be a slight increase in the interest rate.

Cost of Preferred Stock

Preferred stock is the next component of the cost of capital. It is a form of equity that does not have to be repaid to the investor, but for which a dividend must be paid each year. This dividend is not tax-deductible to the company, so preferred stock is essentially a more expensive form of debt. The calculation of the cost of preferred stock is:

$$\frac{\text{Dividend expenditure}}{\text{Amount of preferred stock}} = \text{Preferred stock dividend rate}$$

For example, if a company has $2,000,000 of preferred stock that requires an annual dividend payment of $180,000, then the cost of the stock on a percentage basis is:

$$\frac{\$180,000 \text{ dividend expenditure}}{\$2,000,000 \text{ of preferred stock}} = 9\% \text{ preferred stock dividend rate}$$

Cost of Common Stock

The final component of the cost of capital is common stock, which is a more difficult calculation. The best way to calculate this cost is through the capital asset pricing model (CAPM). The CAPM is comprised of the following three elements:

1. The risk-free rate of return, which is usually considered the return on a U.S. government security.
2. The return on a group of securities considered to have an average risk level, such as the Standard & Poor's 500 or the Dow Jones Industrials. This is considered to be the premium that investors demand above the risk-free rate to invest in the stock market.
3. The beta of the company's stock, which defines the amount by which its stock returns vary from the returns of stocks having an average level of risk. A beta of 1.0 indicates average risk, while a higher figure indicates increased risk and a lower figure indicates reduced risk. Beta is available from a variety of research firms for most publicly-held companies.

The preceding component parts then plug into the following calculation of the cost of common stock:

$$\text{Risk-free return} + (\text{beta} \times (\text{average stock return} - \text{risk-free return})) = \text{Cost of common stock}$$

For example, if the risk-free return is 2%, the return on the Standard & Poor's 500 is 9%, and a company's beta is 1.2, the cost of its common stock would be:

$$\text{2\% risk-free return} + (1.2 \text{ beta} \times (9\% \text{ average stock return} - 2\% \text{ risk-free return})) = 10.4\% \text{ cost of common stock}$$

If a company is privately-held, there will be no beta information for it. Instead, select a publicly-held firm that is operationally and financially similar to the company, and use the beta for this proxy firm. Better yet, use an average of the betas for several similar publicly-held firms, thereby avoiding the risk of using a comparative beta that represents an outlier value.

Weighted Average Cost of Capital

After the cost of each element of the cost of capital has been determined, calculate the weighted average cost of capital (WACC), which is based on the amount of common stock, preferred stock, and debt outstanding at the end of the most recent reporting period. The following table shows how to conduct the calculation. Note that the weighted average of the various elements of the cost of capital in the sample calculation is 12%, which would then be used for the analysis of proposed investments, as described in the next few chapters.

Sample Cost of Capital Calculation

	Outstanding Amount	Interest Rate	Cost
Common stock	$10,000,000	15%	$1,500,000
Preferred stock	2,000,000	8%	160,000
Debt	4,500,000	7%	315,000
Totals	$16,500,000	**12%**	$1,975,000

This section has described the calculation of the WACC at a simplistic level. In the following two sections, we will describe how the inputs to the model can vary, and how the cost of capital can be adjusted for different situations.

Variations in the Cost of Capital

It can be quite difficult to derive an accurate cost of capital. This is not a minor issue, since the cost of capital is used to create discounted cash flow analyses for capital budgeting decisions. If the cost of capital is incorrect by even a small amount, this can alter management's decision to invest in a project. There are a number of ways in which the cost of capital may be incorrectly derived. For example, the following are all methods used to derive the cost of debt in the cost of capital formula:

- *The forecasted interest rate on the next new debt issuance.* This is the cost of the debt needed to fund the next round of capital projects, and so is the most relevant interest rate to include in the WACC formula.
- *The current average rate on debt outstanding.* This is the cost of debt needed to fund the *last* round of capital projects, which may not be applicable if interest rates have changed markedly in the meantime.
- *The historical rate of interest.* This may be the cost of debt that has been retired, and which may not have been applicable for the last few years.

There could be a particularly large difference between the historical and forecasted interest rate, which can result in a significant error in the derivation of the cost of capital. In most cases, the forecasted interest rate (which is the incremental rate) should be used.

A further error arises if the incorrect tax rate is used to derive the net cost of debt. The tax rate that should be used is the company's marginal tax rate that will apply to the specific investment transaction being contemplated. However, some organizations are more inclined to use their average tax rate, which could be significantly different.

The most difficult component of the cost of capital to calculate is the cost of equity, which means that this cost is the most likely to be wrong. Consider the following points:

- *Risk-free rate.* The risk-free rate is an input used to derive the cost of equity; but what is the risk-free rate? Most organizations use the interest rate on U.S. Treasury bonds as a proxy for the risk-free rate, but there is no agreement on which bond. The instruments chosen typically vary from the 90-day bill to the 30-year bond, which presents a wide range of interest rates. Further, some organizations derive an *average* rate from instruments having different maturities, while others may choose to use a *forecasted* U.S. Treasury rate. There may also be inconsistency in using different U.S. Treasury instruments over time.
- *Stock market premium.* The additional return over the risk-free rate that investors demand in order to invest in the stock market is also used to derive the cost of equity. There is a wide range in the assumed amount of this return. Once selected, companies are not in the habit of adjusting the rate, even though there may be changes over time in the comparative level of turmoil in the financial markets that would warrant an adjustment.
- *Beta.* Beta is the amount of variability in the value of a company's stock in comparison to the market. The level of beta will change over time, so there is an issue with the historical time period over which beta should be calculated. A short-duration calculation period may happen to include a radical swing in a company's stock price, which would trigger a high beta. However, a very long-term time horizon would tend to downplay any recent stock price volatility. Thus, the time period covered by the calculation can cause major differences in a company's beta, and therefore in its cost of capital.

We have thus far identified a variety of ways to modify the outcome of the components of the cost of capital. In addition, the assumptions used to assemble these components into a weighted average cost of capital can also result in different outcomes. The most common basis for deriving the WACC is to weight the components based on the book values of debt and equity. However, some organizations elect to derive the weighting based on one of these other methods:

- The targeted amounts of debt and equity that will be on the books as of a later date
- The current market values of debt and equity
- The current market value of debt and the book value of equity
- The book value of debt and the current market value of equity

Ideally, the current market values of debt and equity should be used to derive the WACC, since this most accurately reflects the current expectations of investors regarding the funding mix that the company employs. If management expects that the current round of funding will notably alter the mix of debt and equity, then it can incorporate these changes into its use of the current market values of debt and equity.

It may be acceptable to derive the WACC using the book value of debt, if the company is not expecting to obtain additional debt financing. In this case, the amount recorded on the books is indeed the company's actual cost of debt. The same cannot be said for the cost of equity, which is constantly changing as investors bid the price of a company's stock up or down in accordance with their current expectations for a return on investment.

The method chosen can lead to major differences in the weighting of the debt and equity components of the cost of capital. The problem is especially apparent when a business is in financial difficulties and at least one element of the weighting is based on market value, since the market value is likely to be far less than book value. The following example illustrates the issue.

EXAMPLE

Creekside Industrial issued debt and stock to the public five years ago, after which it has reported reduced financial results that have led investors to believe that the company will have difficulty surviving as an independent business. The result has been a significant decline in the market value of its debt and equity. However, since the bonds payable are classified as senior debt, investors have a reasonable chance of obtaining repayment, so the bonds have retained their value better than the components of equity.

The Cost of Capital

Creekside's CFO is now engaged in a review of the company's cost of capital. She creates the following table, which reveals the book value and market value of its funding sources, as well as their relative proportions:

(000s)	Book Value	Proportion of Total	Market Value	Proportion of Total
Bonds payable	$23,000	30%	$19,000	63%
Preferred stock	11,000	15%	3,000	10%
Common stock	42,000	55%	8,000	27%
Totals	$76,000	100%	$30,000	100%

Based on this information, the CFO derives the following weighted average cost of capital, based separately on book value and market value, which shows a significant 1.9% difference when the market values of debt and equity are employed.

	Book Value Weighting			Market Value Weighting		
	Cost	Weighting	Extended	Cost	Weighting	Extended
Bonds payable	6.0%	30%	1.8%	6.0%	63%	3.8%
Preferred stock	9.5%	15%	1.4%	9.5%	10%	1.0%
Common stock	12.5%	55%	6.9%	12.5%	27%	3.4%
Totals		100%	**10.1%**		100%	**8.2%**

The points made in this section should make it clear that achieving a precise cost of capital is difficult, given the extent to which assumptions can skew the measure. Consequently, it is of some importance to clarify the assumptions used in the derivation of the cost of capital and to update the calculation on a regular basis. Otherwise, an incorrect cost of capital will likely lead to non-optimal investment decisions.

Adjustments to the Cost of Capital

Even after the cost of capital has been derived, questions may be raised concerning when to use it, and when to adjust it. Consider the following situations:

- *Multi-unit business.* A larger corporation may have a number of operating units, each of which operates in environments with different risk characteristics. It may be tempting to derive a separate cost of capital for each of these units, but the calculation requires that each one acquire its own debt and have its shares publicly traded, which is rarely the case for a subsidiary. An alternative is to estimate what the cost of capital would be, based on a mix of comparable companies that are publicly held, and which operate primarily in the same markets as the subsidiary. The result will not be precise, but

could yield a better indication of the real cost of capital than the corporate rate.
- *Single investment.* What if funding is being obtained for a specific investment? For example, a utility issues bonds specifically to build a power plant. In this case, the after-tax cost of the debt used to buy the power plant should be considered the cost of capital for the purpose of making an investment decision about that specific project, rather than the weighted average cost of capital for the entire business.
- *Foreign investment.* What if a multi-national company wants to make an investment in a foreign location? One option is to use the cost of capital for the entire company, since a multi-national is comprised of a portfolio of investments (subsidiaries), which result in an aggregated portfolio risk that can be applied to investments everywhere. If this approach is used, it may be necessary to adjust the cost of capital for any relative difference in the inflation rate between the home and foreign currency. Another option is to derive a local cost of capital, on the grounds that each country has its own environmental factors, such as political risks and tax policy that can strongly influence the rate of return within that country. A third option is to apply a risk premium to the corporate cost of capital that is based on the risk factors in the foreign market. This risk premium is considered to be the interest rate on bonds issued by the foreign government, minus the interest rate on a risk-free bond issued by the home government, adjusted for the difference in the inflation rates of the home and foreign currencies.
- *Lending inefficiencies.* There may be times when it is difficult to obtain funds from a lender at a reasonable rate of interest, no matter how excellent a company's credit history may be. If so and there is variable-rate debt outstanding, the cost of capital should include the most recent interest rate, since that is the rate being charged to the company. Even if there is an expectation of a later decline in the interest rate, the only factual representation of the interest rate is the current inflated rate, which will apply to investments made in the near future.
- *Future expectations.* The beta component of the cost of equity is based on the historical results of a business. Management may feel that this beta figure is not valid, since it expects different results for the company in the future. However, the expectations of management do not always translate into actual results. Also, the market may continue to assign roughly the same beta to the company, simply because of the industry in which it is located. For these reasons, it is better to continue to use the existing beta, perhaps with a weighting that favors the most recent beta for the past year.

Cost of Capital as a Threshold Value

The primary use of the cost of capital is, as the name implies, to establish a cost for the funds that a business employs. Thus, if management is considering the acquisition of a fixed asset, it can judge the acquisition by comparing its projected return on investment to the cost of capital. If the projected return is less than the cost of capital, then the acquisition should be rejected, on the grounds that the cost of the funds required to buy the asset will exceed the return expected from the investment.

Given the variability in the calculation of the cost of capital, as noted earlier, some managers are reluctant to rely upon the cost of capital as a decision threshold. Instead, they may arbitrarily add several percentage points onto the cost of capital and use the result as the threshold for investment decisions. The reasons for doing so include:

- The higher rate allows for any errors that may have been incorporated into the cost of capital.
- The higher rate allows for any errors in the derivation of the capital budgeting proposals being judged.
- The higher rate acknowledges the existence of some investments that have no return at all (such as to meet regulatory requirements), so that other investments must generate a higher return in order to arrive at an average return for all investments that exceeds the cost of capital.

However, arbitrarily adding a few percentage points to the cost of capital reduces the level of quantitative rigor used to evaluate an investment. A better approach is to recognize what the upper and lower boundaries of the cost of capital may be, and to review investment proposals based on these two values.

The cost of capital may also be adjusted based on the perceived risk of a proposed investment. For example, the threshold value may be the cost of capital when a proposed investment pertains to an existing product line, but the threshold is increased by 5% if the investment is for an entirely new product in an untested market. This approach can be used to incorporate a high level of conservatism into the evaluation of riskier projects. However, at some point management must consciously invest in the strategic direction of the business, rather than relying upon quantitative measures to tell it where to spend money. For such strategic decisions, many other factors than the cost of capital must be considered, including the level of competition, government regulations, technology issues, and the perceived duration of any market opportunities.

Summary

This chapter showed how easy it is to derive a cost of capital that is excessively high or low, depending on the assumptions used in the calculation. The cost of capital is a key component of the decision making processes described in the next few chapters, so be sure to spend as much time as possible questioning every aspect of your derived cost of capital. Hopefully, a rigorous review will yield a value that requires minimal inflation to guard against a mistake. Also, it is entirely possible that only a range of values can be derived for the cost of capital, rather than a single figure. If so, it may be necessary to use this range of values when examining investment alternatives, which may make it difficult to reach a purely quantitative decision.

Chapter 19
Discounted Cash Flow Techniques

Introduction

When evaluating investments, it is critical to understand the time value of money, and how it relates to the analysis of cash flows. In this chapter, we address the time value of money concept and describe present and future value tables, followed by descriptions of two discounted cash flow techniques – net present value and the internal rate of return. We also make note of terminal value and the types of information that should be included in a cash flow analysis.

> **Related Podcast Episodes:** Episodes 147 and 214 of the Accounting Best Practices Podcast discuss net present value analysis and issues with discounted cash flows, respectively. The episodes are available at: **accountingtools.com/podcasts** or **iTunes**

Time Value of Money

The foundation of discounted cash flow analysis is the concept that cash received today is more valuable than cash received at some point in the future. The reason is that someone who agrees to receive payment at a later date foregoes the ability to invest that cash right now. The only way for someone to agree to a delayed payment is to pay them for the privilege, which is known as interest income.

For example, if a person owns $10,000 now and invests it at an interest rate of 10%, then she will have earned $1,000 by having use of the money for one year. If she were instead to *not* have access to that cash for one year, then she would lose the $1,000 of interest income. The interest income in this example represents the time value of money.

To extend the example, what is the current payout of cash at which the person would be indifferent to receiving cash now or in one year? In essence, what is the amount that, when invested at 10%, will equal $10,000 in one year? The general formula used to answer this question, known as the *present value of 1 due in N periods*, is:

$$\frac{1}{(1 + \text{Interest rate})^{\text{Number of years}}}$$

Discounted Cash Flow Techniques

The calculation for the example is:

$$\frac{\$10,000}{(1 + 10\%)^{1 \text{ year}}} = \$9,090.91$$

In essence, if the person receives $9,090.91 now and invests it at a 10% interest rate, her cash balance will have increased to $10,000 in one year.

The effect of the present value formula becomes more pronounced if the receipt of cash is delayed to a date even further in the future, because the period during which the recipient of the cash cannot invest the cash is prolonged.

The concept of the time value of money also works in reverse, for expenditures. There is a monetary value associated with delaying the payment of cash, which is known as the *future amount of 1 due in N periods*. The general formula used to address this situation is:

$$\text{Amount deferred} \times (1 + \text{Interest rate})^{\text{Number of years}}$$

For example, if a person could delay the expenditure of $10,000 for one year and could invest the funds during that year at a 10% interest rate, the value of the deferred expenditure would be $11,000 in one year.

One of the common uses of the time value of money is to derive the present value of an annuity. An annuity is a series of payments that occur in the same amounts and at the same intervals over a period of time. An annuity is a common feature of a capital budgeting analysis, where a consistent stream of cash flows is expected for multiple years if a fixed asset is purchased. For example, a company is contemplating the purchase of a production line for $3,000,000, which will generate net positive cash flows of $1,000,000 per year for the next five years. This stream of incoming cash flows is an annuity. The formula used to derive the present value of an *ordinary annuity of 1 per period* is:

$$\frac{1 - \dfrac{1}{(1 + \text{Interest rate})^{\text{Number of years}}}}{\text{Interest rate}}$$

The preceding formula is for an *ordinary annuity*, which is an annuity where payments are made at the end of each period. If cash were instead received at the beginning of each period, the annuity would be called an *annuity due*, and would be formulated somewhat differently.

Present and Future Value Tables

In the last section, we discussed the general concept of the time value of money, and how this value can be translated into the present value formula. The concept is most commonly employed in an electronic spreadsheet. For example, the present value formula in Excel is:

$$(1/(1+\text{Interest rate})^{\wedge}\text{Number of years})$$

As an example, if the discount rate is 10% and you want to determine the discount for cash flows that will occur three years in the future, the Excel calculation is:

$$(1/(1+0.1)^{\wedge}3) = 0.75131$$

The easiest way to calculate present value is to use the preceding formula in Excel for the monetary amount and time period in question. However, what if an electronic spreadsheet is not available? The present value discount factor can also be derived from a present value table, which is commonly available in textbooks and on the Internet. The following present value table states the discount factors for the present value of 1 due in N periods for a common range of interest rates.

Present Value Factors for 1 Due in N Periods

Number of Years	6%	7%	8%	9%	10%	11%	12%
1	0.9434	0.9346	0.9259	0.9174	0.9091	0.9009	0.8929
2	0.8900	0.8734	0.8573	0.8417	0.8265	0.8116	0.7972
3	0.8396	0.8163	0.7938	0.7722	0.7513	0.7312	0.7118
4	0.7921	0.7629	0.7350	0.7084	0.6830	0.6587	0.6355
5	0.7473	0.7130	0.6806	0.6499	0.6209	0.5935	0.5674
6	0.7050	0.6663	0.6302	0.5963	0.5645	0.5346	0.5066
7	0.6651	0.6228	0.5835	0.5470	0.5132	0.4817	0.4524
8	0.6274	0.5820	0.5403	0.5019	0.4665	0.4339	0.4039
9	0.5919	0.5439	0.5003	0.4604	0.4241	0.3909	0.3606
10	0.5584	0.5084	0.4632	0.4224	0.3855	0.3522	0.3220
11	0.5268	0.4751	0.4289	0.3875	0.3505	0.3173	0.2875
12	0.4970	0.4440	0.3971	0.3555	0.3186	0.2858	0.2567
13	0.4688	0.4150	0.3677	0.3262	0.2897	0.2575	0.2292
14	0.4423	0.3878	0.3405	0.2993	0.2633	0.2320	0.2046
15	0.4173	0.3625	0.3152	0.2745	0.2394	0.2090	0.1827

To use the table, move to the column representing the relevant interest rate, and move down to the "number of years" row indicating the discount rate to apply to the applicable year of cash flow. Thus, if an analysis were to indicate $100,000 of cash

Discounted Cash Flow Techniques

flow in the fourth year, and the interest rate were 10%, you would multiply the $100,000 by 0.6830 to arrive at a present value of $68,300 for those cash flows.

The same type of table format is available for determining the future amount of 1 due in N periods. This table is used to derive the amount that you would accept on a future date in exchange for delaying the receipt of cash. The multipliers for this calculation are noted in the following table:

Future Value Factors for 1 Due in N Periods

Number of Years	6%	7%	8%	9%	10%	11%	12%
1	1.0600	1.0700	1.0800	1.0900	1.1000	1.1100	1.1200
2	1.1236	1.1449	1.1664	1.1881	1.2100	1.2321	1.2544
3	1.1910	1.2250	1.2597	1.2950	1.3310	1.3676	1.4049
4	1.2625	1.3108	1.3605	1.4116	1.4641	1.5181	1.5735
5	1.3382	1.4026	1.4693	1.5386	1.6105	1.6851	1.7623
6	1.4185	1.5007	1.5869	1.6771	1.7716	1.8704	1.9738
7	1.5036	1.6058	1.7138	1.8280	1.9487	2.0762	2.2109
8	1.5939	1.7182	1.8509	1.9926	2.1436	2.3045	2.4760
9	1.6895	1.8385	1.9990	2.1719	2.3580	2.5580	2.7731
10	1.7909	1.9672	2.1589	2.3674	2.5937	2.8394	3.1059
11	1.8983	2.1049	2.3316	2.5804	2.8531	3.1518	3.4786
12	2.0122	2.2522	2.5182	2.8127	3.1384	3.4985	3.8960
13	2.1329	2.4099	2.7196	3.0658	3.4523	3.8833	4.3635
14	2.2609	2.5785	2.9372	3.3417	3.7975	4.3104	4.8871
15	2.3966	2.7590	3.1722	3.6425	4.1773	4.7860	5.4736

To use the table, move to the column representing the relevant interest rate, and move down to the "number of years" row indicating the multiplier to apply to the applicable year of cash flow. Thus, if the option were available to delay the receipt of $10,000 for five years, and the funds could be invested at 8% in the meantime, multiply the $10,000 by 1.4693 to arrive at a future value of $14,693 for those cash flows.

The same table format is also available for determining the present value of an ordinary annuity of 1 per period. This table is used to derive the present value of a series of annuity payments. The multipliers for this calculation are noted in the following table.

Discounted Cash Flow Techniques

Present Value Factors for Ordinary Annuity of 1 per Period

Number of Years	6%	7%	8%	9%	10%	11%	12%
1	0.9434	0.9346	0.9259	0.9174	0.9091	0.9009	0.8929
2	1.8334	1.8080	1.7833	1.7591	1.7355	1.7125	1.6901
3	2.6730	2.6243	2.5771	2.5313	2.4869	2.4437	2.4018
4	3.4651	3.3872	3.3121	3.2397	3.1699	3.1024	3.0373
5	4.2124	4.1002	3.9927	3.8897	3.7908	3.6959	3.6048
6	4.9173	4.7665	4.6229	4.4859	4.3553	4.2305	4.1114
7	5.5824	5.3893	5.2064	5.0330	4.8684	4.7122	4.5638
8	6.2098	5.9713	5.7466	5.5348	5.3349	5.1461	4.9676
9	6.8017	6.5152	6.2469	5.9952	5.7590	5.5370	5.3282
10	7.3601	7.0236	6.7101	6.4177	6.1446	5.8892	5.6502
11	7.8869	7.4987	7.1390	6.8052	6.4951	6.2065	5.9377
12	8.3838	7.9427	7.5361	7.1607	6.8137	6.4924	6.1944
13	8.8527	8.3577	7.9038	7.4869	7.1034	6.7499	6.4235
14	9.2950	8.7455	8.2442	7.7862	7.3667	6.9819	6.6282
15	9.7122	9.1079	8.5595	8.0607	7.6061	7.1909	6.8109

The annuity table contains a multiplier specific to the number of payments over which you expect to receive a series of equal payments and at a certain discount rate. When this factor is multiplied by one of the payments, you arrive at the present value of the stream of payments. For example, if you expect to receive five payments of $10,000 each and use a discount rate of 8%, then the factor would be 3.9927 (as noted in the preceding table in the intersection of the 8% column and the row for five years). Then multiply the 3.9927 factor by $10,000 to arrive at a present value of the annuity of $39,927.

Net Present Value

Net present value (NPV) analysis is useful for determining the current value of a stream of cash flows that extend out into the future. It can also be used to compare several such cash flows to decide which has the largest present value. NPV is commonly used in the analysis of capital purchasing requests, to see if an initial payment for fixed assets and other expenditures will generate net positive cash flows.

To calculate net present value, we use the following formula:

$$NPV = X \times [(1+r)^n - 1]/[r \times (1+r)^n]$$

Discounted Cash Flow Techniques

Where:

    X = The amount received per period
    n = The number of periods
    r = The rate of return

It is not that difficult to estimate the amount of cash received per period, as well as the number of periods over which cash will be received. The difficult inclusion in the formula is the rate of return. This is generally considered to be a company's average cost of capital (as described in the Cost of Capital chapter), but can also be considered its incremental cost of capital, or a risk-adjusted cost of capital. In the latter case, this means that several extra percentage points are added to the corporate cost of capital for those cash flow situations considered to be unusually risky.

EXAMPLE

The CFO of Franklin Drilling is interested in the NPV associated with a production facility that the CEO wants to acquire. In exchange for an initial $10 million payment, Franklin should receive payments of $1.2 million at the end of each of the next 15 years. Franklin has a corporate cost of capital of 9%. To calculate the NPV, we insert the cash flow information into the NPV formula:

$$1{,}200{,}000 \times ((1+0.09)^{15}-1)/(0.09 \times (1+0.09)^{15}) = \$9{,}672{,}826$$

The present value of the cash flows associated with the investment is $327,174 lower than the initial investment in the facility, so Franklin should not proceed with the investment.

The NPV calculation can be massively more complicated than the simplified example just shown. In reality, you may need to include the present values of the cash flows related to the following additional items:

- Ongoing expenditures related to the investment
- Variable amounts of cash flow being received over time, rather than the same amount every time
- Variable timing for the receipt of cash, rather than the consistent receipt of a payment on the same date
- The amount of working capital required for the project, as well as the release of working capital at the end of the project
- The amount at which the investment can be resold at the end of its useful life
- The tax value of depreciation on the fixed asset that was purchased

All of the preceding factors should be considered when evaluating NPV for an investment proposal. In addition, consider generating several models to account for the worst case, most likely, and best case scenarios for cash flows.

Internal Rate of Return

The internal rate of return (IRR) is the rate of return at which the present value of a series of future cash flows equals the present value of all associated costs. IRR is commonly used in capital budgeting to discern the rate of return on the estimated cash flows arising from an expected investment. The project having the highest IRR is selected for investment purposes.

The easiest way to calculate the internal rate of return is to open Microsoft Excel and then follow these steps:

1. Enter in any cell a negative figure that is the amount of cash outflow in the first period. This is normal when acquiring fixed assets, since there is an initial expenditure to acquire and install the asset.
2. Enter the subsequent cash flows for each period following the initial expenditure in the cells immediately below the cell where the initial cash outflow figure was entered.
3. Access the IRR function and specify the cell range into which you just made entries. The internal rate of return will be calculated automatically. It may be useful to use the Increase Decimal function to increase the number of decimal places appearing in the calculated internal rate of return.

As an example, a company is reviewing a possible investment for which there is an initial expected investment of $20,000 in the first year, followed by incoming cash flows of $12,000, $7,000 and $4,000 in the next three years. If this information is entered into the Excel IRR function, it returns an IRR of 8.965%.

The IRR formula in Excel is extremely useful for quickly deriving a possible rate of return. However, it can be used for a less ethical purpose, which is to artificially model the correct amounts and timing of cash flows to produce an IRR that meets a company's capital budgeting guidelines. In this case, a manager is fudging the results in his or her cash flow model in order to gain acceptance of a project, despite knowing that it may not be possible to achieve those cash flows.

Incremental Internal Rate of Return

The incremental internal rate of return is an analysis of the financial returns where there are two competing investment opportunities involving different amounts of investment. The analysis is applied to the difference between the costs of the two investments. Thus, subtract the cash flows associated with the less expensive alternative from the cash flows associated with the more expensive alternative to arrive at the cash flows applicable to the difference between the two alternatives, and then conduct an internal rate of return analysis on this difference.

Based just on quantitative analysis, select the more expensive investment opportunity if it has an incremental internal rate of return higher than the minimum return considered acceptable. However, there are qualitative issues to consider as well, such as whether there is an incremental increase in risk associated with the more expensive investment.

If you believe there is additional risk associated with the more expensive investment opportunity, then adjust for this risk by increasing the minimum return considered acceptable. For example, the minimum rate of return threshold for a low-risk investment might be 5%, while the threshold might be 10% for a high-risk investment.

EXAMPLE

Hassle Corporation is considering obtaining a color copier, and it can do so either with a lease or an outright purchase. The lease involves a series of payments over the three-year useful life of the copier, while the purchase option involves more cash up-front and some continuing maintenance, but it also has a resale value at the end of its useful life. The following analysis of the incremental differences in the cash flows between the two alternatives reveals that there is a positive incremental internal rate of return for the purchasing option. Barring any other issues (such as available cash to buy the copier), the purchasing option therefore appears to be the better alternative.

Year	Lease	Buy	Difference
0	-$7,000	-$29,000	-$22,000
1	-7,000	-1,500	5,500
2	-7,000	-1,500	5,500
3	-7,000	-1,500	5,500
Resale		+15,000	15,000
		Incremental IRR	13.3%

Terminal Value

The cash flows associated with an analysis may not have a discernible time horizon – that is, there is no expectation that they will end. In this case, it is customary to derive a terminal value, which is the aggregation of all cash flows beyond the date range for which cash flows are being predicted. Terminal value can be calculated with the *perpetuity formula*, which employs the following steps:

1. Estimate the cash flows associated with the final year of projections, and eliminate from this amount any unusual items that are not expected to occur again in later years.
2. Estimate a reasonable growth rate for this adjusted cash flow figure for later years. The amount should approximate the rate of growth for the entire economy. The rate of sustainable growth should be quite small, and may even be zero or a negative figure.
3. Subtract this growth rate from the company's weighted-average cost of capital (WACC), as derived in the Cost of Capital chapter, and divide the result into the adjusted cash flows for the final year. The formula is:

Discounted Cash Flow Techniques

$$\frac{\text{Adjusted final year cash flow}}{\text{WACC} - \text{Growth rate}} = \text{Terminal value}$$

EXAMPLE

Glow Atomic is reviewing the projected income stream from a new type of fusion plant that could generate electricity in perpetuity. The analysis is broken into annual cash flows for the first 20 years, followed by a terminal value. The expected cash flow for the 20th year is $10,000,000. Glow expects these cash flows to increase at a rate of 1% thereafter. The company has a 15% WACC. Based on this information, the terminal value of the investment opportunity is:

$$\frac{\$10,000,000 \text{ final year cash flow}}{15\% \text{ WACC} - 1\% \text{ growth rate}} = \$71,429,000 \text{ Terminal value}$$

Inclusions in Cash Flow Analysis

There can be a number of variations on the possible cash flows associated with a business decision, making the present value calculation more difficult to derive. The following factors may also need to be considered:

- *Cash from sale of asset*. If an asset is to be purchased, also assume that some cash will be received at a later date from the eventual sale of that asset.
- *Maintenance costs*. If there will be incremental costs incurred to maintain a purchased asset, include the cash flows associated with these costs. Do not include any cash flows related to maintenance personnel who will still be paid, irrespective of the presence of the asset.
- *Working capital*. If there will be an incremental change in the amount invested in accounts receivable or inventory as the result of a purchase decision, include these cash flows in the analysis. If the asset is to be eventually sold off, this may mean that the related working capital investment will be terminated at the same time.
- *Tax payments*. Include any property taxes related to assets that are acquired. Also, include the amount of any incremental income taxes paid, if the acquired asset generates profits.
- *Depreciation effect*. Include the effect on income taxes paid of the depreciation expense associated with an acquired asset. This effect is caused by the tax deductibility of depreciation.

In short, discounted cash flow analysis is an effective way to aggregate and review the cash flows associated with a business decision that are spread over a number of time periods, though some analysis may be required to ensure that all of the relevant cash flows have been included.

Summary

Discounted cash flow is one of the key components of financial analysis. In the next chapter, we will combine the concepts of discounted cash flow with the corporate cost of capital to engage in the analysis of capital budgeting decisions. While discounted cash flow is not the only way to review requests to acquire fixed assets (and is not necessarily the best method), it is considered one of the primary capital budgeting techniques. Consequently, be familiar with how discounted cash flows are constructed and the situations in which they can be used.

Chapter 20
Capital Budgeting

Introduction

The decision to purchase a fixed asset is a key part of financial analysis, since some fixed assets may absorb the bulk of a company's available cash. Given the importance of this decision, a methodology for analyzing fixed asset purchases, called capital budgeting, has been developed.

Capital budgeting is a series of analysis steps followed to justify the decision to purchase an asset, usually including an analysis of the costs, related benefits, and impact on capacity levels of the prospective purchase. In this chapter, we will address the issues to consider when deciding whether to purchase a fixed asset, incorporating information already discussed in the Constraint Analysis and Discounted Cash Flow Techniques chapters.

> **Related Podcast Episodes:** Episodes 45, 144, 145, and 147 of the Accounting Best Practices Podcast discuss throughput analysis, evaluating capital budgeting proposals, capital budgeting with minimal cash, and net present value analysis, respectively. These episodes are available at: **accountingtools.com/podcasts** or **iTunes**

Overview of Capital Budgeting

The normal capital budgeting process is for the management team to request proposals to acquire fixed assets from all parts of the company. Managers respond by filling out a standard request form, outlining what they want to buy and how it will benefit the company. The financial analyst then assists in reviewing these proposals to determine which are worthy of an investment. Any proposals that are accepted are included in the annual budget, and will be purchased during the next budget year. Fixed assets purchased in this manner also require a certain number of approvals, with more approvals required by increasingly senior levels of management if the sums involved are substantial.

These proposals come from all over the company, and so are likely not related to each other in any way. Also, the number of proposals usually far exceeds the amount of funding available. Consequently, management needs a method for ranking the priority of projects, with the possible result that some proposals are not accepted at all. The traditional method for doing so is discounted cash flow analysis, for which the net present value and internal rate of return techniques were covered in the Discounted Cash Flow Techniques chapter.

The trouble with discounted cash flow analysis is that it does not account for how an investment might impact the profit generated by the entire system of production; instead, it tends to favor the optimization of specific work centers, which may have no particular impact on overall profitability. Also, the results of discounted cash flows are based on the future projections of cash flows, which may be wildly inaccurate. Managers may even tweak their cash flow estimates upward in order to gain project approval, when they know that actual cash flows are likely to be lower. Given these issues, we favor constraint analysis over discounted cash flows.

Constraint analysis focuses on how to maximize use of the bottleneck operation. The bottleneck operation is the most constricted operation in a company; to improve the overall profitability of the company, concentrate all attention on management of that bottleneck. This has a profound impact on capital budgeting, since a proposal should have some favorable impact on that operation in order to be approved. Constraint analysis is covered in the Constraint Analysis chapter.

There are two scenarios under which certain project proposals may avoid any kind of bottleneck or cash flow analysis. The first is a legal requirement to install an item. The prime example is environmental equipment, such as smokestack scrubbers, that are mandated by the government. In such cases, there may be some analysis to see if costs can be lowered, but the proposal *must* be accepted, so it will sidestep the normal analysis process.

The second scenario is when a company wants to mitigate a high-risk situation that could imperil the company. In this case, the emphasis is not on profitability at all, but rather on the avoidance of a situation. If so, the mandate likely comes from top management, so there is little additional need for analysis, other than a review to ensure that the lowest-cost alternative is selected.

A final scenario is when there is a sudden need for a fixed asset, perhaps due to the catastrophic failure of existing equipment, or due to a sudden strategic shift. These purchases can happen at any time, and so usually fall outside of the capital budget's annual planning cycle. It is generally best to require more than the normal number of approvals for these items, so that management is made fully aware of the situation. Also, if there is time to do so, they are worthy of an unusually intensive analysis, to see if they really must be purchased at once, or if they can be delayed until the next capital budgeting approval period arrives.

Once all items are properly approved and inserted into the annual budget, this does not end the capital budgeting process. There is a final review just prior to actually making each purchase, with appropriate approval, to ensure that the company still needs each fixed asset.

The last step in the capital budgeting process is to conduct a post-implementation review, in which you summarize the actual costs and benefits of each fixed asset, and compare these results to the initial projections included in the original application. If the results are worse than expected, this may result in a more in-depth review, with particular attention being paid to avoiding any faulty aspects of the original proposal in future proposals.

The Capital Request Form

The capital request form is used to standardize the types of information submitted when a fixed asset is to be acquired. It is intended to provide a summary that identifies a proposed fixed asset, why it is needed, and its impact on the business. The following sample shows how the form could be structured, though it may need to be modified to meet the specific needs of a business. This form is typically treated as a cover page, with additional analyses attached that may cover a number of additional pages.

Sample Capital Request Application

Capital Request Form

Project Name	Project Number		
Project Sponsor	Sponsor Contact Information		Submission Date

Project Type
- ☐ Constraint improvement
- ☐ Cost reduction
- ☐ Environmental/legal requirement
- ☐ Risk reduction
- ☐ Scheduled equipment replacement
- ☐ Other

Project Description

Description Block

Financial Summary

Year 1 Revenue	-	Year 1 Expenses	=	Year 1 Cash Flow
Year 2 Revenue	-	Year 2 Expenses	=	Year 2 Cash Flow
Year 3 Revenue	-	Year 3 Expenses	=	Year 3 Cash Flow

Net Present Value | Internal Rate of Return | Payback Period

Constraint Summary

- Throughput Impact
- Operating Expenses Impact
- ROI Impact

Approvals

All proposals	Financial analyst signature	Attorney signature
< $25,000	Department manager signature	
$25,000+	CEO signature	

The "Project Type" selected on the form dictates the type of analysis that will be applied to the proposal. A constraint improvement will be examined based on the impact of the proposal on company throughput, cost reductions, and/or return on investment. Discounted cash flow analysis can be applied to cost reduction investments, while several of the other project types indicate that the company is required to make an investment, irrespective of the level of return (if any) on the investment.

The Payback Method

The most discerning method for evaluating a capital budgeting proposal is its impact on the bottleneck operation, while discounted cash flow analysis yields a detailed analysis of cash flows. These concepts are discussed in other chapters. The simplest and least accurate evaluation technique is the payback method. This approach is still heavily used, because it provides a very fast "back of the envelope" calculation of how soon a company will earn back its investment. This means that payback provides a rough measure of how long a company will have its investment at risk, before earning back the original amount expended. There are two ways to calculate the payback period, which are:

1. *Simplified.* Divide the total amount of an investment by the average resulting cash flow. This approach can yield an incorrect assessment, because a proposal with cash flows skewed far into the future can yield a payback period that differs substantially from when actual payback occurs.
2. *Manual calculation.* Manually deduct the forecasted positive cash flows from the initial investment amount, from Year 1 forward, until the investment is paid back. This method is slower, but ensures a higher degree of accuracy.

EXAMPLE

Milford Sound has received a proposal from a manager, asking to spend $1,500,000 on equipment that will result in cash inflows in accordance with the following table:

Year	Cash Flow
1	+$150,000
2	+150,000
3	+200,000
4	+600,000
5	+900,000

The total cash flows over the five-year period are projected to be $2,000,000, which is an average of $400,000 per year. When divided into the $1,500,000 original investment, this results in a payback period of 3.75 years. However, the briefest perusal of the projected cash flows reveals that the flows are heavily weighted toward the far end of the time period, so the results of this calculation cannot be correct.

Instead, run the calculation year by year, deducting the cash flows in each successive year from the remaining investment. The results of this calculation are:

Year	Cash Flow	Net Invested Cash
0		-$1,500,000
1	+$150,000	-1,350,000
2	+150,000	-1,200,000
3	+200,000	-1,000,000
4	+600,000	-400,000
5	+900,000	0

The table indicates that the real payback period is located somewhere between Year 4 and Year 5. There is $400,000 of investment yet to be paid back at the end of Year 4, and there is $900,000 of cash flow projected for Year 5. If you assume the same monthly amount of cash flow in Year 5, the final payback should be just short of 4.5 years.

The payback method is not overly accurate, does not provide any estimate of how profitable a project may be, and does not take account of the time value of money. Nonetheless, its extreme simplicity makes it a perennial favorite in many companies.

The accuracy of the payback method can be improved by incorporating the time value of money into the cash flows expected in each future year. However, doing so increases the complexity of this analysis method. To apply the time value of money to the calculation, follow these steps:

1. Create a table in which is listed the expected cash outflow related to the investment in Year 0.
2. In the following lines of the table, enter the cash inflows expected from the investment in each subsequent year.
3. Multiply the expected annual cash inflows in each year in the table by the applicable discount rate, using the same interest rate for all of the periods in the table. No discount rate is applied to the initial investment, since it occurs at once.
4. Create a column on the far right side of the table that lists the cumulative discounted cash flow for each year. The calculation in this final column is to add back the discounted cash flow in each period to the remaining negative balance from the preceding period. The balance is initially negative because it includes the cash outflow to fund the project.
5. When the cumulative discounted cash flow becomes positive, the time period that has passed up until that point represents the payback period.

EXAMPLE

We will continue with the preceding example. Milford Sound has a cost of capital of 7%, so the present value factor for 7% (see the Discounted Cash Flow Techniques chapter) is included in the payback table, with the following results:

Year	Cash Flow	7% Present Value Factor	Cash Flow Present Value	Net Invested Cash
0				-$1,500,000
1	+$150,000	0.9346	+$140,190	-1,359,810
2	+150,000	0.8734	+131,010	-1,228,800
3	+200,000	0.8163	+163,260	-1,065,540
4	+600,000	0.7629	+457,740	-607,800
5	+900,000	0.7130	+641,700	-33,900

The discounted payback calculation reveals that the payback period will be slightly longer than the five years of cash flows presented in the manager's original proposal.

Real Options

Another way to review a capital budgeting decision is to examine the value embedded in different strategic alternatives. This concept is known as a *real option*, which refers to the decision options available for a tangible asset. Most businesses ignore the real option concept, instead choosing to construct a net present value analysis for a single possible outcome. Instead, use the real options concept to examine a whole range of outcomes. For example, a traditional investment analysis in an oil refinery would probably use a single price per barrel of oil for the entire investment period, whereas the actual price of oil will likely fluctuate far outside of the initial estimated price point over the course of the investment. An analysis based on real options would instead focus on the range of profits and losses that may be encountered over the course of the investment period as the price of oil changes over time.

A comprehensive real options analysis begins with a review of the risks to which a project will be subjected, and then models for each of these risks or combinations of risks. To continue with the preceding example, an investor in an oil refinery project could expand the scope of the analysis beyond the price of oil, to also encompass the risks of possible new environmental regulations on the facility, the possible downtime caused by a supply shutdown, and the risk of damage caused by a hurricane.

A logical outcome of real options analysis is to be more careful in placing large bets on a single likelihood of probability. Instead, it can make more sense to place a series of small bets on different outcomes, and then alter the portfolio of investments over time, as more information about the various risks becomes available. Once the key risks have been resolved, the best investment is easier to discern, so that a "bet the bank" investment can be made.

EXAMPLE

An agriculture company wants to develop a new crop strain for either wheat or barley, to be sold for export. The primary intended market is an area in which wheat is currently the preferred crop. The company estimates that it can generate a 20% return on investment by developing a new wheat variant at a cost of $30 million. Since wheat is already the primary type of crop being planted, the odds of success are high. However, if the company can successfully develop a barley variant at a total cost of $50 million, its projected profits are 50%. The key risk with the barley project is farmer acceptance. Given the high profits that could be derived from selling barley, the company makes a small initial investment in a pilot project. If the level of farmer acceptance appears reasonable, the company can then invest an additional $8 million for a further roll out of the concept.

This use of real options allows the company to invest a relatively small amount to test its assumptions regarding a possible alternative investment. If the test does not work, the company has only lost $1 million. If the test succeeds, the company can pursue an alternative that may ultimately yield far higher profits than the more assured investment in wheat.

A concern with using real options is that competitors may be using the same concept at the same time, and may use the placing of small bets to arrive at the same conclusions as the company. The result may be that several competitors will enter the same market at approximately the same time, driving down the initially rich margins that management may have assumed were associated with a real option. Thus, the parameters of real options constantly change, and so must be re-evaluated at regular intervals.

Another concern relates to the last point, that competitors may jump into the same market. This means that a business cannot evaluate the results of its options analyses in a leisurely manner. Instead, each option must be evaluated quickly and decisions made to make additional investments (or not) before the competition gets a jump on the situation.

Capital Budget Proposal Analysis

Reviewing a capital budget proposal does not necessarily mean passing judgment on it exactly as presented. The analyst can attach a variety of suggestions to a proposal, which management may incorporate into a revised proposal. Here are some examples:

- *Asset capacity*. Does the asset have more capacity than is actually needed under the circumstances? Is there a history of usage spikes that call for extra capacity? Depending on the answers to these questions, consider using smaller assets with less capacity. If the asset is powered, this may also lead to reductions in utility costs, installation costs, and floor space requirements.

- *Asset commoditization.* Wherever possible, avoid custom-designed machinery in favor of standard models that are readily available. By doing so, it is easier to obtain repair parts, and there may even be an aftermarket for disposing of the asset when the company no longer needs it.
- *Asset features.* Managers have a habit of wanting to buy new assets with all of the latest features. Are all of these features really needed? If an asset is being replaced, then it is useful to compare the characteristics of the old and new assets, and examine any differences between the two to see if they are really needed. If the asset is the only model offered by the supplier, would the supplier be willing to strip away some features and offer it at a lower price?
- *Asset standardization.* If a company needs a particular asset in large quantities, then adopt a policy of always buying from the same manufacturer, and preferably only buying the same asset every time. By doing so, the maintenance staff becomes extremely familiar with maintenance requirements, and only has to stock replacement parts for one model.
- *Emerging market analysis.* An emerging market is one in which there is a recently-formed infrastructure of laws, business partners, and political institutions. In this type of environment, it is extremely difficult to create a single best-case model of likely cash flows that will actually be achieved. Instead, consider building a number of scenarios that range from the collapse of the local economy to stratospheric market share growth, and many points in-between. The results of this extra work should give a full range of the prospects for an investment. Also, re-model the situation at regular intervals to account for changes in the market, to see if the company should invest further, stand pat, or back away from the market.
- *Extended useful life.* A manager may be applying for an asset replacement simply because the original asset has reached the end of its recommended useful life. But is it really necessary to replace the asset? Consider conducting a formal review of these assets to see if they can still be used for some additional period of time. There may be additional maintenance costs involved, but this will almost certainly be lower than the cost of replacing the asset.
- *Facility analysis.* If a capital proposal involves the acquisition of additional facility space, consider reviewing any existing space to see if it can be compressed, thereby eliminating the need for more space. For example, shift storage items to less expensive warehouse space, shift from offices to more space-efficient cubicles, and encourage employees to work from home or on a later shift. If none of these ideas work, then at least consider acquiring new facilities through a sublease, which tends to require shorter lease terms than a lease arranged with the primary landlord.
- *Investment time horizon.* The period over which cash flows are presented in the proposal may not correspond to the actual life span of the asset. This happens when there is a standard corporate mandate or custom to use a certain projection period, such as five or ten years. In reality, the projected cash

flows should match the life span of the asset, even if doing so results in an unusual projection period. For example, an investment in a software development project may require a very short time horizon, given the uncertainties in this market, while the cash flows associated with a drug development project could span several decades.

- *Monument elimination.* A company may have a large fixed asset, around which the rest of the production area is configured; this is called a monument. If there is a monument, consider adopting a policy of using a larger number of lower-capacity assets. By doing so, you avoid the risk of having a single monument asset go out of service and stopping all production, in favor of having multiple units, among which work can be shifted if one unit fails.

The sponsors of capital proposals frequently do *not* appreciate this additional review of their proposals, since it implies that they did not consider these issues themselves. Nonetheless, the savings can be substantial, and so are well worth the aggravation of dealing with annoyed managers.

Complex Systems Analysis

When analyzing a possible investment, it is useful to also analyze the system into which the investment will be inserted. If the system is unusually complex, it is likely to take longer for the new asset to function as expected within the system. The reason for the delay is that there may be unintended consequences that ripple through the system, requiring adjustments in multiple areas that must be addressed before any gains from the initial investment can be achieved.

It may initially appear that the multitude of factors to consider in a complex system can be accounted for by creating an equally complex analysis model. However, virtually all models, no matter how complex, are not entirely complete; there are always additional factors that have not been considered that can impact a model in unexpected ways. Further, some factors may interact in unexpected ways, resulting in outcomes that are well outside of what the analyst might expect.

EXAMPLE

ABC Airlines is modeling whether to offer its customers a new route into Denver from Kansas City. ABC must consider a number of factors that can impact flight service, such as the impact of snowfall on the number of travelers to the area's ski resorts, whether a new high-speed train from Kansas City to Denver will impact the number of paying passengers, the extent to which upstart low-cost airlines may drive down prices, and how the price of aviation fuel will drive up ticket prices. ABC elects not to provide service, after which the International Olympic Committee grants Denver the next Winter Olympics, which triggers an upsurge in travel even in advance of the games. Thus, an outlier event arises that would not normally have been factored into the decision, but which has an impact on the decision.

A basic rule of investing in a complex environment is that it is impossible to understand the full impact of the investment. There may be any number of adjustments required that will call for additional investments of both time and money. Consequently, the more complex the environment, the more time and money should be allocated to an investment, even if there may not appear to be any immediate need for the additional investment.

Research and Development Funding Analysis

The funding process for research and development (R&D) projects tends to result in the funding of less-risky projects. The reason is that there is usually not enough cash available to fund all proposed projects, so a ranking system must be imposed to determine which projects will receive funding. The ranking is driven by a discounted cash flows analysis, for which a higher discount rate is imposed on the riskier projects. Since this analysis tends to reduce the cash flows associated with riskier projects, only safer R&D projects are funded. The typical result is that a business pours more cash into the extension of its existing product lines, which are considered safe investments, and little cash into real innovation.

One way to break through this safety-driven selection process is to deliberately allocate cash to several classifications of R&D projects, of which one is for high-risk endeavors. The amount allocated to each classification will vary, depending on management's willingness to lose money on high-risk projects. In general, this concept will increase the probability that a business will come up with a breakthrough product that can lead to an entirely new product line.

When cash is deliberately invested in high-risk R&D projects, there will inevitably be a number of project failures, either because the results will not be commercially viable or because the project is an outright failure. The real problem is when there are *few* failures, because it indicates that the company is not investing in sufficiently risky projects, with their attendant high returns.

To determine the amount of project failure being experienced, summarize the total expense related to projects that have been cancelled (known as *R&D waste*). While this metric can be deliberately altered by delaying the date on which a project is cancelled, it can still provide relevant input into the amount of project risk being incurred over multiple periods.

Even when the allocation of funding into different classifications increases the odds of funding a riskier R&D project, it is still necessary to allocate funds *within* each classification. A possible approach for deciding between projects is to use *expected commercial value* (ECV), which amalgamates the probabilities of success into a more standard net present value calculation. The formula is:

(((Project net present value × probability of commercial success) − commercialization cost) × (probability of technical success)) − product development cost

EXAMPLE

Entwhistle Electric is considering an investment in a tiny battery for cell phone applications. There is some risk that the battery cannot be developed in the necessary size. Facts pertaining to the project are:

Project net present value	$8,000,000
Probability of commercial success	90%
Commercialization cost	$1,500,000
Probability of technical success	75%
Product development cost	$3,500,000

Entwhistle's financial analyst derives the following ECV for the project from the preceding information:

((($8,000,000 Project NPV × 90% probability of commercial success) – $1,500,000 commercialization cost) × (75% probability of technical success)) – $3,500,000 product development cost

Expected commercial value = $775,000

An ECV analysis will inevitably result in some projects not being funded. However, not being funded does not necessarily equate to being permanently cancelled. These projects might become more tempting prospects for funding at a later date, depending on changes in such areas as:

- Competitor actions
- Legal liability
- Price points for adjacent products
- Raw materials availability
- Technical advances

Because of these issues, it may make more sense to schedule an occasional review of projects that have failed the ECV test, to see if circumstances now make them worthy of an investment.

The Outsourcing Decision

It may be possible to avoid a capital purchase entirely by outsourcing the work to which it is related. By doing so, the company may be able to eliminate all assets related to the area (rather than acquiring more assets), while the burden of maintaining a sufficient asset base now shifts to the supplier. The supplier may even buy the company's assets related to the area being outsourced. This situation is a well-established alternative for high technology manufacturing, as well as for information technology services, but is likely not viable outside of these areas.

If outsourcing is a possibility, then the cash flows resulting from doing so will be highly favorable for the first few years, as capital expenditures vanish. However, the supplier must also earn a profit and pay for its own infrastructure, so the cost over the long term will probably not vary dramatically from what the company would have experienced if it had kept a functional area in-house. There are three exceptions that can bring about a long-term cost reduction. They are:

- *Excess capacity.* A supplier may have such a large amount of excess capacity already that it does not need to invest further for some time, thereby potentially depressing the costs that it would otherwise pass through to its customers. However, this excess capacity pool will eventually dry up, so it tends to be a short-term anomaly.
- *High volume.* There are some outsourcing situations where the supplier is handling such a massive volume of activity from multiple customers that its costs on a per-unit basis decline below the costs that a company could ever achieve on its own. This situation can yield long-term savings to a company.
- *Low costs.* A supplier may locate its facility and work force in low-cost countries or regions within countries. This can yield significant cost reductions in the short term, but as many suppliers use the same technique, it is driving up costs in all parts of the world. Thus, this cost disparity is useful for a period of time, but is gradually declining as a long-term option.

There are also risks involved in shifting functions to suppliers. First, a supplier may go out of business, leaving the company scrambling to shift work to a new supplier. Second, a supplier may gradually ramp up prices to the point where the company is substantially worse off than if it had kept the function in-house. Third, the company may have so completely purged the outsourced function from its own operations that it is now completely dependent on the supplier, and has no ability to take it back in-house. Fourth, the supplier's service level may decline to the point where it is impairing the ability of the company to operate. And finally, the company may have entered into a multi-year deal, and cannot escape from the contract if the business arrangement does not work out. These are significant issues, and must be weighed as part of the outsourcing decision.

The cautions noted here about outsourcing do not mean that it should be avoided as an option. On the contrary, a rapidly growing company that has minimal access to funds may cheerfully hand off multiple operations to suppliers in order to avoid the up-front costs associated with those operations. Outsourcing is less attractive to stable, well-established companies that have better access to capital.

The Post Installation Review

It is very important to conduct a post installation review of any capital expenditure project, to see if the initial expectations for it were realized. If not, then the results of this review can be used to modify the capital budgeting process to include better information.

Another reason for having a post installation review is that it provides a control over those managers who fill out the initial capital budgeting proposals. If they know there is no post installation review, then they can wildly overstate the projected results of their projects with impunity, just to have them approved. Of course, this control is only useful if it is conducted relatively soon after a project is completed. Otherwise, the responsible manager may have moved on in his career, and can no longer be tied back to the results of his work.

It is even better to begin a post installation review while a project is still being implemented, and especially when the implementation period is expected to be long. This initial review gives senior management a good idea of whether the cost of a project is staying close to its initial expectations. If not, management may need to authorize more vigorous management of the project, scale it back, or even cancel it outright.

If the post implementation review results in the suspicion that a project proposal was unduly optimistic, this brings up the question of how to deal with the responsible manager. At a minimum, the proposal reviews can flag any future proposals by this manager as suspect, and worthy of especially close attention. Another option is to tie long-term compensation to the results of these projects. A third possibility is to include the results of the reviews in personnel analysis, which may lead to a reduction in employee compensation. A really catastrophic result may even be grounds for the termination of the responsible party.

EXAMPLE

Milford Sound has just completed a one-year project to increase the amount of production capacity at its speaker production work center. The original capital budgeting proposal was for an initial expenditure of $290,000, resulting in additional annual throughput of $100,000 per year. The actual result is somewhat different. The analyst's report includes the following text:

> **Findings:** The proposal only contained the purchase price of the equipment. However, since the machinery was delivered from Germany, Milford also incurred $22,000 of freight charges and $3,000 in customs fees. Further, the project required the installation of a new concrete pad, a breaker box, and electrical wiring that cost an additional $10,000. Finally, the equipment proved to be difficult to configure, and required $20,000 of consulting fees from the manufacturer, as well as $5,000 for materials scrapped during testing. Thus, the actual cost of the project was $350,000.
>
> Subsequent operation of the equipment reveals that it cannot operate without an average of 20% downtime for maintenance, as opposed to the 5% downtime that was advertised by the manufacturer. This reduces throughput by 15%, which equates to a drop of $15,000 in throughput per year, to $85,000.

Recommendations: To incorporate a more comprehensive set of instructions into the capital budgeting proposal process to account for transportation, setup, and testing costs. Also, given the wide difference between the performance claims of the manufacturer and actual results, to hire a consultant to see if the problem is caused by our installation of the equipment; if not, we recommend not buying from this supplier in the future.

Summary

This chapter addressed a variety of issues to consider when deciding whether to purchase a fixed asset. We put less emphasis on discounted cash flow analysis, which has been the primary capital budgeting tool in industry for years, because it does not take into consideration the impact on throughput of a company's bottleneck operation. The best capital budgeting analysis process is to give top priority to project proposals that have a strong favorable impact on throughput, and then use discounted cash flows to evaluate the impact of any remaining projects on cost reduction.

When reviewing a capital budgeting proposal, do not assume that the scenario stated in the proposal must be evaluated "as is." Instead, suggest improvements to the proposal to enhance the projected cash flows, and consider adding additional scenarios to provide a more complete basis of information on which an investment decision can be made.

Chapter 21
The Lease or Buy Decision

Introduction

After a company makes the decision to acquire an asset, it must decide how to finance the purchase. A common decision is whether to buy the asset with cash or to lease it. In this chapter, we discuss the nature of the lease or buy comparison, the circumstances under which leasing is a beneficial alternative, and the lease terms that can potentially increase the cost of a lease.

The Lease Arrangement

A lease is an arrangement where the lessor agrees to allow the lessee to use an asset for a stated period of time in exchange for a series of fixed payments. The arrangement typically requires that the asset be returned after a stated interval, though the lessee may have the option to extend the lease or buy the asset at the end of the lease term. Depending on the terms of the lease, it may be treated in one of two ways:

- *Capital lease*. The lessee records the leased asset on its books as a fixed asset and depreciates it, while recording interest expense separately. This option is only available if the lease terms have the characteristics of a long-term loan.
- *Operating lease*. The lessor records the leased asset on its books as a fixed asset and depreciates it, while the lessee simply records a periodic lease payment. This option is more common, and involves lease terms that essentially establish the ownership of the asset by the lessor.

The Lease or Buy Decision

There are a multitude of factors that a lessor includes in the formulation of the monthly rate that it charges, such as the down payment, the residual value of the asset at the end of the lease, and the interest rate, which makes it difficult to break out and examine each element of the lease. Instead, it is much easier to create separate net present value tables for the lease and buy alternatives, and then compare the results of the two tables to see which alternative is better from a cash flow perspective. The following example illustrates the use of net present value for this analysis.

The Lease or Buy Decision

EXAMPLE

Milford Sound is contemplating the purchase of an asset for $500,000. It can buy the asset outright, or do so with a lease. Its cost of capital is 8%, and its incremental income tax rate is 35%. The following two tables show the net present values of both options.

Buy Option

Year	Depreciation	Income Tax Savings (35%)	Discount Factor (8%)	Net Present Value
0				-$500,000
1	$100,000	$35,000	0.9259	32,407
2	100,000	35,000	0.8573	30,006
3	100,000	35,000	0.7938	27,783
4	100,000	35,000	0.7350	25,725
5	100,000	35,000	0.6806	23,821
Totals	$500,000	$175,000		$360,258

Lease Option

Year	Pretax Lease Payments	Income Tax Savings (35%)	After-Tax Lease Cost	Discount Factor (8%)	Net Present Value
1	$135,000	$47,250	$87,750	0.9259	$81,248
2	135,000	47,250	87,750	0.8573	75,228
3	135,000	47,250	87,750	0.7938	69,656
4	135,000	47,250	87,750	0.7350	64,496
5	135,000	47,250	87,750	0.6806	59,723
Totals	$675,000	$236,250	$438,750		$350,351

Thus, the net purchase cost of the buy option is $360,258, while the net purchase cost of the lease option is $350,351. The lease option involves the lowest cash outflow for Milford, and so is the better option.

Leasing Concerns

There is an undeniable attraction to acquiring assets with a lease, since it replaces a large up-front cash outflow with a series of monthly payments. However, before signing a lease agreement, be aware of the following issues that can increase the cost of the arrangement:

- *Buyout price.* Many leases include an end-of-lease buyout price that is inordinately high. If the lessee wants to continue using a leased asset, the buyout price may be so outrageous that the only realistic alternative is to

continue making lease payments, which generates outsized profits for the lessor. Therefore, always negotiate the size of the buyout payment before signing a lease agreement. If the buyout is stated as the "fair market value" of the asset at the end of the lease term, the amount can be subject to interpretation, so include a clause that allows for arbitration to determine the amount of fair market value.
- *Deposit.* The lessor may require that an inordinately large deposit be made at the beginning of the lease term, from which the lessor can then earn interest over the term of the lease.
- *Deposit usage.* The terms of a lease may allow the lessor to charge any number of fees against the up-front deposit made by the lessee, resulting in little of the deposit being returned at the end of the lease.
- *Lease fee.* The lessor may charge a lease fee, which is essentially a paperwork charge to originate the lease. It may be possible to reduce or eliminate this fee.
- *Rate changes.* The lessor may offer a low lease rate during the beginning periods of a lease, and then escalate the rates later in the lease term. Be sure to calculate the average lease rate to see if the implicit interest rate is reasonable. In these sorts of arrangements, a rate ramp-up usually indicates an average interest rate that is too high.
- *Return fees.* When the lease term is over, the lessor may require that the leased asset be shipped at the lessee's cost to a distant location, and sometimes even in the original packaging.
- *Termination notification.* The lease agreement may require the lessee to notify the lessor in writing that it intends to terminate the lease as of the termination date stated in the contract. If the lessee does not issue this notification in a timely manner, it is obligated to continue leasing the asset, or to pay a large termination fee. Whenever this clause appears in a lease agreement, always negotiate it down to the smallest possible termination notification period.
- *Wear-and-tear standards.* A lease agreement may contain unreasonable standards for assigning a high rate of wear-and-tear to leased assets when they have been returned to the lessor, resulting in additional fees being charged to the lessee.

In short, many lessors rely upon obfuscation of the lease terms to generate a profit, so it makes sense to delve into every clause in a lease agreement and to be willing to bargain hard for changes to the terms. Also, have a well-managed system in place for retaining lease agreements and monitoring when the key dates associated with each lease will arise. Finally, conduct a cost review after each lease agreement has been terminated, to determine the total out-of-pocket cost and implicit interest rate; the result may be the discovery that certain lessors routinely gouge the company, and should not be used again.

In addition to the issues just noted, the lessee also loses access to any favorable changes in the residual value of leased assets, since the lessor usually retains ownership of the assets. Also, the lessee cannot take advantage of the tax benefits of depreciation when a lease is classified as an operating lease; instead, the lessor records the depreciation and takes advantage of the related tax benefits. This latter issue may not be a concern if the lessee has minimal taxable income that could be reduced by a depreciation charge, and does not expect to be able to use a net operating loss carryforward in future years.

The list of concerns with leasing arrangements may appear formidable. However, they also have a number of advantages, as explained in the next section.

Leasing Advantages

The leasing concerns just described should introduce a note of caution into dealings with lessors, since a careful analysis of lease terms may reveal an inordinately high cost. However, there are also a number of advantages to leasing, which include:

- *Asset servicing.* The lessor may have a sophisticated asset servicing capability. Though the cost of this servicing may be high, it can result in fast servicing intervals and therefore extremely high equipment usage levels. In some cases, the presence of a servicing capability may be the main attraction of a leasing deal.
- *Competitive lease rates.* A lessor can offer quite competitive lease rates. This situation arises when a lessor buys assets in such high volumes that it can obtain volume purchase discounts from suppliers, some of which it may pass along to lessees. The lessor may also be able to borrow funds at a lower rate than the lessee, and can share some of the cost differential.
- *Financing accessibility.* A lessor is more likely to enter into a leasing arrangement with a company that is experiencing low profitability than a traditional lender. This is because the leased asset is collateral for the lessor, which can take the asset back if the lessee is unable to continue making timely lease payments. Conversely, a traditional lender might have a considerably more difficult time accessing company assets, and so would be less inclined to lend funds for the purchase of assets.
- *New technology.* A non-monetary advantage of leasing is that a company is continually swapping out old equipment for newer and more technologically advanced equipment. This can present a competitive advantage in those cases where the equipment is being used within a core function, or used to enhance products or services.
- *Off-balance sheet transaction.* Depending on the terms of a leasing arrangement, it may be possible for a lessee to avoid having to state its remaining lease payment liabilities on its balance sheet. By doing so, the balance sheet shows the company as having fewer obligations than is really the case, and so the business appears more solvent. However, it may still be necessary to reveal the annual amount of future lease payments in the accompanying financial statement disclosures.

- *Reserve available debt.* The company can reserve room on its existing line of credit by instead using a lease to buy an asset.
- *Short-term usage.* A leasing arrangement can be an effective alternative for those assets that are expected to have little value by the end of their lease terms, or for which the company expects to install a replacement asset at about the time of the lease termination.

Summary

We have spent a large proportion of this chapter addressing the ways in which a lease can turn sour, due to terms that may be hidden deep within a lease agreement. Though the result can be an inordinately high financing cost, leasing can still prove to be an excellent alternative to buying assets outright. The keys to a successful leasing deal are to be aware of the situations in which leasing makes the most sense, reviewing lease terms with great care before signing the agreement, and complying with all lease terms.

Chapter 22
Acquisition Valuation

Introduction

There are many ways to value a business, which can yield widely varying results, depending upon the basis of each valuation method. Some methods assume a valuation based on the assumption that a business will be sold off at bankruptcy prices, while other methods focus on the inherent value of intellectual property and the strength of a company's brands, which can yield much higher valuations. There are many other valuation methods lying between these two extremes.

We need all of these methods, because no single valuation method applies to all businesses. For example, a rapidly-growing business with excellent market share may produce little cash flow, and so cannot be valued based on its discounted cash flows. Alternatively, a company may have poured all of its funds into the development of intellectual property, but has no market share at all. Only through the application of multiple valuation methods can we discern what the value of a business may be.

In this chapter, we cover how to arrive at an acquisition valuation. You will see not only the calculation methodology, but also the assumptions underlying each one, and the situations to which they might be applied. They are presented beginning with those likely to yield the lowest valuations, and progress through other methods that usually result in higher valuations. The methods are summarized at the end of the chapter, in the Valuation Floor and Ceiling section.

Liquidation Value

Liquidation value is the amount of funds that would be collected if all assets and liabilities of the target company were to be sold off or settled. Generally, liquidation value varies depending upon the time allowed to sell assets. If there is a very short-term "fire sale," then the assumed amount realized from the sale would be lower than if a business were permitted to liquidate over a longer period of time.

The liquidation value concept is based on the assumption that a business will terminate, for one that continues in business has additional earning power from its intellectual property, products, branding, and so forth. Thus, liquidation value sets the lowest possible valuation for a business. The concept is useful for the acquirer to address even in cases where it intends to pay a great deal more for a target company. The reason is that the difference between the liquidation value and the amount actually paid is the amount for which the acquirer is at risk, in case there are problems with the target company that require it to be liquidated.

The owners of a business would be foolish to sell at the liquidation price, since they could just as easily liquidate the business themselves as sell it to someone else and have *them* liquidate it. Nonetheless, if a business is suffering from any number of factors related to its operations or the business environment, it is possible that an astute acquirer might actually complete a purchase at a valuation relatively close to the liquidation value of the target.

Real Estate Value

If a company has substantial real estate holdings, they may form the primary basis for the valuation of the business. This approach only works if nearly all of the assets of a business are various forms of real estate. Since most businesses lease real estate, rather than owning it, this method can only be used in a small number of situations.

EXAMPLE

High Noon Armaments is interested in acquiring Home Caliber, a chain of gun shops. Upon further investigation, High Noon finds that the shops are barely profitable, but that Home Caliber owns both the land on which its stores are situated and the stores themselves. The CFO of High Noon elects to compile a valuation based on the underlying real estate, rather than the cash flow fundamentals of the business.

If the acquirer has no experience in dealing with real estate, and plans to sell off the real estate, then it may apply a discount to the real estate values that it derives. However, since the real estate valuation is being used as the primary source of information for the valuation, and the acquirer expects to sell the real estate, this brings up the issue of why the acquirer is making an offer at all.

From the perspective of a seller that wants to be sold, it may make more sense to gradually sell off the real estate in such a manner as to maximize prices, and use the funds to either buy back shares or issue a large cash dividend to shareholders. This approach shifts all of the cash directly to the shareholders, without worrying about any discount that might be applied by a prospective acquirer. Company management can then pursue the sale of the remainder of the business to realize any residual cash, which also goes to the shareholders.

Relief-from-Royalty Method

What about situations where a company has significant intangible assets, such as patents and software? How can a valuation be created for them? A possible approach is the relief-from-royalty method, which involves estimating the royalty that the company would have paid for the rights to use an intangible asset if it had to license it from a third party. This estimation is based on a sampling of licensing deals for similar assets. These deals are not normally made public, so it can be difficult to derive the necessary comparative information.

Under this method, any savings from not licensing an asset are considered on an after-tax basis. The reason is that, if the company had indeed licensed the rights from a third party, there would have been a licensing expense that reduced taxable income.

The relief-from-royalty method is hardly one that can be used to value an entire enterprise, since it only addresses intangible assets. Nonetheless, it is one of the few methods available for putting a price tag on intangible assets, and so can be of use in situations where intangibles comprise a large part of the assets of a target company.

Book Value

Book value is the amount that shareholders would receive if a company's assets, liabilities, and preferred stock were sold or paid off at exactly the amounts at which they are recorded in the company's accounting records. It is highly unlikely that this would ever actually take place, because the market value at which these items would be sold or paid off might vary by substantial amounts from their recorded values. There could be particularly large disparities between the recorded and market values of items in the following areas:

- *Inventory*. If a company uses the last in, first out method of inventory costing, this could mean that some portions of the inventory are assigned a cost that could be a number of years old. Also, if a company is located in an industry where inventory obsolescence occurs quickly, then the recorded cost of inventory may be much higher than the amount at which it could actually be sold.
- *Fixed assets*. Fixed assets are recorded at their purchase costs. That cost is reduced over the useful life of the assets with depreciation. However, the depreciation charge does not necessarily relate to the decline in the market value of an asset over time. Instead, there can be a significant difference between the net book value of a fixed asset and its sale price.
- *Intangible assets*. Intangible assets are recorded at their purchase costs, which are then reduced over the useful life of the assets with amortization. There can be very large differences between the market value of these assets and their net book value. For example, a patent may have an increasing market value that greatly exceeds its recorded cost.
- *Contingent liabilities*. There may be any number of contingent liabilities that are not recorded in the accounting records of a business at all, and yet represent significant liabilities. For example, there may be a potential for adverse judgments in lawsuits, or as a guarantor for a debt.

Book value is an imprecise measure of the value of a business, since it simply reflects a variety of accounting standards used to record accounting transactions. It does not necessarily reflect the value of a business at all. In general, it may be used as a baseline around which more valid valuation results may fall.

Book value may also be used as the denominator in the calculation of sale price to book value for the sales of similar businesses. Thus, if a mix of other companies in the same industry sold for a multiple of five times book value, then one might apply that same relationship to another prospective sale when determining a price for it.

EXAMPLE

High Noon Armaments wants to determine the sales price to book value ratio for recent sales in the armaments industry, to see what types of multiples it should apply when formulating offer prices for other businesses. It compiles the following information about five other sale transactions that were completed within the past 12 months:

Transaction	Sale Price	Book Value	Sale-to-Book-Value Ratio
A	$10,000,000	$3,800,000	2.6x
B	27,500,000	8,900,000	3.1x
C	42,650,000	10,900,000	3.9x
D	16,250,000	5,800,000	2.8x
E	6,500,000	4,800,000	1.4x
Totals	$102,900,000	$34,200,000	3.0x

Upon further examination of the underlying information, High Noon's CFO finds that Transaction E involved the sale of a business that was in severe financial difficulties, so he throws out the outlier ratio that resulted from that transaction. The remaining transactions yield an average sale-to-book-value ratio of 3.3x.

There are a number of problems with using the sale price to book value ratio as the basis for a valuation. They are:

- *Intellectual property.* Another business may have garnered an unusually high price in comparison to its book value, because it had unusually excellent intellectual property that may not have even been recorded as an asset in its accounting records.
- *Early-sale effect.* If there is a surge in acquisitions within an industry, typically the highest-quality firms are snapped up first. This means that the highest ratios of sale price to book value appear early in an acquisition cycle; the ratio should decline later in the cycle, as lower-quality firms are purchased.
- *Asset efficiency.* Some companies are much more efficient in the use of their assets than others, leading to significant disparities in the ratio.

In short, book value is of dubious use in deriving the valuation of a target company. Do not use it as the sole basis for deriving a valuation.

Enterprise Value

What would be the value of a target company if an acquirer were to buy all of its shares on the open market, pay off any existing debt, and keep any cash remaining on the target's balance sheet? This is called the enterprise value of a business, and the calculation is:

+	Market value of all shares outstanding
+	Total debt outstanding
-	Cash
=	Enterprise value

Enterprise value is only a theoretical form of valuation, because it does not factor in the effect on the market price of a target company's stock once the takeover bid is announced. Also, it does not include the impact of a control premium on the price per share (see the Control Premium section). In addition, the current market price may not be indicative of the real value of the business if the stock is thinly traded, since a few trades can substantially alter the market price. Further, the removal of cash from the target company does not indicate the need for that cash in order to continue operating the target business. Nonetheless, enterprise value is of some use in determining the "raw" valuation prior to estimating the control premium and other factors that typically boost the valuation of a business.

EXAMPLE

High Noon Armaments is preparing the valuation of a target company, and the CFO wants to know the amount of its enterprise value. The target has one million shares, and today's market price is $12.50 per share. According to its most recent quarterly Form 10-Q filing, the target has $2.4 million of outstanding debt, and $200,000 of cash on hand. Based on this information, its enterprise value is:

+ Market value (1,000,000 shares × $12.50/share)	$12,500,000
+ Debt	2,400,000
- Cash	-200,000
= Enterprise value	$14,700,000

Multiples Analysis

It is quite easy to compile information based on the financial information and stock prices of publicly-held companies, and then convert this information into valuation multiples that are based on company performance. These multiples can then be used to derive an approximate valuation for a specific company. The typical approach is as follows:

Acquisition Valuation

1. Create a list of the top ten publicly-held companies most comparable to the company for which a valuation is being compiled.
2. Find the current market valuation for each business, which is easily obtained through Yahoo Finance or Google Finance.
3. Obtain the revenue information for the past 12 months for each business, either from SEC filings or the Internet sites just noted. Compare revenues to the total company market valuation to arrive at a sales-to-market-value multiple.
4. Obtain the EBITDA information for the past 12 months for each business, either from SEC filings or the Internet sites just noted. EBITDA is earnings before interest, taxes, depreciation, and amortization. Compare EBITDA to the total company market valuation to arrive at an EBITDA-to-market-value multiple.
5. Multiply the target company's revenue and EBITDA amounts for the past 12 months by the median multiples for the target group to derive valuations.

The following example illustrates the concept.

EXAMPLE

High Noon Armaments routinely acquires other businesses within the firearms industry, and so conducts an annual review of the revenue and EBITDA multiples associated with the smaller publicly-held companies in the same industry. Accordingly, the acquisitions staff prepares the following multiples analysis.

Multiples Analysis
Firearms Industry
As of January 10, 20xx
(000s)

Name	Market Capitalization	One Year Revenues	One Year EBITDA	Revenue Multiple	EBITDA Multiple
Arbuckle Weapons	$145,000	$174,000	$19,300	1.2x	7.5x
Billy the Kid Designs	90,000	117,000	11,500	1.3x	7.8x
Heston Shotguns	128,000	160,000	24,200	0.8x	5.3x
Patton Siege Guns	210,000	210,000	30,000	1.0x	7.0x
Plasma Weapons	52,000	24,000	3,900	2.2x	13.2x
Quigley Artillery	360,000	240,000	42,400	1.5x	8.5x
Rifled Custom Guns	76,000	19,000	3,200	4.0x	24.0x
Totals	$1,061,000	$944,000	$134,500	1.1x	7.9x

Thus, the review shows a weighted-average revenue multiple of 1.1x and a weighted-average EBITDA multiple of 7.9x.

Acquisition Valuation

One month later, High Noon is engaged in a valuation analysis of a prospective acquisition, which has annual sales of $6.8 million and EBITDA of $400,000. Based on the multiples analysis, High Noon arrives at the following possible valuations for the company:

	Revenue	EBITDA
Target company results	$6,800,000	$400,000
× Industry average multiple	1.1x	7.9x
= Valuation based on multipliers	$7,480,000	$3,160,000

The results suggest quite a broad range of possible valuations, from a low of $3,160,000 to $7,480,000. It is possible that the target company has unusually low EBITDA in comparison to the industry, which is causing its EBITDA-based multiplier to be so low. This means that High Noon might want to push for a lower valuation if it proceeds with the acquisition.

It is most common to multiply the valuation multiples by the revenue and EBITDA information for the target company for its last 12 months. This is known as *trailing revenue* or *trailing EBITDA*. This is the most valid information available, for it represents the actual results of the business in the immediate past. However, if a target company expects exceptional results in the near future, then it prefers to use *forward revenue* or *forward EBITDA*. These measurements multiply expected results for the next 12 months by the valuation multipliers. While the use of forward measurements can create a good estimate of what a business will be worth in the near future, it generally incorporates such optimistic estimates that it tends to result in excessively high valuations.

> **Tip:** If a target company is allowed to derive its valuation based on forward revenue or EBITDA, then insist that the target does so based on its internal budgeted information for the projected period, and only if it has a solid track record of having met its budgeted numbers in the past.

A multiplier analysis that is based on revenues is useful in cases where a business is in high-growth mode, where there are typically fewer profits. This is because such businesses have elevated expenditure levels to hire staff, acquire more facilities, and other issues related to faster growth. However, creating a valuation based solely on revenues is dangerous, since a target company may be generating those revenues by selling at such rock-bottom prices that it will be impossible for the acquirer to turn a profit. Also, high revenues do not mean that a business is being run well. In short, a revenue-based multiplier should be supplemented by other valuation techniques.

The EBITDA multiple is a much better basis for a valuation than the revenue multiple, since it reflects the ability of a business to generate a profit. However, examine the EBITDA for the past few years as well, to see if the management of the target company is cutting back on expenditures in the current year in order to make the business appear more profitable.

> **Tip:** Apply both the revenue *and* EBITDA multiples to each acquisition. If the revenue multiple results in a lower valuation than the EBITDA-based valuation, then the target company has higher profits than the average for the industry. This may indicate that the business is not investing in its infrastructure. The reverse situation indicates lower-than-average profitability, which can be caused by many factors. In either case, the relationship between the valuation levels can be used as the basis for additional due diligence.

There are several problems with multiples analysis to be aware of. They are:

- *Company size.* The information used for multiples analysis comes from publicly-held companies, and those companies are generally larger ones. Thus, the multiples that they command may not be applicable to smaller, privately-held organizations.
- *Conglomerates.* If a target company dabbles in multiple industries, then it is extremely difficult, if not impossible, to construct a multiples analysis for it. This is a particular problem when a target company insists on a valuation for the entire company that is based on the subsidiary located in an industry where multiples are highest. Given the difficulty of analysis, it may be better to use the discounted cash flows method instead (see the Discounted Cash Flows section).
- *Market capitalization.* A very large publicly-held company may have higher multiples than smaller companies, if only because it has a more liquid market for its shares and more institutional investors authorized to own its shares. Thus, comparing a larger firm's multiples to a small private company can be misleading.
- *Outliers.* It is quite common for a few companies in the comparison analysis to have unusually high or low multiples. It is also common for an acquirer to fixate on those businesses with the lowest multiples, while target companies do the reverse. Instead, throw out the high and low outliers and focus on the median multiples, which give the best general idea of valuation.
- *Price swings.* The stock price of a company may vary significantly over just a few days, so the specific date on which a multiples table is compiled can have a resounding impact on multiples. Some of this difficulty can be avoided by using the average stock price for the past month.
- *Thin trading.* A public company whose shares trade over-the-counter rather than on a stock exchange will likely be thinly traded, which means that even a few trades may significantly alter share prices, resulting in unusual multiples.
- *Transitory revenue.* Both the revenue and EBITDA multiples can be skewed if the target company has recorded transitory sales. These are typically larger, one-time sales that are not expected to recur. Examine the underlying details of a business and strip away these sales before applying any revenue or EBITDA multiples.

- *Underlying quality.* A major problem with using multiples to derive valuations is that you are assuming the business being valued is about the same as every other company included in the multiples analysis. If the business has much better fundamentals than other companies, such as a more recent product line, then it may be worth much more than the multipliers would indicate. Conversely, a poorly-run business with low-quality assets may not justify the valuation that a multiplier analysis would indicate for it.

The last point, regarding the underlying quality of a target company, underscores the main problem with multiples analysis. In short, this may seem to be an ideally quantitative type of analysis that yields a strong justification for a particular valuation, but in reality it only suggests what an average business may be worth, based on a cluster of other average businesses. A company with unusual business fundamentals could be worth substantially more, or less, than multiples analysis would indicate.

Discounted Cash Flows

One of the most detailed and justifiable ways to value a business is through the use of discounted cash flows (DCF). Under this approach, the acquirer constructs the expected cash flows of the target company, based on extrapolations of its historical cash flow and expectations for synergies that can be achieved by combining the two businesses. A discount rate is then applied to these cash flows to arrive at a current valuation for the business. The steps in the process are:

1. Create an estimate of the cash flows to be derived from the target company in each of the next five years, including any expected synergies.
2. After the five-year period, estimate a second set of cash flows that are assumed to continue in perpetuity at a certain rate of growth (or decline) per year. This is typically based on the cash flows in year five. We use this approach after year five, because it is impossible to estimate cash flows with much precision so far in the future.
3. Calculate the net present value of all future cash flows, using a discount rate. The result is the present value of the target company.

Post Five-Year Cash Flows

The preceding itemization of the steps to follow for a DCF included the assumption of a perpetual rate of growth or decline in the target company following five years of detailed cash flow analysis. This is an extremely difficult number to arrive at, for slight changes in the rate of growth or decline can have a major impact on the valuation of the target. Here are several options for dealing with these post five-year cash flows:

- *Ignore.* The acquirer can base its valuation on only five years of cash flows, and ignore any further cash flows. This argument is based on the quite likely position that there is significant risk that the acquisition will not work, and

so there is a significant chance that there will be no cash flows after five years.
- *Risk adjustment.* If the acquirer elects to use a perpetual rate of growth or decline, it can use an extremely high discount rate to reduce the present value of these cash flows to quite a small amount. The discount rate applied to the first five years of cash flows may be substantially smaller, since those cash flows are in the near future, and so can be more easily predicted.
- *Assume sale of the business.* The acquirer can assume that it will sell the target company to a third party at the end of year five. This brings up the issue of what the business might be worth in five years, which is difficult to determine, and which may call for a higher discount rate to reduce its present value.

In general, the acquirer does not want to deal with post five-year cash flows, due to their uncertainty, while the target company wants them to be considered in order to increase the valuation of the business. The result may be any of the preceding options. The author has generally ignored cash flows more than five years in the future, based on considerable experience with being unable to predict such flows. Actual cash flows have nearly always been lower than predicted even a few years in the future, so any use of post five-year cash flows should be reduced to the greatest extent possible. Otherwise, the acquirer will almost certainly assign too high a valuation to a business.

Negotiation of DCF Contents

There can be some manipulation involved in adjusting the items to be included in a discounted cash flow analysis. The seller invariably wants to exclude selected expenses from the calculation, on the grounds that they were one-time events that the acquirer will not experience in the future. The seller will also identify a large number of expense exclusions that are based on presumed synergies. The result, according to the seller, is likely to be startlingly high cash flow that the target would be unlikely to ever achieve in practice. It is the task of the acquirer to sort through these alleged expense reductions and verify which ones may actually be achieved.

The following example illustrates the compilation of cash flows for a target company, as well as their reduction to net present value using a discount rate.

EXAMPLE

The CFO of High Noon Armaments is constructing a discounted cash flow forecast for Sinclair Side Arms. The CFO begins with the cash flow for the preceding 12-month period, which was $5,800,000. The Sinclair management team claims that the following items should be added back to the cash flow figure:
- Unusual charge of $200,000 related to lawsuit judgment
- One-time bonus payment of $120,000 made to the management team
- Elimination of $60,000 for CEO travel and entertainment expenses that would go away once the CEO is terminated

Acquisition Valuation

- Reduction of $400,000 in salary and payroll taxes related to the CEO, who will be terminated
- Reduction of $92,000 for a leased warehouse that the management team had not quite gotten around to terminating on its own

The CFO does not exclude the $200,000 lawsuit judgment, on the grounds that Sinclair has incurred a series of similar judgments from such lawsuits in the past, and there is a significant possibility that it will continue to do so in the future. The CFO also does not exclude the $120,000 bonus payment, since further investigation reveals that this was a performance-based bonus, and there is an expectation in the industry for this type of bonus to be paid; further, the amount is not unreasonable. The CFO accepts the combined $460,000 expense reduction related to the CEO, since that expenditure will not be required in the future. Finally, the CFO elects not to exclude the $92,000 warehouse lease, on the grounds that there is no evidence yet that the company can operate without the additional warehouse space.

In addition, the CFO's due diligence team comes up with the following suggestions, which are added back to the cash flow report for valuation purposes:

- $200,000 for duplicated corporate staff who can be terminated
- $80,000 from volume purchasing discounts
- $320,000 from the consolidation of leases
- $38,000 from the elimination of duplicated software maintenance charges

The due diligence team also notes that Sinclair's fixed assets are very old, and will require $2,000,000 of expenditures in years two, three, and four to bring them up to standard.

Finally, the due diligence team prudently recommends that High Noon assume that Sinclair's cash flow will likely drop 5% in the year following the merger, as uncertainty causes some customers to switch to competitors. Cash flow growth thereafter should be 5% per year.

The CFO combines this information into the following table, in which he estimates the most likely cash flow scenario for the next five years. High Noon has a cost of capital of 9%, which is used to derive the discount rates noted in the table.

	Year 1	Year 2	Year 3	Year 4	Year 5
Beginning* cash flow	$5,800,000	$6,608,000	$6,938,000	$7,285,000	$7,649,000
Base level % change	-290,000	+330,000	+347,000	+364,000	+382,000
CEO expense reduction	+460,000				
Fixed asset replacements		-2,000,000	-2,000,000	-2,000,000	
Duplicate staff	+200,000				
Volume discounts	+80,000				
Lease consolidation	+320,000				
Software maintenance	+38,000				
Net cash flow	$6,608,000	$4,938,000	$5,285,000	$5,649,000	$8,031,000

Acquisition Valuation

	Year 1	Year 2	Year 3	Year 4	Year 5
Discount rate	0.9174	0.8417	0.7722	0.7084	0.6499
Present value of cash flows	$6,062,000	$4,156,000	$4,081,000	$4,002,000	$5,219,000
Present value grand total	$23,520,000				

* Considered to be the cash flow for the year, based on prior year results, not including fixed asset replacements

The CFO did not include any valuation for Sinclair after five years, citing the uncertainty of cash flow projections that far in the future.

Note: You may also need to factor into the DCF model any expected changes in working capital requirements for the target company. For example, if there is an expectation of increased sales through the forecast period, it would be reasonable to assume a reduction in cash flow based on the need for more accounts receivable and inventory to support the incremental increase in sales.

If the target company has exhibited unstable cash flows in the past, it is a very good idea to create several DCF models for it, in which you test the key factors that appear to be causing its cash flows to vary. For example, you could model the loss of a major customer, or a sudden increase in raw material costs, or the loss of a patent lawsuit – whatever is indicated by the circumstances. These extra analyses may point out specific weaknesses or potential strengths that may lead the acquirer to adjust the size of its offer to a target company.

In summary, the DCF model incorporates considerable detail about the cash flows of a target company and the synergies to be expected from it, though there is an increasing amount of uncertainty as cash flows go further into the future. The resulting model gives what is likely to be the most realistic view of the valuation of a business. However, it also incorporates many estimates regarding future events, so the model must be constructed carefully to yield results that can be attained in practice.

Replication Value

An acquirer can place a value upon a target company based upon its estimate of the expenditures it would have to incur to build that business "from scratch." Doing so would involve building customer awareness of the brand through a lengthy series of advertising and other brand building campaigns, as well as building a competitive product through several iterative product cycles. It may also be necessary to obtain regulatory approvals, depending on the products involved. There is also the prospect of engaging in a price war in order to unseat the target company from its current market share position. Here is a summary of the more likely expenditures to include in the derivation of replication value:

- Product development
- Production design and investment in new production equipment
- Working capital to support new product line
- Startup scrap and spoilage costs
- Branding expenditures
- Expenditures to set up and support a new distribution channel
- Cost of additional sales force or retraining of existing sales force

Further, if the acquirer could have bought a target company at once to avoid the preceding replication expenses, also include in the replication value the present value of foregone profits that the company could have earned during the process of replicating the business of the target company. In short, it is usually a very expensive process to replicate a business.

EXAMPLE

A target company is resisting a $5 million buyout offer by High Noon Armaments, so High Noon examines the cost of replicating the product line that it wants to acquire. It estimates the following information:

	Cost Estimate	Time Estimate
Product development	$420,000	10 months
Production line redesign	100,000	2 months
Startup scrap costs	20,000	--
Branding expenditures	180,000	6 months
New distribution setup	110,000	4 months
	$830,000	22 months

The analysis shows that the replication value is less than $1 million. Also, High Noon estimates that the present value of the profits that it would forego in the next 22 months by *not* purchasing the company is $500,000. This leaves an incremental acquisition cost of $3.6 million associated with buying the company right now. Also, the replication process will require nearly two years.

High Noon needs to decide if it is worth offering more than the $3.6 million incremental cost of buying the company in order to be in the market with an active product line right now, rather than in two years.

The replication cost requires an additional analysis, which is how long the replication will take. If the acquirer wants to jump into a market in the near future, replication of a target company is a near impossibility, since doing so nearly always requires multiple years of effort. Thus, the analysis of replication cost and time may lead an acquirer to assign quite a high price to a target company. In many instances, this results in what may appear to be an inordinately high valuation for a target company that is not generating much cash flow.

The analysis of replication value is an interesting one, for it involves the collection of estimates from within the company about replication costs, rather than the more typical analysis of a target company. This does not mean that the resulting information is more accurate – on the contrary, the acquirer does not own the products and businesses under consideration, and so may arrive at quite inaccurate estimates of replication costs. For this reason, always consider replication cost to be a supplemental analysis method, and use a more detailed analysis, such as discounted cash flows, as the primary valuation technique.

Comparison Analysis

A common form of valuation analysis is to comb through listings of acquisition transactions that have been completed over the past year or two, extract those for companies located in the same industry, and use them to estimate what a target company should be worth. The comparison is usually based on either a multiple of revenues or cash flow. In rare instances, the analysis may be based on recurring (contract) sales. Information about comparable acquisitions can be gleaned from public filings or press releases, but more comprehensive information can be obtained by paying for access to any one of several private databases that accumulate this information.

The Comparison of Sales Multiples

A common approach for deriving the value of a business is to assemble the ratio of sale price to revenues for a group of comparable companies, and apply that ratio to the sales of the target company. This is a very easy approach, since the information is available in a number of merger and acquisition databases. Any company that wants to be sold will engage the services of an investment banker who will use sales multiples to derive the value of the business. However, there are a number of problems with the sales multiple valuation method, including the following:

- *Link to profits.* A target company may generate sales by setting its prices extremely low. Doing so means that profits and cash flow will be low, if they exist at all. Thus, someone paying a multiple based on sales may find that it has acquired an essentially worthless business that will never generate a profit.
- *Comparison group.* The seller will attempt to match itself to whichever industry niche has generated the highest sales multiples. The acquirer must verify that the target company actually engages in the same line of business as those in the comparison group, and not a different group in another industry niche for which sales multiples are lower.
- *Fundamentals.* Another company may have obtained a high sales multiple, but for a very specific reason that was attractive to the acquirer, such as a key patent or distribution channel. If the target company does not have a

- *Outliers.* A target company may collect a group of unusually high sales multiples from other transactions and attempt to apply them to the proposed sale transaction. The acquirer should be wary of these selective comparable transactions, which may in fact be outliers in comparison to the normal sales multiples typically obtained in the industry.

In short, the sales multiple is more of a tool for the target company, not for the acquirer. It can distort the valuation of a business, since the comparison solely to sales does not account for any other factors, such as profitability or cash flow, with which an acquirer should be deeply concerned.

The Comparison of Cash Flows

If a valuation is created based on a comparison of cash flow multiples elsewhere, be aware that these multiples vary widely by industry. For example, the cash flow multiple for software may exceed 20x, while manufacturing multiples are in the range of 5-10x, and retail is typically 2-4x. Consequently, be very clear about which cash flow multiples are being included in a comparison. This is a particularly difficult comparison when reviewing the results of a sale that involves businesses in multiple industries, since the multiple cannot easily be assigned to a single industry area.

The Comparison of Contract Revenues

If a target company is situated in the government sector, or in any other sector where revenues are associated with large contracts, a possible valuation technique is a multiple of recurring yearly contracts. There is a large difference between one-time contracts and those expected to renew for a number of years, since a recurring contract represents more reliable cash flow. There may be a history of prior sales for which contract multiples are available, in which case it could be applied to a valuation. However, there are several considerations that can alter a valuation based on this type of multiple:

- *Remaining contract period.* The group of contracts to which the contract multiple will be applied will be of different lengths. Some may be funded only for the next year or two, while others may have considerably longer terms. You may need to apply a reduced contract multiple if the bulk of the contracts are scheduled to expire sooner, rather than later.
- *Prospects for renewal.* The multiple may require modification if the preponderance of contracts have a high or low likelihood of renewal. Also, even if a contract is very likely to be renewed, what if the period of the renewed contract is only a few months or a year? This can also impact the multiple. Determining the prospects for renewal is very judgmental, and so can result in great variability from actual results.

- *Prospects for new contracts.* Any acquisition candidate always makes a strong case for the business that it has almost closed, and how that should be included in the valuation. See the Earnout section for a discussion of this issue.
- *Margins on contracts.* There could be a broad range of profit margins associated with the various contracts, but you are applying a single contract multiple to the entire group of recurring contracts. If there are substantial profit differences by contract, it may make sense to divide the contracts into groups by profit ranges, and apply a different multiple to each one.

The preceding list of considerations should make it evident that applying a single multiple to a group of contracts is an extremely rough way to calculate the valuation of an acquisition target. If you intend to use this method, it would be better to adopt a high degree of precision and apply different multiples to groups of contracts, based on their remaining duration, profitability, and prospects for renewal.

52-Week High

The seller of a publicly-held business tends to be fixated on the highest stock price that it achieved over the preceding 52 weeks, and will insist on selling at a price near that price point. There are two reasons for this fixation:

- *Psychological.* No matter how much the stock price may have subsequently declined, the 52-week high represents a relatively recent valuation, and the seller still believes it is worth that amount.
- *Lawsuit risk.* The board of directors may feel that selling at this price point reduces the risk that they will be sued by shareholders for not negotiating a fair price.

It may be difficult for the acquirer to justify paying a price anywhere near the 52-week high, especially if the stock price has declined markedly since then. If so, it would be best to walk away from the deal and wait for the buyer's expectations to decline.

Influencer Price Point

A potentially important point impacting price is the price at which key influencers bought into the target company. For example, if someone can influence the approval of a sale, and that person bought shares in the target at $20 per share, it could be exceedingly difficult to offer a price that is at or below $20, irrespective of what other valuation methodologies may yield for a price.

Further, if influencers have held their shares for some time, they may expect a rate of return on their initial investment, which the acquirer can roughly estimate. Thus, if an influencer bought shares at $20 one year ago, and a similar investment in the same time period should have yielded a return of 10%, then the influencer will probably not accept a purchase offer of less than $22 per share.

The influencer price point has nothing to do with valuation, only the minimum return that key influencers are willing to accept on their baseline cost. If the amount they want is nowhere near what more rational valuation methods state the business is actually worth, then it may be best to walk away from the deal. It is possible that, once sufficient time has passed, key influencers may want to shift their holdings into other investments, and will therefore take a reduced price once rational thinking has set in.

The Initial Public Offering Valuation

A privately-held company whose owners want to sell it can wait for offers from potential acquirers, but doing so can result in arguments over the value of the company. The owners can obtain a new viewpoint by taking the company public in the midst of the acquisition negotiations. This has two advantages for the selling company. First, it gives the company's owners the option of proceeding with the initial public offering and eventually gaining liquidity by selling their shares on the open market. Also, it provides a second opinion regarding the valuation of the company, which the sellers can use in their negotiations with any potential acquirers.

However, this approach also has some problems. First is the million-dollar cost usually associated with taking a company public. Also, the IPO process requires an enormous amount of effort, and can seriously interfere with management's ability to run the business. And finally, the sellers may find that they are required to hold their shares in lockup agreements as a condition of taking the company public, and so cannot liquidate their shares for at least six months after going public.

The problems just noted keep most companies from engaging in the IPO ploy to obtain a high valuation. Nonetheless, it may be worthwhile for a privately-held business that is sufficiently large to go through with an IPO, and which is having a difficult time convincing suitors to propose a valuation that the owners believe properly values the business.

The Strategic Purchase

The ultimate valuation strategy from the perspective of the target company is the strategic purchase. This is when the acquirer is willing to throw out all valuation models and instead consider the strategic benefits of owning the target company. For example, an acquirer can be encouraged to believe that it needs to fill a critical hole in its product line, or to quickly enter a product niche that is considered key to its future survival, or to acquire a key piece of intellectual property. In this situation, the price paid may be far beyond the amount that any rational examination of the issues would otherwise suggest.

The downside of a strategic purchase is that the buyer is more likely to dismantle the target company and fully integrate it into its own operations, on the grounds that the strategic value gained must be maximized by rolling it into the acquirer's business to the greatest extent possible. Thus, this type of valuation certainly

Acquisition Valuation

maximizes the return to shareholders, but sometimes at the cost of the complete elimination of the underlying business as a cohesive unit.

Intellectual Property Valuation

We have previously noted that an acquirer's interest in a target company may be primarily focused on its intellectual property, such as unique manufacturing processes, patents, and brands. It can be difficult to arrive at a reliable valuation for these assets, so we have noted several possible methods in this section.

It is not possible to assign an exact value to intellectual property, since the underlying notion is so vague. Instead, several valuation methods are used to develop a range of possible valuations. The acquirer then uses this information to develop an initial offer price, as well as a permissible range of increased prices that reasonably encompass the calculated value of the intellectual property. The more common methods used to value intellectual property are as follows:

- *Replication cost.* This is the cost that the acquirer would have to incur in order to replicate the intellectual property. There is also a time component to this calculation, in that the acquirer might require years of effort in order to create the intellectual property. If the acquirer wants access to the property immediately, it should be willing to pay a premium to buy it from the acquiree.
- *Market price.* This is the price that third parties would pay for the intellectual property if it were put up for bid in a fair market, with multiple bidders. An acquirer may want to pay more than this amount in order to avoid a bidding war with potential competitors.
- *Discounted cash flows.* This is the present value of the cash flows currently generated by the intellectual property, with certain assumptions included regarding possible changes in those cash flows over future years. The rate at which these cash flows are discounted to a present value is subject to interpretation and negotiation.
- *Relief from royalty.* This approach is based on the cost that the acquirer would otherwise incur if it were required to pay a royalty for access to the intellectual property. This approach may not work if access to the intellectual property cannot be obtained through a licensing arrangement.

While it may not be necessary to calculate a valuation using all of the preceding methods, one should employ several of them, in order to gain a perspective on the range of possible valuations.

Extraneous Valuation Factors

An acquirer may be unduly influenced by a number of factors that have little to do with the intrinsic value of a target company. These other factors may increase the price it is willing to pay to levels that are well beyond the results of any reasonable quantitative analysis. For example:

- *Purchase by competitor.* There may be a considerable value associated with keeping a target company away from a competitor, if only to acquire intellectual property that could interfere with the business of that competitor.
- *Speed.* The acquirer may be interested in closing a deal fast for a number of reasons, such as meeting an acquisition target by year-end, or prior to a shareholders meeting.

The Control Premium

When investors purchase stock in a business, they gain the right to dividends, any appreciation in the market price of the stock, and any final share in the proceeds if the business is sold. If an investor buys at least a 51% controlling interest in a business, then it also obtains the right to redirect the business in any way it chooses. Consequently, obtaining a controlling interest is worth an additional price, which is known as the control premium. This premium can be an insignificant issue if the target is on the verge of bankruptcy, since the presumably short-term nature of the business makes the control premium essentially irrelevant. However, if the target is a robust business that can be enhanced by the acquirer, then the control premium can be a significant factor. Historical evidence shows that control premiums for healthy businesses can range from 30% to 75% of the market price of a company's stock.

The control premium is not a black-and-while concept, where the first 51% of ownership is more valuable than the remaining 49%. Instead, consider the multitude of situations where ownership is split among many owners. For example, what if there are three shareholders, with two owning 49% and one owning 2% of the shares? In this case, the 2% shareholder owns an extremely valuable piece of the business, given its ability to impact votes, and which would certainly command a premium. Alternatively, what if there are hundreds of small shareholders and one shareholder who owns 35% of a business? Owning that 35% might not result in outright control of the business, but it may be so much easier to obtain in comparison to the pursuit of hundreds of other shareholders that it commands a premium.

The control premium concept is a key reason why acquirers sometimes reduce their offer prices for any remaining shares outstanding in a two-tier acquisition. If an acquirer has already attained control over a business, there is no longer a control premium associated with any additional shares, which therefore reduces their value.

The Earnout

A significant problem for the acquirer is a seller that insists upon a valuation that is based on future expectations for the business. For example, the target company may be "just a few months" away from landing a major new contract, or launching a new product, or opening up a new distribution channel. The seller may believe that these prospective changes will have immense value, while the acquirer rightfully feels that these future prospects are entirely unproven, and may never occur or generate additional cash flow. These differences of opinion can cause major differences in the assumed valuation of the business.

When future expectations are causing a difference of opinion regarding valuation, one solution is to put off the acquisition until such time as the projected change has occurred, and its impact appears in the financial statements. However, these changes may take months or years to be completed, and may never occur at all. If so, the two entities are never able to close an acquisition deal.

An alternative that bridges the valuation gap between the two parties is the earnout. An earnout is a payment arrangement under which the shareholders of the target company are paid an additional amount if the company can achieve specific performance targets after the acquisition has been completed. It has the following advantages:

- *Payment source.* The improvements generated by the target company will likely generate sufficient cash flow to pay for all or a portion of the earnout, so the acquirer may be cash flow neutral on the additional payment.
- *Target achievement.* The shareholders of the target company will push for the completion of the performance targets, so that the acquirer pays the earnout. This helps the acquirer, too (despite having to pay the earnout), since the results of the target company will have been improved.
- *Tax deferral.* The shareholders of the target company will be paid at a later date, after the earnout is achieved, which means that the income tax related to the earnout payment is also deferred for the payment recipients.

Despite these advantages, an earnout is generally not a good idea. The trouble is that, even after purchasing it, the acquirer must leave the target company as a separate operating unit, so that the target's management group has a chance to achieve the earnout. Otherwise, there is a risk of a lawsuit in which there is a complaint that the acquirer's subsequent actions to merge it into the rest of the company impair any chance of completing the earnout conditions. It is risky for the acquirer to leave a newly acquired company alone in this manner, since doing so means that it cannot engage in any synergistic activities designed to pay for the cost of the acquisition – such as terminating duplicate positions or merging the entire business into another part of the acquirer.

Further, the management of the acquired business will be so focused on achieving the earnout that they ignore other initiatives being demanded by the acquirer – and the acquirer may not be able to fire them for insubordination until the earnout period has been completed. In short, agreeing to an earnout clause subjects the acquirer to an uncomfortable period when it cannot achieve its own goals for the target company.

This does not mean that earnouts are impossible, only that they should be very strictly defined. Here are several tips for mitigating the issues associated with them:

- *Earnout period.* Keep the period over which the earnout can be earned as short as possible, so that the acquirer does not have to wait too long to enact its own synergy-related changes.

- *Continual monitoring*. Have a performance tracking system in place that keeps all parties aware of the progress toward the earnout goal, so that no one is surprised if the goal is not reached. This lessens the risk of a lawsuit, since expectations were managed.
- *Sliding scale*. Pay the earnout on a sliding scale. For example, if the target company achieves 80% of the target, it is paid 80% of the earnout. This is much better than a fixed target, where no bonus is paid unless an exact profit figure is achieved. In the latter case, the shareholders of the target company are much more likely to initiate a lawsuit, since they are not paid at all even if there is only a slight performance shortfall.

In summary, earnouts appear to present a neat solution for acquirers that have a substantial gap in valuation perception with their targets, but this solution can be a thorny one. There are ways to mitigate the risk, but the acquirer needs to be willing to pay out the full amount of an earnout, just to avoid lawsuits claiming that it impeded the actions of the target company in trying to achieve its earnout goals.

Synergy Analysis

It is standard practice to evaluate a potential acquisition in terms of the types of synergies that can be attained by merging the companies together. For example, it may be possible to consolidate employees in a single building, thereby eliminating a building lease, or perhaps some duplicate positions can be eliminated.

Synergies related to expense reduction are one of the best areas in which to find value in an acquisition, because they are entirely under the control of the acquirer. It is easy enough to prepare a list of exactly which expense reduction synergies are expected when formulating a purchase price, and then follow up after the acquisition to ensure that the expenses are realized.

Expense reduction synergies are usually expected in the areas of facilities and personnel, but it is possible to find reductions in other areas, too. Consider the following areas of duplication in which expense reductions may be found:

- *Salaries and wages*. Particularly applies to duplicated administrative positions, especially when the two corporate staffs are combined. The following expenses are also automatically reduced when employees are terminated.
    - Payroll taxes
    - Benefits
    - Telephone charges
    - Travel and entertainment
    - Office supplies
    - Parking fees
- *Facility reduction*. Usually involves extra space made available through either the termination of employees or the consolidation of manufacturing and storage facilities. In a retail environment, this can also mean that stores

will be consolidated. The following expenses are affected when facilities are eliminated or their usage is reduced.

- o Utilities
- o Janitorial services
- o Building insurance

- *Equipment reduction.* Usually involves the elimination of manufacturing equipment within facilities that are also eliminated, or simply equipment for which there is no need for the additional capacity. The following expenses are also affected when facilities are eliminated or their usage is reduced:

  - o Maintenance staff
  - o Maintenance parts
  - o Utilities

- *Marketing.* Typically involves the consolidation of advertising and other marketing campaigns, as well as back-office operations. The following expenses are also affected when marketing costs are reduced:

  - o Salaries, payroll taxes, and benefits

- *Research and development.* The combined entity could combine its research operations, which may lead to expense reductions in the following areas:

  - o Outsourced research contracts
  - o Salaries, payroll taxes, and benefits
  - o Legal costs associated with patent defense

- *Procurement.* It is entirely possible that businesses operating in the same industries can combine their purchasing activities to buy from fewer suppliers in larger volume, thereby driving down supplier prices. This can impact costs in all parts of the business, not just in the area of raw materials for manufacturing operations.

In addition to the preceding areas of duplication, consider the reduction of costs associated with the owners of a closely-held company. There may be excessive expenditures in any of the following areas, all of which can be eliminated:

- Above-market senior manager compensation packages
- Wages paid to friends, family, and other related parties
- Over-market lease payments made to entities owned by the shareholders
- Unusually high expenditures for travel and entertainment by senior management
- Insurance premiums for policies where the company is not the beneficiary
- Excessive benefit and pension plans for senior managers
- Fixed assets exclusively used by the shareholders and senior managers, such as condominiums and airplanes

The expenses just noted for a closely-held company may have been designed to exactly offset company profits, so the business does not have to pay income taxes. This approach is so prevalent that the financial statements of many businesses may cloak highly profitable operations; it takes an excellent valuation team to strip away these excess expenditures to find the hidden value of a target company.

When arriving at a list of synergies related to expense reductions, be sure to offset them with the one-time costs associated with those same synergies. For example, there may be severance payments associated with employee terminations, or termination fees associated with the early expiration of facility leases. Also, if equipment is eliminated, the company may recognize a loss on any maintenance parts that it had in stock, and which it must sell off at a loss.

When evaluating synergies, be particularly wary of those related to revenue. An acquirer may believe that it can combine sales forces and have this aggregated group sell the products of both businesses. Or, it can combine the products of both companies in a single web store – and so on. The trouble with revenue synergies is that they rely upon the agreement of customers that this is, indeed, a good thing, resulting in more sales. Instead, it is exceedingly common for customers not to respond as planned, resulting in little or no sales boost from an acquisition. If anything, it is more common for nervous customers to be picked up by competitors, thereby *reducing* sales. Thus, it is best to either minimize or eliminate from consideration any revenue synergies.

The Valuation Floor and Ceiling

We have presented a number of ways to create a valuation for a target company. The trouble is that if you were to use all of them, there would be an incredibly broad range of possible valuations from which to choose. There may be orders of magnitude between the valuation indicated by a liquidation analysis and the price an acquirer might be willing to pay for a strategic purchase. How do you find your way amongst these numbers?

The key issue is that, eventually, most acquisitions must present positive cash flow to the acquirer, even if it takes some optimistic forecasts to arrive at positive cash flow projections. The only valid reason for paying more than what any cash flow projection indicates is when the purpose of the deal is to keep the target company away from a competitor. Consequently, the discounted cash flow model should be the key valuation methodology that every acquirer uses.

While a discounted cash flow analysis can always be used, this does not mean that it should be used to the exclusion of all other methodologies. In the following bullet points, we have clustered those valuation methods that tend to yield low, medium, and high valuations. Select one valuation method from each of these clusters in order to establish a range of valuations. Doing so gives some leeway in regard to what the final price will be. Thus, you will be comfortable using the valuation based on discounted cash flows, but will push for a price closer to liquidation value, and may accept a price closer to the amount indicated by a strategic purchase analysis. The valuations are:

Acquisition Valuation

Low valuation tendency

- *Liquidation value.* Tends to yield the lowest possible valuation. This is useful for establishing the amount the acquirer can sell the business for if an acquisition does not go as planned, rather than for establishing the price the acquirer will insist on paying.
- *Real estate value.* Tends to be close to liquidation value, and only applies to target companies with significant real estate holdings.
- *Relief-from-royalty method.* Is only used to measure the royalties avoided by owning an intangible asset.
- *Book value.* States the amount at which a business could be sold at the values stated in its balance sheet. Actual results likely vary considerably from book value.

Medium valuation tendency

- *Enterprise value.* States the current amount at which a business could be bought. It only applies to those businesses for which there is a ready market for its stock, and does not include a control premium. Thus, it tends to be one of the lower valuations.
- *Multiples analysis.* Is based on the valuations of other publicly-held businesses in the same industry, and so is similar to the enterprise measurement approach; and like that measurement, it does not include a control premium. Thus, it also tends to be one of the lower valuations.
- *Discounted cash flows.* Based on estimated future cash flows. If these cash flows are carefully reviewed and tested against historical results, this can yield excellent results. The results tend to be in the middle of the cluster of valuations.
- *Replication value.* Indicates the "go it alone" cost required to duplicate a business that an acquirer wants to buy. This can yield one of the higher valuations. Since it is largely based on estimates, it is not sufficient as the sole source of valuation information.
- *Comparison analysis.* Estimates the valuation based on the prices paid when similar businesses were sold in the recent past. This analysis includes the control premium, and so tends to yield a higher valuation.

High valuation tendency

- *52-Week high.* Based on an arbitrary high point in the stock price in the past year. If that high point was an outlier price, the resulting valuation could be inordinately high. This only works if there is an active market for the company's stock.
- *Influencer price point.* Based on the price at which a decision maker bought into the target company. This price point could be anywhere, ranging from very low to very high.

- *IPO valuation.* Based on the price at which the target company intends to go public. This can be a very high valuation. Due to the cost of an IPO, this option is rarely used.
- *Strategic purchase.* Based on other considerations than cash flow, and can yield a startlingly high price.

In summary, consider spending a modest amount of time establishing liquidation value, certainly calculate a detailed discounted cash flow, possibly also compile a comparison analysis, and then establish the high-end valuation by engaging in a strategic purchase review.

Summary

Of the various valuation methods described in this chapter, the most quantitatively precise one is the discounted cash flows method. However, even that method is derived from a variety of estimates of future results, as well as estimates of expenses that can be eliminated due to synergies. In short, even the DCF method can yield results that turn out to vary widely from subsequent actual results.

Valuation depends to a great extent upon the timing of the situation. If the target company finds itself in a difficult financial situation and there are few potential bidders, then an acquirer may be able to snap it up for an amount at the far lower end of what would normally be considered reasonable. Conversely, a business that is carefully built to provide a strategic advantage in a new market, and for which multiple bidders see a strong strategic advantage, may sell at a price far beyond the price created by most rational valuation calculations.

Chapter 23
The Enhancement of Shareholder Value

Introduction

A business should be managed so that the returns generated for shareholders are maximized. There are a number of ways to do so through return on equity analysis, including higher profitability, the use of leverage, and maximizing the use of assets. Alternative methods for arriving at value enhancement are economic value added, cash flow analysis, the opportunity cost of capital, and key success factors. In this chapter, we address each of these concepts, as well as several issues related to the enhancement of shareholder value.

Return on Equity

The return on equity (ROE) ratio reveals the amount of return earned by investors on their investments in a business. It is one of the metrics most closely watched by investors. Given the intense focus on this measurement, ROE is frequently used as the basis for bonus compensation for senior managers.

ROE is essentially net income divided by shareholders' equity. ROE performance can be enhanced by focusing on improvements to three underlying measurements, all of which roll up into ROE. These sub-level measurements are:

- *Profit margin.* Calculated as net income divided by sales. Can be improved by trimming expenses, increasing prices, or altering the mix of products or services sold.
- *Asset turnover.* Calculated as sales divided by assets. Can be improved by reducing receivable balances, inventory levels, and/or the investment in fixed assets, as well as by lengthening payables payment terms.
- *Financial leverage.* Calculated as assets divided by shareholders' equity. Can be improved by buying back shares, paying dividends, or using more debt to fund operations.

Or, stated as a formula, the return on equity is as follows:

$$\text{Return on Equity} = \frac{\text{Net income}}{\text{Sales}} \times \frac{\text{Sales}}{\text{Assets}} \times \frac{\text{Assets}}{\text{Shareholders' equity}}$$

EXAMPLE

Hammer Industries manufactures construction equipment. The company's return on equity has declined from a high of 25% five years ago to a current level of 10%. The CFO wants to know what is causing the problem, and assigns the task to a financial analyst, Wendy. She reviews the components of ROE for both periods, and derives the following information:

	ROE		Profit Margin		Asset Turnover		Financial Leverage
Five Years Ago	25%	=	12%	×	1.2x	×	1.75x
Today	10%	=	10%	×	0.6x	×	1.70x

The information in the table reveals that the primary culprit causing the decline is a sharp reduction in the company's asset turnover. This has been caused by a large buildup in the company's inventory levels, which have been caused by management's insistence on stocking larger amounts of finished goods in order to increase the speed of order fulfillment.

The multiple components of the ROE calculation present an opportunity for a business to generate a high ROE in several ways. For example, a grocery store has low profits on a per-unit basis, but turns over its assets at a rapid rate, so that it earns a profit on many sale transactions over the course of a year. Conversely, a manufacturer of custom goods realizes large profits on each sale, but also maintains a significant amount of component parts that reduce asset turnover. The following illustration shows how both entities can earn an identical ROE, despite having such a different emphasis on profits and asset turnover. In the illustration, we ignore the effects of financial leverage.

Comparison of Returns on Equity

	ROE		Profit Margin		Asset Turnover
Grocery Store	20%	=	2%	×	10x
Custom manufacturer	20%	=	40%	×	0.5x

Usually, a successful business is able to focus on either a robust profit margin *or* a high rate of asset turnover. If it were able to generate both, its return on equity would be so high that the company would likely attract competitors who want to emulate the underlying business model. If so, the increased level of competition usually drives down the overall return on equity in the market to a more reasonable level.

    A high level of financial leverage can increase the return on equity, because it means a business is using the minimum possible amount of equity, instead relying on debt to fund its operations. By doing so, the amount of equity in the denominator of the return on equity equation is minimized. If any profits are generated by funding activities with debt, these changes are added to the numerator in the equation, thereby increasing the return on equity.

The trouble with employing financial leverage is that it imposes a new fixed expense in the form of interest payments (see the Financial Leverage chapter). If sales decline, this added cost of debt could trigger a steep decline in profits that could end in bankruptcy. Thus, a business that relies too much on debt to enhance its shareholder returns may find itself in significant financial trouble. A more prudent path is to employ a modest amount of additional debt that a company can comfortably handle even through a business downturn.

EXAMPLE

The president of Finchley Fireworks has been granted a bonus plan that is triggered by an increase in the return on equity. Finchley has $2,000,000 of equity, of which the president plans to buy back $600,000 with the proceeds of a loan that has a 6% after-tax interest rate. The following table models this plan:

	Before Buyback	After Buyback
Sales	$10,000,000	$10,000,000
Expenses	9,700,000	9,700,000
Debt interest expense	---	36,000
Profits	300,000	264,000
Equity	2,000,000	1,400,000
Return on equity	15%	19%

The model indicates that this strategy will work. Expenses will be increased by the new amount of interest expense, but the offset is a steep decline in equity, which increases the return on equity. An additional issue to be investigated is whether the company's cash flows are stable enough to support this extra level of debt.

A business that has a significant asset base (and therefore a low asset turnover rate) is more likely to engage in a larger amount of financial leverage. This situation arises because the large asset base can be used as collateral for loans. Conversely, if a company has high asset turnover, the amount of assets on hand at any point in time is relatively low, giving a lender few assets to designate as collateral for a loan.

> **Tip:** A highly successful company that spins off large amounts of cash may generate a low return on equity, because it chooses to retain a large part of the cash. Cash retention increases assets and so results in a low asset turnover rate, which in turn drives down the return on equity. Actual ROE can be derived by stripping the excess amount of cash from the ROE equation.

Return on equity is one of the primary tools used to measure the performance of a business, particularly in regard to how well management is enhancing shareholder value. As noted in this section, there are multiple ways to enhance ROE. However, we must warn against the excessive use of financial leverage to improve ROE, since the use of debt can turn into a considerable burden if cash flows decline.

A case can be made that ROE should be ignored, since an excessive focus on it may drive management to pare back on a number of discretionary expenses that are needed to build the long-term value of a company. For example, the senior management team may cut back on expenditures for research and development, training, and marketing in order to boost profits in the short term and elevate ROE. However, doing so impairs the ability of the business to build its brand and compete effectively over the long term. Some management teams will even buy their companies back from investors, so that they are not faced with the ongoing pressure to enhance ROE. In a buyback situation, managers see that a lower ROE combined with a proper level of reinvestment in the business is a better path to long-term value.

Economic Value Added

A different view of shareholder value is provided by using the economic value added (EVA) measurement. In essence, this metric compares the cost of capital of a business (see the Cost of Capital chapter) to the rate of return it generates, to see if the business is creating any value in excess of its cost of funds. If the economic value added measurement turns out to be negative, this means a business is destroying value on the funds invested in it. It is essential to review all of the components of this measurement to see which areas of a business can be adjusted to create a higher level of EVA.

To calculate EVA, determine the difference between the actual rate of return on assets and the cost of capital, and multiply this difference by the net investment in the business. Additional details regarding the calculation are:

- Eliminate any unusual income items from net income that do not relate to ongoing operational results.
- The net investment in the business should be the net book value of all fixed assets, assuming that straight-line depreciation is used.
- The expenses for training and research and development should be considered part of the investment in the business.
- The fair value of leased assets should be included in the investment figure.
- If the calculation is being derived for individual business units, the allocation of costs to each business unit is likely to involve extensive negotiation, since the outcome will affect the calculation for each business unit.

The formula for EVA is:

$$\text{Net investment} \times (\text{Actual return on investment} - \text{Percentage cost of capital})$$

The Enhancement of Shareholder Value

EXAMPLE

The president of the Hegemony Toy Company has just returned from a management seminar in which the benefits of EVA have been trumpeted. He wants to know what the calculation would be for Hegemony, and asks his financial analyst to find out.

The financial analyst knows that the company's cost of capital is 12.5%, having recently calculated it from the company's mix of debt, preferred stock, and common stock. He then reconfigures information from the income statement and balance sheet into the following matrix, where some expense line items are instead treated as investments.

Account Description	Performance	Net Investment
Revenue	$6,050,000	
Cost of goods sold	4,000,000	
General & administrative	660,000	
Sales department	505,000	
Training department		$75,000
Research & development		230,000
Marketing department	240,000	
Net income	**$645,000**	
Fixed assets		3,100,000
Cost of patent protection		82,000
Cost of trademark protection		145,000
Total net investment		**$3,632,000**

The return on investment for Hegemony is 17.8%, using the information from the preceding matrix. The calculation is $645,000 of net income divided by $3,632,000 of net investment. Finally, he includes the return on investment, cost of capital, and net investment in the following calculation to derive the EVA:

($3,632,000 Net investment) × (17.8% Actual return − 12.5% Cost of capital)

= $3,632,000 Net investment × 5.3%

= $192,496 Economic value added

Thus, the company is generating a healthy EVA on the funds invested in it.

Cash Flow Analysis

An alternative way to enhance shareholder value is to focus on the generation of cash flow. A business can be valued based on the amount of cash it can generate, since investors should pay more for the shares of a business that pays them a large dividend or would distribute a large amount of cash as part of its liquidation or sale to an acquirer. Strong cash flow also reduces the risk that a business will be unable to continue operating due to poor results, since it should maintain significant cash reserves. Further, positive cash flow gives a business the funding needed to pay for its growth, so there is little need to use riskier debt funding for this purpose. Thus, it is easy to tie strong cash flows to shareholder value.

If management elects to make cash flow its main focus in the pursuit of enhanced shareholder value, there are a multitude of operational methods for doing so that, in essence, involve tight and innovative oversight of the business. For example, the following methods all result in enhanced cash flow:

- Just-in-time inventory deliveries reduce the amount of cash invested in inventory.
- Cellular manufacturing reduces the overall investment in all types of inventory.
- Bottleneck scheduling focuses attention on the bottleneck operation of a business, which must be maximized in order to generate more throughput (defined as sales minus all variable expenses).
- Target costing is used to develop products that will have specific feature sets that can be sold at a predetermined price point in order to generate a predetermined profit.
- Month-end promotions are avoided, since they trigger excessive overtime costs and overload the manufacturing system.
- All early payment discounts are taken that exceed the company's cost of capital.
- Cost objects are terminated that do not contribute to throughput and which absorb too many invested funds in proportion to the amount of cash that they spin off.
- Credit policy is tightened in order to reduce the time period over which receivables are outstanding.
- Throughput analysis is employed to see if proposed capital expenditures actually improve the total throughput of a business or reduce costs.

In short, there are many ways to enhance the operations of a business so that cash outflows are improved, and cash investments are reduced. If pursued consistently, this can result in superior cash flows in comparison to competitors, which in turn should yield a higher corporate value for shareholders.

Opportunity Cost of Capital

The opportunity cost of capital is the incremental return on investment that a business foregoes when it elects to use funds for an internal project, rather than investing cash in a marketable security. Thus, if the projected return on the internal project is less than the expected rate of return on a marketable security, one would not invest in the internal project, assuming that this is the only basis for the decision. The opportunity cost of capital is the difference between the returns on the two projects. Close attention to this issue can trigger an incremental increase in shareholder value.

For example, the senior management of a business expects to earn 8% on a long-term $10,000,000 investment in a new manufacturing facility, or it can invest the cash in stocks for which the expected long-term return is 12%. Barring any other considerations, the better use of the cash is to invest $10,000,000 in stocks. The opportunity cost of capital of investing in the manufacturing facility is 2%, which is the difference in return on the two investment opportunities.

This concept is not as simple as it may first appear. The person making the decision must estimate the variability of returns on the alternative investments through the period during which the cash is expected to be used. To return to the example, senior management may be certain that the company can generate an 8% return on the new manufacturing facility, whereas there may be considerable uncertainty regarding the variability of returns from an investment in stocks (which could even be negative during the cash usage period). Thus, the variability of returns should also be considered when arriving at the opportunity cost of capital. This uncertainty can be quantified by assigning a probability of occurrence to different return on investment outcomes, and using the weighted average as the most likely return. No matter how the issue is addressed, the main point is that there is uncertainty surrounding the derivation of the opportunity cost of capital, so that a decision is rarely based on completely reliable investment information.

Key Success Factors

The enhancement of shareholder value is by no means managed solely through the manipulation of profit, asset turnover, and financial leverage. These are the core financial metrics, but below them are many competitive advantages that must be adroitly managed. Ultimately, the true value of a business lies in these competitive advantages, rather than the financial ratios generated from them. Consequently, true shareholder value is derived from (for example) the following key success factors:

- *Gate leases.* An airline has acquired long-term leases to gates in a major airport, which it can use to block competitors from gaining access to that airport.
- *Inventory replenishment.* A retail chain has devised a system for creating new clothing designs and restocking its stores with these goods within a very short period of time. The result is an ability to sell new designs weeks before competitors can begin to sell similar products.

- *License protection.* A taxi company has obtained a license to exclusively operate its cabs within a city. The license effectively blocks all competition, creating a monopoly situation.
- *Patent protection.* A consumer products company obtains a patent on a key product design, which it can use to block competitors from building similar products.
- *Product design.* An automobile company has assembled the finest group of car designers in the industry; this group routinely issues leading-edge designs for which customers are willing to pay a premium.
- *Real estate acquisition.* A retail chain has the unique capability to acquire leases on property in areas with high levels of foot traffic, so that it can generate more sales per square foot than its competitors.
- *Truck stops.* A company has acquired long-term leases on locations adjacent to several major highways, on which it has built full-service truck stops. Since few of these plots of land are available, the company essentially has a monopoly on the servicing of trucks along the designated highways.

This list of key success factors does not begin to touch the multitude of such factors that can give a business a long-term competitive advantage. From a financial analysis perspective, the goal is to identify these factors, and then work with management to ensure that they are protected and enhanced over time. Any improvements in financial ratios are essentially a byproduct of the proper nurturing of these success factors.

Stock Price Enhancement

If a company is publicly-held, shareholders are likely to be more interested in the market price of their shares than in the return on equity or economic value added measurements. If so, some steps can be taken to shore up the market price of the stock, such as:

- An increased investor relations effort, to ensure that information about the company is widely distributed in the marketplace
- Hiring an investor relations firm to assist with marketing the company's stock
- Buying back shares if the market price drops below a certain threshold level
- Returning funds to investors in the form of dividends

However, a large part of the stock price is based on changes in the market as a whole, and so is well beyond the control of any individual company. For example, if there is a general economic downturn, it is likely that the prices of a broad range of stocks will suffer, even if companies continue to report excellent results. Further, rumors about a business – even if unsubstantiated – can impair the stock price. Consequently, though management may be tempted to aggressively support the stock price, it may be best to simply keep the investment community fully informed of company results, and let the stock price fluctuate based on that information.

Long-Term and Short-Term Value Considerations

There are significant differences between the maximization of shareholder value over the short term and the long term. If the focus is purely on the short term, management could decide to terminate any further investment in the business, liquidate high-value items, and turn the resulting cash flow over to shareholders. While this payout might be greeted with some enthusiasm by shareholders, they might not be so happy once they realize that the business has essentially been gutted in order to maximize short-term returns. However, this approach is an entirely valid one under the following (or similar) circumstances:

- The company does not have any prospects for high-return products or services that are worthy of a long-term investment.
- The business is family-run, and the next generation of family owners wants to cash out, rather than continuing to operate the company.
- The company has received a major one-time cash influx from a lawsuit settlement or sale of a subsidiary, and does not need the extra cash for its operations.

Conversely, there are circumstances under which it makes sense to reduce the short-term return to shareholders, and instead invest for a longer-term increase in value. Consider the following scenarios where this situation may arise:

- The industry is in a cyclical downturn, where the company routinely generates minimal returns at the bottom of the business cycle. The best option is to use excess cash to snap up competitors at a low price, rather than paying out dividends.
- Sales are growing at a high rate, and all cash is needed to fund the continuing expansion of the business, rather than making a dividend payout to shareholders.
- Increasing sales is more important than taking the company public, so a public offering is deferred until a later date. Shareholders cannot sell their shares until the public offering has been completed.
- Shareholders have a long-term objective of selling the business, and so have directed management to invest additional funds in fixed assets, to spruce up facilities to impress potential buyers.

Thus, the decisions made to increase shareholder value must encompass the circumstances under which a business finds itself, and the needs of its shareholders.

The Industry Setting

When devising methods for enhancing shareholder value, it is of some importance to understand the context within which a company operates – its industry. Each industry forces certain financial and operating limitations on a business, which it must deal with when devising strategy. For example, a company located in the steel fabrication, car rental, or power generation industries must deal with a large asset base, which mandates low asset turnover. Given the low turnover rate, companies will be driven toward the options of either high financial leverage or high profitability in order to generate adequate returns for investors. Thus, the choice of industry dictates how returns can be generated.

The choice of industry also carries with it the existing competitive structure of that industry. For example, if there is a dominant low-cost provider, all other competitors will likely find it necessary to pursue a niche strategy in order to generate adequate profits. Going head-to-head against a dominant competitor is a near-certain way to generate minimal profits, and so is not an option from a shareholder value perspective. As another example, if a company is located in a regulated industry, such as power generation, there must be recognition that many aspects of the business will be controlled, such as the prices charged to customers. If so, these aspects of shareholder value are essentially static, so management must turn to other methods for generating enhanced shareholder returns.

In summary, the particular characteristics of the industry within which a business is located has a profound effect upon its ability to generate shareholder returns – not only in regard to the size of the returns, but also the manner in which returns are generated. This means that the development of strategy must take into account the restrictions imposed on a company by its environment.

Summary

This chapter has included discussions of the return on equity and economic value added. Though these measurements are commonly associated with an analysis of shareholder value, it does not mean that managers should manipulate the information underlying these measurements in order to increase the outcome. Instead, use a clear vision of where to take the company to arrive at the long-term enhancement of shareholder value. This vision should include an analysis of the key success factors of the business, and how they are to be managed in order to maximize value. Thus, shareholder value is ultimately based on the proper management of operations and how a business competes, rather than manipulation of a few key measurements.

Glossary

A

Accelerated depreciation. A depreciation method designed to charge the bulk of the depreciable amount of a fixed asset to expense as soon as possible.

Accrual basis of accounting. A system for recording revenues when earned and expenses as incurred.

B

Balance sheet. A report that summarizes all of an entity's assets, liabilities, and equity as of a given point in time.

Bill and hold. The practice of recording revenues even when goods have not yet been shipped to a customer.

Bond. The sale of a fixed payment obligation to investors.

Borrowing base. The total amount of collateral against which a lender will lend funds to a business.

Bottleneck. An operation that impedes the ability of a process to generate goods or services.

Breakeven point. The sales level at which a business earns a zero profit.

Budget. A quantified expectation for what a business wants to achieve.

C

Call option. An agreement giving the buyer the right to buy an investment instrument at a certain price and within a certain time period.

Capital budgeting. The analysis of requests to acquire assets.

Capital expenditure. A payment made to acquire or upgrade an asset. A capital expenditure is recorded as an asset, not an expense.

Capital lease. A lease in which the lessor only finances the lease, and all other rights of ownership transfer to the lessee.

Capital structure. The mix of long-term funds employed by a business.

Capitalization limit. The threshold beyond which expenditures may be classified as fixed assets.

Cash basis of accounting. A system for recording revenues when cash is received and expenses when cash is paid out.

Cash equivalent. A short-term, very liquid investment that is easily convertible into a known amount of cash.

Constraint. A bottleneck that caps the amount of output that can be generated.

Glossary

Contribution margin. Sales minus all variable costs associated with those sales.

Control premium. The additional value associated with shares that will give the purchaser control over a business.

Cost based pricing. Prices that are derived from the costs of the underlying products.

Cost object. An item for which a cost is compiled, such as a product service, project, customer, or activity.

Cost of capital. The cost of funds for a business.

Credit rating. A standard score assigned to an entity, based on its financial and operational condition, and which is used to evaluate the credit terms granted to the entity.

Cross price elasticity of demand. The percentage change in the demand for one product when the price of a different product changes.

Current ratio. The current assets of a business, divided by its current liabilities.

Current value accounting. The practice of recording assets and liabilities at their current values.

D

Deleveraging. The reduction of debt obligations and other liabilities.

Depreciation. The gradual charging to expense of an asset's cost over its useful life.

Discount rate. The interest rate used to discount a stream of future cash flows to their present value. Depending upon the application, typical rates used as the discount rate are a firm's cost of capital or the current market rate.

Dividend payout ratio. A comparison of dividends paid to net earnings, used to evaluate the level of dividend payments made by a business.

E

Earnout. An additional payment made to the shareholders of an acquired company if it can meet certain performance objectives.

EBITDA. Earnings before interest, taxes, depreciation, and amortization. It is a rough measure of the cash flows of a business.

Enterprise value. The market value of the shares of a business, plus its outstanding debt, less its cash balance.

Expected commercial value. A technique for combining net present value analysis with the probability of success of a product in the market.

Expiry date. The expiration date of a contract.

F

Factoring. The sale of accounts receivable to a third party for cash.

Glossary

FICO score. A credit quality score calculated for individuals, as developed by the Fair Isaac Corporation.

Financial statements. A collection of reports that describe the financial results, condition, and cash flows of an entity.

Fiscal year. The 12-month period over which a business reports its financial results.

Fixed cost. A cost that does not vary in the short term, irrespective of changes in activity levels.

Forecast. A forecast of the results that a business expects to achieve.

Functional currency. The currency that an entity uses in the majority of its business transactions.

H

Hedging. Actions taken to reduce the volatility of cash flows, earnings, and/or the value of investments.

Horizontal analysis. The comparison of historical financial information over a series of reporting periods.

I

Income statement. A financial report that summarizes an entity's revenue, cost of goods sold, gross margin, other costs, and net income or loss.

Internal rate of return. The discount rate at which the net cash flows associated with an investment equal zero.

L

Lease. An arrangement where the lessor agrees to allow the lessee to use an asset for a stated period of time in exchange for a series of fixed payments.

Leverage. The use of borrowed funds to increase profits.

Line of credit. A commitment from a lender to pay a company whenever it needs cash, up to a pre-set maximum limit.

Liquidation value. The amount of funds that would be collected if all assets and liabilities of a company were sold off or settled.

M

Margin of safety. The reduction in sales that can occur before the breakeven point of a business is reached.

N

Net book value. The original cost of an asset, less any accumulated depreciation, accumulated amortization, and accumulated impairment.

Glossary

Net present value. The difference between the present values of all cash inflows and outflows associated with an investment.

Notional amount. The face amount used to calculate payments on a financial instrument, such as an option or interest rate swap.

O

Operating lease. The rental of an asset from a lessor.

Other comprehensive income. A classification within the financial statements that contains all changes not permitted in the main part of the income statement.

P

Payback method. A technique for reviewing fixed asset purchase requests, based on the time required to earn back the original investment.

Present value. The current value of a sum of money not to be received until a future date.

Price elasticity of demand. The degree to which changes in price impact the unit sales of a product or service.

Pro forma earnings. The practice of adjusting reported earnings at the discretion of the issuing entity, usually to report enhanced results.

Put option. An agreement giving the buyer the right to sell an investment instrument at a certain price and within a certain time period.

Q

Quick ratio. The ratio of cash, marketable securities, and accounts receivable to current liabilities. The ratio does not include inventory or prepaid expenses.

R

R&D waste. The expense related to research and development projects that have been cancelled.

Real option. The range of possible actions available for an investment decision.

Reference rate. An interest rate used as the basis for an interest rate swap, floating rate security, interest rate option, or forward rate agreement.

Relief-from-royalty method. The assignment of value to an intangible asset, based on the royalty that would have been paid for the rights to use the asset if it were licensed from a third party.

Replication value. A valuation technique that involves estimating the cost to replicate a target company.

Rolling forecast. The recasting of a company's financial prospects on a frequent basis.

Glossary

S

Shelf registration. Stock that is registered with the Securities and Exchange Commission before there are plans to issue the stock.

Shell company. A business entity for which there are minimal assets, liabilities, or business activity.

Sole proprietorship. A business that is not incorporated, so that a single individual is entitled to the entire net worth of the business, and is personally liable for its debts.

Statement of cash flows. A part of the financial statements that summarizes an entity's cash inflows and outflows in relation to financing, operating, and investing activities.

Statement of retained earnings. A part of the financial statements that summarizes changes in equity during a reporting period.

Straight line depreciation. When the same amount of depreciation for an asset is charged to expense in each period.

Strategic pricing. Prices that are set to drive away competitors or position a business within a market.

Strategic purchase. The purchase of a business for strategic reasons, rather than being based on a more quantitative valuation model.

Strike price. The price at which an option or other similar contract can be exercised.

T

Tax shield. An income tax reduction caused by the use of an allowable tax deduction.

Teaser pricing. Prices that are kept low on a few products to attract customers.

Terminal value. The aggregation of all cash flows beyond the date range for which cash flows are being predicted.

Throughput. Revenues minus totally variable costs.

Transaction exposure. The risk of loss from a change in exchange rates during the course of a business transaction.

Translation exposure. The risk of a reported change in value of a company's assets and liabilities, if they are denominated in a foreign currency.

V

Value based pricing. Prices that are based on customer perceptions of the value of products.

Variable cost. A cost that varies in relation to changes in production or other activity volume.

Glossary

Vertical analysis. The proportional analysis of a financial statement, where each line item is stated as a percentage of another item.

W

Warrant. A call option issued by a company on its own shares.

Window dressing. Actions taken by management to improve the appearance of a company's financial statements.

Y

Yield curve. A line that plots the interest rates associated with an investment having different durations. A normal yield curve reveals a gradual increase in interest rates as maturity dates increase. An inverted yield curve reveals declining interest rates as maturity dates increase.

Index

52-week high valuation 303

Accelerated depreciation 44
Accounting policies 27
Accounts payable turnover 59
Accounts receivable turnover 60
Accrual basis of accounting 37
Administration budget 226
Agency financing 157
Angel investors 161
Auditor certification 49

Balance sheet
    Common size 19
    Comparative 21
    Overview of 16
Beta 254
Bill and hold transaction 41
Bond rating, planning for 178
Bonds 156
Book value 290
Borrowing base 149
Bottleneck, cost of 119
Breakeven point 65, 75
Budget scenarios 228
Budgets, system of 224

Capital budget 226
Capital budgeting
    Analysis of 275
    Overview of 269
    Request form 271
Capital investment decision 127
Capital structure
    Analysis 173
    Optimal 172
Cash basis of accounting 38
Cash coverage ratio 56
Cash flow analysis 318
Cash forecast 233
Clearing dates 240
Common size balance sheet 19
Common stock cost 252
Comparison analysis 301
Complex systems analysis 277

Constraint
    Model 122
    Overview 117
    Terminology 116, 121
Contingencies 29
Contribution margin 73
    And growth 244
    Income statement 13
Control premium 306
Convertibility risk 190
Cost assignment 103
Cost object analysis 102
Cost of capital
    Adjustments to 256
    Derivation of 251
    Reduction of 178
    Variations 253
Cost of goods sold budget 225
Cost plus pricing 86
Cost-volume-profit analysis 79
Covenants 175
Credit increases, requests for 142
Credit monitoring 139
Credit rating systems 132
Credit ratings
    Errors 137
    Overview 131
    Third party 135
    Use of 137
Credit scores, evaluation of 136
Cross price elasticity of demand 99
Crowdfunding 162
Currency option 198
Current ratio 57
Current value accounting 45
Customer
    Acquisition costs 106
    Costs 104
    Lifetime value 107
Customers
    Demanding 144
    Risky 143
Cylinder option 200, 213

Debt cost 251
Debt for equity swap 163

Debt funding	147	Netting	201
Debt maturity structure	176	Reserves	194
Debt paydown	177	Risk management	191
Debt service coverage ratio	181	Swaps	201
Debt to equity ratio	64	Forward rate agreement	205
Deleveraging	158	Freemium pricing	88
Delinquency indicators	138	Future value table	262

Depreciation
- Accelerated 44
- Straight line 44
- Usage based 44

Direct labor budget	224	Goodwill disclosures	30
Direct materials budget	225	Gross profit ratio	66
Direct method	23		
Disclosures	27		

Growth
- Constraints 247
- Funding of 242
- Ideal rate of 249
- Negative effects of 248

Discounted cash flows	296		
Dividend payout ratio	183	Headline earnings	47
Dividend policy	183	High low pricing	89
Dynamic pricing	87	Horizontal analysis	53
Early payment discounting	150	Illusory profits	46
Earnout valuation	306	Impairment disclosures	31
EBITDA	68		
Economic value added	316		

Income statement
- Contribution margin 13
- Multi-period 15
- Multi-step 13
- Overview of 9
- Single-step 12

Employee cost	108	Incremental internal rate of return	265
Enterprise value	292	Indirect method	24
Equity funding	158	Influencer price point	303
Factoring	153	Interest coverage ratio	180
FIFO method	43		

Financial analysis
- Concepts 2
- Judgment 4
- Precision of 5
- Purpose of 1

Interest rate
- Futures contract 207
- Hedging 204
- Options 211
- Risk management 203
- Swap 209
- Swaption 214

Financial analyst, role of	7	Internal rate of return	265

Financial leverage
- Compensation effects 170
- Concept 165
- Issues impacting 168
- Risks 169

		Inventory budget	224
		Inventory costing methods	42
		Inventory financing	153
		Inventory turnover	61
Financial statement interpretation	51	Investment disclosures	31
Financing budget	226	Investment time horizon	276
Fiscal year effects	39	Invoice discounting	152
Fixed asset turnover	62	IPO valuation	304
Fixed charge coverage	65		

Foreign exchange
- Forward contract 196
- Futures contract 198
- Hedging 194

Key success factors 319

Lease or buy decision 283
Leasing 154
    Advantages 286
    Problems 284
LIFO method 43
Line of credit 148, 174
Liquidation value 288
Liquidity index 58
Loan, long term 155

Manufacturing overhead budget 225
Margin of safety 78
Modified cash basis of accounting 39
Multiples analysis 292

Negative cash 42
Net present value 263
Net profit ratio 67
Non-price determinants of demand 100
NOPAT 69

Opportunity cost of capital 319
Optimization, local 120
Organic growth 245
Outsourcing decision 126, 279

Payback method 272
Pension disclosures 32
Political risk 190
Post installation review 280
Preferred stock cost 252
Premium pricing 90
Present value table 261
Price elasticity of demand 98
Price reduction decision 125
Private investment in public equity 163
Pro forma earnings 47
Product cancellation decision 128
Product cost 109
Product line costs 111
Production budget 224
Psychological pricing 84
Purchase order financing 154

Quick ratio 57

Ratio analysis, limitations of 70
Real estate value 289
Real options 274

Recapitalization 182
Receipts and disbursements method ... 234
Regulation Crowdfunding 162
Related party disclosures 33
Relief-from-royalty method 289
Replication value 299
Research and development analysis 278
Restricted stock 159
Return on equity 313
Return on net assets 68
Revenue forecasting 219
Revenue recognition
    Bill and hold 41
    Disclosures 33
    Gross or net 40
Risk-free rate 254
Rolling forecast 229
Run rate 217

Sales and marketing budget 226
Sales channel costs 113
Sales mix 81
Sales to working capital ratio 63
Segment disclosures 34
Sensitivity analysis 218
Specific identification method 43
Sprint capacity 118
Statement of cash flows
    Direct method 23
    Indirect method 24
    Overview of 22
Statement of retained earnings 25
Step costs and growth 245
Stock buybacks 186
Stock dividend 187
Stock price enhancement 320
Straight line depreciation 44
Strategic purchase valuation 304
Subsequent events 35
Synergy analysis 308

Target balance 237
Tax shield 175
Terminal value 266
Time and materials pricing 92
Time value of money 259
Transaction exposure 189
Transfer risk 190
Translation exposure 189

Unrestricted stock 160

Valuation floor and ceiling 310
Value based pricing 94
Venture capital 161

Vertical analysis 54
Warrants 160
Weighted average cost of capital 253
Weighted average method 43
Window dressing 48

CPSIA information can be obtained
at www.ICGtesting.com
Printed in the USA
LVHW101619210720
661235LV00006B/345

9 781938 910968